MUIRHEAD LIBRARY OF PHILOSOPHY

An admirable statement of the aims of the Library of Philosophy was provided by the first editor, the late Professor J. H. Muirhead, in his description of the original programme printed in Erdmann's *History of Philosophy* under the date 1890. This was slightly modified in subsequent volumes to take the form of the following statement:

'The Muirhead Library of Philosophy was designed as a contribution to the History of Modern Philosophy under the heads: first of Different Schools of Thought—Sensationalist, Realist, Idealist, Intuitivist; secondly of different Subjects—Psychology, Ethics, Aesthetics, Political Philosophy, Theology. While much had been done in England in tracing the course of evolution in nature, history, economics, morals and religion, little had been done in tracing the development of thought on these subjects. Yet "the evolution of opinion is part of the whole evolution".

'By the co-operation of different writers in carrying out this plan it was hoped that a thoroughness and completeness of treatment, otherwise unattainable, might be secured. It was believed also that from writers mainly British and American fuller consideration of English Philosophy then it had hitherto received might be looked for. In the earlier series of books containing, among others, Bosanquet's *History of Aesthetic*, Pfleiderer's *Rational Theology since Kant*, Albee's *History of English Utilitarianism*, Bonar's *Philosophy and Political Economy*, Brett's *History of Psychology*, Ritchie's *Natural Rights*, these objects were to a large extent effected.

'In the meantime original work of a high order was being produced both in England and America by such writers as Bradley, Stout, Bertrand Russell, Baldwin, Urban, Montague, and others, and a new interest in foreign works, German, French and Italian, which had either become classical or were attracting public attention, had developed. The scope of the Library thus became extended into something more international, and it is entering on the fifth decade of its existence in the hope that it may contribute to that mutual understanding between countries which is so pressing a need of the present time.'

The need which Professor Muirhead stressed is no less pressing today, and few will deny that philosophy has much to do with enabling us to meet it, although no one, least of all Muirhead himself, would regard that as the sole, or even the main, object of philosophy. As Professor Muirhead continues to lend the distinction of his name to the Library of Philosophy it seemed not inappropriate to allow him to recall us to these aims in his own words. The emphasis on the history of thought also seemed to me very timely; and the number of important works promised for the Library in the very near future augur well for the continued fulfilment, in this and other ways, of the expectations of the original editor.

H. D. LEWIS

MUIRHEAD LIBRARY OF PHILOSOPHY

General Editor: H. D. Lewis
Professor of History and Philosophy of Religion in the University of London

Action by SIR MALCOLM KNOX
The Analysis of Mind by BERTRAND RUSSELL
Belief by H. H. PRICE
Brett's History of Psychology edited by R. S. PETERS
Clarity is Not Enough by H. D. LEWIS
Coleridge as a Philosopher by J. H. MUIRHEAD
The Commonplace Book of G. E. Moore edited by C. LEWY
Contemporary American Philosophy edited by C. P. ADAMS and W. P. MONTAGUE
Contemporary British Philosophy first and second Series edited by J. H. MUIRHEAD
Contemporary British Philosophy third Series edited by H. D. LEWIS
Contemporary Indian Philosophy edited by RADHAKRISHNAN and J. H. MUIRHEAD 2nd edition
Contemporary Philosophy in Australia edited by ROBERT BROWN and C. D. ROLLINS
The Discipline of the Cave by J. N. FINDLAY
Doctrine and Argument in Indian Philosophy by NINIAN SMART
Essays in Analysis by ALICE AMBROSE
Ethics by NICOLAI HARTMANN translated by STANTON COIT 3 vols
The Foundations of Metaphysics in Science by ERROL E. HARRIS
Freedom and History by H. D. LEWIS
The Good Will: A Study in the Coherence Theory of Goodness by H. J. PATON
Hegel: A Re-examination by J. N. FINLAY
Hegel's Science of Logic translated by W. H. JOHNSTON and L. G STRUTHERS 2 vols
History of Aesthetic by B. BOSANQUET 2nd edition
History of English Utilitarianism by E. ALBEE
History of Psychology by G. S. BRETT edited by R. S. PETERS abridged one volume edition 2nd edition
Human Knowledge by BERTRAND RUSSELL
A Hundred Years of British Philosophy by RUDOLF METZ translated by J. N. HARVEY, T. E. JESSOP, HENRY STURT
Ideas: A General Introduction to Pure Phenomenology by EDMUND HUSSERL translated by W. R. BOYCE GIBSON
Identity and Reality by EMILE MEYERSON
Imagination by E. J. FURLONG

Muirhead Library of Philosophy

EDITED BY H. D. LEWIS

G. E. MOORE
ESSAYS IN RETROSPECT

G. E. MOORE
ESSAYS IN
RETROSPECT

EDITED BY
ALICE AMBROSE

AND

MORRIS LAZEROWITZ

Sophia and Austin Smith Professors of Philosophy
Smith College

LONDON · GEORGE ALLEN & UNWIN LTD
NEW YORK · HUMANITIES PRESS INC

PRINTED IN GREAT BRITAIN
IN 11 ON 12 PT IMPRINT
BY UNWIN BROTHERS LIMITED
WOKING AND LONDON

PREFACE

George Edward Moore (1873–1958) was one of the most influential philosophers of the twentieth century, and the outcome of the changes he introduced into our ways of thinking in philosophy cannot yet be foreseen. Philosophy after Moore can never again be what it was before Moore, because of the standards of exactness and refinement he brought to the doing of philosophy, but more importantly, because of the direction he gave to philosophical investigation. His analytical method, and particularly his method of translation into the concrete, have awakened philosophers to certain features of their views and arguments to which they cannot again close their eyes. And it is to be hoped, as Moore would have hoped, that further investigations will add to the light his work has thrown on a subject which stands in great need of better understanding. This is the motivation of the present collection of essays. Contributors of the papers in this book examine various views to which Moore gave his attention, and assess his claims and the central method he used to discover evidence for them. All of the papers were written in or after 1958, by philosophers whom Moore respected, and may be viewed as appraisals of his work in retrospect. The editors wish to express their special thanks to the contributors of the new essays and particularly to Professor H. D. Lewis, editor of the Muirhead Library, who, perhaps more than anyone else, has a clear view of Moore's fundamental importance for the progress of philosophy.

For permission to reprint previously published papers we are indebted to the editors of *Philosophy*, *The Proceedings of the British Academy*, *The Philosophical Review*, *The Journal of Philosophy*, and *Inquiry*; and to the following publishers: Prentice-Hall, Inc., George Allen & Unwin Ltd., Oxford University Press,

University of Nebraska Press
Northampton, Massachusetts
November 1968

ALICE AMBROSE
MORRIS LAZEROWITZ

Bibliography of works of G. E. Moore to which references are made throughout these essays

Principia Ethica, Cambridge University Press, 1903.

Ethics, Oxford University Press, 1912.

Philosophical Studies, Routledge & Kegan Paul, 1922.

'A Defence of Common Sense', *Contemporary British Philosophy* (second series), edited by J. N. Muirhead, George Allen & Unwin Ltd., 1925. Also in *Philosophical Papers*, George Allen & Unwin Ltd., 1959.

'Proof of an External World', *The Proceedings of the British Academy*, Vol. XXV, 1939. Also in *Philosophical Papers*, George Allen & Unwin Ltd., 1959.

'A Reply to My Critics', *The Philosophy of G. E. Moore*, The Library of Living Philosophers, Vol. IV, edited by P. A. Schilpp, Open Court Publishing Co., 1942.

'Russell's "Theory of Descriptions"', *The Philosophy of Bertrand Russell*, The Library of Living Philosophers, Vol. V, edited by P. A. Schilpp, Open Court Publishing Co., 1944.

Some Main Problems of Philosophy, George Allen & Unwin Ltd., 1953.

Philosophical Papers, George Allen & Unwin Ltd., 1959.

Commonplace Book 1919–53, edited by Casimir Lewy, George Allen & Unwin Ltd., 1962.

Lectures on Philosophy, edited by Casimir Lewy, George Allen & Unwin Ltd., 1966.

NOTE

The papers in this book which have been previously published originally appeared as follows:

'George Edward Moore 1873–1958', by R. B. Braithwaite, in *The Proceedings of the British Academy*, Vol. XLVII (Oxford University Press, 1961).

'Reflections on *Some Main Problems of Philosophy*', by O. K. Bouwsma, in *The Philosophical Review*, Vol. XLIV, 1955, and in *Philosophical Essays*, University of Nebraska Press, 1965.

'Philosophy', by C. D. Broad, extracted by C. D. Broad from papers published in *Inquiry*, Vol. I, no. 2, 1958.

'G. E. Moore's Latest Published Views on Ethics', by C. D. Broad, in *Mind*, Vol. LXX, no. 280, 1961.

'Intrinsic Value: Some Comments on the Work of G. E. Moore', by Austin Duncan-Jones, in *Philosophy*, Vol. XXXIII, 1958.

'Some Neglected Issues in the Philosophy of G. E. Moore', by J. N. Findlay, in *Language, Mind and Value*, George Allen & Unwin Ltd., 1963.

'G. E. Moore on the Naturalistic Fallacy', by Casimir Lewy, in *The Proceedings of the British Academy*, Vol. L (Oxford University Press, 1964).

'George Edward Moore', by Norman Malcolm, in *Knowledge and Certainty. Essays and Lectures*, Prentice-Hall, Inc., 1963.

'Three Aspects of Moore's Philosophy', by Alice Ambrose, in *The Journal of Philosophy*, Vol. LVII, no. 26, 1960, and in *Essays in Analysis*, George Allen and Unwin Ltd., 1966.

'Moore's Commonplace Book', by Morris Lazerowitz, in *Philosophy*, Vol. XXXIX, 1964, and in *Philosophy and Illusion*, George Allen & Unwin Ltd., 1968.

CONTENTS

16 CONTENTS

GEORGE EDWARD MOORE,[1] 1873–1958

by R. B. BRAITHWAITE

George Edward Moore was born on November 4, 1873, at Upper Norwood, London. His father, Daniel Moore, M.D., had been in general practice as a doctor at Hastings; but being a man of private means he had moved to London, and ceased to practise, a year or two before G. E. Moore was born.

Daniel Moore's father, George Moore (1803–80; in *D.N.B.*), had also practised medicine, and had been the author of several successful books on what would now be called 'popular philosophy'. Moore's mother, Henrietta Sturge, was the daughter of two first cousins, both Sturges and members of that well-known Quaker family. Joseph Sturge the philanthropist (1793–1859; in *D.N.B.*) was her uncle. Moore was the fifth child in a family of eight, four boys and four girls; so the recently built red-brick house at Upper Norwood, with half an acre of garden, on the western slope of the hill rising to where was then the Crystal Palace, contained, as Moore has said, 'enough of us to make plenty of company for one another'. His eldest brother, Thomas Sturge Moore, the poet, artist, and critic, had a great influence on the formation of his opinions: Moore attributed to him a large share of responsibility for the falling away of his religious beliefs before he had left school. (The Moore parents were Baptists.) In the very characteristic thirty-nine-page 'Autobiography' which Moore wrote to prefix to the collection of articles in *The Philosophy of G. E. Moore* (ed. P. A. Schilpp: 1942) [referred to as *PGEM*], he makes no reference to the characters of his parents; but he leaves no doubt that he had a happy childhood, both at home and at school.

One of the reasons for the Moore family moving to Upper Norwood was that the sons should be able to be day boys at Dulwich College under its great first headmaster A. H. Gilkes. Moore went there at the age of 8, and stayed there for ten years and two terms, walking (or running) the mile between home and

[1] Reprinted from *The Proceedings of the British Academy*, Vol. XLVII, 1961. (Oxford University Press.)

school four times four days of the week and twice on Wednesdays and Saturdays. The account Moore has given of his formal education there will curdle the blood of any modern educationalist devoted to the cause of a balanced education. Moore was good at classics and went up the school rapidly on the 'classical side', and his last six years (*aet.* $12\frac{3}{4}$–$18\frac{1}{2}$) were spent in the top two forms where almost all his time was devoted to Greek and Latin, mostly to translation into these languages in prose or verse. Moore never regretted this concentration upon classics: he said that the variety of English passages which he was required to translate made him appreciate their qualities. Though Moore learned little mathematics and no science, he was well grounded in German; and the head of the musical department (E. D. Rendall) gave him private lessons in singing and introduced him to Schubert's and other *Lieder*, which later Moore used to sing, accompanying himself on the piano, to the great delight of his friends.

It is evident from Moore's account that his enjoyment of the Sixth Form at Dulwich was largely due to two great teachers— W. T. Lendrum, who later became a Fellow of Gonville and Caius College, Cambridge (and changed his name to Vesey), and the headmaster, A. H. Gilkes. Moore's portrait of Gilkes (*PGEM*, 9) compares him to the Platonic Socrates: the talks he gave to the Sixth Form in their weekly classes with him, and the essays which they wrote for him on the 'astounding variety of different subjects' of these talks, must have provided in themselves a liberal education.

It is not surprising that when Moore went up to Trinity College, Cambridge, in October 1892 (with a Major Entrance Scholarship) to read for Part I of the Classical Tripos, he found that the work to be done during his first two years at Cambridge largely repeated what he had done at Dulwich. Moore profited in these years by forming, for the first time, 'intimate friendships with extremely clever people. . . . Until I went to Cambridge, I had had no idea how exciting life could be' (*PGEM*, 13). Many of these men were a year or two his senior, and Moore was surprised that they should make friends with him. But if they impressed Moore by their brilliance combined with 'very great seriousness', there is no doubt of the remarkable impression which Moore made upon them. Bertrand Russell has written:

'In my third year I met G. E. Moore, who was then a freshman, and for some years he fulfilled my ideal of genius. He was in those days beautiful and slim, with a look almost of inspiration, and with an intellect as deeply passionate as Spinoza's. He had a kind of exquisite purity' [*Portraits from Memory and other Essays*, 1956, p. 68].

Russell introduced him to J. E. McTaggart, then a young Fellow of Trinity College; and Moore believed that it was the way he held his own argument with McTaggart at their first meeting which made Russell think that he had 'some aptitude for philosophy' and encourage him to read moral science in his third year.

Many of Moore's friends were members of the 'Apostles' discussion society; and Moore was elected to this in his second year. This Society played a large part in Moore's life during his first period in Cambridge (and till quite late in life he attended its meetings on special occasions); and Moore played a leading part in the Society. Leonard Woolf, describing in his recent auto-biography the Society as he knew it in 1901, has written:

'Throughout its history, every now and again an Apostle has dominated and left his impression, within its spirit and tradition, upon the Society. Sidgwick was one of these, and a century ago he dominated the Society, refertilizing and revivifying its spirit and tradition. And what Sidgwick did in the fifties of last century, G. E. Moore was doing when I was elected' [*Sowing*, 1960, p. 130].

Further testimony to the influence at this time of Moore's 'combination of clarity, integrity, tenacity, and passion' (Woolf's words) will be found in the biographies of G. Lowes Dickinson by E. M. Forster (p.110) and of J. M. Keynes by R. F. Harrod (p. 75). And those of us who knew Moore twenty years later would not have written differently.

To go back to 1894. Moore got his First that year in Part I of the Classical Tripos (and won the University Craven Scholarship in January 1895) and took to philosophy. In his Autobiography he records his debt to four of his teachers, James Ward, G. F. Stout, McTaggart (lecturing on Hegel), and Henry Jackson (lecturing on Plato and Aristotle, for Moore was simultaneously reading Ancient Philosophy for the Classical Tripos). After obtaining a First Class, with a mark of distinction, in Part II of the Moral Sciences Tripos in 1896 (and in the same month a Second Class in Part II of the Classical Tripos), he worked for a Trinity College Fellowship, submitting a dissertation on 'Freedom' in 1897. He added a concluding chapter on 'Reason' for the annual election of 1898, when he was elected to what was then called a 'Prize' fellowship with a tenure of six years. Thus Moore had full freedom to develop his philosophical ideas 'living in a set of Fellows' rooms on the north side of Nevile's Court—a very pleasant place and a very pleasant life'. Moore reported in 1942 that he did a respectable, 'but, I am afraid, not more than respectable', amount of work (and he went on to explain how lazy he was by nature: *PGEM*, 24–5). Since in these six years Moore published, besides many articles in philosophical journals and in Baldwin's *Dictionary of Philosophy*, the book which made his philosophical reputation, *Principia Ethica* (1903), 'magnificent' would seem a more appropriate epithet to apply to Moore's performance as a prize fellow.

Moore's philosophical teachers (except Henry Sidgwick) were all, one way or another, philosophical Idealists; and Moore, like Russell, started his philosophizing as a Bradleyan–Hegelian Idealist. (F. H. Bradley's *Appearance and Reality* had appeared in 1893.) Moore's first published writing was a contribution to an Aristotelian Society symposium on the sense in which past and future time exist: he concluded it by saying: 'Time must be rejected wholly, its continuity as well as its discreteness, if we are to form an adequate notion of reality . . . neither Past, Present, nor Future exists, if by existence we are to mean the ascription of full Reality and not merely existence as Appearance' (*Mind*, vi, 1897, p. 240). And a few months later, 'the arguments by which Mr. Bradley has endeavoured to prove the unreality of Time appear to me perfectly conclusive' (*Mind*, vii, 1898, p. 202). When twenty years later Moore tore these conclusions to pieces (*Philosophical Studies*, 1922 [*PS*], chap. vi), he was making amends for the sins of his youth. However, Moore passed out of his Idealist phase very quickly, carrying Russell along with him. The Aristotelian Society paper 'The Nature of Judgement' (*Mind*, viii, 1899, pp. 176 ff.), developed out of Moore's second fellowship dissertation, shows him insisting, in opposition to Bradley, that fact is independent of experience. From the end of 1898 Moore separated himself completely from the dominant Idealist school, and his famous 1903 *Mind* article entitled 'The Refutation of Idealism' (*PS*, chap. i) directly attacked the proposition, 'essential to Idealism', that *esse* is *percipi*.

The ethical system which Moore expounded in *Principia Ethica*

[*PE*] is firmly rooted in his philosophical Realism. Just as yellow-
ness is a simple unanalysable property of things in the world so
also is goodness. This thesis of the unanalysability of goodness
has been regarded by professional philosophers for the last thirty
years as the most important part of the book; but for his Cambridge friends what came as a revelation was the combination of
this thesis with the insistence that there are many different sorts
of things which are good in themselves ('worth having *purely for
their own sakes*'), by 'far the most valuable' of which are 'certain
states of consciousness, which may be roughly described as the
pleasures of human intercourse and the enjoyment of beautiful
objects' (*PE*, 188). J. M. Keynes (*Two Memoirs*, 1949, pp. 81 ff.)
and Leonard Woolf (*Sowing*, pp. 144 ff.) have given fascinating
accounts of the impact of *Principia Ethica* upon the Cambridge
intellectuals of the time. The considerable difference between their
two accounts may arise partly from the fact that each had attached
most importance to that in it which spoke to his own condition.
What spoke to the condition of my generation in the immediate
post-First-World-War period, when *Principia Ethica* was as
widely read by intelligent undergraduates as ever before, was its
non-hedonistic and pluralistic utilitarianism ('Ideal Utilitarianism', as W. D. Ross later called it); and we would have agreed with
Leonard Woolf that

'Moore's distinction between things good in themselves or as ends
and things good merely as means, his passionate search for truth
in his attempt in *Principia Ethica* to determine what things are
good in themselves, answered our questions, not with the religious
voice of Jehovah from Mount Sinai or Jesus with his Sermon from
the Mount [nor, we would have added, with the authoritarian
voice of the State telling us what it was our duty to do], but with
the more divine voice of plain common-sense' [p. 148].

When Moore's prize fellowship at Trinity College ran out in
1904, the recent death of both his parents had left him with some
private means; and he went to live at Edinburgh, sharing an
apartment in Buccleuch Place with his friend A. R. Ainsworth who
held a lectureship at Edinburgh University. In 1908 Moore moved
south to set up house with two of his sisters on the Green at
Richmond, Surrey; and in 1911 he returned to Cambridge on his
appointment to a university lectureship there. Except for four

years in America during the Second World War the rest of his life
was spent in Cambridge.

Moore said that during these seven years away from Cambridge
he 'worked at philosophy as hard as, though no harder than' he
had worked during the six years of his fellowship. Besides writing
the book *Ethics* for the Home University Library series (1912) and
articles on William James's pragmatism and Hume's philosophy,
he started on a line of thought about the philosophical problems of
perception which he continued all the rest of his life and which,
by his Cambridge lectures as well as by his published writings, has
profoundly influenced Anglo-American philosophy. Moore centred
his discussion upon the notion of things which are 'directly
apprehended' in sense-perception, which he first called 'sense-
contents' (*PS*, 79) but later 'sense-data'. This was the term which
Moore used in the lectures he wrote out for delivery at Morley
College in London in 1910: although these lectures were not
published until 1953 (under the title of *Some Main Problems of
Philosophy* [*SMPP*], see p. 30), Russell had read this part of the
manuscript when, in his Home University Library volume *The
Problems of Philosophy* (1912), he gave wide publicity to the term
and notion of 'sense-datum'.

For Moore the fundamental question in the philosophy of
perception was the relation of these sense-data to material objects.
In the six pages devoted to this problem in the famous article 'A
Defence of Common Sense' which he contributed to *Contemporary
British Philosophy* (second series: ed. J. H. Muirhead) in 1925
(reprinted in *Philosophical Papers*, 1959 [*PP*]), Moore gave three
possible types of answer to the question: what do I know about a
visual sense-datum when I know that it is a sense-datum of my
hand? The first answer was that I know that the sense-datum is
part of the surface of my hand (*direct realism*). The second type of
answer (*representativism*) was that what I know is that there is a
unique part of the surface of my hand which stands in an 'ultimate
relation' R to the sense-datum. The third type (*phenomenalism*)
was that all that I know is a whole set of hypothetical facts to the
effect that, if certain conditions had held, I should have perceived
other sense-data intrinsically related in certain ways to this sense-
datum. [The type-names in italics are mine.]

Consideration of the arguments for and against answers of these
three types frequently took up the whole year (forty or sixty
lectures) of one of Moore's lecture courses at Cambridge in the

twenties. Besides discussing answers of the different types put forward by various philosophers (after first elucidating exactly what it was they wanted to say), Moore invented several forms of answer which were less open to objection. Hardly any of these highly original philosophic-theory-construction analyses are to be found in Moore's own publications, though some of them found their way, with due acknowledgement, into the justly celebrated writings of philosophers who had sat at his feet.

One reason why Moore, in his prime of life, never wrote a book on perception (or indeed on anything else) is, I suspect, that he saw the reasons against any view so clearly that he could never make up his mind which was on the whole the most defensible, especially since he was ingenious in recasting every theory into its least objectionable form. More of his thinking about direct realism—that the visual sense-data which we directly see are parts of surfaces of material objects—survives in his published writings than of his thinking about representativism or about phenomenalism (which is only discussed in some ten pages: *SMPP*, 132–5; *PS*, 188–92, 250–1; *PP*, 57–8). Perhaps because of this some present-day direct realists have claimed him as their master. I have no doubt at all that Moore would have liked to be a direct realist if his intellectual conscience had permitted him. But after sitting on the fence for forty years he definitely decided against direct realism in his last paper ('Visual Sense-Data', in *British Philosophy in the Mid-Century*, ed. C. A. Mace, 1957). Moore left no indication as to which of the other views he would prefer; but in his Cambridge lectures in the middle thirties phenomenalism received a far more favourable treatment than might have been expected.

Moore never lectured on ethics in Cambridge, and the developments of his ethical theory since *Principia Ethica* are to be found in his published writings. In *Principia Ethica* he had taken the goodness of the consequences of an action as defining the 'rightness' of the action; but in subsequent works he regarded rightness and goodness as independently given notions interrelated by logical relations. The only one of his later ethical writings which breaks really new ground is the ethical part of his 'Reply to My Critics' (*PGEM*, 535 ff.). Here among other things he discusses the 'emotive' theory of ethics, as it was then called, which had been put forward by C. L. Stevenson in his criticism of Moore, according to which the essential function of an ethical statement lies in its *emotive* and not in its *cognitive* meaning. Moore, indeed, goes further than Stevenson in suggesting that an ethical statement might have no cognitive meaning whatever ('nothing whatever that could possibly be true or false'). This view Moore admitted would be paradoxical, but he thought that 'very possibly it may be true' (*PGEM*, 542). Indeed at the end of his discussion he says that he is both inclined to think that ethical words have merely emotive meaning and inclined to think the contrary, and 'I do not know which way I am inclined most strongly' (*PGEM*, 554). It is rare to find a philosopher open-minded enough to be prepared, in his sixty-ninth year, to speak in this manner of a view which cuts away the presupposition of a doctrine that had made him famous in his youth and that he had maintained all his life.[1]

When Moore returned to Cambridge in 1911 as University Lecturer in Moral Science, it was arranged, to suit the teaching requirements, that he should give the lectures on Psychology for Part I of the Tripos. But, as is the Cambridge practice, the lecturer was given pretty complete freedom in deciding how to treat his subject. Moore has described how, influenced by the fact that C. S. Myers was giving lectures on Experimental Psychology, he designed his course as one on the Philosophy of Mind. He gave this course, three times a week throughout the three terms, for fourteen years. But from 1918 onwards he also lectured on Metaphysics, at least twice a week until 1925 (when he succeeded James Ward in his professorship) and three times a week after that until his retirement in 1939. Moore held discussion classes in connexion with each of his courses, and frequently it happened that a point raised in discussion made him revise in his next lecture what he had previously said. Moore never took sabbatical leave, and very seldom missed a lecture through illness; so any philosopher wishing to know how Moore was thinking could rely on finding him in Cambridge lecturing three times a week. Particularly after 1925, when 'A Defence of Common Sense' caused rumours of his 'method of analysis' to spread throughout the English-speaking philosophical world, there was hardly a year in which there were not one or two British or American philosophers, junior and senior, who had contrived, sometimes with great difficulty, to spend a term or a year in Cambridge to sit at Moore's feet.

[1] A. C. Ewing has recently reported that, in a conversation he had with Moore at some date after 1953, Moore said that 'he still held to his old view [that ethical statements have cognitive meaning], and further that he could not imagine whatever in the world had induced him to say that he was almost equally inclined to hold the other view' (*Mind*, lxxi, 1962, p. 251).

Whatever the subject-matter or nominal title of the lectures, examples of philosophic analyses were what Moore provided. In 'A Defence of Common Sense' Moore insisted, with respect to an unambiguous expression (like 'The earth has existed for many years past'), that 'the question whether we understand its meaning (which we all certainly do)' must be distinguished from 'the entirely different question whether we *know what it means*, in the sense that we are able to *give a correct analysis* of its meaning' (*PP*, 37). Moore's lectures were searches for correct analyses. One possible analysis was propounded, and elucidated in great detail; it was found defective in various ways, but could be modified to avoid these defects. But then the modifications had other defects. After worrying at and improving one type of analysis throughout some twenty lectures, Moore would then pass to another possible type and repeat the process of elucidating, criticizing, modifying, and criticizing again. In 1922–23, when I attended both courses of Moore's lectures, we hunted the correct analysis of propositions about the self on Monday, Wednesday, and Friday mornings and the correct analysis of propositions of the form 'This is a pencil' on Tuesday, Thursday, and Saturday mornings throughout the year. By the end of May, when lectures had to stop because the triposes started, Moore would have got through about two-and-a-half of the possible kinds of analysis. The lectures were quite inconclusive: Moore saw grave objections to any of the analyses he had discussed being the *correct* analysis, and the audience dispersed to sit their examinations, or to return to their homes across the Atlantic, without any idea as to which of the analyses had the best claim to correctness. Of course Moore was concealing nothing: he himself did not know which solution to prefer. In his 'Reply to My Critics', where he commented upon L. S. Stebbing's defence of him against Rudolf Metz's judgement that 'though we may call Moore the greatest, acutest and most skilful questioner of modern philosophy, we must add that he is an extremely weak and unsatisfying answerer' (*PGEM*, 521), he said: 'I did want to answer questions, to give solutions to problems, and I think it is a just charge against me that I have been able to solve so few of the problems I wished to solve.' And he added that he thought that probably one of the reasons for this was that he had 'not gone about the business of trying to solve them the right way' (*PGEM*, 677).

The way in which he went about trying to solve these problems was the way of 'analysis'; but Moore rarely directly attacked the question of what it is to give an analysis, and there are only eight pages in his published writings devoted explicitly to this question (*PGEM*, 660–7). Here he is concerned with the analysis of a concept (e.g. being a brother) and the analysis of a proposition (e.g. John is a brother); and from the examples of analysanda which Moore always takes in other places it is clear that he regarded an analysis of a proposition as the fundamental notion in terms of which the analysis of a concept was to be explained. For the purpose of analysis a concept cannot be treated in isolation: it must be considered in the contexts of the propositions in which it can occur. In lectures (which I attended) given in Cambridge in 1933–34, Moore went further than this: he said that sometimes a proposition cannot be analysed in isolation, but must be considered in relation to propositions which are its logical consequences. Here the system of logically related propositions would be the fundamental unit for analysis, and the analysis of the proposition would be given by means of its logical relations to propositions whose analysis was of a different kind. In mentioning this possibility Moore may perhaps have been influenced by F. P. Ramsey's ideas on the understanding of 'Theories', posthumously published in 1931 in a book to which Moore wrote a preface. Certainly what Moore was here suggesting, and the emphasis throughout his lectures on the relevance to analysing a proposition of what are its logical consequences, was in line with some of the things that Rudolf Carnap was about to say in his *Logische Syntax der Sprache* (1934). When I lectured on this book a few years later, I was able to make Carnap's way of thinking appear less alien to Cambridge philosophers by pointing out similarities to what Moore had been saying in an entirely different manner.

I have tried to indicate how it was that those of us who sat at Moore's feet regarded him as a far more original thinker, and one whose thought was always developing more, than did those whose knowledge of him was confined to his published writings. During the twenty-eight years of his teaching life at Cambridge Moore's conscientiousness in preparing his lectures, which were never the same from year to year, and his editorship after 1921 of *Mind*, left him little time for writing for publication. Almost all he published during this period were contributions to symposia at the Joint Sessions of the Aristotelian Society and the Mind Association, where Moore did what he was asked to do by discussing and criticizing most lucidly what had been said by other philosophers, but rarely added any ideas of his own. The great exception is 'A Defence of Common Sense' to which I have frequently referred (since for me it is the work most characteristic of Moore at the height of his powers); but this article only whets the appetite for a meal which the cook appears to be saving for his Cambridge *clientèle*. To use contemporary jargon, the public 'image' which Moore presents to many of his readers—that of a modern Johnson refuting the modern Berkeleys by holding up his hands instead of kicking a stone—is quite different from that of a philosopher with subtle and original ideas upon a great variety of important philosophical issues which is the 'image' that his pupils in the twenties and thirties formed of him. To give some examples from my own experience, Moore produced for us original ideas on causal theories of perception, on the analysis of 'If . . . then . . .' propositions, on the 'incomplete symbols' of *Principia Mathematica*, on how one gets to know logical truths, on the relations of expressions to one another and to what they mean (and the interrelationships of these various relations), on the importance of criteria of identity in giving analyses. Frequently, when I read excellent books and articles by distinguished contemporary philosophers, I find points which I remember hearing from Moore. [Indeed one of Moore's earliest publications contains the argument that 'in virtue of the deterministic hypothesis itself, the knowledge that a certain course of action was about to be pursued must always . . . make the result different from what was foreseen after a consideration of all the other elements that would contribute to it' and hence that 'the results of human volition, alone among causes, must *of necessity* remain incapable of prediction' (*Mind*, vii, 1898, p. 187), an argument which has been very prominent in recent free-will discussions, where it is usually attributed to an unpublished paper by Gilbert Ryle in the thirties.] After Moore's death there was found among his papers a 'Commonplace Book' in which he had recorded ideas for his private use: a selection of these entries is being prepared by Casimir Lewy for publication and will, I hope, show the wide variety of the questions with which Moore was concerned.

The main feature in the public image of Moore is his appeal to 'common sense' in his refutation of what Hume called 'excessive scepticism'; but how this appeal should be understood has been the subject recently of fierce controversy. In 'A Defence of

Common Sense' Moore, after giving examples of propositions such as 'My own and many other human bodies live on the earth' which are fundamental features of the 'Common Sense view of the world', says that 'I am one of those philosophers who have held that the "Common Sense view of the world" is, in certain fundamental features, *wholly* true'. And he goes on to say: 'According to me, *all* philosophers, without exception, have agreed with me in holding this: . . . the real difference . . . is only a difference between those philosophers, who have *also* held views inconsistent with these features in "the Common Sense view of the world", and those who have not' (*PP*, 44). This would seem to be clear enough. But several commentators on Moore have thought that he could not be speaking literally when he spoke of philosophers who held 'sincerely, as part of their philosophical creed, propositions inconsistent with what they themselves *knew* to be true' (*PP*, 41), since it is impossible for philosophers to hold views which they know to be false (Morris Lazerowitz, *PGEM*, 380). These commentators have therefore wished to say that what is important in Moore's argument is his pointing out that philosophers who make statements which appear to contradict common sense are using words in ways which deviate from the ordinary use of language. Norman Malcolm, for example, regards Moore's 'so-called defence of Common Sense, in so far as it is an interesting and tenable philosophical position', as being 'merely the assertion, in regard to various sentences, that those sentences have a correct use in ordinary language' (*Mind*, lxix, 1960, p. 97). Malcolm adds: 'This makes it into a very simple idea, but that is what good ideas sometimes are.'

But what Moore was concerned with was an even simpler and better idea—that philosophers ought not to contradict themselves. As Moore said in 1942, in reply to Lazerowitz, 'there is no reason whatever to suppose that this is impossible' (*PGEM*, 675), and, in a similar connexion in 1903, 'it is very easy to hold two mutually contradictory opinions' (*PS*, 13). And Moore knew what he was talking about, for in his early short Bradleyan phase he had indulged in exactly that type of 'double thinking' which he was to castigate in his maturity. Moore's anti-sceptical protest was directed against the temptation to which every philosopher (and linguistic philosopher) is subject, to be carried away by the apparent self-evidence of his premises or cogency of his argumentation into believing ridiculous conclusions—ridiculous because they contradict those common-sense beliefs which he has no intention of discarding. Hume oscillated between the 'philosophical melancholy and delirium' of 'excessive scepticism' and being merry playing backgammon with his friends. Moore rejected such a double life: the backgammon player, while philosophizing, must never forget that he continues to hold his common-sense beliefs. Moore's attack on the inconsistency of double thinking was as much moral as intellectual; and G. J. Warnock has rightly emphasized the influence upon philosophy of 'the *character* of G. E. Moore' (*English Philosophy since 1900*, 1958, pp. 11–12).

In his Autobiography Moore mentions the works of Bertrand Russell, W. E. Johnson, and C. D. Broad as those which had provided points upon which he had lectured in detail, and Johnson and F. P. Ramsey as those with whom he had long discussions on philosophy. Moore saw a good deal of Ludwig Wittgenstein in 1912–14, and after 1929 attended many courses of his lectures, 'always with admiration': after Wittgenstein's death he published an account of the contents of courses which he had attended between 1930 and 1933 (*PP*, 252–324). 'How far he has influenced positively anything that I have written, I cannot tell', Moore wrote in 1942. (My own view is that no positive influence is detectable.) But Wittgenstein made him 'very distrustful about many things which, but for him, I should have been inclined to assert positively' and 'think that what is required for the solution of philosophical problems which baffle me, is a method quite different from any which I have ever used—a method which he himself uses successfully' (*PGEM*, 33). Moore never attempted to employ Wittgenstein's or any other method of 'linguistic philosophy'; in his lectures in the thirties he discussed at length relations between synonymous expressions, but this was always in connexion with the analyses of the concepts or propositions for which these expressions stood. If, as some present-day philosophers suggest, Moore's anti-scepticism and method of analysis will take their place in the history of philosophy as *intimations* of a philosophy grounded on considerations as to how language is used, they will only be intimations in a Wordsworthian sense. For me Moore marks the end of one epoch rather than the beginning of another, though I should agree that the new epoch could hardly have begun if Moore had not definitely refuted the 'excessive scepticism' which has been such a temptation to post-Cartesian philosophers.

I have devoted so much space in this memoir to Moore's philosophical thinking partly because it has been misunderstood, partly because Moore's published writings do not display his full originality, but chiefly because, in his public character, Moore was a philosopher and nothing but a philosopher. In this is included being an educator of philosophers: Moore's single-minded and passionate devotion to the search for truth inspired all who came into contact with him. Moore was no respecter of persons. In the discussions following his lectures, at the weekly meetings of the Cambridge Moral Science Club which Moore regularly attended, and at the Joint Sessions of the Aristotelian Society and the Mind Association held annually at different universities, the beginner in philosophy who ventured with trepidation to raise a difficulty would find Moore assisting him to put his point more clearly, while a scholar of world-wide renown might find Moore telling him that he was talking utter nonsense. Moore's interventions were accompanied by gestures of his pipe and his whole body and with characteristically over-emphasized words ('*Oh*! you *really* think *that*?') which made it impossible for anyone to take offence. Moore's mere presence raised the tone of a philosophical discussion: it made flippancy or sarcasm or bombast impossible. We were compelled, sometimes against our wills, to be as serious, and to try to be as sincere, as Moore so obviously was himself.

Moore's endearing directness and simplicity showed itself also in university committees; and I will give two characteristic examples which continue to give me great pleasure. The first occurred in 1929 when Wittgenstein, returned to Cambridge, submitted his *Tractatus Logico-Philosophicus* as his Ph.D. dissertation. Russell and Moore were appointed his examiners; and Moore's written report to the Moral Science Degree Committee concluded as follows (I quote from memory): 'I myself consider that this is a work of genius; but, even if I am completely mistaken and it is nothing of the sort, it is well above the standard required for the Ph.D. degree.'

The second example concerns the title of the Chair which Moore occupied. When Moore was elected to it in 1925 it was the Professorship of Mental Philosophy and Logic, a title doubtless chosen in 1896 to give free scope to its first holder, James Ward. In 1933 the Council of the Senate thought that difficulties might be presented to the electors in the many cases of Cambridge chairs which had conjunctive titles, and asked the Faculty Board of Moral Science to consider omitting the reference to Logic in the title of the Chair so that the two philosophical chairs would be respectively of Mental Philosophy and of Moral Philosophy (the latter being the seventeenth-century Knightbridge Chair then held by C. D. Broad). We on the Faculty Board did not wish to perpetuate the obsolescent term 'Mental Philosophy', particularly since a Professorship of Experimental Psychology had recently been established; and we had a high philosophic discussion as to the best titles for the two chairs. Moore proposed that his Chair should be called that of *Theoretical* Philosophy and the Knightbridge Chair that of *Practical* Philosophy, citing Sidgwick as the authority for this dichotomy. We took a lot of time persuading Moore that such titles would give rise to ribaldry at our expense, for his proposal seemed to him so sweetly reasonable. Finally it was settled that the Knightbridge Chair should continue to be that of Moral Philosophy, but that Moore's Chair should be the Professorship of Philosophy with no qualifying adjective.

Moore had at different times been Secretary and Chairman of the Faculty Board of Moral Science, and for four years (1933–36) he was a member of the General Board of the Faculties as one of the two representatives of the group of four faculties which included Moral Science. Moore was no innovator in university matters, though he was open-minded to reforms suggested by others. His strength in council was his judicial cast of mind; and he was an excellent examiner and writer of testimonials. When he became professor in 1925 he was re-elected a Fellow of Trinity College (as a Professorial Fellow); and he served a four-year term as a member of the College Council. But he is most remembered in Trinity for *Die beiden Grenadiere*, which he sang each year at the party following the Commemoration Feast.

In 1921 Moore succeeded G. F. Stout as editor of *Mind*, and the twenty-six years of his editorship enhanced the high reputation of that journal. Moore took enormous trouble in corresponding, in his own hand, with contributors and in suggesting improvements in exposition; many young philosophers are deeply grateful to him for the informal 'tutorials' they thus received. The co-operation of Lewy in Cambridge enabled him to continue being editor through the years 1940–44 when he was in America; but increasing infirmity compelled him to resign in 1947.

Moore took a Cambridge Litt.D. degree in 1913, and in 1918

was given an Honorary LL.D. by St Andrews and elected a Fellow of the British Academy. He was President of the Aristotelian Society for the year 1918–19. In June of 1951 he was appointed to the Order of Merit. By a fortunate coincidence the Cambridge Vice-Chancellor was giving a garden party in Pembroke in honour of the newly-installed Chancellor on the day on which the Honours List was published. It was a brilliantly fine afternoon; and Moore (*aet.* 77) was able to attend, and to sit in a chair to receive our congratulations and to learn (if he did not know it before) how much we all respected and loved him.

In 1915–16 Moore made the acquaintance of Dorothy Ely, a Newnham College graduate who was attending his lectures in her fourth year; and they were married in December 1916. They first lived in a flat at 17 Magdalene Street, nearly opposite Magdalene College. Two sons were born of the marriage, and Moore became a devoted family man. In the early twenties one would meet him any fine afternoon pushing a perambulator along the Backs. In 1922 the Moores moved to a house in a terrace in Chesterton Road, about three-quarters of a mile from the centre of the town, which was to be their home for the rest of his life. All visitors to the house were received with an easy welcome; and one of the pleasures of being a Tripos examiner with Moore as chairman was that we met at 86 Chesterton Road and, when our morning's business was concluded, we descended into the semi-basement for a delicious luncheon, ending with glasses of Canary sack. It is impertinent to comment on happy marriages: all that I shall say is that the Moores provided a model of a way of living in which simplicity and seriousness were combined with an extroverted enjoyment of the good things of life.

In September 1939 Moore retired from his Cambridge Chair, having reached the age of 65. He became Emeritus Professor of Philosophy and remained a Fellow of Trinity College. During the Michaelmas Term of 1939 he went over once a week to Oxford to lecture—to a larger audience, as he reports, than had ever attended his lectures before. In August 1940 his American friends and former pupils Alice Ambrose and Morris Lazerowitz thought it better that he should think and teach philosophy in the United States than assist, at his age, in the Battle of Britain; and he was invited to be Neilson Visiting Professor at Smith College in Massachusetts for the autumn semester. He and his wife arrived in America in October and stayed there until May 1944. During the spring of 1941 he lectured at Princeton University; and in the summer Moore went west to be Howison Lecturer at the University of California in Berkeley, living (and also teaching) at Mills College near San Francisco. During this year Moore was largely occupied in writing the 145-page 'Reply to My Critics' (in *PGEM*), the most substantial and important work of his later life. At the end of the year the Moores returned to the eastern states; and Moore lived in New York and taught at Columbia University for two consecutive semesters in 1942 and throughout the academical year 1943–44. During the spring of 1943 he lectured at Swarthmore College in Pennsylvania. Moore gave single lectures at many other universities, and the Moores were able to visit their American friends during vacations. Moore had never been to the United States before, and was deeply appreciative of the kindness shown to him and Mrs Moore in these difficult years. From the American side Morton White (who had not sat at Moore's feet in Cambridge) has testified to the great impression Moore made upon the young New York philosophers. 'I believe that Moore, more than any of his distinguished contemporaries, communicated to his students the feeling that they could share his method even when they did not accept his philosophical beliefs.' ' "Do your philosophy for yourself" . . . was one of Moore's great messages to the young' (*The Journal of Philosophy*, lvii, 1960, p. 807).

Moore had had a few illnesses in America; and on his return to Cambridge in 1944 his doctor, to our great disappointment, forbade him the over-excitement that would result from his taking part in discussions at the Moral Science Club. For the rest of his life Moore rarely appeared in public, though he was able for some years to dine weekly in Trinity. He gave great pleasure to a group of European philosophers by appearing for an informal discussion about sense-data at a symposium organized for them at Peterhouse in 1953 by the British Council; and he wrote the short paper 'Visual Sense-Data' (already mentioned) specially for the volume that arose out of the symposium. Up to the end of his life he was able to talk philosophy for limited periods with individual friends, particularly Casimir Lewy and John Wisdom. But he was gradually getting feebler, and for the last few years osteoarthritis confined him to his house, though not to his bed. In the summer of 1958 he had to go into Addenbrooke's Hospital with a painful illness; and he died in Cambridge on October 24 eleven days before his eighty-fifth birthday.

B

GEORGE EDWARD MOORE[1]

by NORMAN MALCOLM

I

I should like to say something about the character of G. E. Moore, the man and philosopher, whom I knew for the last twenty years of his life. He was a very gentle and sweet-natured human being, as anyone acquainted with him would testify. For one thing, he had a wonderful way with children. When he read or told a story or explained something to a child, the scene was so delightful that the adults within hearing were enthralled, as well as the child. He liked to spend time with children. To one son, Moore gave a music lesson every day from his third year until he went away to prep school; and that son is now a music teacher and composer. Moore loved to sing and play the piano. He also took great joy in flowers and plants, and was anxious to learn their names.

Moore was himself a childlike person. One thing that contributed to this quality in him was an extreme modesty. It was as if the thought had never occurred to Moore that he was an eminent philosopher. I recall that once when lecturing before a small class he had occasion to refer to an article that he had published some years before, and he went on to remark, without embarrassment, that it was a *good* article. I was much struck by this. Most men would be prevented by false modesty from saying a thing of this sort in public. Moore's modesty was so genuine that he could say it without any implication of self-satisfaction. How many times, both in public and private, did he declare that some previous work of his was a 'dreadful muddle' or 'utterly mistaken'!

Another aspect of the childlike in him was the constant freshness of his interest, his eager curiosity. This was manifest in all things, but was particularly surprising and impressive in his philosophical work. During the approximately two and a half years I spent in Cambridge at two different periods, I had regular weekly discussions with him; also I went to his weekly 'at-homes', which were given over to discussion with whomever showed up. I was amazed

---

[1] Reprinted from *Knowledge and Certainty. Essays and Lectures*, Prentice-Hall, Inc., 1963.

at the way he reacted whenever anyone proposed a problem for discussion. He was all eagerness: never casual, never bored, never suggesting in his manner, 'Oh, yes, I have heard of that problem before'. His reaction was rather as if he had not known of it before and was anxious to look into it at once! This was so even if the topic was one that the others and himself had been thinking about together for many months. In the course of a discussion he would listen to everyone's remarks with breathless attention, as if what they were saying was entirely new and extraordinarily exciting. His younger son, who was then about seventeen years of age and a freshman at Cambridge, began to attend Moore's lectures, and I recall how in the course of a discussion that occurred after the lecture, Moore listened with this same intensity to a comment made by the young man, a beginner in philosophy and his own offspring! This continuously fresh interest and eager desire to learn was certainly one of Moore's most remarkable qualities as a philosopher.

Another aspect of the childlike in Moore was his simplicity. This was exhibited in both his speech and his writing. Although he had a mastery of the classical languages, as well as of French and German, he did not ever adorn his prose with phrases from those languages. And his writing is largely free of the jargon that philosophers typically fall into. He wrote in the plainest possible English, employing no elegant variation but rather continuous repetition. Rarely did he ever use any of the technical phrases or terms of art of philosophy; and when he did, he went to great pains to explain their meaning in the common language of everyday life.

Moore wrote an 'Autobiography', which is printed in the volume entitled *The Philosophy of G. E. Moore*.[1] In it he describes a striking episode of his youth. When he was eleven or twelve years old, he was converted by a group of young men whose evangelical views were similar to those of the Salvation Army. Moore says he felt it to be his duty to try to convert others as he had been converted, but that he 'had to fight against a very strong feeling of reluctance'. He did, however, drive himself to do various things which he 'positively hated'—for example, to distribute religious tracts. 'But I constantly felt', he says, 'that I was not doing nearly as much as I ought to do. I discovered that I was very

---

[1] The Library of Living Philosophers, Vol. IV, edited by P. A. Schilpp (Open Court Publishing Co., 1942).

deficient in moral courage.'[1] The three features of Moore's child-like quality that I have mentioned, his modesty, freshness, and simplicity, present themselves very clearly in his account of this incident, which I will not quote in full.

As a philosopher he was not very imaginative. He was not fertile in ideas, as was Russell. He was not a profound thinker, as was Wittgenstein. I believe that what gave Moore stature as a philosopher was his *integrity*, an attribute of character rather than of intellect. He had the depth of seriousness. When he addressed himself to a philosophical difficulty what he said about it had to be *exactly* right. Philosophical problems vexed him: but it was impossible for him to get one out of the way by ignoring some aspect of it with which he did not know how to deal. His lectures at Cambridge were always freshly written, and during a course of lectures he would continuously revise or take back what he had previously said. His lecturing was always new research, which is perhaps one reason why he never availed himself of sabbatical leave. His labour on any piece of philosophical writing was intensive and prolonged. To one paper, 'Four Forms of Scepticism',[2] he applied himself for some fifteen years. He gave the Tarner Lectures in Cambridge, but could not bring himself to publish them and therefore received no fee for the lectures.

The address that Moore delivered to the British Academy, entitled 'Proof of an External World', caused him a great deal of torment in its preparation. He worked hard at it, but the concluding portion displeased him, and he could not get it right as the time approached for his appearance before the Academy. On the day of the lecture he was still distressed about the ending of the paper. As he was about to leave the house to take the train to London Mrs Moore said, in order to comfort him, 'Cheer up! I'm sure they will like it'. To which Moore made this emphatic reply: 'If they *do*, they'll be *wrong*!'

The anecdote is entirely typical of Moore. It is not what people *believe* that matters, but the truth and only the truth. When I dwell in my mind on this true love of the truth, it disturbs me. A thinker with that kind of devotion to truth must go it alone, and this is awesome and frightening.

Moore's steady, immovable integrity was exhibited in every

---

[1] *Op. cit.*, pp. 10–11.
[2] Published posthumously in G. E. Moore, *Philosophical Papers* (New York: The Macmillan Company, 1959).

lecture, every discussion, everything he wrote. He had a stubbornness, not of pride, but of honesty.

Along with his perfect honesty there was another thing that contributed to Moore's stature, namely, his utter absorption in philosophy. He worked at it the better part of each day. He worked very slowly with intense concentration, and he came back to the same topics again and again. The philosophical problems stayed with him; they were part of his nature; for Moore to have given up philosophy would have been inconceivable.

Let me relate another anecdote which helps to point up this side of Moore. He was awarded the Order of Merit, the highest honour that a man of letters can receive in the British Empire. The presentation was to be made by King George VI, in a private audience. Moore and his wife went to London on the day appointed and took a cab to Buckingham Palace. Mrs Moore waited in the cab while Moore went into the palace. There he was met by the King's secretary and taken to the King's library. The secretary was a man of culture and also a Cambridge man, and while they waited for the King, he and Moore chatted about Cambridge. The King entered. He invited Moore to sit down and they talked for a while. Then the King presented the medal to Moore. After some further conversation the King arose, indicating that the audience was at an end. They shook hands and Moore was taken back to the gates of the palace. He re-entered the cab and, leaning over excitedly, said to Mrs Moore: 'Do you know that the King had never heard of *Wittgenstein*!'

This exclamation of Moore's illustrates not only his naïveté, but also his complete preoccupation with philosophy. Here is philosophy, the most exciting thing in the world; here is Wittgenstein, the most exciting figure in philosophy; and here is the King, who had not even heard of Wittgenstein!

Finally, Moore had an acute and energetic mind. He could hold together all of the strands of a long, complex, and subtle discussion. As he pushed deeper and deeper into a topic he would always know what the road behind had been, how he had got to the place he was in the argument.

Thus the qualities that contributed to Moore's philosophical eminence (and by eminence I do not mean fame, but rather the quality of being first-rate) were, I think, these: complete modesty and simplicity, saving him from the dangers of jargon and pomposity; thorough absorption in philosophy, which he found endlessly exciting; strong mental powers; and a pure integrity that accounted for his solidity and his passion for clarity. These were the primary ingredients in the nature of this remarkable philosopher.

II

Let us turn now to Moore's philosophical work. He made interesting contributions on many topics: perception, knowledge, facts and propositions, the reality of time, hedonism, idealism, universals and particulars; whether goodness is a quality, whether existence is a predicate; the proof of an external world, the nature of philosophical analysis: these are some of the topics on which Moore wrote. But as I reflect on his writings, his lectures, and his oral discussions, the thing that stands out most prominently for me is his so-called 'Defence of Common Sense'. I suspect that if Moore is remembered in the history of philosophy it will be because of this theme embedded in his philosophical thought. It was not there merely as an implicit assumption. He made it an explicit principle of his philosophy, so much so that in 1925 when he published an essay intended to describe his philosophical position he actually entitled it 'A Defence of Common Sense'.

Now what did Moore mean by 'Common Sense' and what is its importance in relation to philosophy? Writing in 1910, Moore said the following: 'There are, it seems to me, certain views about the nature of the Universe, which are held, nowadays, by almost everybody. They are so universally held that they may, I think, fairly be called the views of Common Sense.'[1] He goes on to say: 'It seems to me that what is most amazing and most interesting about the views of many philosophers is the way in which they go beyond or positively contradict the views of Common Sense.'

He proceeds to mention some of these 'views of Common Sense'. For example: 'We certainly believe that there are in the Universe enormous numbers of material objects, of one kind or another. We know, for instance, that there are upon the surface of the earth, besides our own bodies, the bodies of millions of other men; we know that there are the bodies of millions of other animals; millions of plants too; and, besides all these, an even greater number of inanimate objects—mountains, and all the stones upon

---

[1] G. E. Moore, *Some Main Problems of Philosophy* (New York: The Macmillan Company, 1953), p. 2.

them, grains of sand, different sorts of minerals and soils, all the drops of water in rivers and in the sea, and moreover ever so many different objects manufactured by men; houses and chairs and tables and railway engines, etc., etc.'[1] 'All this we now believe about the material Universe', he says; 'It is surely Common Sense to believe it all.' Another 'Common Sense belief' is this: 'We believe that we men, besides having bodies, also have minds.'[2] And another belief of Common Sense is that we *know* all of the things that have just been mentioned.[3]

In his essay 'A Defence of Common Sense', published fifteen years later,[4] Moore put down another list of 'Common Sense beliefs'. Among the sentences on this list are the following: 'I am a human being'; 'There exists at present a living human body, which is my body'; 'This body was born at a certain time in the past, and has existed continuously ever since'. He declares that each of us *knows* these things to be true of himself, and that it would be 'the height of absurdity' for any philosopher 'to speak with contempt' of these Common Sense beliefs.

It might be useful to stop for a moment to examine this phrase 'common sense'. To me it sounds odd to speak of 'a common sense belief', whereas the phrases 'common belief' and 'common knowledge' are quite familiar. It is, for example, a common belief that colds can be transmitted from one person to another. I doubt that we should call it a 'common sense belief' or a 'common sense view'. How do we actually use this expression 'common sense'? I can imagine one person saying to another: 'If you want so very much to enter the Civil Service, then it is common sense that you have to start preparing yourself for the examination.' 'It is common sense' means here 'It is the obvious conclusion'. I am inclined to think that this is how we commonly use the phrase 'common sense'. Something falls under that heading if it is an obvious conclusion from information at hand. In this common use of 'common sense', common sense has nothing to do with views about the universe, nor with the so-called 'belief' that there are enormous numbers of material objects in the world. We say of one person that he is lacking in common sense, and of another that he has lots of common sense. What this means is that the former has a tendency to arrive at conclusions which ignore obvious facts, and that the latter does not have this tendency. In general, the

[1] *Some Main Problems of Philosophy.*, pp. 2–3.   [2] *Ibid.*, p. 4   [3] *Ibid.*, p. 12.
[4] Republished in *Philosophical Papers*.

expression 'lacking in common sense' means 'lacking in good judgement'. Thomas Reid, the eighteenth-century Scotsman, who, like Moore, made 'an appeal to common sense' a foundation of his philosophical work, connected 'common sense' quite explicitly with good judgment:

'A man of sense is a man of judgment. Good sense is good judgment. Nonsense is what is evidently contrary to right judgment. Common sense is that degree of judgement which is common to men with whom we can converse and transact business.'[1]

A man of common sense is a *sensible* man—one who makes sensible judgments. He is not to be identified as a man who holds a certain set of *views*—about the world or anything else.

Suppose that a mother has a daughter, sixteen years of age, who takes singing lessons and is said by her teacher and others to have a pretty voice. Suppose this lady tries to persuade her husband to sell his prosperous business in the small town where they live and move to New York City, so that their daughter can study in a famous school of music. Her idea is that after six months of training, during which time they will live on savings, their daughter will become an opera and concert singer, and support them for the rest of their lives. This mother's proposal could be said to be extravagant and unrealistic on a number of counts. It could also be said to show a complete lack of common sense. Her husband, in arguing against this proposal and pointing out various objections, is showing common sense. He takes a common sense view of the matter. This is a faithful example of the actual use of the expression 'a common sense view' whereas to say that it is 'a common sense view' that there are an enormous number of material objects in the universe is to violate the ordinary use of the expression 'common sense'. It is not a matter of common sense at all. Common sense has nothing to do with it.

III

Since, as I hold, the examples that Moore gives of alleged 'common sense views of the world' actually are not examples of common sense, let us ask whether they are 'common beliefs',

[1] *Reid's Essays on the Intellectual Powers of Man*, A. D. Woozley, ed. (New York: The Macmillan Company, 1941), pp. 330-1.

or 'widespread beliefs', or 'universal beliefs', or 'things which we all commonly assume to be true', as Moore says they are. There is one item on Moore's list of which some, at least, of the above things are true: namely, the belief that 'the sun and moon and the visible stars are great masses of matter, most of them many times larger than the earth'.[1] This might even be said to be common knowledge, whereas at one time it was not. But consider the following examples: 'There are enormous numbers of material objects'; 'Acts of consciousness are quite definitely *attached* in a particular way to some material objects';[2] 'Our acts of consciousness . . . occur *in the same places* in which our bodies are';[3] 'There exists at present a living human body, which is my body'; 'I am a human being'. Is it right to say that nearly everyone assumes these things to be true, and even knows them to be true?

If you stop to think about the things on this list you will begin to see that all of them are queer sentences. Their queerness is brought out if we ask of each of them a question that Wittgenstein taught us to ask, namely, 'What is supposed to be the *use* of the sentence?' When would you seriously say it to someone? What would the circumstances be? What would be the purpose of saying it? Would it be to give someone information, or to admonish or warn him, or to remind him of something, or to teach him the meaning of a word, or what?

Let us try out this kind of inquiry with the sentence 'I am a human being'. When would you say this to someone or to yourself? If you think about it a bit, certain ways in which this sentence might be used will occur to you: (*a*) The first example that I think of is this: Suppose we lived in a region where there were beings who looked like bears but who talked our language, so that if you heard someone talking in the next room, you often could not tell whether it was a human being or a bear. If I were to knock on someone's door he might ask me through the door, 'Are you a bear?' and I could reply, 'I am a human being'. (*b*) Second example: A child might ask me, 'What is a human being?' and I could reply, 'I am a human being; you are a human being; the cat there is not a human being; the baby is a human being, but the dog is not'. Here I should be trying to teach him, by examples, to master the range of application of the expression 'human being'. (*c*) Third example: Suppose that someone had been falsely informed of my

---

[1] *Some Main Problems of Philosophy*, p. 3.
[2] *Ibid.*, p. 6. [3] *Ibid.*

death. When I appear before him he exclaims in terror, 'Are you a ghost?' I reply: 'I am a human being.'

Those are three sorts of cases in which you could seriously say the sentence 'I am a human being' and if we tried we could think of still others. Now when Moore wrote and spoke the sentence 'I am a human being', in which of these circumstances was he using it? In none of them, of course. Did he believe that someone somewhere supposed he might be a bear? No. Was he trying to teach someone the application of the expression 'human being'? No.

There is an inclination to think that if anyone were to utter the sentence 'I am a human being', he would be stating an *obvious fact*. But there is something wrong with this. I should not know whether he was stating an obvious fact until I knew how he was using the sentence: to what question he was addressing himself or what doubt he was trying to remove. I do not think this is over-sophisticated. If some stranger should come up to me and say, 'I am a human being', I should probably be at a loss as to what he meant. (Is he complaining of unfair treatment?) I should not know whether or not he was stating an obvious fact.

I am not holding, of course, that the sentence 'I am a human being' is meaningless. On the contrary, it is a sentence for which we can, without much effort, imagine various contexts of use. But if I hear or see that sentence and it is not clear to me what the context of its use is, then it is not clear to me what the person meant by that sentence on that occasion. It would be useless for him to reply, 'I meant that I am a human being!' That would be repeating the sentence without explaining what he meant by it.

One is strongly tempted to make something like the following reply: 'There is a certain assertion that a person normally makes when he speaks or writes the sentence "I am a human being". The sentence is ordinarily used to make that assertion. You may not know what the speaker's *purpose* is (Moore's, for example) in making the assertion in question. But you know that Moore used the sentence in its *ordinary sense* to make the assertion that it is normally used to make.'

Let us leave aside the cases in which one would not have made *any* assertion at all by saying that sentence. (For example, alone in my study, thinking about the 'Defence of Common Sense', I say aloud, 'I am a human being'. Have I made an assertion?) Why should we suppose that when the sentence is used to make an assertion, there is some *one and the same* assertion that is 'normally' made? How does one tell whether it is the same assertion that is made in different cases? Does not the particular doubt, the particular question at issue, have some bearing on this? In one of our examples the speaker *informed* someone that he was *not a bear*; in another, that he was *not a ghost*; in another that he is *called* a 'human being' (in contrast to a dog or a cat). If these differences in what is in doubt, in what comparisons are made, in what information is given, do not make for differences in *what is asserted*, then it will have no definite meaning to speak of one assertion as being 'different' or the 'same' as another one.

When Moore says 'I am a human being', I do not wish to agree or to disagree. It is not clear to me what he is saying. Of course he is addressing himself to philosophers, and it would be reasonable to assume that his utterance is relevant to some philosophical view. But what view? Could it be some thesis of Cartesian philosophy? But which one? What philosophical thesis has the implication that Moore is not a human being? When Moore's sentence is, instead, 'I *know* I am a human being', it is much easier to supply philosophical surroundings for it.

My general point is that not only does the famous 'Defence of of Common Sense' have no clear relationship to *common sense* but, furthermore, if we go through Moore's list of so-called 'Common Sense views' it is far from clear, with regard to some at least, either what assertions he was making or that he was making any at all.

IV

So far I have not succeeded in explaining why the 'Defence of Common Sense' was an important development in philosophy. I do not doubt that it was. I was strongly influenced by it, and so were many others. *Prima facie* it is not easy to understand what philosophical interest it has. Of what possible interest could it be to remind us that it is a universal or widespread belief that the sun is many times larger than the earth? Moore's list of 'common sense views' is an odd assortment. Some of the items in it, like the one just mentioned, are genuine common beliefs—but they have no apparent philosophical relevance. Some, like 'I am a human being', cannot be said to express common beliefs, nor am I certain that they have any philosophical relevance.

But there are some that are of real philosophical interest,

although they are neither 'common sense views' nor 'common beliefs'. An example in this category is the following statement from 'A Defence of Common Sense':

'I have often perceived both my own body and other things which formed part of its environment, including other human bodies; I have not only perceived things of this kind, but have also observed facts about them, such as, for instance, the fact which I am now observing, that that mantel-piece is at present nearer to my body than that book-case.'[1]

Considering that some philosophers have said that it is impossible for a person to perceive a material thing, this statement of Moore's has philosophical interest. In another work Moore discusses what he calls 'judgments of perception', and his examples are seeing an inkstand, or a door, or a finger. He makes this remark:

'Some people may no doubt think that it is very unphilosophical in me to say that we ever can perceive such things as these. But it seems to me that we do, in ordinary life, constantly talk of seeing such things, and that, when we do so, we are neither using language incorrectly, nor making any mistake about the facts—supposing something to occur which never does in fact occur. The truth seems to me to be that we are using the term 'perceive' in a way which is both perfectly correct and expresses a kind of thing which constantly does occur. . . . I am not, therefore, afraid to say that I do now perceive that that is a door, and that that is a finger.'[2]

In still another work Moore was commenting on a feature of Hume's philosophy, which has the consequence that no person can ever know of the existence of any material thing. He says:

'If Hume's principles are true, then, I have admitted, I do *not* know *now* that this pencil—the material object—exists. If, therefore, I am to prove that I *do* know that this pencil exists, I must prove, somehow, that Hume's principles, one or both of them, are *not* true. In what sort of way, by what sort of argument, can I prove this?

'It seems to me that, in fact, there really is no stronger and better argument than the following. I *do* know that this pencil

---

[1] *Philosophical Papers*, p. 33.
[2] *Philosophical Studies* (New York: Harcourt, Brace & World, Inc., 1922), pp. 226-7.

exists; I could not know this, if Hume's principles were true;
therefore, Hume's principles, one or both of them, are false. I
think this argument really is as strong and good a one as any that
could be used; and I think it really is conclusive.'[1]

Here there appears to be some sort of issue joined between
Moore and some other philosophers. But I expect that some will
be puzzled as to how anyone in his right mind can *deny* that we
see doors and know that pencils exist. Others, who feel no difficulty
about this, will be perplexed as to how Moore could think of
himself as *disproving* these views; for all he does is to declare that
he *does* see a door and does know that there is a pencil in front of
him; so he appears to be begging the question. I should like to say
something on both of these points.

With regard to the first point, anyone who begins to study
problems in the philosophy of perception will soon come upon a
number of arguments which appear to prove that it is impossible
to see a material thing. For example, H. A. Prichard, who held a
chair at Oxford and wrote and lectured from about 1910 to 1940,
produced various arguments to prove that it is impossible to see
bodies. Prichard accepted these arguments, and I expect he had
many followers. Speaking of the 'view' that we do see such things
as chairs, tables, and boats going downstream, he remarked: 'It
need hardly be said that this view, much as we should all like to be
able to vindicate it, will not stand examination.'[2] He said that the
'consideration of any so-called illusion of sight . . . is enough to
destroy this view'.[3]

I will not try to give a detailed account of how he thought that
the occurrence of 'illusions of sight' proves that we do not see
bodies, but the gist of the argument is something like this: If you
are to really see a body then 'the whole fact of seeing must include
the thing seen',[4] and furthermore the body cannot 'look other than
what it is'.[5] 'A body, if it be really seen and seen along with other
bodies, can only present to us just that appearance which its
relations to the other bodies really require'.[6] For example, if a
body were really seen it could not 'present the appearance which a
body similar but reversed as regards right and left can present', as
happens when we 'see' something in a mirror.[7] When it seems to

---

[1] *Some Main Problems of Philosophy*, pp. 119–20.
[2] *Knowledge and Perception* (New York: Oxford University Press, 1950), p. 53.
[3] *Ibid.*   [4] *Ibid.*, p. 53.   [5] *Ibid.*, p. 54.   [6] *Ibid.*, p. 53.   [7] *Ibid.*

us that we see a man moving in front of us (we are looking in a mirror), if 'that state, activity, or process which really only seems to us to be seeing a man move across in front of us had an intrinsic character of its own, in virtue of which it was only *like*, without *being*, seeing a man move thus, then that character ought to be recognizable at the time, in an act of self-consciousness, and if so it need not be true, as in fact it always is, that we can still have the illusion even though we are not taken in by it'.[1] 'If the state had a character other than being just like seeing a man move across, we ought to be able while in this state to recognize that it has this character, and if we did we should no longer have the illusion.'[2] There is no difference in 'intrinsic character', Prichard is saying, between what is ordinarily *called* seeing a body and the cases in which we are under an illusion of seeing a body. If there is no difference in 'intrinsic character' between two 'states', then if one of them is not seeing a body neither is the other. 'No one doubts that in certain cases we have or are under an illusion, and all I have been doing is to contend that all so-called seeing involves an illusion just as much as that so-called seeing which everyone admits to involve an illusion.'[3]

The argument may be briefly recapitulated as follows: Suppose there are two 'states', or 'states of mind',[4] A and B. They are states of either seeing or seeming to see a man in front of us. When state A occurs there actually is a man in front of us; state B is an illusion produced by a mirror. States A and B have the *same intrinsic character*—that is, if we considered state B 'in itself we could not say that it was not a state of seeing' a man in front of us.[5] State A, therefore, which is ordinarily *called* 'seeing a man in front of us' is not actually seeing a man in front of us, any more than is the admittedly illusory state B.

The reasoning is undoubtedly obscure; but at the same time it is extremely persuasive, and it is extremely difficult to put one's finger on any serious error in it. It is one of a number of attractive arguments that Prichard and others have used to prove, to the satisfaction of many philosophers, that we do not see bodies, and that what we really see are 'sense-data' or 'sensations'. Those arguments and that conclusion, in one form or another, dominated the philosophy of perception for centuries. If you consider Moore's remark, 'I am not . . . afraid to say that I do now perceive

---

[1] *Knowledge and Perception*, p. 50.   [2] *Ibid.*
[3] *Ibid.*   [4] *Ibid.*, p. 49.   [5] *Ibid.*

that that is a door and that that is a finger', and view it against this background of the history of philosophy, you will appreciate it as being a bold line to take.

This brings us to the second point, namely, what does Moore *achieve* by insisting that he does see material things? Is not this merely a stubborn refusal to accept the various arguments against it? Distinguished philosophers have given ingenious and persuasive proofs that we do not see material things. Moore says that we do, and that the proofs are wrong. But he does not say *how* they are wrong; so is he not begging the question?

It must be admitted that Moore never gave a satisfactory account of what he was doing; and so we ourselves must supply some explanation of this particular feature of the so-called 'defence of common sense', if we are to attribute any cogency to it. In the following I will attempt an explanation.

Prichard and the others must admit that we use such sentences as 'See my finger', 'Now you see the dog', 'Now you don't see him', every day of our lives; and furthermore that we are taught to use such sentences and teach their use to others. We are taught and do teach that the correct way to speak, in certain circumstances, is to say 'I see the dog', and in other circumstances to say 'I don't see him now', and in still other circumstances to say 'I think I see him', and so on. Undoubtedly Prichard used such forms of speech every day (and taught them to his children, if he had any) and would have acknowledged in various ways in practical life that they are correct forms of speech.

His philosophical position, however, stands in opposition to this obvious fact. I believe that Prichard was contending that we *cannot* see bodies, not merely that we do not. He says: 'I, of course, take it for granted that if it can be shown in certain cases that what we see cannot be a body, the same thing must be true of all cases.'[1] He implies, I believe, that if there is just *one* case in which someone is under the illusion of seeing a certain body in front of him then no one ever sees a body. As we noted, he offers the example of seeing something in a mirror as an instance of illusion.[2] I do not believe, however, that Prichard's real point could have been that visual illusions do occur *in point of fact*. Suppose that

---

[1] *Knowledge and Perception*, p. 54.
[2] J. L. Austin justly remarks that, normally, seeing something in a mirror is *not* an illusion (*Sense and Sensibilia* [New York: Oxford University Press, 1962], p. 26).

they should cease to occur (e.g., there are no more mirrors or reflecting surfaces): would Prichard be willing to admit then that we see bodies? Obviously not. The 'state' that we call 'seeing a body' would not have changed its 'intrinsic character' and could not do so. Visual illusions would be logically possible, and this would be enough to prove that we do not see bodies. Prichard says: 'A body, if it be really seen and seen along with other bodies, can only present to us just that appearance which its relations to the other bodies really require.'[1] It cannot cease to be a logical possibility that a body should present an appearance 'different from what its relations to the other bodies really require'. Prichard is holding that if we could see bodies then visual illusions could not occur. The actual occurrence of illusions is not necessary for his position. The logical possibility of illusions suffices. The logical possibility of visual illusions is an *a priori* truth. When Prichard's view is drawn out in the only direction it can go, it turns out to be the claim that it is an *a priori* truth that we cannot see bodies. He is holding that the very notion of *seeing a body* is absurd. It contains a requirement that *could not* be satisfied, namely, that visual illusion should be logically impossible. In order for this requirement to be satisfied the concept of seeing a body would have to be identical with the concept of seeing an after-image—which is an impossibility of an *a priori* sort.[2] Prichard is holding that there is a conceptual absurdity in saying such a thing as 'I see a raccoon in your corn patch', or in making *any* affirmative statement expressed by a sentence whose main verb is some form of the verb 'see', used in a visual sense and taking for its object the name of a body.

If those sentences embodied some conceptual absurdity then they would not have a correct use. They could never express true statements. But those sentences do have a correct use. A child is taught that he is wrong when he says 'I see pussy cat' while he is looking the wrong way, but that he is right when his eyes are following the cat's movements. If the sentence involved a conceptual absurdity he would never be right and he would not be told that he was. The language has the use that we give it.

To come back to Moore: When he said, against the sceptics, such a thing as 'I now see that door', it did not matter whether he

[1] Prichard, *Knowledge and Perception*, p. 53.
[2] The two concepts are compared in 'Direct Perception', *Knowledge and Certainty*, pp. 85–7.

was actually looking at a *door*. He did not have to produce an example of a *true* perceptual statement. In order to refute the claim that there is an absurdity in the concept of seeing a body, Moore did not have to present a *paradigm* of seeing a body, as I once thought.[1] He only had to remind his listeners and readers that the sentence 'I see a door over there' has a correct use and, therefore, *can* express a true statement. On one famous occasion Moore was actually in error in his example. This delighted his sceptical opponents in the audience. On my view he was right even when he was wrong.

I believe that Moore himself was confused about what he was doing, as is often so when one makes a philosophical advance. He always *tried* to present his audiences with examples of *true* perceptual statements. And he made a point of remarking that sentences such as 'I have often seen pennies' or 'I have often seen the moon' 'are correct ways of expressing propositions which are true. I, personally, have in fact often seen pennies and often seen the moon, and so have many other people'.[2] Why does he have this interest in giving examples of perceptual statements which are *true*, if it is irrelevant whether they are true? Part of the explanation (perhaps all of it) is Moore's mistaken idea that when he is dealing with a proposition put forward by a philosophical sceptic he is dealing with an *empirical* proposition. That Moore has this idea is shown, for one thing, by his famous 'proof' of the existence of external things.[3] In 'A Reply to My Critics', he states explicitly that a philosopher who holds that there are no external objects is 'making a false empirical statement'.[4] Undoubtedly he would be inclined to say the same thing about Prichard's proposition that we do not see bodies, or about the common philosophical view that no one has absolutely certain knowledge of any empirical fact. But the examination of a typical argument for the latter view makes it plain that what is being held is that it is *logically* impossible for anyone to know with certainty the truth of any empirical statement.[5] Our brief study of Prichard's claim shows that, on his

[1] I misunderstood this point when I first wrote on Moore. In 'Moore and Ordinary Language', I said that Moore's replies to various sceptical assertions consist in presenting *paradigms* of knowing something for certain, seeing bodies, and so on. *The Philosophy of G. E. Moore*, p. 354.

[2] 'Visual Sense-Data', *British Philosophy in the Mid-Century*, C. A. Mace, ed. (New York: The Macmillan Company, 1957), p. 205.

[3] 'Proof of an External World', *Philosophical Papers*, pp. 145–6.

[4] *The Philosophy of G. E. Moore*, p. 672.

[5] See 'The Verification Argument', *Knowledge and Certainty*, especially p. 56.

view, we could not see bodies unless something which is a logical possibility (visual illusion) were to become a logical impossibility—which is itself a logical impossibility. In replying to Prichard, therefore, it is both unnecessary and misleading for Moore to assert that he has often seen the moon. It does not matter whether he has. What is necessary and sufficient, and also puts the view he is attacking in its true light, is to point out that the sentence 'I see the moon' has a correct use. It is surprising that anyone should think it has not: but philosophical reasoning has a peculiar power to blind one to the obvious.

It has been claimed that in previous writings I identified Moore's 'appeal to common sense' with his 'appeal to ordinary language', and that this is a mistake because they are different.[1] I want to insist, however, that if Moore's so-called 'defence of common sense' has any cogency, then it is not really about *common sense* or *common beliefs*, for neither of these things is relevant to the philosophical issues in which Moore is involved. I take the philosophers with whom he is engaged to be asserting that the notion of seeing a body (or of having absolutely certain knowledge of an empirical truth, and so on) contains a logical absurdity. The actual efficacy of Moore's reply, his misnamed 'defence of common sense', consists in reminding us that there is a proper use for sentences like 'I see the broom under the bed' or 'It is known for certain that he drowned in the lake'. As Moore remarks, when we say such things we are not 'using language incorrectly'.[2] We should be *if* those sentences did embody some logical absurdity. The philosophical positions that Moore opposes can, therefore, be seen to be false *in advance* of an examination of the arguments

---

[1] Alan R. White, *G. E. Moore: A Critical Exposition* (Oxford: Basil Blackwell & Mott, 1958): see Chapters 1–3. V. C. Chappell has an interesting discussion of various interpretations of Moore's 'defence of common sense' in his article 'Malcolm on Moore' (*Mind*, LXX, no. 279, July 1961, 417–25). Chappell mentions two interpretations that differ from the one put forward here. One is ascribed to Moore himself. Its principal feature is the assertion that Moore's opponents are maintaining empirical theses. But in order to find out what kind of thesis a philosopher is maintaining, we have to consider the kind of support he offers for it. Prichard's reasoning, for example, clearly implies that his thesis is nonempirical. The other interpretation, put forward by A. Ambrose and M. Lazerowitz in their essays in *The Philosophy of G. E. Moore*, contains the claim that Moore's opponents are essentially making 'verbal recommendations'. But there is no natural sense of 'recommend' in which Prichard, for example, can be said to have *recommended* that we should no longer *speak* of seeing bodies.

[2] *Philosophical Studies*, p. 226.

adduced in support of them. We can know that something is wrong with Prichard's reasoning before we study it.

We are able to see now why Moore was not begging the question against Prichard: for when we understand the latter's position we realize that he was contending for something that is, beyond question, false. That is just the point that Moore made. He was not begging the question because the point he made (without fully realizing it) was that it is *not even a question* whether those sentences of ordinary language have a correct use.

Here there comes to light a genuine connection with common sense. Prichard showed a lack of common sense, in the ordinary meaning of the words. He was led by persuasive reasoning into losing sight of the obvious fact that it is correct to speak of seeing bodies. He was blind to something that was right before his eyes. In contrast, Moore resisted that temptation. In tenaciously keeping sight of the obvious he showed common sense.[1] And also he 'appealed to common sense', in the common meaning of the words, when he reminded other philosophers of the plain facts of language.

Why should we not say that what Prichard was blind to was the fact that we do see bodies? Because, as I tried to show, his denial that we see bodies is really the claim that it is logically impossible to see bodies. Moore's assertion that we do see the moon and pennies and doors can be taken as a *reply* to Prichard only if it is understood as the assertion that there is no logical absurdity in the notion of seeing a body. But is it a 'common sense view' or a 'common belief' that it is logically possible to see bodies? No. It is the kind of observation that only a philosopher makes or understands.

V

I believe that Moore's misnamed 'defence of common sense' was a philosophical step of first importance. Its effect is to alter one's conception of the nature of philosophy and thereby to change one's philosophical practice. Clearly Prichard would have looked at

---

[1] I owe this observation to Professor G. H. von Wright. (I would not be thought to be extolling common sense as the supreme virtue of a philosopher. Many first-rate contributions to philosophy have been made by thinkers who developed their ideas in disregard of absurd consequences. They would rather be rigorous than right. As Austin remarks: 'In philosophy, there are many mistakes that it is no disgrace to have made: to make a first-water, ground-floor mistake, so far from being easy, takes one (*one*) form of philosophical genius.' J. L. Austin, *Philosophical Papers*, J. O. Urmson and G. J. Warnock, eds. [New York: Oxford University Press, 1961], p. 153.)

what he was doing in an entirely different way had he seen the soundness of Moore's position. He would have realized that he could not possibly prove that it is impossible to see bodies! He might have been unable to detect anything wrong in his reasoning. But he would have known that *something* was wrong in it. His attitude toward his own philosophical work would have been different.

Wittgenstein says: 'A philosophical problem has the form: "I don't know my way about."'[1] That is: 'I am confused'; 'I am in a muddle'. But I think a philosophical problem can take this form only if one sees the soundness of Moore's defence of ordinary language. One is tempted to hold that certain ordinary expressions *cannot* have a correct use: at the same time one realizes that of course they *do*. Then one knows that one is in a muddle.

Prichard did not have that attitude towards this view of his about seeing. If that had been his attitude he would have thought: 'Here I am inclined to hold something absurdly false, namely, that we cannot see bodies. Where in my thinking do I go *wrong*?' Instead, he said that the 'common view' that we see bodies 'will not stand examination'. He really thought that our ordinary language of perception needs to be corrected.

Wittgenstein says: 'Philosophy may in no way interfere with the actual use of language; it can in the end only describe it.'[2] This conception of philosophy is entirely different from Prichard's. He thought that philosophy *could* 'interfere with the actual use of language'. To think of philosophy as Prichard did is enormously different from thinking of a philosophical problem as a confusion. Philosophy has a different *feel* in the two conceptions, and the actual steps one will take in conducting one's philosophical inquiry will be different.

I believe that in order to grasp Wittgenstein's idea that a philosophical problem is essentially a confusion in our thinking, and that philosophical work cannot interfere with the actual use of language but must 'leave everything as it is' (that is, leave our actual use of language as it is, not leave everything in philosophy as it is)—in order to grasp this idea, one must understand what is right in Moore's defence of ordinary language. The latter was an advance in philosophy because it brought us nearer to a true understanding of philosophy itself.

[1] Ludwig Wittgenstein, *Philosophical Investigations*, tr. G. E. M. Anscombe (New York: The Macmillan Company, 1953), sec. 123.
[2] *Philosophical Investigations*, sec. 124.

MOORE'S COMMONPLACE BOOK[1]

by MORRIS LAZEROWITZ

G. E. Moore was one of the philosophical titans who changed the course of philosophy and our way of doing it. The appearance of his *Commonplace Book* is thus an event of special importance, not only for those philosophers who, in varying degrees, do their work under his influence, but also for those who resist it. Moore kept philosophical notebooks between 1919 and 1953, nine altogether; and Dr Casimir Lewy has published a selection of the entries, in chronological order, under the title Moore gave to his last six notebooks. The reflections recorded in the notebooks, which Moore intended for his private use, are indeed a welcome addition to the things he published during his lifetime: they exemplify the same ideal of clarity and accuracy that his known writings do, and they will undoubtedly add to the effect Moore has already had on the practice of philosophy.

In his memoir of Moore, Professor Braithwaite writes that '. . . after 1925, when "A Defence of Common Sense" caused rumours of his "method of analysis" to spread throughout the English-speaking philosophical world, there was hardly a year in which there were not one or two British or American philosophers, junior and senior, who had contrived, sometimes with great difficulty, to spend a term or a year in Cambridge to sit at Moore's feet.'[2] Moore's 'method of analysis' has of course become an established way of doing philosophy, and it is continuously exemplified in his *Commonplace Book*. There can be no doubt whatever that the effect Moore's analytical method, and particularly that part of it which goes under the name of 'translation into the concrete', has had on philosophy is deep, permanent, and salubrious, and that, despite expected reactions against it, academic philosophy will become less and less available as a sanctuary for intellectuals who work on the premise that depth of thought is incompatible with clarity of thought and who have a predilection for the former.

[1] Reprinted from *Philosophy*, Vol. XXXIX, 1964.
[2] 'George Edward Moore 1873–1958', *Proceedings of the British Academy*, Vol. XLVII, 1961, p. 300.

At one important university an attempt has been in process to revive a way of thinking in philosophy which was popular before Moore's work sobered philosophers, before it brought them down to the earth of Common Sense. But its revival is uneasy, and it is safe to say that the prospects of its having a considerable duration and influence are not excellent—because of what Moore has done for philosophy. What was all right before Moore is not all right after Moore. The two most important things which Moore did for philosophy, to give a general characterisation, were first, to bring philosophical talk into connection with ordinary language, which no philosopher really gives up or even modifies to make it square with his philosophical talk, and second, to show philosophers, by the example of his own work over the years, how to use the technique of analytical elucidation. The first tended to bring to our awareness the splitting mechanism which kept our philosophical talk psychologically sealed off from our everyday use of language. And this awareness enabled us to scrutinise philosophical statements with improved vision. The second, the method of analysis as practised with Moore's enormous skill and in combination with an intellectual integrity which everywhere shows through, enabled us to see, or to begin to see, what the limits of philosophical investigations are, what sort of information analysis can yield. Socrates gave us the formula: follow the argument wherever it leads. Moore's actual practice gives us the formula, not easy to adhere to: follow the analysis *impersonally* wherever it leads. *The Commonplace Book*, which covers Moore's private reflections for a period of thirty-four years, is a continuous illustration of Moore's method. It will easily be realised that this is a book for thoughtful browsing, not for reading straight through.

Braithwaite states in his memoir that 'Moore rarely directly attacked the question of what it is to give an analysis, and there are only eight pages in his published writings devoted explicitly to this question'.[1] This is substantially correct, and it is interesting that in the *Commonplace Book* also very little is expressly given over to the question as to what the conditions are which govern the correct analysis of a concept. The first entry in Notebook VI reviews some of Moore's discussion in the eight pages referred to in *The Philosophy of G. E. Moore* and contains several interesting and useful observations on the difference between statements

[1] 'George Edward Moore 1873–1958', *Proceedings of the British Academy*, Vol. XLVII, p. 301.

which display what might be called a 'decomposition' analysis of a concept and statements whose apodoses are not, either explicitly or implicitly, 'contained in', 'part of', or 'included in' their protases, yet follow logically from them. Thus, although according to the logician's book of rules, the disjunctive statement 'cats mew v dogs bark' formally, or logically, follows from the first disjunct, the statement cannot according to Moore's criteria be properly said to constitute an *analysis* of the disjunct, as it is not contained in or a part of 'cats mew'. A common way of characterising an analytic proposition is to say that it is one the consequent of which is *identical with* some part of the antecedent, so that the joint assertion of the antecedent and the negation of the consequent is self-contradictory. But 'cats mew v dogs bark' is not identical with part (nor the whole) of 'cats mew', although 'cats mew. $\sim$ (cats mew v dogs bark)' is self-contradictory. The criterion of the contradictoriness of the denial is, as Moore by implication maintains, not a condition for analyticity: a proposition may be an instance of a law of formal logic and not be analytic. It is important to point this out, in order to make modern logicians look again at some, at least, of their elementary formulas. The formula '$q. \supset .p \vee q$' is not analytic, in that '$p \vee q$' is not an *analysis* of 'q', although '$p \vee q$' is said to *follow from* 'q'. We might be inclined to justify our saying that '$p \vee q$' follows from 'q' by pointing out that '$q: \sim p. \sim q$' is self-contradictory. It could be charged, however, that 'q' has been smuggled into the formula via an inconsistency in which it plays no sort of role. Whatever has happened to create a rift between the criteria of 'Moore-analyticity' and the criterion of the self-contradictoriness of the opposite, the rift needs to be called to the attention of logicians. In the same entry, Moore criticises Professor Hempel who, with other logicians, has put forward the claim that a proposition which is a specification of '$(\exists x)\phi x$' is also a specification of '$(\exists x)\phi x. \sim (\phi x. \sim \phi x)$', that, e.g. 'Something is a cat' is the *same* proposition as 'Something is a cat and it is not the case that it is both a cat and not a cat'. The consequence of this claim that Moore brings out is that 'every tautology is the same as every *other* tautology', which is to say that there is only *one* tautology. But it would seem obvious that 'It is not the case that there is something which is both a beetle and not a beetle' is not the same proposition as 'It is not the case that there is something which is both a granite mountain and not a granite mountain'. In accordance with the conditions Moore has laid down for anything being an analysis, he points out that '$(\exists x)\phi x. \sim (\phi x. \sim \phi x)$' is not *contained* in '$(\exists x)\phi x$' and thus is not an analysis of it. A cleavage is shown thereby to exist between logical entailment and Moore-analyticity. The underlying point of this would seem to be, to put the matter quite generally, that '$p. \supset . \sim p \vee p$' and also '$pq. \supset . \sim q \vee \sim q$' are logicians' formulas[1] which need further looking at: the negation of the first produces a contradiction between *antecedent* and *part* of the denied consequent (which would indicate that the other part has been smuggled in), while the negation of the second produces no contradiction *between* antecedent and negated consequent.

The *Commonplace Book* contains something under 190 entries, varying in length from two lines to as many as six pages; and as those who got to know Moore would expect, there are no reflections on 'the meaning of life' and related popular topics.[2] With perhaps one exception, Moore throughout addresses himself to technical points, and always with an absence of flamboyance and with meticulous regard for accuracy. The topics touched on or dealt with at substantial length, and in many instances returned to again and again, are varied, including points about time, causality, necessity, language, entailment, propositions and sentences, sense-data, motion, universals, certainty, existence, number. The weight of the subject-matter in roughly the first half of the *Commonplace Book* is theory of perception: the weight of the subject-matter in the latter part is logic and language, although, of course, these subjects are not treated exclusively in one or the other parts of the book. Moore's passionate and abiding desire for truth, or to use a word which carries with it less of an emotional aura than the word 'truth' does, his passionate and constant wish to get at the *facts*, make him come back to and re-examine many times points he had made and analyses he had performed. Moore had a deep respect for philosophy and he approached its problems with the attitude of a scientist. He did not deliver himself with blithe abandon on a plethora of subjects, an intellectual abandon which in so many shows an underlying disrespect for their subject.

[1] The first formula results from simple substitution on '$q. \supset .p \vee q$' and the second, in Lewis' notation written '$p. \prec .q \vee \sim q$', is argued for in Lewis and Langford's *Symbolic Logic*, p. 251.

[2] Moore sometimes surprised his friends with the unexpected. Some of us who enjoyed musical sessions with him expected him to have a strong preference for Bach as against such romantics as Schumann and Hugo Wolf, but it was just the other way round.

In his private notebooks as in the writings Moore published while alive he shows the steadfast concern of the scientist to make sure of his findings; and his limitations are the same as those of a research scientist.

A few comments may be made about two or three of the major topics in the book. As is well known, Moore's published writings played an absolutely central role in the modern development of sense-datum theory, but in none of them, with the exception of his last paper, 'Visual Sense-Data', which appears in the volume *British Philosophy in the Mid-Century* edited by Professor C. A. Mace, did he come to a decision about the question of whether visual sense-data are ever parts of the surfaces of physical things. In his last paper he decides against the view that they are. It therefore comes as a surprise to read in one of his early entries (p. 78) 'Double images have convinced me that the sense-datum of which I am speaking when I say "That's a sofa" is *not* identical with any part of the surface of the sofa'. His argument, in this entry, is that when I see the sofa or my finger double (1) 'the two images are two different *things*' and (2) it cannot be 'that one of the two is the surface of my finger, & the other something else, not identical with any physical object'. The conclusion to be drawn from this line of reasoning would seem to be that visual sense-data are *images*, the same in their intrinsic nature as after-images one sees with closed eyes: they are open-eye images, so to speak. The question arises (p. 79) as to 'whether sense-data continue to exist when we don't see them', and this question would seem to have a categorical answer, namely, that they cannot. After-images which we have with closed eyes, like dream images, are the kind of things that do not exist unperceived; and if visual sense-data are *images* they too are the kind of things that do not exist unperceived. A dream does not go on in the absence of a dreamer, nor an image in the absence of a perceiver. Nevertheless to Moore the visual sense-datum of a sofa [the example in the entry changes to that of a visual sense-datum of a jug] is something which when he stops seeing it 'seems only a cessation of [his] seeing it, *not* of the coloured thing [he] saw' (p. 79). So far as I am aware Moore does not resort to the Humean sort of explanation of how we come to have the idea of 'independent and continu'd things', the bogus explanation, that is, of how we form an idea which, according to Hume's own showing, we cannot have.

To restate the matter linguistically, in terms of what it makes sense and does not make sense to say, the terms 'image' (in the sense of mental image) and 'surface of a material thing' have a use which makes the expression 'image which is part of the surface of a material thing' descriptively senseless. They also make senseless, rule out from having any application in the language, such expressions as 'image which exists but which no one has', and such a philosophical form of words as 'independent and continued image'. If, now, the visual appearances that things present are identified with visual sense-data, which in turn are counted as images, then no visual appearance can be identical with part of the surface of a physical thing, and no thing can, logically, be as it looks. For if the surface of a thing could have the visual colour, say, it appears to have, we could picture to ourselves parts of the surface. But what we can picture could, theoretically, be presented to our senses, which is to say that it is a possible appearance, or a possible sense-datum. If, however, a sense-datum is an image, it would make no sense to say that any part of the surface of a material thing is as it looks, as that would imply that part of the surface of a material thing is or could be an image. Furthermore, it would seem clear that if the surface cannot, logically, be as (supposedly) it appears, i.e. cannot have a property ϕ which the putative appearance endows it with, then it cannot present the appearance of having the property. The outcome of the view that sense-data are images would seem to be that it makes no sense to say, e.g., 'The top surface of the button is round and blue', and this implies that it makes no sense to say 'The top surface of the button looks round and blue'. Material things could not present visual appearances.

In several entries other considerations which Moore adduces lead to this result, and also to a further result, of which, perhaps he was unaware, and which he might have rejected, of course. In one place he writes (p. 225): 'You can say that in "This book is *red*", "I'm having a red after-image", *red* is used in the *same* sense, and that in saying of a book that it "*is* red" and of an after-image that it "*is* red", "is" is being used in a different sense, but "red" in the same: that "is" in the first case = "would look to a normal eye by good light", and in the second something indefinable. "*Is* red", "*was* red", "*will be* red" certainly have different meanings in the 2 cases, but *one need not say* ⟨?⟩ that "red" has.' In another place he writes (p. 147): 'It is quite certain that when you say of a physical surface that it "looks blue", "blue" is being used in the same sense as when you say of an after-image (closed eye) that it *is* blue. Why? (It is a necess. condition of its looking blue to you, that you should see the colour blue, in the same sense as when you see an after-image which is blue.) But this being so, the phrase "it looks blue, but it isn't blue" is deceptive, because it *looks as if* you were saying of the very same quality which the thing looks to have, that it hasn't got it; whereas if I am right that "*is* blue" in this usage = "would look blue to normal persons in good daylight at a proper distance", it's really only a play on words. . . . On my view, it throws a curious light on the use of "looks" of physical things: we only say "looks φ" when φ is a property which no physical thing *could* possibly have—which it's nonsense to attribute to any.'[1] The implication this would seem to have is that things cannot, logically, *appear* to have properties of colour and shape. For if it is logically impossible for anything *to be* blue, then it is logically impossible for anything to look *to be* blue, and if 'it's nonsense to attribute' φ to *x* (e.g. weight to numerical oddness) it is nonsense to attribute to *x* the appearance of its *looking to be* φ. What a thing looks to be it could, in principle, be, and what it cannot, in principle, be it cannot sensibly appear to be: we cannot with sense 'say "looks φ" when φ is a property which no physical thing could possibly have—which it's nonsense to attribute to [it]'.

The result that material things cannot sensibly look to have colour or shape is strange, as Moore notes. Stranger still, perhaps, is the further consequence that *nothing* could appear to have properties of colour and shape (and other sensible properties also, of course). On the present view sense-data cannot be said to have the properties material things sensibly *look* to us to have, and it might be contended that sense-data themselves cannot, therefore, exist. Putting this aside, however, and looking instead at a common characterization of sense-data, namely, that they '. . . always really have the qualities which they sensibly appear to us to have',[2] it can be maintained that sense-data cannot themselves present sensible appearances. In the ordinary use of 'appears' and 'looks' according to which it is intelligible English to say, e.g., '*x* looks (or appears to be) blue but that is not its actual colour', it is literal nonsense to say, 'My sense-datum looks blue, and as closer

---

[1] It is interesting that in *Some Main Problems of Philosophy*, p. 38, Moore had said: 'It seems very probable . . . that *none* of the sizes and shapes seen were the size or the shape of the real envelope.'

[2] 'A Defence of Common Sense', *Philosophical Papers*, p. 56.

inspection shows, actually is blue', just as it is not intelligible English to say, 'My after-image looks blue, but perhaps it isn't; I shall have to look again'. When a philosopher makes the statement 'A sense-datum has the properties it sensibly appears to have', he means to say, 'A sense-datum *necessarily* has the properties it sensibly appears to have'. It is clear that in his philosophical use of 'appears', to say with regard to a sense-datum, or an after-image, that it looks blue is to say *the same thing as to say* that it is blue: 'A sense-datum has the colour it appears to have' says the same thing as 'A sense-datum has the colour it has'. In the ordinary, non-philosophical sense of 'appear' and 'look' it is 'nonsense to attribute' appearances to sense-data: 'in the case of a [closed eyes] after-image there is no sense in saying that it would look red under certain circumstances, but doesn't look red now' (p. 327). If it is logically impossible for a sense-datum to look blue or round, and also logically impossible (on the view that Moore was trying out) for material objects to look blue or round, then the plain consequence is: *nothing* can, logically, look blue or round. Moore undoubtedly would have said about this, as he does say about the consequences he elicits, that its 'strangeness might be used as an argument that it isn't true' (p. 147). Common Sense is his final criterion, and it is interesting to realize that a good many years ago he was impelled to write about a type of view under frequent discussion in recent years: 'Broad says, & Russell commends his opinion, that I can never tell (even with the smallest probability?) that when I judge with certainty that a particular colour is a shade of blue, what I mean by using the words "is a shade of blue" is the same as what anyone else means. This view seems to me to be nonsense. I know not only with great probability but with certainty, that *I* mean by "is a shade of blue" what other people mean by it: though *how* I know this I cannot tell' (p. 18).

Two closely related topics which Moore considers in a number of entries are universals and propositions, with regard to which he consistently takes a Platonic position, i.e. he holds that universals and propositions are a kind of entity. Braithwaite states that he has not been able to detect any positive influence whatever on Moore by Wittgenstein, and certainly Moore's thinking on universals and propositions was not in any way affected by the various things, now so much in vogue, that Wittgenstein said about them. Moore confided to me only a few years ago that in his opinion *all* that Wittgenstein meant by 'rule of grammar' was what he, Moore, meant by 'necessary proposition'. Moore and Wittgenstein respected each other, but neither succeeded in influencing the other. And perhaps this was as it should be, for each had his own things to say.

To return to universals and propositions, in one place, interestingly enough, Moore asks the question 'But what *is* a proposition?', rather than the question (the form of which he made famous) 'What is the analysis of the meaning of the word "proposition"?' One has the impression that he was never satisfied that he knew *what* a proposition was, its breed. With the great clarity which was almost unique with him, he distinguishes in various ways between sentences and propositions, between saying a sentence, understanding a sentence, asserting a proposition, etc. To give one example of a distinction he makes, whose implications it is worth-while to try to get clear about, he writes (p. 359): 'The words (or sentence) "He said it *was* raining" obviously don't mean the same as the words "He said the words 'It *was* raining'". A man may quite well have said it was raining without saying those words; & he might quite well have said those words without saying that it was raining.' There are a few places where Moore slips into using the word 'proposition' to mean sentence (p. 260). However, with typical accuracy he distinguishes in a number of enlightening and useful ways between the uses of 'proposition' and 'declarative sentence'. He remarks on the 'illegitimate sense in which people use [the word "true"] when they say that sentences are *true*' (p. 231), and later he says (p. 375): 'Every proposition which is true, except propositions about sentences, *could* have been true, even if there had been no sentences: from the fact that it's true that the sun is shining it doesn't follow that there are any sentences, since if the sun *is* shining, it follows that it's true that it is, & it obviously does not follow that there are any sentences.'

It is not easy to see how philosophers like F. P. Ramsey and A. J. Ayer would, following Moore's carefully drawn distinctions, be able to meet Moore's Platonic claim about propositions, without invoking the so-called Verification Principle. And it hardly needs to be said that Moore knew the Verification Principle and was perfectly familiar with its application to statements about universals and propositions. Moore's version of Ramsey's view about propositions is that '. . . a proposition is a class of sentences, grouped together as having the same meaning' (p. 359). Ayer's statement of the position is the following: '. . . we may define a proposition as a class of sentences which have the same intensional significance for anyone who understands them. Thus, the sentences, "I am ill", "Ich bin krank", "Je suis malade" are all elements of the proposition "I am ill".[1] Against this view Moore could say (p. 375): 'It is *not true* that if there were no instances of sentences there would be no propositions; since, even if there had never been any sentences, some propositions might have been true & others false. . . .' A curious consequence of the Ramsey view would seem to be that understanding an indicative sentence in one language implies knowing sentences in all languages which translate into it. For understanding 'I am ill' implies knowing the proposition it expresses; and if the proposition is the class of sentences which have the same meaning as or translate into the sentence, then understanding it implies knowing the sentences 'Ich bin krank', 'Je suis malade', and their equivalents in all other languages.

Moore's analyses were always guided by considerations of correct language, and it may not be too far off the mark to say that facts of correct or proper usage were the ultimate facts for him. Indeed, if we stop to reflect on the matter we may wonder what it is a philosopher is doing who goes against usage. Moore, as is well known, represents him as making a 'mere mistake'; and if this is not the final explanation of what the philosopher does, it is a necessary step towards the right explanation. In one entry he observes (p. 258): 'To talk of *deducing* one sentence from another sentence is not English. What these people must mean is deducing *what is expressed by* one sentence from *what is expressed* by another.' To point this out is important, and it is also important to point out, as he does elsewhere, differences in use between the 'if p, q' of ordinary language and the logician's '$p \supset q$' (p. 391): 'And it is certain that a person who knew either of these 3 possibilities $[p.q, \sim p.q, \sim p. \sim q]$ to be the case would be deceiving you if he said "if p, q". If you asked him "How do you know that 'if p, q'?" & he said "because I know $\sim p$", or said "because I know q", we should say that it is *not* a good reason for saying "if p, q"—it doesn't shew that you know "if p, q"; whereas it would be a good reason for $p \supset q$.' Being told this would help students of formal logic and it might also have a moderating effect on logicians.[2]

---

[1] *Language, Truth and Logic*, 2nd edition, p. 88.

[2] In one way or another the two so-called paradoxes of material implication, '$q. \supset . p \supset q$' and '$\sim p. \supset . p \supset q$', tend to be represented as exhibiting astonishing properties of 'if p, q' rather than uninteresting properties of disjunction artificially freed from conditions of relevance.

A final fragment of analysis should be cited which occurs in the last entry of the *Commonplace Book*. The whole entry is something more than a page and bears the title *Free Will*. It contains the following sentences: 'What is a "voluntary movement"? When a bird flies away, that is a voluntary movement; but the bird doesn't "choose" to make it. And in general we don't *choose* our voluntary movements, or *decide* to make them.' This presents a distinction which is enlightening, for it calls attention to similarities and differences between 'Mary blushed furiously', 'Mary slipped but managed to right herself', 'She sat down', 'She wrote a letter', 'She decided to go to the cinema'. It is also, perhaps, a piece of autobiography. Moore, more than anyone I have ever known or know about, could with inner dignity come to terms with what has to be.

SOME NEGLECTED ISSUES IN THE PHILOSOPHY OF G. E. MOORE[1]

by J. N. FINDLAY

I propose to speak to you this evening on some neglected sides of the thought of G. E. Moore. It might seem strange that one can find anything neglected in a philosopher so much admired and so frequently cited as G. E. Moore. The fact is, however, that, as in the case of a great philosopher like Leibniz, whose fame among his contemporaries was vast, Moore's general 'image', even among philosophers, is very far from doing justice to the actual thinker: in some respects, I should say that he really is the unknown philosopher. The people who read him, teachers and pupils alike, generally read him by the way, as leading up to or throwing light on other people: he is rather like Padua or Verona, with their incomparable art-treasures, in which people spend a few hours on their journey to Venice. There is, if you will read some recent writing on Moore—I shall refer particularly to Professor Wisdom's Foreword to *Some Main Problems of Philosophy* and to Mr Alan White's in many ways excellent book—a note of faint patronage, of historical relegation, in the way people speak of Moore: he is spoken of much as the Germans used to talk of *der gute Locke*. I wish to suggest this evening that Moore is undoubtedly the greatest British philosopher of the present century, and that he stands with perhaps William of Ockham and David Hume among the three greatest philosophers we have ever produced. No one has at all approached him in dialectical accuracy, or in the ability to talk with unfailing clearness on the most difficult of philosophical issues. Even as a stylist I should hold him unsurpassed. Why then is it the case that he is so comparatively unappreciated?

The reason for such under-valuation lies, I think, in the fact that Moore, like some immense central peak in a mountain range, always managed to be partially occluded or overshadowed by less eminent but nearer peaks, as a background to which he was

[1] A paper given at the Cambridge Moral Sciences Club and the Royal Institute of Philosophy. Reprinted from *Language, Mind and Value*, George Allen & Unwin, Ltd., 1963.

invariably seen. For the first quarter of the century we have the period of his occlusion by Russell, an immensely dazzling philosopher, whose greatness at that period, though inferior to Moore's, I should not wish to abate in the least. For the second quarter of the century we have the period of his occlusion by Wittgenstein, a man whose wonderful but somewhat confusing genius was assisted to immense influence by his unique personal magic, an influence which has declined steadily since his death. Why did Moore, whom I think more penetrating and more responsively constructive than either of these thinkers, allow himself to be thus occluded? The answer lies in his incredible personal modesty which was not, as perhaps in the case of Socrates, at all ironic: in other ways, however, he was more like Socrates than any philosopher that has ever lived. Socrates you may remember—we may for the moment pretend that the *Phaedo* is history—spent a lot of his time in youth studying the books and attending the lectures of the philosophers, and wondering why on earth they said the queer things they said, and this study was the stimulus which led him on to his own inquiries: Moore in much the same way was jolted into philosophy by the queer statements of McTaggart, Bradley and other idealist philosophers, and without their stimulus would never have developed his profound analysis of common sense. Moore was essentially a man who required prodding, a great lazy genius, who would produce a masterpiece if asked to give a lecture to some quite unimportant body of amateurs, but who, if not asked, preferred to take refuge in the dream world of *Redgauntlet* or Mr Pickwick. Moore, like Cézanne, thought little of his work: his remarkable book *Some Main Problems of Philosophy*, which he gave as extension lectures to Morley College, was never published at all. I am immensely glad that Professor Lewis has rescued it from oblivion, and that I urged him to go and look for the treasures that Moore might have in store. A great deal of Moore's most valuable thought is, I believe, still contained in lecture notes, and will be published by Dr Lewy.

With this really small opinion of his own performance went a great and generous admiration for the intellectual performance of others: being slow and infinitely cautious, he admired the meteoric swiftness of Russell, the wonderful mental versatility of Ramsey, the brilliant queerness of Wittgenstein. Moore liked to be a commentator on other people's work: 'Russell has said, Broad thinks, I know Wittgenstein maintains though I am not quite sure that I

c

understand it', etc. etc. I shall not pretend, of course, that he admired everyone's intellectual performance, and where he did not admire it, he either showed or said it. But the generosity of his spirit meant that he constantly let himself be silenced by others: while he was starting to construct one of his incomparable, scrupulous sentences, others less scrupulous had already leapt into the breach, and Moore readily deferred to them. All this was a little unfortunate, since his utterances, when he developed them fully, had a quality that no one else's could approach.

Another reason for Moore's general overshadowing is that his most brilliant philosophical work, like that of Russell, was early: it extends to about 1925. In that period Cambridge thought as a whole was overshadowed by Oxford idealism: at Oxford, if one referred to Cambridge thinkers at all, it was only to utter epigrams. When Cambridge thought began to gain on that of Oxford in the 'thirties, Moore's genius was in decline: he made few fundamental innovations, and became more and more absorbed in the minutiae of correct expression, which led the historical or legendary Chinese student to remark that while Moore might have taught him little about the universe, he had certainly taught him much about the English language. It also led to the monumental misinterpretation of Moore by Malcolm—a misinterpretation whose interest I do not deny—which made Moore refute philosophical errors merely by showing them to be stated in bad English. I have, I think, said enough of the reasons why Moore has not been properly appreciated. I hope that some people here who knew Moore better than I did and over a longer period, will be able to resolve some of my perplexities, and perhaps also criticize some of my interpretations and assessments.

What now are the aspects of G. E. Moore that I think particularly worth stressing? I think that by far the most interesting, characteristic thing about G. E. Moore is not his ordinariness, his common sense, but the *gnostic* character of his philosophical approach. Moore claims that we know certain truths, e.g. that this is a pencil or that a human hand, and that we know independently that we have knowledge of them, and that this knowledge, though its existence and detailed content may be mysterious, is incomparably firmer than any premiss dragged up to confute it, or any argument used to subvert it. What I think it important to stress is that Moore means his claim to know certain things to be a remarkable, *substantive* claim, something it would not be at all senseless or contrary to usage to deny. This is shown, first of all, by the fact that Moore says that we are incomparably *more* sure of what we know than of any premiss or argument that could be used to show it false, or that could be used to show it true. There are certainly passages where Moore suggests that we cannot, in some sense of 'cannot', be wrong about what we know, but I do not think that his claims to knowledge make any use of the infallibilism thus merely written into the notion of knowledge. What he in effect means by knowledge is just what he says: it is for something to be much more certain than any premiss used to prove it false, and also much more certain than any premiss used to prove it true. It is to occupy a supreme, an unchallengeable place on the ladder of certainty, not a place differing wholly from any other place. And of course what we know need not be logically necessary, and does not in this way differ from what we merely believe.

I think, further, that the substantive character of Moore's claim to knowledge comes out in the fact that he uses it most impressively in the case of *singular* certainties, in regard to which there is what may be called an *immediate* element. I do not primarily know *general* propositions about material realities and their relation to sense-experience, dreams, etc., about other minds and their relation to behaviour, about the past and its relation to memory, etc. etc. What I primarily know is that *this* pencil exists, that *this* is a human hand and so is *that*, that the name 'Moore' was uttered by myself a few moments ago, that Professor Stace whom I now see has thoughts and that I am not dreaming that I see him, however much it may be the case that I often have dreams in which I seem to meet intelligent people. The *singularity* of the Moorean gnosis is all-important, and it is here that Moore is quite at variance with Malcolm who thinks that one produces human hands, etc., merely to show that certain expressions have a use, and that provided one knows they have a use, one might dispense with the particular illustrations. Moore does not think that one can dispense with the particular examples, nor does he regard them as mere illustrations: they yield the necessary premisses on which our more general knowledge reposes. It is quite possible *in general* that I might be dreaming when I seem to confront someone like Professor Stace, and there may be no living person of that name at all: when I confront Professor Stace in the lecture room, however, I cannot doubt that I am face to face with a living person, with thoughts as well as with a body, etc. etc.

I think it important to stress, further, that my knowledge of all these singular matters of fact does not merely mean that the situation is appropriate to my making certain utterances, that it is the sort of situation in which such utterances have a use. Moore thinks that the gnosis involved in such situations goes beyond anything palpably contained in them, and that it would therefore not be inappropriate or stupid to refuse to make my gnostic statements: only I should then know them to be false. 'Where therefore I differ from Russell', Moore says, 'is in supposing that I do know certain things that I do not know immediately, and which also do not follow from anything which I do know immediately.' The message of the somewhat confused *Proof of an External World*—Moore was right in not thinking it one of his best writings—has been widely misconceived, by myself among others: it may be taken to mean that, since I can correctly say 'This is a human hand and that is also', therefore it is certain that two human hands, and therefore two material objects exist. What it is all-important to note is that Moore only thinks the proof valid because he thinks that he *knows* the premises, and the knowledge involved in those premises is for him immense and substantial, and goes far beyond the immediate situation. It is in fact amazing that we have such knowledge, though the fact is that we undoubtedly do have it. It includes the knowledge that one is not dreaming, that what one is seeing could have existed even if no one had experiences, etc. etc. At no point does Moore think that it would not make sense to say that one was dreaming: he merely thinks that one sometimes knows that this is not the case, and that the unwary statements of philosophers who say that all is a dream, show that they really all know that this is not the case. I therefore come to my second major puzzle regarding Moore: why, since his views are plainly not those of Malcolm, did Moore never repudiate Malcolm's account of his views? Why did he never correct Malcolm when he put forward these views as Moore's own? Why did he allow Malcolm to persuade many people to think that Malcolm's linguistic-use interpretation of Moore's gnosis was Moore's view? Malcolm has of course admitted that his whole interpretation was a 'theory', based, it seems clear, on a conflation of Moore with Wittgenstein. Why did Moore permit all this? I leave it to those better acquainted with Moore to provide a full answer.

Moore's gnosis may seem to be attenuated by the comparatively commonplace character of what he claims to know: it covers what he calls the *common-sense* view of the world. It is worth emphasizing, however, that what Moore puts into this common-sense view is not anything and everything that men are disposed to believe, but matters concerning instances of what may be called the *main categories* of existent things and their essential properties and relationships, matters whose acknowledgement is so wrought into, so presupposed by, organized discourse that such discourse is largely disrupted by their denial. What he knows of is the existence of many material bodies occupying space and standing in spatial relations to one another, that have existed in long ages of the past and will presumably exist in the future; he likewise knows of the existence of acts of consciousness in connection with the body he calls *his* own, and of parallel acts of consciousness in connection with other similar living bodies: he also knows about the knowledge he has of various facts and about the precisely parallel knowledge of other persons of other corresponding facts, etc. etc. What the gnosis reveals are the existence of the main types of furnishings of the experienced world and their essential interrelations, and though it may reveal them primarily in the immediate, individual case, yet it would not seem to arrive at its total world-picture through a process of piecemeal extension. There is in fact something very Kantian about the world professedly open to common-sense, an impression strengthened by the use of transcendental arguments to buttress its main certainties, arguments which show these certainties to be presupposed by all our arguments, even by such as seek to undermine them. But however much the structure and main contents of the common-sense world may be basic to discourse, Moore still thinks that they may with some effort be questioned. We may speak as if they did not exist or obtain, without committing absurdity in doing so, but we shall *know* that we are not then speaking truly.

The substantive character of the Moorean gnosis is of course plainer when we turn to his views on analysis. Moore plainly treated his analyses with the greatest of seriousness. There is even a sense in which one might say that his common-sense certainties are ambiguous: they might mean A, they might mean B, they might mean C, etc. etc. In making common-sense assertions, we are for Moore committing ourselves to *one* out of a number of queer alternatives, and the whole task of philosophical analysis consists in finding *which* of the queer alternatives is the true one.

This is fortunately a point on which Moore *has* committed himself to a definite assertion. In reply to the suggestion of Lazerowitz that his various revolutionary analyses are merely linguistic recommendations, proposals to alter the language ordinarily used in certain situations, Moore tells us that he definitely does not think this was all he was trying to do, that he certainly holds that analysis is of concepts, not of verbal usages, etc. etc. I think therefore that Moore is positively misrepresented as a philosopher of what most people understand by 'common-sense', even though he may himself have adopted the designation. For Moore thinks there are abysses of incomprehension even in our most commonplace certainties. And many of the queer things that other philosophers assert in controversion of commonplace certainties Moore asserts in analysing commonplace certainties. The views of Moore are in fact *more* queer than those of the metaphysicians he attacks, for while they say that certain commonplace beliefs are false, and other queer things true, Moore says that certain commonplace beliefs are really the *same in content* as certain wildly strange beliefs. So far from really holding that 'Everything is what it is and not some other thing', Moore may be said to have held that everything when scratched shows itself to be something quite unsuspected.

I think we must not forget the immense substance Moore packs into his analyses: he is so sure that this pencil exists, that he knows it exists, that he is prepared to think that he may know that something exists which he has never observed and never will observe, and that it stands in a relation he also has not observed nor will observe to what the senses reveal of the pencil. And he is prepared, if nothing else will do, to refute Hume and Hume's principles by this drastic piece of gnosis. And he is prepared to maintain, in the face of all immediate appearances, that when I say 'That is a door', the ultimate subject of my judgment is not a door, but something, a 'sense-datum', of which most people have never heard at all, and which is in fact introduced just to *be* the real subject of this sort of judgment. It is worth emphasizing, too, that while Moore thought the analysis of commonplace certainties more likely to end in failure than success, he was still gnostic about analysis. We can certainly, if we reflect, know that we *don't* include certain things in certain of our concepts, that certain analyses *won't* work at all. Thus Moore never falters in repudiating idealistic accounts of material-object statements, though surprisingly he is not unwilling to accept phenomenalist accounts, perhaps because a possibility of sensation has something objective about it. Propositions as entities are likewise very decisively rejected because we see that the relation of a mind to a proposition *cannot* be what obtains when we consider cases of false belief, and this in the face of the fact that Moore admits, both early and late, that a perfectly good sense can be given to the statement that there are propositions. That statements can be given a perfectly good sense, and have a use, does not therefore make them correct as analyses.

What is now the role of ordinary language in this queer analytic *approfondissement*? Ordinary language we may say is the net in which we catch the fish (or the dolphin or mermaid) which we then get to perform in our analytic aquarium: alternatively it is the press gang that captures the man of whom we then proceed to make an able seaman. The role of ordinary language is to ensure that we have a *genuine* notion before us for analysis, that we are not merely playing with words and saying nothing at all. Let me take a case of Moore's use of ordinary language from the brilliant but forgotten article 'The Subject Matter of Psychology' published in 1909. Moore says: 'I wish here to define as clearly as I can those kinds of entities which seem to me to be undoubtedly mental and to consider how they differ from those which are not mental. To begin with then: I see, I hear, I smell, I taste, etc., I sometimes feel pain; I sometimes remember entities which I have formerly seen or heard, I sometimes imagine and I sometimes dream; I think of all sorts of different entities; I believe some propositions, and think of others without believing them; I take pleasure in certain events and am displeased at others; and I sometimes resolve that certain actions shall be done. All these things I do, and there is nothing more certain to me than that I do them all. And because, in a wide sense, they are all of them things which I do, I propose to call them all "mental acts". By calling them acts I do not mean to imply that I am always particularly active when I do them. No doubt I must be active in a sense, whenever I do any of them. But certainly when I do some of them I am sometimes very passive. Now I think we may say that, whenever I do any of these things, I am always "conscious of" something or other. Each of these mental acts consists, at least in part, in my being conscious of something. I do not mean to say that in the case of each of them I am conscious of something in one and the same sense. For instance when I actually see a colour I am certainly conscious of that colour in a very different sense from that in which I am conscious of it when I remember it half an hour afterwards and do not any longer see it. And I am not sure that there is anything whatever in common to these two senses of "consciousness". But still I think the name can certainly be rightly applied to what occurs in both these cases, and that similarly we are, in *some* proper sense of the word, conscious of something whenever we do any of the acts I have named.'[1]

The above is a marvellous piece of Moorean concept-trapping. We trap a concept by taking a number of ordinary phrases in regard to which we are sure that they have an application, and we introduce various other phrases, e.g. 'mental act', by connecting them precisely with some of these. Even here Moore does not teach that the mere fact that we use a word in certain circumstances shows that there is a clear and consistent concept behind that use: in certain cases, however, we do know this, and the ground is now prepared for further analysis. It may be noted how Moore is willing to gather together concepts under a new concept which may never have previously existed, e.g. mental act, and how he also allows that a word which appears to have one sense may be found to cover a number of quite distinct concepts, e.g. 'consciousness'. What is remarkable in the whole process is how firmly it secures the existence of its subject-matter by using ordinary words that we *know* have an application, and how resolutely it then moves from that ordinary starting-point towards goals more and more extraordinary. There is in Moore no great respect for the suggestions made to philosophers by ordinary language: he thinks in fact, as a famous passage testifies, that it is sometimes so constructed as systematically to mislead them.

We must in philosophy get our concept away from the net in which we have trapped it; we must make it *perform* in our analytical aquarium, in which special environment we may find it doing astonishing things that it never did in ordinary contexts. The kind of tests we put it through consist in trying to detect affinities and differences not ordinarily noted, and using in this connection the now standard method of conceptual experiment. Moore asks, e.g., if we can conceive a case in which there might be an act of consciousness which had not that relation to other acts of consciousness which is ordinarily expressed by the phrase 'belonging to the same mind', and decides that he *can* conceive of it, or at least that he isn't clear that he cannot. This experiment reveals the

[1] *Aristotelian Society Proceedings*, n.s., Vol. 10, 1909–10.

independence and distinctness of two concepts: mentality in the sense of being an act of consciousness, and mentality in the sense of belonging to a mind, which are not normally kept apart at all. Only last week I heard the same method elaborately applied at Oxford: we had to deal with people who couldn't move their own limbs directly, but who could move remote objects directly, and their own limbs indirectly by them, etc., etc. I do not myself think the method of conceptual experiment a safe one in philosophy, tending as it does to cut off the vague penumbra which is implied by, rather than included in, a concept, but it remains a conceptual technique which has *some* importance even now, as it had in the time of Descartes and again of Moore. In all this procedure Moore makes us think of Plato's procedure as described in the Seventh Epistle. In philosophical thought we don't deal with mere words, definitions, illustrations, etc., we have to rub them all together in the mind until reason flashes forth. We may start with the routines of ordinary usage, but we may end with our thought and language utterly transformed.

I have given you two aspects of Moore not sufficiently regarded: his profound gnosticism, and his use of ordinary language to make sure that we *have* a substantial gnosis and not a mere verbal appearance of one. I now wish to consider a number of other aspects I regard as very fundamental. The first is Moore's assertion of the unique nature of consciousness, its complete categorial difference from anything attributive. In this respect he brought to full clearness in England a perception which Brentano and Husserl clarified on the Continent, that being conscious is not at all like being blue, that the one is *of* things in a way in which the other is not. Moore possibly got this idea from a reading of Brentano who also influenced his ethics profoundly, but his main interest in it was of course as a tool to combat epistemological idealism and to put epistemological realism in its place. The source of this interest explains why Moore's analysis of consciousness remains rather rudimentary and in fact ends in failure: Moore is unable to give more than a very partial analysis of the thought of the non-existent, and never worked out a complete map of the forms of consciousness as was done by Husserl. The very faulty 'Refutation of Idealism' has, however, as its main merit, the insistence on the unique character of consciousness, and also the insistence on its accessibility. Consciousness represents something of which, though it may be retiring and evanescent, we can in some circum-

c*

stances be directly aware. I think it clear that Moore never gave up his belief in the reality and seizable character of what he called 'conscious acts', that for him such words as 'apprehension' and 'knowledge' meant more than peculiar series of sense-contents or of considered and correct speech and action: they meant something interior and episodic, realizable in an instant and fitly described by way of metaphors derived from illumination and light. In apprehension and knowledge something appeared to, was before the mind, and this appearing or being before the mind was itself something that could be taken note of or apprehended. At the time when Russell was trying to get away from intentionalism in the *Analysis of Mind*, Moore was unable to go the whole way with him. He pointed out that in mental contexts we never merely have loud sounds, red patches, etc., but sounds heard *as* loud, patches seen *as* red, etc., that more or less disengaged universals play a part in mental contexts that they do not in physical ones, and that one cannot in consequence adopt Russell's oversimple picture of two modes or arrangement of sense-contents giving rise to the mental and physical worlds. Hints of these views are to be found in the paper 'Are the materials of sense affections of the mind?' published in 1920.

I must confess, however, that I do not understand what Moore meant by his strange statements in the 'Defence of Commonsense' (1925) that he feels 'doubtful whether there is any intrinsic property expressed by the words "I am conscious now"', and 'that the proposition that he has had experiences does not necessarily entail the proposition that there have been any events which were experiences, and that he cannot satisfy himself that he is acquainted with any events of the supposed kind'. It is really very obscure how one can have experiences without there being events, things which happen to one, which *are* experiences. I should have said the one was entirely tantamount to the other. Perhaps the stress is on the word 'intrinsic', and Moore means to hold some view of consciousness as a *relation* among a number of entities. If this is so, I think it wholly obscure what he thought this relation was. Perhaps he was at this time in a genuine wobble about consciousness, as he was at a later time in a wobble about the predicate 'good', as where he remarks amusingly that he is inclined to think that the predicate 'good' is not the name of a characteristic, that it has merely 'emotive' and not cognitive meaning, but that he is also inclined to think that this is *not* the case, and that he cannot say in which way he is inclined more strongly. I have heard it said that Moore in his later years definitely came out of this particular wobble, and *was* more inclined to believe once more in the unique non-natural character of goodness, and on the only occasion on which I discussed consciousness with Moore his remarks suggested that he had come out of his 1925 wobble also, and that he again believed consciousness to be something unique, irreducible and well known.

Moore then had something valuable and important to say about consciousness: I think he also had something valuable and important to say about universals and other *entia rationis*. Moore assumed in his early writings that we are asking substantial questions if we ask whether or not such *entia rationis* have being, if they have being in the same or a different sense from concrete particulars, and into how many distinct sub-varieties they fall. The Morley Lectures, chapters xvi-xx, contain in my view one of the most brilliant, interestingly argued ontologies or sorting out of categories with which I have any acquaintance. On reading them one feels that what I may call the peculiar treachery of *entia rationis*, their proneness to antinomy, of which Plato had such disillusioning experience when he wrote the *Parmenides*, has been dispelled: it is really possible, it would seem, to talk clearly and without contradiction about entities of reason. In this ontology, whose details I recommend to you for study, Moore maintains that there are at least three basic categories all of which have being univocally: there are particulars, there are truths or facts, and there are universals or general ideas which are in no sense mental. What is interesting about Moore's treatment of universals is his cold attitude to qualitative universals, such as salmon-pink and whiteness. He readily admits that there are relations and relational properties, but of qualitative universals all sorts of elaborate relational reductions are attempted. In the end colour is admitted to the rank of genuine entities while salmon-pink is not. I should not wish anyone to accept these opinions—I am quite unpersuaded myself—but they afford a unique piece of philosophical discussion of which I seem the only student and admirer. What should be noted is that Moore's loyalty to his *entia rationis* was not changed by the nominalistic climate through which he lived: for him the being of facts and universals never became a mere question of how one chooses to speak. This is shown by the remarkable Appendix to *Some Main Problems to Philosophy*, written in 1952, where Moore makes various corrections to his 1909 views, and discovers some 'gross mistakes' in them. What is important, however, is that Moore proposes no fundamental revision of these earlier views: they are broadly endorsed once the 'gross mistakes' have been discounted.

I shall not say anything about the peculiar contributions of Moore to ethics since, whatever else they may have been, they have not been neglected. Perhaps, however, it is worth calling attention to the remarkable degree to which Moore appeals to synthetic *a priori* connections in his ethics, connections held to be necessary and not empirical, and yet not tautological. I should also have said that the system of values set up in *Principia Ethica* represents a far more daring flight of *a priori* moralizing than any found in the idealist moralists: what is for Moore good or right had nothing to do with what is ordinarily thought so, nor with the ordinary use of ethical words.

I have now created what I feel to be a reasonably true image of Moore as a philosopher, laying my main emphasis on his neglected aspects. I wish to stress that these neglected sides were never discarded by Moore, and that without them it is not possible to appraise him properly. I now wish to say something about the philosophical importance of these peculiar Moorean aspects. Are they of contemporary interest, or do they perhaps belong wholly to the past, to the 'philosophical palaeontology' into which contemporary thinkers so readily relegate what they do not regard with sympathy?

I should like first of all to stress the immense, permanent value of the *gnostic* element in G. E. Moore, the doctrine that there are things of which we are much more sure than of any premiss or argument devoted to their overthrow, and of the Moorean extension to this view to the effect that there are interpretations of the gnosis which the gnosis itself rejects, or which at least cannot readily be squared with it. It does seem to me that the presence of this gnostic element is an essential element in a philosophy, and that it differentiates what I should call a responsible philosophy from one which, though brilliant, is also irresponsible. A responsible philosopher seems to me one who, when certain assumptions and methods lead to plainly preposterous conclusions, will begin to suspect something invalid in the assumptions and methods he has been employing, not draw the preposterous conclusions, and who will never accept *any* mode of argument, however persuasive, which makes nonsense of *too* much of what he knows very much better. This is not to say that a philosopher who is sound will not be prepared to try out assumptions and methods as far as they will go, and to see whether their results will square with what he knows very much better, but only that he will remain possessed of what he fundamentally knows, and will judge all assumptions and methods in terms of this. Now it seems to me that the main fault of three brilliant philosophies of meaning successively launched upon the world—I shall speak here of the philosophy of meaning as mirroring, of meaning as verification and of meaning as use—is their grave lack of a regulative gnosis. They have been remarkable schizoid fantasies irresponsibly launched in the void without regard to the preposterous character of their outcome. I do not need to particularize elaborately, but the kind of thought which at one stage teaches us that we cannot talk about our friends' experience without talking about the possible movements of their bodies, and which at a later stage teaches that we cannot identify or distinguish our own experiences except to the extent that there is a public check on what we say of them, obviously lacks all gnostic regulation. For we certainly do understand what it is for experiences to belong to different minds, and what it is for such experiences to be similar or different, and that their similarities or differences are not similarities in anything bodily and linguistic, and we not only understand all this, but we know that we understand it, and we know it to express truth, and we are much more sure of all this than we can ever be of any theory of meaning. If a theory of meaning, therefore, makes it seem dubious or impossible that we should understand or know any of these things, or if it forces us to interpret them in a fashion that we know not to accord with their meaning, then it is the theory of meaning that must be sacrificed or altered, not the certainties in question. In the same way we understand what it is for one thing to be better than another, or to be something that we absolutely ought to do, and we likewise *know* that there are some things better than others, and some things that we ought absolutely to do, and we know further that these things, though discerned with difficulty, do not differ from one man or society to another. We have now various theories of the use of ethical terms which do not readily accord with this claim, or which do so only with a great deal of subtle trimming. What must one do? Must one discard philosophical ethics as the systematic study of absolute values and norms, or reduce it to a meta-ethical branch of linguistics? Not at all. One must question the theories which fail to make sense of a fundamental enterprise, which we know to be feasible, even if we are then left with the hard task of finding out just how it is 'feasible' and where the opposing theories are mistaken.

Does this all mean that I am proposing a new movement of 'Back to Moore'? By no means. The movement in question has, I think, been going on covertly for a long time. Contemporary philosophy has, in my view, considerable elements of the saving gnosis. Professor Ayer, e.g., has long shed his early behaviouristic analyses of other people's experiences, simply because he found he could not believe them, i.e. he knew them to be false, and he has had much to say in criticism of the dogmatic thesis of the impossibility of a private language. No one would likewise accuse a contemporary thinker like Austin of being prone to preposterous theses: he is in fact an analyst after the manner of Moore, except that he conducts his analysis largely by considering the use of words, which is from a Moorean point of view legitimate, since the content of a concept certainly comes out in our verbal usages. Nor is a philosopher like Austin a mere worshipper of ordinary speech, though his occasional tidying up of our usage certainly does not go as far as the analyses of Moore.

What I should myself like to complain of in Moore is not that he was a gnostic, but that he did not carry his gnosticism far enough. To me it seems that in addition to the hard core of certainties rightly defended by Moore—certainties about material objects, other minds, time and space, knowledge, etc.—we have an immense number of softer near-certainties, things of which we are not indeed more sure than of *any* premiss or argument brought in to confound them, but of which we are certainly more sure than of *many* such premisses and arguments. I am, I fear, a philosopher who thinks the air positively thick with the synthetic *a priori*, that there is hardly a sphere of experience or knowledge in which we do not have important advance intimations of various sorts, even though these intimations may at times prove delusive, and even though their content is often only probabilistic, and permits of empirical exceptions. It is not, however, my business to give you *my* gnosis nor to oppose it to Moore's, but only to insist that to have a gnosis in philosophy is quite essential if one's thinking is not to be vain and sterile.

I should like, in closing, to criticize another aspect of Moore: the precise form taken by his analyses of common-sense certainties. I believe Moore right in thinking that the accounts one ultimately arrives at in thinking over and rethinking ordinary certainties will be startingly different from the accounts one starts with, that philosophical assertions can't be a mere reassertion of what one ordinarily says. But I should gravely object to the form in which Moore often tried to cast his analyses, and I believe it largely responsible for his inability to reach satisfactory results. I should say that Moore was unduly obsessed by a misleading model of *whole and parts*: whenever one has a many-sided reality to deal with, one must resolve it into a set of *constituents* put together in a certain way. Thus if one is analysing the consciousness of blue, one must split it up into two elements, consciousness pure and simple, and blue pure and simple, or if one is analysing a good thing like personal affection one must split it up into a natural psychological activity, on the one hand, and a non-natural value-predicate, on the other. Now I think this whole-part type of analysis completely mistaken, and that whole and part is a category simply not applicable to most of the facts that have interest for philosophy. For I think it plain that in some sense our notions have other notions 'built into' them, that they are *of* this or of that, or are oriented to this or to that, without having this or that as a part or constituent, and I think that a notion can only be philosophically grasped when it is seen in its place in a total notional economy, each of whose members realizes the living paradox of doing little more than take in the others' washing. Now it is plain why Moore avoided this built-in, internal analysis: he thought too readily that it was logically absurd, and he was also reacting to the exaggerations of Bradley's *Appearance and Reality*. But his determination 'to chop everything up into little bits' resulted in the failure of his philosophical psychology, the failure of his theory of perception, the failure of his theory of our knowledge of the physical world and the failure of his ethics. And from that failure has sprung the slow nihilism that has sapped British philosophy for so long, but which is now, I hope, at its dying gasp. I am sorry to end on a critical note, but I do not wish to diminish the greatness of Moore. Moore, like Socrates, was a great philosophical watershed. Socrates produced Cynics, Cyrenaics and logic-chopping Megarians as well as the great synthetic thought of Plato. Moore likewise has been the father of much triviality and of much valuable thought. Of the advent of his Plato, however, there is as yet no sign.

THREE ASPECTS OF MOORE'S PHILOSOPHY[1]

by ALICE AMBROSE

It is reported that a Chinese who came to Cambridge commented on his philosophical pilgrimage as follows: 'I came to Cambridge to study philosophy with Professor Moore, and what I learned was something about the English language.' The aspect of Moore's philosophical activity which these words suggest is nowadays perhaps the one uppermost in the minds of Moore's critics and of all the subsequent school of analysts to whom Professor Brand Blanshard attributed 'that preoccupation with language which is one of the most curious aspects of the current philosophy of analysis'.[2] There are, however, other aspects of Moore's doing of philosophy which have also acted as powerful determinants of the direction philosophy has taken, perhaps the most familiar being his defence of common sense. This defence of common sense had as a by-product, very probably not consciously intended by Moore, a defence of ordinary language. It may not be possible consistently to interpret the work of his lifetime as directed to both of these ends at once, but it is undeniable that various philosophers have interpreted it as directed to one or the other and sometimes to both. Either interpretation is plausibly supported by placing different constructions on the technique Moore made use of, namely, analysis. With this technique for clarifying concepts, i.e., for clarifying the meanings of words, Moore's name has come to be associated—not because he made important use of it for the first time in the history of philosophy, for in fact many historical figures have used it, but because through him the technique of analysis became very explicit and was used by him in a characteristic way. The defence of common sense, the defence of ordinary language, the clarification of concepts—each in its way has had an

[1] This is a revised version of a paper read at a meeting in memory of G. E. Moore, Columbia University, January 15, 1959. Reprinted from *The Journal of Philosophy*, Vol. LVII, no. 26, 1960.
[2] 'The Philosophy of Analysis', *Proceedings of the British Academy* (1952), p. 63.

enormous influence on philosophy in the English-speaking world. I should like to comment on each, and thereby to attempt to do at this memorial meeting in honour of Professor Moore the kind of critical philosophical study for which he has set the standard.

Moore's role as the great refuter is so familiar that one is likely to forget the basic purpose of his refutations. Moore conceived philosophy as having a positive task, namely, 'to give a general description of the *whole* of the Universe, mentioning all the most important kinds of things which we *know* to be in it . . .';[1] and he thought what he called the Common Sense view on these matters to be true and hence views in contradiction to it false. Moore commented that 'what is most amazing and most interesting about the views of many philosophers, is the way in which they go beyond or positively contradict the views of Common Sense: they profess to know that there are in the Universe most important kinds of things, which Common Sense does not profess to know of, and also they profess to know that there are *not* in the Universe (or, at least, that, if there are, we do not know it), things of the existence of which Common Sense is most sure'.[2] Some of the views which go beyond Common Sense Moore is not concerned to attack, and in fact certain of his own accounts of what there is in the Universe certainly are of this kind. But the point not to be lost sight of is that his refutations of other views about the Universe are intended to leave the field to Common Sense.

It is worth while characterizing more exactly the views which go against Common Sense, i.e., which go against those beliefs men have had 'almost as long as they have believed anything'[3] and which have not changed with our progress in knowledge. In the case of all these views it is natural to express them negatively, as asserting that something does *not* exist, that something is *not* known, that something is *not* as it appears. Bradley says that material objects do not exist, Hume that no one can know that they do, Parmenides that they merely appear to undergo change but in fact do not. And some of these metaphysicians, in condemning the sense world as mere appearance, are in the position of the proponents of negative theology, who can only say of the real what it is not. Bradley's assertion of a supra-sensible Whole, in which the self-contradictoriness of its predicates is resolved, Hume's account of genuine knowledge, which it is logically

---

[1] *Some Main Problems of Philosophy* (London: Allen & Unwin, 1953), p. 1.
[2] *Ibid.*, p. 2.   [3] *Ibid.*, p. 3.

impossible for sense-evidence to achieve, certainly go beyond the
views of Common Sense; but at the same time they are destructive
of the views of Common Sense, without making any clear positive
claim. They might be characterized as negative metaphysics, the
philosophical counterpart of the *via negativa*.

From a number of Moore's writings it is clear that he thought
these views were factually false, and he used analysis in his
characteristic manner to try to show them to be false. His disagreement with the negative metaphysicians might be called a family
quarrel, a disagreement between brother metaphysicians over what
is the true state of affairs. He at no time took them to be saying
nothing at all. Although the claims of logical positivists were well
known to Moore and appeared at a time when he was at the height
of his philosophical activity, he did not subscribe to the thesis
that the statements of these metaphysicians were pieces of literal
nonsense. In fact, in lectures I attended in 1934–35 he criticized
Professor A. J. Ayer for saying metaphysical sentences have no
meaning at all while defining them by the kind of meaning they
have (i.e., as asserting something unverifiable). Ayer held that 'A
good example of the kind of utterance that is condemned by our
criterion as being not even false but nonsensical would be the
assertion that the world of sense experience was altogether unreal
. . . it is plain that no conceivable observations . . . could have
any tendency to show this'.[1] Moore, on the other hand, set out a
criterion for concluding to the falsity of a metaphysical proposition,
not to the literal meaninglessness of the sentence expressing it.

I want to say something about this criterion and the technique
by which he made use of it. The criterion is to the effect that any
view which implies either the falsity or self-contradictoriness of a
belief of Common Sense is itself false or self-contradictory. The
criterion can be construed as a double criterion, one as a means
for defending ordinary language, the other as a means for defending Common Sense. But for the moment let us consider its use to
ward off attacks on the truth of common sense beliefs, i.e., of such
beliefs as 'There are in the Universe a great number of material
objects',[2] that the earth has existed for many years past, that there
are other human beings than oneself, each of whom, like oneself,
has had various experiences. Now the technique by which Moore
made use of this criterion involves what he called 'translation into

---

[1] *Language, Truth and Logic* (London: Victor Gollancz, 1936), pp. 26–7.
[2] *Some Main Problems of Philosophy*, p. 3.

the concrete'. He made this process explicit in his treatment of the view that Time is unreal when he suggested that one 'try to translate the proposition into the concrete, and to ask what it *implies*. . . .'[1] 'Time is unreal' he translated into 'There are no temporal facts', and this implies that nothing ever happens, has happened, or will happen. Similarly, to consider, for variety's sake, a different philosophical view, 'Physical objects are unreal' implies that there are no objects external to our minds. And if we try to think what this 'really comes to, [we] at once begin thinking of a number of different *kinds* of propositions, all of which plainly must be untrue . . .'[2] if physical objects are unreal. It will not be true that the earth exists, or the mountains on it, or human bodies, or any other animate bodies. The falsity of all these propositions is implied by 'There are no external objects' in the same way as 'There are no blue things' is implied by 'There is nothing coloured'. As is well known, Moore ostensibly brings the logical consequences of the theory—what it implies—into confrontation with the facts: the claim that there are no hands, for example, into confrontation with the fact he makes evident to everyone by holding up each of his two hands and saying, 'Here is a hand'. Translated into the concrete, the theory can be seen to imply the falsity of what everyone knows to be true, and hence must itself be false. According to Moore, it is sufficient proof of the commonsense belief that there are external objects to exhibit a pair of hands.

Moore made it clear in his 'Reply to My Critics'[3] that he took 'There are external objects' to be an empirical proposition, and of course its negation as well. In fact the statement 'There are no external objects' he supposed could express both an empirical proposition and the non-empirical one that 'There are external objects' is self-contradictory,[4] presumably on the ground, which to me is questionable, that ' "p" is self-contradictory' entails that 'p' is false, i.e., that ' "There are external objects" is self-contradictory' entails that 'There are external objects' is false. One would expect a refutation of the one sort of proposition to differ radically from that of the other. It is possible that Moore's refutation of 'There are no external objects', with its avowed aim

[1] *Philosophical Studies* (London: Routledge & Kegan Paul, 1922), p. 209.
[2] *Ibid.*, p. 209.
[3] *The Philosophy of G. E. Moore*, Library of Living Philosophers, edited by P. A. Schilpp, Vol. IV (Open Court Publishing Co.).
[4] *The Philosophy of G. E. Moore*, p. 672.

of defending a belief of Common Sense, may not be what it has been taken to be. An interpretation has been placed on his argument which throws it into a very different light, an interpretation which makes out Moore's translation into the concrete to be defending not a common belief, but ordinary language. Some of Moore's earlier contemporaries had charged him with begging the question, pointing out that anyone who maintained that there are no external objects would also maintain all that it apparently implies, that there are no hands, no mountains, no animate bodies, no earth. A Bradleian, or a sceptic, would refuse to accept the proof Moore gave of external objects by exhibiting a pair of hands, on the ground that it assumes the thing in question. The charge of circularity would effectively stalemate the argument, interpreted as an attempt to refute a factual claim about the world. In order to maintain that Moore's argument *is* a refutation, some other construction had to be placed on it and also on the Bradleian claim against which it was directed. This Professor Norman Malcolm attempted to do.[1] He maintained that 'the essence of Moore's technique of refuting philosophical statements consists in pointing out that these statements go against ordinary language'.[2] Malcolm interpreted negative metaphysicians as not disagreeing with Common Sense over any empirical facts but rather as disagreeing over the language used to describe those facts. He supposed them to be attacking Common Sense for what they consider improper forms of speech, their own language being a more correct way of speaking.[3] If a negative metaphysician who asserts 'There are no external objects' is claiming that it is improper language to say 'There are mountains', then I think Malcolm was right in saying that it is his claim, not ordinary usage, which is erroneous. And *if* what Moore does in his proof is to remind us that it is correct to describe some states of affairs by 'There are mountains', then he has sufficiently refuted a person who says it is not.

Now there is something puzzling about the thesis, perhaps no longer held by Malcolm but nevertheless interesting on its own account, that the negative metaphysician is misdescribing the use of language. It is just as absurd that he should hold ordinary usage to be incorrect while knowing it is correct as that he should hold common sense beliefs to be false while knowing the facts which make them true. In either case he makes an incredible

---

[1] 'Moore and Ordinary Language', *The Philosophy of G. E. Moore.*
[2] *Ibid.*, p. 349.   [3] *Ibid.*, pp. 350–3.

mistake. And something even more puzzling has been pointed out by Professor Morris Lazerowitz in his paper 'Moore and Philosophical Analysis', namely, 'how the two kinds of mistake [about usage, and about non-linguistic matter of fact] could be made in the same utterance. . . . [For] in making a linguistic mistake a philosopher is not mistakenly denying matter of fact and in mistakenly denying matter of fact he is not making a linguistic mistake'.[1] The point of Moore's translations into the concrete cannot be to correct Bradley's use of the *term* 'physical object' by showing him that the factual belief expressed by 'physical objects are unreal' is false.[2] It therefore appears that his refutations cannot be construed as having to do two jobs at the same time, to defend the truth of common sense beliefs and to defend the propriety of ordinary language. It can indeed by argued that despite appearances to the contrary they do have one of these two tasks, the defence of ordinary language, but not if this defence rests on Malcolm's charge that philosophers are misdescribing it. The defence will take an entirely different form. Moore's work does, I think, constitute a defence of the language of Common Sense. One of its undeniable consequences has been its enormous influence in holding philosophers to the use of ordinary language and in making a use in conflict with it a criterion for repudiation of a view. But that it should do this presents a puzzle: How can his translations into the concrete, i.e., his making explicit the implications of *propositions* and *concepts*, be construed as having a bearing on the use of *expressions*?

Let us consider what the analysis of a concept is taken to come to. In his 'Reply to My Critics' Moore stated that analysing a concept is not the same thing as defining a word,[3] although in the first lecture of his which I attended in 1932 he said that analysis of concepts is resolved into something very like the definition of words and that 'in a strictly limited sense' the analysis of a notion is identical with the definition of a word. To make use of Moore's example, clearly it is incorrect to say '"Brother" means male sibling' and 'A brother is a male sibling' are identical, since one is an empirical linguistic statement and the other is not. But it is also undeniable that in defining the word 'brother' one has analysed the concept *brother* which the word stands for. Furthermore, the

---

[1] *Philosophy*, Vol. XXXIII, July 1958, p. 218.
[2] *Ibid.*, pp. 218–19.
[3] *The Philosophy of G. E. Moore*, pp. 664–5.

words used in the expression of the analysans name the criteria for
the application of the word which denotes the analysandum, and
this is what any sentence correctly expressing a complete analysis
does. So there is a close connection between the analysis of a
concept and the use of an expression, and further, between a
correct analysis and correct usage. Another way of showing the
connection is given by Lazerowitz' account of sentences of the
form 'It is logically impossible that $\sim p$', which are equivalent to
'"p" is necessary'.[1] The fact that the English sentence 'It is
logically impossible for there to be a brother who is not a male
sibling' expresses a necessity implies that the phrase 'brother but
not a male sibling' has no use in English to describe any creature.
If it did, then it would describe something which would falsify the
necessary proposition the sentence expresses. This fact about the
way language is used prevents the sentence from saying anything
falsifiable. And anyone who understood a given sentence expressing
a necessary proposition would know a fact about the use of words.

Now among the philosophical views Moore was concerned to
refute are those which assert the unreality of physical objects,
selves, etc., the ground for these assertions being that the concepts
physical object, *self*, etc., are self-contradictory. This non-empirical
ground Moore takes as implying that propositions expressed by
such sentences as 'The earth has existed for many years past'
and 'There are other human beings than myself' will always be
false. And whether or not Moore made it explicit, this ground
also assure a linguistic fact about terms occurring in such sentences: if the concepts *physical object* and *self* are self-contradictory,
then physical-object terms or terms referring to persons will be
self-contradictory. Hence, expressions ordinarily used to describe
a thing or person will now describe nothing at all, as no self-
contradictory expression has a descriptive use. Bradley's view could
with apparent plausibility be taken to imply that many everyday
expressions have no use. But although it is sometimes the case
that we do not know an expression to be self-contradictory, clearly
an expression which in everyday speech has an application,
whether to things, states of affairs, or persons, cannot be self-
contradictory.

For Moore to maintain against a philosopher that a certain
concept is not self-contradictory is in effect to argue that in the
language in which the philosopher expresses himself the word

[1] *Op. cit.*, pp. 206–8.

denoting the concept has a use. Looked at verbally, translations
into the concrete show that certain words do not lack application.
But as already remarked, negative metaphysicians are perfectly
familiar with facts about the usual applications of words and can
hardly be supposed to be misdescribing language. It has been
maintained that Moore's seemingly empirical refutations, which
he expressed in the idiom used to refute factual claims rather than
in that used to attack linguistic claims, are actually linguistic
counter-moves against attempts to change the language of Common Sense. I do not want to develop or argue for this thesis which
has been explicated in detail by Lazerowitz in the paper previously
cited. The thesis, in addition to justifying the claim about Moore's
work that it urges preserving the linguistic *status quo* and opposes
idle innovations in ordinary language, has the merit of escaping
the difficulty in the two most natural claims about his work: that
it shows a belief about the world which contradicts Common
Sense to be false, that it shows a philosopher's claim about
linguistic usage to be mistaken. And it resolves the puzzle I set
out earlier in supposing that it defends at one and the same time
both the truth of common beliefs and the propriety of ordinary
language. Moore's work is instead construed as urging that
ordinary language not be changed. 'The propositions he lays down
as truisms . . . are not statements of fact as to what exists and
what things are, but examples of the kind of everyday utterance
which are not to be tampered with by metaphysically inclined
philosophers under the guise of making . . . analyses.'[1]

It seems to me that Moore's refutations, effected by translations
into the concrete, are much more convincing when taken as
arguments whose import is linguistic than when taken as defending
a factual truth. I call attention to the two divergent interpretations
to which Moore's work lends itself, as opposing those theories
about reality which go against commonsense beliefs, and as
opposing the linguistic correlates of such theories, to make clear
what it is that has changed the direction of philosophy. The one
interpretation has eventuated in the resurgence of philosophical
realism, the other in meta-philosophical studies of philosophers'
language.

There is a third contribution which Moore's work has made to
philosophy, and which I shall mention briefly because of a somewhat different direction philosophy has taken recently. Moore

[1] 'Moore and Philosophical Analysis', p. 219.

stated, and by practice implied, that analysis is one of the proper businesses of philosophy.[1] Inevitably this involves the close examination of the usage of expressions. In virtue of the kind of philosophical work on systems of metaphysics and ethics current when Moore began to write, it was natural that Moore's attention turned to certain expressions of key importance in the statements of these positions. When he belaboured philosophers for 'the attempt to answer questions, without first discovering precisely *what* question it is which [they] desire to answer',[2] he had in mind questions about such concepts as *good* and *right*, and he accordingly examined the uses of the terms 'good' and 'right'. Moore's analyses were always anchored in an obvious way in philosophical positions. Recently the work of certain philosophers has moved away from such anchorage, the result being a type of lexicography whose relation to the solution of philosophical problems is unclear. But there can be no doubt that attempts, for example, by Professor J. L. Austin, to clarify the meanings of nearly synonymous terms has its impetus from Moore's earlier attempts at analysis. Possibly this is a third direction into which Moore's thought will turn philosophers. That it has already turned some of them away from negative metaphysics and that it has produced a school devoted to the defence of ordinary language is clear.

[1] *The Philosophy of G. E. Moore*, p. 676.
[2] *Principia Ethica* (Cambridge University Press, 1922), p. vi.

G. E. MOORE'S 'THE NATURE OF JUDGMENT'

by GILBERT RYLE

Between 1897 and 1900 Moore published in *Mind* five substantial pieces and one short review, namely: (1) in 1897, his contribution to the symposium between Bosanquet, Shadworth Hodgson and himself 'In what sense, if any, do Past and Future Time exist?'; (2) in 1898, an article 'Freedom'; (3) in 1899, the article 'The Nature of Judgment'; a Critical Notice of Russell's *Essay on the Foundations of Geometry*; and a short review of a book on Ethics by F. Bon; (4) in 1900, an article 'Necessity'.

Moore seems not to have been very proud of these early publications. He did not republish them; and in his Autobiographical Statement in *G. E. Moore* (ed. Schillp), he says little about any of them and nothing about some of them. Most of them exerted little or no influence, and their interest for us is chiefly that of biographical pointers. But 'The Nature of Judgment' did have an influence. Russell's *Principles of Mathematics* (1903), especially Chapter IV; his three *Mind* articles (1904) 'Meinong's Theory of Complexes and Assumptions'; and his Lectures on Logical Atomism of 1918 all need to be read as, *inter alia*, developments out of Moore's 'The Nature of Judgment', and doubtless also out of things that were being said *viva voce* in Cambridge by Moore, Russell and others at the turn of the century. Wittgenstein's *Tractatus Logico-Philosophicus* (1922) is, in its earlier parts, a revival or exhumation of the Moore–Meinong–Russell Logical Atomism of the 1899–1905 period. His 'objects', 'simples', and 'complexes' are Moore's 'concepts' and 'complex concepts' of 1899; and his 'facts' and 'states of affairs' descend partly from Meinong, but partly also from what became of Moore's 'true propositions' after 'subsisting falsehoods' went out of favour. Maybe Wittgenstein's 'Objects from the Substance of the World' echoes Moore's denial on pp. 192–3 that there is anything adjectival about concepts (later, 'objects') '. . . in the end, the concept turns out to be the only substantive, or subject, and no one concept either more or less an adjective than any other'.

'The Nature of Judgment' could be described as the *De Interpretatione* of early twentieth-century Cambridge logic.

I. TIME

In his contribution to the symposium on Time in *Mind*, 1898, Moore explicitly adopts, on pp. 238 and 240, arguments of Bradley and a conclusion of Bosanquet in favour of the inferior reality of the temporal and temporary *vis-a-vis* the superior reality of what is eternal or timeless. In his 'Freedom' of the following year he is an outspoken Bradleian on the unreality of time (p. 202). '. . . the arguments by which Mr Bradley has endeavoured to prove the unreality of time appear to me perfectly conclusive.' Through to 1903, when *Principia Ethica* came out, he continues to downgrade the temporary *vis-a-vis* the non-temporary. During this period the epithets 'temporal', 'natural', 'existent' and 'empirical' are given the same extension; all alike are somewhat derogatory expressions. Some notions, like *True, Good, Two* and *Four*, cannot be defined either directly or indirectly in terms of anything that exists. For to exist is to exist at and for a time, but these notions belong to the superior, Transcendental realm, the 'objects' in which are exempt from changing and from ageing, and from having dealings with anything that does change or age. To assert that these objects do not exist and are non-natural is not a slur, but a tribute. In *Principia Ethica* 'naturalistic' is a comminatory title just because 'natural' is still a relatively derogatory, tense-connoting adjective. What Ethics is essentially about is proudly outside the orbit of the mere natural sciences, including psychology and sociology. However, by 1903 the status of the temporal is beginning to rise a little—if only because Ethics would have nothing to prescribe unless people existed for periods of time to do things at moments of time (§ 68).

So when in 1917, in 'The Conception of Reality' Moore argues against Bradley for the unqualified truth of some tensed statements, he is criticizing a view which he himself had once accepted; and when in his Autobiographical Statement he records how, as an undergraduate, he had, no less than in his later years, found McTaggart's doctrine of the unreality of Time 'a perfectly monstrous proposition', he forgets that he had not found it perfectly monstrous in the late 1890s and the very early 1900s. Then he was going to need this absolute contrast between the inferior temporal and the superior non-temporal in order to define in terms of it the, for him, crucial dichotomy between the inferior empirical and the superior *a priori* truths. The former are, directly or indirectly, tensed truths, the latter are untensed. Russell endorses this definition on p. 209 of the first Meinong article. It is worth noticing *en passant* that Moore's preoccupation with Time is not matched by any similar preoccupation with Space.

II. KANT

In 'Freedom' and in the second half of 'The Nature of Judgment' (especially pp. 183-4, 190, 192) Moore avows himself a Kantian. He does not pretend to be a very obsequious one. He had said in the first paragraph of 'Freedom' (1898) 'My object is to emphasize and defend . . . certain points in Kant's doctrine in which I believe him to be right and to criticize others in which I believe him to be wrong'. On p. 200 '[Kant] supplies, as it seems to me, more materials for a true view than anyone else. . . .'

Now, 1899, he says, on p. 183,'. . . it [Moore's theory] retains the doctrine of Transcendentalism. For Transcendentalism rests on the distinction between empirical and *a priori* propositions.' On p. 190, 'The Transcendental Deduction contains a perfectly valid answer to Hume's scepticism, and to empiricism generally'. Moore does indeed vigorously criticize his master, sometimes for ordinary mistakes, but sometimes for departing from the true Critical philosophy. Moore says of himself, in 'Freedom', first paragraph, 'I think that reference to the views of the philosopher with whom you are most in agreement is often the clearest way of explaining your own views to an esoteric audience. . . .'

Moore wholeheartedly accepts Kant's distinction between *a priori* and *a posteriori* truths; and with this, he accepts in principle Kant's two-floor doctrine of the noumenal and the phenomenal realms. Indeed he says on p. 195 of 'Freedom', speaking apparently in *propria persona*, 'This supersensible reality is the world as a whole, it is the reason of everything that appears; and, as such, it has Freedom'. Moore himself avoids the Kantian labels 'noumenal' and 'phenomenal'; and is, in fact, much less interested in the sorry phenomenal-ness of the objects on the lower floor than he is in their sorry temporal-ness. He never grumbles that something is mere Appearance; his grumble is that it is mutable and short-lived. What is true of it today is false of it tomorrow (p. 188). In 'Necessity', 1900, he disallows such mutable truth-values (p. 296). It is as a Kantian and with purportedly Kantian whips that Moore castigates English empiricism. Some of his complaints against Kant in his 'Freedom' are that Kant has un-Critically assimilated to the Transcendental something that is merely psychological, and therefore occurrent, natural and empirical. Words like 'mental', 'consciousness' and even 'will' carry no capital letters for Moore. It is not intelligences but intelligibles that occupy his upper floor.

In *Principia Ethica* the honorific epithet 'Transcendental' has been replaced by the still fairly honorific epithet 'Metaphysical'. True, Moore severely scolds actual metaphysicians for crediting or discrediting non-natural objects with existence, albeit non-temporal existence; they should have said that non-natural objects, including truths, *are*. It is a bad error to say that they exist. But he can still say, in the middle of § 66, 'I admit that "metaphysics" should investigate what reasons there may be for belief in such a supersensible reality, since I hold that its peculiar province is the truth about all objects which are not natural objects'. However, metaphysics, just as much as the natural sciences, must be forbidden to infringe the absolute autonomy of Ethics.

We need to remind ourselves that the Vienna Circle is still over a quarter century ahead, and that Bradley and McTaggart still have a score more years to live.

III. 'THE NATURE OF JUDGMENT'

In his *Principles of Logic* Bradley had vigorously attacked the accounts of thinking that were given by English empiricists. Their basic theory of 'ideas' had culminated in the view that the description of thought and judgment could and should be given entirely in terms of what the thinker's introspections would reveal. His judgment, say, that *yonder animal is a horse* would consist just in his having these together with those momentary experiences—perhaps of his having a visual image and, with it or after it, another visual image. Against any such psychologizing view Bradley had argued forcibly and correctly that for truth and false-hood to be possible, and so for judging that something is the case to be possible, the predicate-word, say, of a declaration of opinion must convey a meaning, an 'universal meaning' or 'logical idea'. Truths are no processions of introspectibles.

With all of this Moore, in the beginning of his 1899 article, is in complete agreement. His complaint is that Bradley does not go far enough. Bradley's theory of abstraction is still an attempt, however cathartic, to extract or distil out of a fleeting state of mind the immutable 'universal meaning' that is to be predicated of yonder animal. The de-psychologizing must be total. Nothing in the truths or falsehoods that may be considered by people owes anything to anything that happens to or in these people. Accordingly Moore here totally eschews the word 'idea' because of its psychological connotations, except once or twice for Bradley's phrase 'logical idea'. Instead he operates, in 1899 only, with the Kantian word 'concept'. A concept or a combination of concepts is what a person thinks; it is the 'object of his thought' when he thinks of *red*, *roses*, or *that the roses are red*. *What* he thinks is not a state of his mind or anything to do with any state of his mind— unless *per accidens* he thinks about his states of mind.

Some concepts, like *red*, are simple. There is no defining them, no analysing them into component concepts, since they have no components. Some concepts, like *rose* and *horse*, are complex, and therefore analysable into their ultimate, unanalysable component concepts. But some syntheses or combinations of concepts constitute complex concepts or complexes of a special sort; for they constitute propositions, i.e. truths and falsehoods. These are expressed by sentences, and not just by phrases or single words. They are what we judge, and not just what we make judgments *about*. It is indeed an important part of Moore's task in this article to throw light on these notions of the *truth* and *falsity* that qualify some complex concepts, namely propositions.

It may be useful at this point to digress for a moment, and consider some differences and similarities between the terminology of Moore's 'The Nature of Judgment' of 1899 and that of his *Principia Ethica* of 1903. By 1903 the word 'concept' has disappeared, and no explanation is given of its disappearance. Instead we frequently find the doublet 'object or notion', and less frequently the doublet 'object or idea'; 'notion' by itself is quite common, as is 'object' by itself; 'object of thought' occurs now and then; 'term' rarely. All of these expressions are proxies for his earlier 'concept'; it is they that are simple or else complex; that are, or are not definable or analysable; that are or are not what something else is analysable into; that are what we judge or else what we make our judgments about; that are either the constituents, i.e. the subject-terms or the predicate-terms of truths and falsehoods, or else are themselves integral truths or falsehoods.

It is of great historical importance that one of Moore's new and quite unexplained proxies for his former 'concept' is 'object', whether by itself or in the phrases 'object of thought', 'object or notion', and 'object or idea'. Even with the rider '. . . of thought', but especially without it, 'object' already promises to be a trouble-carrier. How well it fulfilled that promise! For it made it fatally easy and tempting to equate—or 'meta'-equate—things with word-meanings or phrase-meanings, Socrates with the predicates of certain propositions, horses with what is conveyed by '. . . . is [not] a horse'; and the parts of horses with the parts of the definition of *Horse*. It helped to 'meta'-evaporate the Referents of expressions into parts of their Senses, e.g., the luminous and remote objects studied through telescopes by astronomers into the 'objects', i.e. proposition-components, that are studied by logicians without telescopes; what a grammatical subject names, designates, describes, or misdescribes into what it means.

To return to Moore's meaning-theory of 1899: Partly from the realist's desire to remove nuisances from epistemology, but probably much more from the desire to remove nuisances from the theory of inference (p. 183, middle), Moore completely depsychologizes the notions of truth and falsehood, and, therewith, the notions both of the components or terms of truths and falsehoods, and of the connexions between propositions. Concepts, simple or complex, are *what* we do or might think about and *what* we do or might think about them. But there is nothing mental or even temporally existent or occurrent in them. They are what we mean by our sentences, and by their subject-words and predicate-words; but they are not themselves things uttered or written. They possess most, though not all of the impressive, if rather promissory attributes with which Plato distinguished his Forms, including that of immutability *par excellence*.

We might here notice one unsurprising and one surprising feature of Moore's 1899 doctrine of concepts. (*a*) It is not surprising that at this date Moore pays no attention to nonsensical phrases and sentences. Nothing that he says insures against impossible complexes. So far, all concatenations of words stand for complex 'objects [of thought]'. Russell is not yet tackling paradoxes. (b) It is surprising that there is in this article no vestige of Mill's account of the import of propositions, of denotation *versus* connotation, of the meanings, if any, *versus* the things designated by proper names, by many-worded names (= definite descriptions), and by singularly referring pronouns and demonstratives. Indeed Moore does not here operate with *names* at all. With one important, though only partial exception, all words are taken by Moore, after Bradley, to convey 'universal meanings'; so, but for this partial exception, all sentences can convey only general or unparticularized truths and falsehoods. The single partial exception is this: we can give *time*-particularizations. 'Now', once 'this' (p. 179, para. 2), and other ways of specifying dates and moments of time do enable us to state particular matters of natural fact. But Moore does not tell us whether *now* and *midnight tonight* are or are not themselves concepts or 'universal meanings'. This is his only concession, and a largely unconscious concession to the differences noticed by Frege and, in effect, by Mill between Sense and Reference. Hence the radical ambiguity of Moore's words 'concept', 'object [of thought]', 'notion', 'constituent' and 'term'; and hence the troubles that this ambiguity had in store.

Moore now gives his arid answer to the question What is Truth? or rather to the question What are Truth and Falsehood? Truth is not a relation e.g. a relation of matching or corresponding with realities or existents external to the proposition that is true. It is an internal property of that proposition, just the special way in which its constituent concepts are interrelated inside that proposition. As later with *Good*, so already with *True*, we have an ultimate, unanalysable, indefinable or simple notion. We can recognize that propositions are true and false, but there is no answer to the question What makes them true or false?

The vehemence with which Moore criticizes relational or matching-theories of *True* reminds us of the vehemence with which he later criticizes relativizing theories of *Good*. Correspondence-theories reduce *True* to a relation between a proposition and external existent, much as naturalistic theories reduce *Good* to a relative property of existents. The autonomy of ethics is challenged by the one theory, the autonomy of logic is challenged by the other. Somewhat as Moore, later on, argues that *Good* cannot be defined in terms of any natural thing or process, since for any such thing or process the question 'But is it Good?' is askable, so here, *True* cannot be defined directly or indirectly in terms of anything existent, since about any putative existent the question is askable 'But is the predicate *existent* truly ascribed to it?' The argument is not above suspicion, but what is of interest is that alike in 'The Nature of Judgment' and in *Principia Ethica* Moore demands that some concepts, notions or 'objects' are superior to natural or empirical ones. They are non-temporal and therewith non-existent. They *are*, but not where and when the mere natural scientist finds the things that he studies. In *Principia Ethica* § 66 Moore emphatically includes truths among the objects, such as *Two* and *Good*, which are, but do not exist. Perhaps inequitably he here concentrates on one specially eminent class of truths, namely those which are 'universal', tenseless and non-empirical. He omits to say whether or not falsities still enjoy the status to which, *qua* complex objects [of thought] possessing the unanalysable, non-natural property of falsity, they would seem to be entitled. Before long Russell was to feel some qualms in crediting falsities with subsistence. Subsistent Facts then replace Moore's subsistent Truths. Subsistent objects answering to nonsensical word-combinations will be ostracized as soon as they are noticed.

Moore regards it as Kant's great merit that he had separated off the noumenal from the phenomenal sphere, a separation which, for Moore, coincides with the separation of *a priori* from empirical truths, and therewith of their *a priori* and non-natural 'objects', i.e. subject-terms, from empirical ones. It is for rescuing from Hume these non-empirical truths about these non-natural 'objects' that Kant's Transcendental philosophy, as Moore sees it, is the right philosophy.

Although Moore rejects as *lèse-majesté* any Correspondence-theory of truth, it would be a mistake to credit him with any form of Coherence-theory. He does not here even mention any such theory. There are lots of truths, not just one Truth; and though some truths certainly follow from some other truths, the truth of each is, so to speak, not their communal but its domestic concern.

More startling than this somewhat unnourishing theory of truth, and partly accounting for it, is Moore's dissolution of everything else whatsoever into the concepts and complexes of concepts of which all knowable truths and all thinkable truths and falsehoods consist. 'All that exists is thus composed of concepts necessarily related to one another in specific manners, and likewise to the concept of existence.' (p. 181.) 'It seems necessary then to regard the world as formed of concepts. These are the only objects of knowledge; ... A thing becomes intelligible first when it is analysed into its constituent concepts. ... The opposition of concepts to existents disappears, since an existent is seen to be nothing but a concept or complex of concepts standing in a unique relation to the concept of existence.' (pp. 182–3.)

'They [concepts] cannot be regarded as abstractions either from things or from ideas; since both alike can, *if anything is to be true of them*, be composed of nothing but concepts.' (p. 182, italics added.) What is this argument? If anything is to be true of Socrates, must he be composed of nothing but concepts? No flesh or bone? With wisdom after the event, we, I suggest, can see that, filled out, the argument would be: A proposition is true—or else false— of what it is about. What it is about is the subject-term of which its predicate is predicated. This subject-term is, or is normally, what is signified by the nominative-expression in the sentence that expresses that proposition. What this nominative signifies is part of what the whole sentence signifies. But this is a proposition, and a proposition is a special sort of complex of constituent concepts. So what the nominative-expression contributes to the proposition as a whole is *both* a simple or complex concept or 'universal meaning' and what the proposition is true or false of. A proposition which is true or false of the snub-nosed teacher of Plato, is therefore *about* the complex concept that is signified by 'the snub-nosed teacher of Plato'. Socrates *is* this complex concept or proposition-constituent. So a proposition A that is about the Morning Star, one B that is about the Evening Star and one C that is about Venus are about irreducibly different 'objects of thought', since the nominatives to the sentences expressing these propositions are not synonyms; so they 'mean' different objects. Different planets?

As in Graz, Jena and Freiburg, so in Cambridge the requisite de-psychologizing of the thinkable has begun by engendering an omniverous ontology of 'meanings' or 'objects [of thought]'. Here is an adolescent Logical Atomism, in which Plato's snub-nosed teacher is, mercifully *post mortem*, 'meta'-translated into what is undyingly conveyed by 'Plato's snub-nosed teacher . . .'

Against this backcloth of concepts and propositions, i.e. 'objects [of thought]' being what everything is composed of, Moore's famous and subsequently repented confusion in *Principia Ethica*

D

(§ 7 and § 8) between the parts of horses and the parts of the definition of *Horse* becomes understandable. Since all objects, including animated, four-legged objects have to *be* simple or complex 'objects or notions', it can, for a short time, seem that the hooves which are the nether and clattering parts of horses *are* the *hoof-having* which is a part, though not a nether or a clattering part of the definition of *Horse*. What we had talked about straight can seem to dissolve into what we must write about with the help of inverted commas.

At the bottom of p. 183 of 'The Nature of Judgment', less than half-way through the article, Moore disappoints us by moving on from his ambitious conceptual and propositional ontology to a sustained examination of the distinction between *a priori* and empirical truths. In particular he tries to correct defects in Kant's ways of distinguishing between them. Neither Universality nor Necessity gives Kant the criterion that he rightly desiderates. It is non-temporality that gives the right criterion. Part of our disappointment may be due to the fact that the conceptual ontology or Logical Atomism of the first part of the article nowadays interests us a lot, both for its own sake and for its links with twentieth-century Logical Atomism; while the distinction between *a priori* and empirical truths is now rather boring to us. It no longer promises to us, as it then did to Moore, a new Heaven, or at least a new earth. The *Tractatus* has intervened. But our disappointment is probably uncalled-for. At this stage Moore seems to have been deeply preoccupied *both* with the opposition between the temporal and the non-temporal *and* with the opposition between the *a posteriori* and the *a priori*. His heart was in a Transcendental Philosophy of a semi-Kantian kind, providing a two-floors reality, with the important, non-natural things on its clock-less upper floor. So very likely his interest in the non-natural and so non-psychological components of truths and falsehoods was from the start derivative from his interest in that realm of 'objects of thought' which provided the subjects for the *a priori* truths of which Transcendental philosophy is the study—including pre-eminently truths about *Good*, but also truths about numbers, and about truths. To de-psychologize the idea-doctrines of empiricists was a necessary step, but only a step towards emancipating, *inter alia*, Ethics from all naturalistic relativisms. That there are Truths on a floor higher than that of the truths of the mere natural sciences seemed to Moore to require that there be 'objects [of thought]' on a floor higher than that occupied by the objects in Nature, which merely exist. So maybe Moore Platonized the thinkable chiefly in order to be able to justify the *Grundlegung* to man. Much of what Frege did for the sake of arithmetic Moore did for the sake of Ethics.

At the end of the second paragraph on p. 189 Moore startles us by saying 'But we have now to point out that even existential propositions have the essential marks which Kant assigns to *a priori* propositions—that they are absolutely necessary'. A few lines later he says 'If now we take the existential proposition "Red exists", we have an example of the type required . . . when I say this my meaning is that the concept "red" and the concept "existence" stand in specific relation to one another *and to the concept of time*. [Italics added.] I mean that "Red exists now . . ."' and this connexion of red and existence with *the moment of time I mean by "now"* [italics added] would seem to be as necessary as any other connexion whatever. If it is true, it is necessarily true, and if it is false, necessarily false. If it is true its contradictory is as fully impossible as the contradictory of $2 + 2 = 4$.'

Moore here seems to have gone temporarily crazy—though sane again by p. 191, where he says 'No existential proposition of any sort seems discoverable, which might not thus be false; not even the famous "cogito" is indubitable'. In his article 'Necessity' of the following year there is no echo of the view that 'even existential propositions . . . are absolutely necessary'. But Russell echoes it in the first of his 1904 Meinong articles, on pp. 208-9.

Moore's aberration is likely to derive from the following source. Having already labelled as a 'concept' whatever can be a simple or complex constituent of a proposition; and having denied that the truth of a proposition is a contingent matching-relation between that proposition and what happens independently to be real or existent, he has to say that all the connexions that combine its elements into this true proposition, or into that false proposition, are conceptual connexions, and not just *de facto* ones. It would not be *this* truth if anything in it were different or differently connected with anything else in it. Moore seems to be overlooking the fact that there are conceptual tolerations as well as necessitations. It is a conceptual truth that what is yellow can be sweet and can be, not sweet, but sour. But this oversight is only tributary to Moore's basic mistake which is to conflate, e.g., the moment of time I

mean by 'now' with the concept of *time*, and even with the more
specific concept of *the present time*; or, more generally, to conflate
what a referring expression refers to with the sense or meaning of
that referring expression, its *denotatum* with its *significatum*. He—
in very respectable company—equates what a proposition is true
or false *of* with a constituent, namely the subject-term of that
proposition; equates, that is, Socrates with what the translator
finds a French expression for before he reaches the verb, when
translating, say, 'The snub-nosed teacher of Plato died in 399 B C'.
A proposition being true or false of a part of itself—Shades of
Epimenides!

Unlike Frege or Mill, Moore has, as yet, no idea of the distinction between Sense and Reference, or, therefore, between objects
and 'objects of thought', i.e. concepts of notions. He is alive to it
in 'The Conception of Reality' (1917), p. 216 of *Philosophical
Studies*. So no territory is retained for actualities and unactualities;
only conceivabilities *are*. Though Philonous's 'ideas' have been
hygienically de-subjectivized into 'Ideas', Hylas should still be
dissatisfied. Some objects, or rather every object in the cosmos
has been left uncaptured after Logical Atomism has captured
between its inverted commas every single 'object of thought'.
Socrates cannot go into quotes. Nor can his potion of hemlock;
or his death.

We may, in conclusion, raise the personal question Why was
Moore, in the late 1890s, so deeply concerned to separate off a
non-temporal field of non-natural, non-empirical objects from the
lowly field that belongs to the natural sciences, including psychology? What made it imperative for him to reinforce Kant's two-
floored mansion? No answer is afforded by Moore's Autobiographical Statement. We have to speculate.

The vehemence of his attack on the naturalistic fallacy in
Principia Ethica, together with concordant things in his article,
'Freedom', of 1898, and his short review of F. Bon in 1899
(*Mind* pp. 420-2), suggests that the notion of *Good*, together with
those of *ought*, *right* and perhaps *End*, had been for him, all along,
of quite special importance. So it may be that his epistemological
anti-empiricisms and anti-psychologisms got their heat from his
ethical anti-relativism. Perhaps for him the Categories of Kantian
philosophy were only ancillaries to its Categorical Imperative;
and perhaps its noumenal floor was for Moore rather the asylum
of intrinsic goods than the asylum of super-natural agents,

faculties and agencies. Nor, to speculate further, would Moore have been alone among new converts to agnosticism or atheism if he had felt a homesickness not so much for the theistic beliefs as for the moral certitudes of his former days. Surely Good is, even though God is not.

MOORE AND LINGUISTIC
PHILOSOPHY

by MORRIS LAZEROWITZ

Academic philosophy has undergone a striking metamorphosis in recent years, one so radical that a philosophical Rip van Winkel would indeed have to rub his eyes to recognize his subject in it. The attention of philosophers has become more and more concentrated on language; and linguistic considerations, which were once introduced incidentally, for the sake of clarifying a question or an argument, now occupy a central place in the doing of philosophy. It may be that the inner substance of philosophy has remained unchanged and that what philosophers seek now is what philosophers have always sought. But there can be no doubt that the approach to problems has, apparently, gone through a change which is as strange and disconcerting to some able philosophers as it is exciting and promising to others. In the *Phaedo* Socrates says that he tried to determine 'the truth of existence' by recourse to concepts: this is the traditional image of the philosopher. And Moore's distinction between knowing the meaning of a common word and knowing the analysis[1] of its meaning fitted in with the picture of the philosopher looking more deeply into concepts than does the ordinary man and discovering basic facts about things. Wittgenstein, it will be remembered, told us not to ask for the meaning of a word but rather to ask for its use; and in line with this recommendation many present day philosophers examine linguistic usage with the traditional aim, apparently, of establishing facts of ontology.

I

Wittgenstein, who even more than Moore, has directed the attention of philosophers to language, declared that philosophers reject

---

[1] The currently popular word is 'unpacking', which carries with it associations that are unmistakable. The image the philosophical analyst creates of himself is that of someone who digs below the surface to discover unexpected contents: he is a kind of semantic archaeologist.

a form of words while imagining themselves to be upsetting a proposition about things, and that what they need in order to rid themselves of their fantasy is a clear understanding of the workings of language. Some philosophers, however, seem to have the idea that the study of language can bring to light basic features of reality, that facts about things can be inferred from facts of linguistic usage. Professor C. D. Broad, who identifies Moore's famous essay, 'A Defence of Common Sense', as an important source of this idea, writes that it '. . . has led many able men, who might have contributed to solving the real problems of the philosophy of sense-perception, to waste time and labour and ingenuity in semi-linguistic studies of the usages of ordinary speech in the language with which they happen to be familiar. To imagine that a careful study of the usages, the implications, the suggestions, and the *nuances* of the ordinary speech of contemporary Englishmen could be a substitute for, or a valuable contribution towards, the solution of the philosophical problems of sense-perception, seems to me one of the strangest delusions that has ever flourished in academic circles.'[1] Bertrand Russell, who also cannot accept the present day linguistic approach to philosophy, has characterized it as consisting in 'reasoning from the actual use of words to answers to philosophical problems, or from a conflict in actual uses to the falsehood of a philosophical theory'.[2]

A. J. Ayer, in one place at least, provides us with an illustration of the notion that analytical lexicography is capable of yielding ontological information. He tells us that 'what we obtain by introducing the term "sense-datum" is a means of referring to appearances without prejudging the questions what it is, if anything, that they are appearances *of*, and what it is, if anything, that they are appearances to'.[3] This introduction of a term into the language of perception seems aseptic enough; its use is to refer to appearances, pure and simple, i.e., without linking the term to a philosophical theory, and it merely substitutes for expressions which are already in the language. But the point of introducing the term 'sense datum' is not merely to extend philosophical patronage to a word: 'The idea is that it helps you to learn something about

---

[1] 'Philosophy', *Inquiry*, Vol. I, no. 2 (1958).
[2] Introduction to Ernest Gellner's *Words and Things* (London: Victor Gollancz, 1959), p. 13.
[3] *Philosophical Essays* (London: Macmillan & Co. Ltd., 1954), p. 131.

the nature of physical objects, not in the way that doing science does, but that you come to understand better what is meant by propositions about physical objects, what these propositions amount to, what their "cash value" is, by restating them in terms of sense-data. That is, the fact that you *can* restate them in this way, *if* you can, tells you something important about them.'[1] It is not easy to see how what a philosopher wishes to learn about the *nature* of physical objects differs from what science might teach him; but it seems clear, at any rate, that Ayer has the idea that the analysis of linguistic usage, aided by the introduction of the term 'sense-datum', can yield information about the nature of such things as stones and sheets of paper.

Norman Malcolm provides us with an example of a philosopher who 'refutes' a philosophical view by recourse to linguistic usage. In his opinion, H. A. Prichard's philosophical view that we do not really see physical objects is upset by the fact that such expressions as 'sees a sheet of paper' have a use in the language. 'Prichard and others', he writes, 'must admit that we use such sentences as "See my finger", "Now you see the dog", "Now you don't see him", every day of our lives; and furthermore that we are taught to use such sentences and teach their use to others. We are taught and do teach that the correct way to speak, in certain circumstances, is to say "I see the dog", and in other circumstances to say "I don't see him now", and in still other circumstances to say "I think I see him", and so on. Undoubtedly Prichard used such forms of speech every day (and taught them to his children, if he had any) and would have acknowledged in various ways in practical life that they are correct forms of speech. His philosophical position, however, stands in opposition to this obvious fact.'[2] The correct inference to draw, it would seem, is that Prichard's philosophical view is false, and that what shows it to be false is a matter of linguistic usage.

These two examples are sufficient to illustrate Broad's reproach that some philosophers labour under the notion that by recourse to language alone it is possible to solve some, or perhaps all, philosophical problems. One philosopher thinks, or seems to think, that the scrutiny of linguistic usage will reveal facts about the nature of things, another that it is sufficient to refute a philosophical theory about our perception of things; and still a third

---

[1] *Philosophical Essays*, p. 141.
[2] *Knowledge and Certainty* (Prentice-Hall, Inc., 1963), p. 177.

philosopher, it might be added, professed to demonstrate the existence of free will from the linguistic fact that the term 'free will' has a correct use. To sum up, the idea at work behind linguistic philosophy is that linked with lexicography, which records the usages of common speech, there is something which might be called ontological lexicography, the study of which enables us to determine the truth-values of philosophical theories and to obtain knowledge of what exists, and of what does not exist. Broad characterizes this idea, specifically in connection with the philosophical problems of perception but undoubtedly quite in general, as a delusion.

Taken at fact value, it is an odd idea, one which we might not be surprised to find alive in people who have yet to emerge from the stage of magic thinking, but which we should be astonished to find active in the professional work of sophisticated thinkers. No philosopher, regardless of his special persuasion, is so unrealistic in the usual conduct of life as to believe that any sort of study of language will by itself reveal to him that amber has electrical properties, that pelicans exist, and that phlogiston does not exist. If, as appears at first glance to be the case, linguistic philosophers believe that ontology can be learned from the study of linguistic usage, then indeed they suffer from a bizarre delusion, but one, it is hardly necessary to point out, which is confined to philosophy. It is a professional delusion, and must be bound up in some way with the nature of philosophy itself. It would seem that we have to think either that a considerable number of outstanding philosophers labour under a curious idea, one which is wholly inappropriate to their subject, or that the idea is in some way appropriate and that the nature of the subject has not been clearly perceived. We may be less inclined to reject the second alternative if we do not push out of our minds the strange fact that in its long history philosophy has not been able to produce a single uncontested result.

Broad lays the present unwelcome development in philosophy at Moore's door; and there are many things in the 'Defence of Common Sense', undoubtedly the most sober treatise in the history of a discipline not known for its sobriety, which point towards linguistic philosophy. Indeed, it is not too much to say that after Moore the only direction in which philosophy could go was towards linguistic analysis. And there are many things, not only in his 'Defence of Common Sense', but in a number of other

D*

papers, which propelled philosophy in the direction it did take. To mention one of Moore's observations, his pointing out the shocking fact that philosophers have been able to hold sincerely philosophical propositions inconsistent with what they knew to be true[1] could not fail to have had great impact on the thinking of philosophers, all the greater, perhaps, for doing its work in the underworld of the mind. If the philosophical statement that Reality is an undifferentiated unity is inconsistent, for example, with the proposition that there are fifteen students, twelve men and three women, in the lecture room, the inconsistency is *conspicuous*; and if the philosophical statement that no one can really know that another person feels pain is inconsistent with the proposition that I *know* that Jones feels pain (because he winces whenever I jab him with a pin), the inconsistency is *conspicuous*. It is not a trade secret that philosophers are not made to give up their everyday statements by their professional views, nor their professional views by their everyday statements. The strange situation to which Moore's Paradox has directed the attention of philosophers demands an explanation, and continues to do so even when pushed out of the forefront of one's thinking. The attempt to explain it can, in the end, lead us in one direction only.

Many philosophers have, as was to be expected, taken refuge in what might be called intellectual solipsism. Like Galileo's colleagues who would not look through his telescope, they go on with their work as if Moore had never stated his paradox. If forced to give *some* explanation of the situation, they reassure themselves with the Berkeleian formula: speak with the vulgar, but think with the learned. But there is no serious question that they not only speak with the vulgar but that they also *think* with the vulgar. Their using the speech of everyday life is not a hypocritical concession, intended to spare them the rude comments of the gross. Their beliefs are the beliefs of the ordinary commonsense man, and in consequence of Moore's paradox their taking a stand with philosophy against whole classes of everyday statements has come to acquire an air of unreality. The impression created is that a *game* is being played.

Another possible explanation, one which seems to be implied by Moore's Paradox, is that philosophers really believe their philo-

---

[1] *Contemporary British Philosophy* (London: George Allen & Unwin, 1925), edited by J. Muirhead, Vol. II, p. 203.

sophical statements. But this is to imply that philosophers actually suffer from strange delusions, for example, that they do not really know that others feel pain or that there is a number of students in a room. The picture of the philosopher which is conjured up is that of a person who simultaneously lives in two worlds, the ordinary world of everyday experience and everyday talk and an exotic world of odd convictions. But although this is a possibility, it is certainly not a realistic possibility. There is no observational evidence that the picture applies to the philosopher, and it offers no satisfactory explanation of the situation to which Moore has directed our attention.

One path remains open. This is to suppose that there is no inconsistency between the philosophical views which appear to go against everyday propositions and the everyday propositions themselves. But to suppose that there is no inconsistency between what a person says on a given occasion who uses the sentence 'I know that he is in pain' and what the philosopher expresses by the sentence 'No one really knows whether anyone else feels pain' is to imply that the two sentences are not about the same subject matter, that they do not refer to the same sort of thing. What could not fail to suggest itself, independently of various things that Moore said, is that the philosophical sentence, despite the non-verbal mode of speech in which it is framed, makes a verbal claim, to the effect that the expression 'knows that someone else feels pain' has no correct application.

A number of observations Moore made prodded philosophers in the direction of a linguistic interpretation. In 'Some Judgments of Perception' he wrote: 'This, after all, you know, really is a finger: there is no doubt about it: I know it, and you all know it.'[1] The strong impression these words make on one is that a pretence is being exposed and that philosophers are being cajoled out of it. But the pretence obviously is not like that of the youngest son in the fairy tale who pretends stupidity. One idea which is bound to suggest itself is that, whether consciously or not, Moore is trying to free philosophers from a wrong way of looking at their own utterances, from a misunderstanding of their views, and that he is trying to straighten them out about facts of ordinary language.

In his 'Defence of Common Sense' he remarked: 'In what I have just said, I have assumed that there is some meaning which is *the* ordinary or popular meaning of such expressions as "The

[1] *Philosophical Studies* (London: Routledge & Kegan Paul, 1922), p. 228.

earth has existed for many years past". And this, I am afraid, is
an assumption which some philosophers are capable of disputing.
They seem to think that the question "Do you believe that the
earth has existed for many years past?" is not a plain question,
such as should be met either by a plain "Yes" or "No", or by a
plain "I can't make up my mind", but is the sort of question
which can be properly met by: "It all depends on what you mean
by 'the earth' and 'exists' and 'years': if you mean so and so, and
so and so, and so and so, then I do; but if you mean so and so,
and so and so, and so and so, or so and so, and so and so, and so
and so, or so and so, and so and so, and so and so, then I don't,
or at least I think it is extremely doubtful." It seems to me that
such a view is as profoundly mistaken as any view can be. Such
an expression as "The earth has existed for many years past" is
the very type of unambiguous expression, the meaning of which
we all understand.'[1] This, as a moment's sober reflection shows,
is not a caricature of the philosopher, nor of philosophical discussions. And it brings out in startling relief the difference between the philosopher, who can surround every statement and
every question with clouds of verbal dust, and the same man in
ordinary discussions. When an important and greatly respected
philosopher holds up the mirror to his colleagues the image that
looks back at them must make an impression which cannot simply
be shrugged off. It leaves an active residue in the mind.

One more of Moore's remarks should be recalled. In 'Some
Judgments of Perception' he wrote: 'Some people may no doubt
think that it is very unphilosophical in me to say that we *ever* can
perceive such things as [doors and fingers]. But it seems to me
that we do, in ordinary life, constantly talk of *seeing* such things,
and that, when we do so, we are neither using language incorrectly,
nor making a mistake about the facts—supposing something to
occur which never does in fact occur. The truth seems to me to
be that we are using the term 'perceive' in a way which is both
perfectly correct and expresses a kind of thing which constantly
does occur, only that some philosophers have not recognized that
this is a correct usage of the term and have not been able to define
it.'[2] Joined to his remark two pages later that 'The questions
whether we ever do know such things as these, and whether there
are any material things, seem to me therefore, to be questions

---

[1] *Contemporary British Philosophy*, Vol. II, p. 198.
[2] *Philosophical Studies*, p. 226.

which *there is no need to take seriously*',[1] the point is clear. What needs to be taken seriously is the *failure* by philosophers whose views go against everyday statements to 'recognize' cases of correct usage. Wittgenstein said that 'philosophical problems . . . are, of course, not empirical problems; they are solved, rather, by looking into the workings of our language',[2] and that what philosophers need is to get a 'clear view of our use of words'.[3] There can be no doubt that Wittgenstein had his most important roots in Moore, whose defence of common sense began to emerge as a defence of the language of common sense, i.e., the language in everyday use.

There has been disagreement in recent years over whether the linguistic interpretation of Moore's defence of Common Sense is correct. I might say that in the course of a philosophical discussion in Cambridge Moore told me that he accepted the interpretation Norman Malcolm placed on his defence in 'Moore and Ordinary Language'. To introduce a personal note, he rejected forcefully, even with some heat, my own account of what his defence came to, but thought that the account which made him out to be correcting philosophers' mistaken ideas about usage was correct. Moore's work made many philosophers aware of the linguistic character, or what first appeared to be the linguistic character, of a particular type of philosophical theory, and Wittgenstein went on to throw a linguistic shadow over the whole of philosophy. The idea which began to take its place among the standard ideas as to *what* philosophy is, to put it somewhat metaphorically, is that language is the stuff philosophy is made of.

What Moore's Paradox could not fail to suggest is the idea that philosophical theories which seem to be inconsistent with ordinary assertions are *not* inconsistent with them, but instead go against the *language* used to give them utterance. This is the idea which emerged about the nature of paradoxical theories, those which appear to flout common sense; and this idea can easily be seen to apply also to more sober and more scientific sounding theories which seem antithetical to large classes of ordinary statements. To illustrate, take the philosophical question regarding what is implied by the physical fact that light takes time to travel from an object to its perceiver. Does this physical fact imply that we never see a material thing, e.g., a book that is being read, at any of the

---

[1] My italics.
[2] *Philosophical Investigations* (Oxford: Basil Blackwell, 1953), p. 47.
[3] *Ibid.*, p. 49.

times it seems to us that we are seeing it? Light waves from the nearest star take four years to reach the earth, which implies, according to some philosophers, that a star gazer, to whom it seems that he is 'seeing' the star, is not in fact seeing it. At best, it is argued, he can be said to be perceiving what was in the past, not the star as it is at the time of his perception, if indeed it is still in existence then. The philosophical outcome is that we do not see remote objects such as stars. But like Zeno's argument which applies to fractions of a distance to be traversed as well as to the entire distance, the consideration which applies to astronomically far objects applies equally to near objects. The consequence, which is drawn by many philosophers, is that at no time do we see the thing it seems to us we are seeing, and thus that we do not see physical things. Some philosophers, under the influence of things Moore has said, would place a linguistic interpretation on this claim, rather than, as is natural, a scientific interpretation, the reasoning being somewhat as follows. A philosopher who holds that we never see things at the times we seem to be seeing them implies that the ordinary use of 'see' as it occurs in such phrases as 'sees a sheet of paper' and 'sees a finger' is incorrect. He cannot, to use Wittgenstein's expression, say *what it would be like* to see things, as against only seeming to see them, and is thus holding, directly or indirectly, that such an everyday phrase as 'sees a finger' has no use to describe anything. The view that we do not really see things does not say anything about what does not or cannot happen physically. It declares the logical impossibility of seeing physical things, and thus implies that such an ordinary expression as 'sees a finger', like 'whole number which is half of 7', has no use in the language.[1]

Once having brought out what he takes to be the linguistic character of the view, once having made explicit the verbal claim behind the non-verbal sentence 'We do not really see things at the times it appears to us we are seeing them', a so-called ordinary language philosopher would bring linguistic evidence against the view, by pointing out that perception words like 'sees' have a correct use which is not confined to their occurrence in phrases like 'seems to see'. It will be clear that a linguistic philosopher who infers that we do really see things from the fact that such an expression as 'sees a sheet of paper' has a correct use is pointing

---

[1] What lies behind the velocity of light argument is the wish to mark the difference between seeing a physical object and 'seeing' a mental image.

out that it is logically possible to see things. The proposition his linguistic evidence supports is of the same type as the proposition that his linguistic evidence is intended to upset: what it is brought against is the claim that it is logically impossible to see things at the times we would be said to see them; and therefore what it is adduced for is the proposition that it is logically possible to see them at those times. In fact, the inference from usage to the philosophical proposition that we do see things consists of nothing more than giving two reports of the same fact in two different modes of speech: the verbal report that expressions like 'sees a sheet of paper' has a correct use and the indirect non-verbal report of the same fact in the idiom of logical possibility.

One important outcome of Moore's Paradox is the position which construes philosophical views opposed to common sense as attacks on everyday language. This is certainly one of Wittgenstein's constructions, as it is also of some philosophers after Wittgenstein. Where Moore says that philosophical doubts about the existence of things, etc., need not be taken seriously, Wittgenstein tells us that philosophical attacks on common sense are not to be countered by 'restating the views of common sense'.[1] The relevant and correct way to deal with them is to straighten out 'misunderstandings concerning the use of words'.[2] The implication, quite apart from other of Wittgenstein's remarks, is that they are, in substance if not in outward appearance, misdescriptions of ordinary language, to be corrected by recourse to the actual use of terminology.[3] This explanation of the paradoxical utterances helps us understand how a philosopher can say the odd things he says without embarrassment and without making others uneasy about him, but it raises a question on which it throws no light. It tells us why a philosopher who attacks common sense is not corrected by the facts and how he can make his pronouncements in the presence of the facts. But it does not help us understand what makes it possible, supposing it to happen, for a philosopher

---

[1] *The Blue Book* (Oxford: Basil Blackwell, 1938), p. 59.

[2] *Philosophical Investigations*, p. 43.

[3] To my knowledge, Wittgenstein nowhere says this outright; but it is certainly one of his ideas. In *The Blue and Brown Books* he states, for example, 'Ordinary language is all right' (p. 28); and in the *Yellow Book* he states, 'What the bedmaker says is all right, but what the philosophers say is all wrong'. (The so-called *Yellow Book* consists of notes taken in the intervals between dictation of *The Blue Book*.) The idea which comes through here, as in other places, is that what the philosopher says about ordinary language is wrong, that he misdescribes it.

persistently to misdescribe usage in the presence of actual usage. It leaves unexplained why he does not, to use Moore's word, *recognize* actual usage, which he does not give up, nor why, instead of accepting linguistic correction, he takes refuge in such questions as 'What is ordinary language?' and 'Does the fact that a philosophical term occurs in a standard dictionary make it part of ordinary language?' Nevertheless, this linguistic way of looking at many philosophical theories, the sober alike with the unsober, improves our understanding of the troubling question as to why they can remain in unending debate.

It should be noted that there is a further kind of philosophical position which is not open to the interpretation of describing, truly or falsely, ordinary language (or to the interpretation of misusing language). This instead seems open to the charge that it misconceives the causal powers of language. Professor W. V. Quine, for example, gives the impression of thinking that the contents of the world can be changed by changing linguistic categories.[1] Occam laid down the principle that entities should not be multiplied unnecessarily, which, apart from the Platonic theory it was directed against, would be taken to refer only to the *postulation* of entities. In the view of some philosophers, so it would seem at any rate, by manœuvring with language ontology can be enlarged or decreased. For example, by widening the category of singular terms, entities are introduced into the world, are brought into existence; and by narrowing the category of singular terms, by not counting indicative sentences as names, for instance, certain kinds of objects are barred from existence. Quine has written: 'When we say that some dogs are black, $(\exists x)$ (x is a dog. x is black), we explicitly admit some black dogs into our universe, but we do not commit ourselves to such abstract entities as dog-kind or the class of black things; hence it is misleading to construe the words "dog" and "black" as names of such entities.'[2]

We do not, of course, 'admit' black dogs into the universe by *saying* that some dogs are black, any more than an Irishman actually peoples Erin with leprechauns by saying that some leprechauns have beards. Not having the powers of Divinity, saying so-and-so does not bring so-and-so about; and it is out of

[1] This does not prevent him from also holding that entities are being postulated, rather than created, as is suggested by phrases like 'a theory's commitment to objects'.

[2] 'Semantics and Abstract Objects', *American Academy of Arts and Sciences*, Vol. 80–1, p. 93.

the question to suppose that any philosopher might think the contrary, regardless of the suggestions his language carries with it. But in philosophy things are not as they are in ordinary life. There is an atmosphere of bewitchment in it that is not encountered in ordinary work and talk, and language which would be considered inappropriate in connection with an everyday statement, as just a way of speaking, might not be just a way of speaking when used in the expressions of a philosophical position. Thus, when Quine writes that it is important 'to show how the purposes of a segment of mathematics can be met with a reduced ontology' the implication of the words is that ontology can be reduced, i.e., that the number of things there are can be decreased. And the suggestion created by his language has to be taken seriously: the implication of the words is not merely that a decreased ontology can be postulated but that ontology can be decreased by grammatical fiat. How this is to be effected may be gathered from a number of different remarks. The following, in addition to those already cited, should suffice: 'In discussing the theory of meaning I did urge the uselessness of meanings as entities. My thinking was, in effect, that no gain is to be sought in quantifying over such alleged entities as meanings',[1] and 'I prefer not to regard the general terms and statements as names at all'.[2] The idea which comes through is that by 'widening the category of terms that name'[3] entities considered by Quine to be useless are *made* part of ontology, that by grammatically turning 'dog' and 'Friction generates heat' into names or singular terms, abstract entities are created, and that by excluding such expressions from the category of names, entities are barred from existence. The idea appears to be that ontology, the content of the world, is subject to control by grammatical fiat.[4] In one place Ayer speaks of creating a new domain of private entities by a 'stroke of the pen', and from other philosophers the comparable impression is gained that by grammatical gerrymandering, i.e., by manœuvring with linguistic categories, various kinds of abstract entities are either made part of what is or subtracted from what is. Indeed, the thought which forces itself on one is that unlike such everyday things as shoes

[1] *Ibid.*, p. 94.   [2] *Ibid.*, p. 93.

[3] 'Semantics and Abstract Objects', *American Academy of Arts and Sciences*, Vol. 80–1, p. 92.

[4] This notion is given oblique expression in James S. Miller's witticism which Quine quotes on the frontispiece of his *Word and Object*: 'Ontology recapitulates philology'.

and tables, abstract entities are the production of language. To extend Broad's Paradox to philosophers of this general persuasion, we should say that some linguistic philosophers labour under the delusion that by changing language in certain ways reality itself is made to suffer change. It will be clear that the explanation which has been applied to philosophical views falling under Moore's Paradox does not apply to this position.

To come back to the linguistic outcome of Moore's defence of common sense, there can be no doubt that Moore has changed the course of philosophy. His perceptions started a trend that has continued on its own. After Moore it was a natural step to proceed from the notion that a false philosophical theory is one which mis-describes actual usage to the notion that a true philosophical theory is one which correctly describes usage. The whole of philosophy becomes linguistic in character. Thus, Wittgenstein in the *Yellow Book* speaks of the 'confusion which considers a philosophical problem as though such a problem concerned a fact of the world instead of a matter of expression'.

Many philosophers have viewed the linguistic turn which philosophy has taken since Moore with the greatest consternation, since it deflates philosophical questions into 'mere questions about words'.[1] Broad, who deplores the effects of Moore's 'Defence of Common Sense' on the doing of philosophy, is led to think that linguistic philosophers must suffer from the delusion that from an examination of word usage they can learn facts about things. By deciphering an ancient piece of writing, which requires learning the use certain symbols once had, historical facts are learned; but the facts are learned from the statements into which the symbols enter and not from the fact that the symbols have a certain use. Anyone who thought that the study of the use of terms alone will yield information which is more than just information about a language, that it is capable in addition of yielding information given by statements using the terminology, would be suffering from a delusion of some sort.[2] And a philosopher who has the idea that the study of perception-terminology, for example, could lead to an explanation of what takes place when a person is said to be perceiving a thing would also be suffering from an intellectual

[1] Moore's expression.

[2] There is much talk these days about ordinary language being 'theory laden'. Without going into this philosophical notion, it would seem plain enough that a language in which rival theories can be expressed is not laden with or based on any of them.

delusion, one comparable to the idea that it is possible to discover the properties of a substance by studying its name. Moore's Paradox, which is about traditional philosophers, has led to a way of doing philosophy which has created a paradox of its own, one which might be called Broad's Paradox of Linguistic Philosophy. This is that it is a strange fact that many philosophers actually believe they can solve 'real' philosophical problems by studying the usage of ordinary speech.

Broad's description of linguistic philosophers has two obvious implications. One is that the real problems of philosophy are problems about the nature and existence of phenomena of various sorts, the solution of which will establish 'truths of existence'. The other is that linguistic philosophers want from philosophy what philosophers have always wanted from it, or have appeared to want from it. A sceptical note is perhaps not out of place here. Freud has remarked that what we get from science we cannot get elsewhere, and it only calls attention to what cannot have escaped anyone to remark that for information about *things* philosophers along with others go to science. Not to pursue this, however, Broad is undoubtedly right in thinking that linguistic philosophers seek what conventional philosophers seek, that their goals are the same, although their approaches appear to be utterly different. The words of one important linguistic philosopher are a clear enough indication of this. J. L. Austin has written: 'When we examine what we should say when, what words we should use in what situations, we are looking again not *merely* at words (or "meanings", whatever they may be) but also at the realities we use the words to talk about: we are using our sharpened awareness of words to sharpen our awareness of, though not as the final arbiter of, the phenomena.'[1] Parenthetically, it is interesting to compare Austin's statement that a sharpened awareness of words is not a 'final arbiter' of phenomena with Ayer's observation that a philosopher who adopts the 'sense-datum' notation learns something about the nature of physical objects but not what a physicist by his work learns about it. Both seem to hint at a kind of recognition of what philosophy cannot give us and thus of what it does give us, what its actual 'domain of discourse' is.

The question which comes up is whether the 'real' problems of philosophy are the kind of problems whose solutions, like those

[1] *Philosophical Papers*, edited by J. O. Urmson and G. J. Warnock (Oxford University Press, 1961), p. 130.

of chemistry, will establish facts about the existence and behaviour of phenomena. Moore's Paradox throws much of traditional philosophy into a strange light, some of the strangeness of which is removed by placing a linguistic interpretation on it. Broad's paradox throws linguistic philosophy into a strange light, on the assumption that the traditional problems of philosophy are not questions about the uses of words. But since Moore and Wittgenstein this assumption can no longer be taken for granted. It cannot be taken for granted any longer that traditional philosophy, behind the fact-stating idiom it employs, is different in content from that of linguistic philosophy: the one may be related to the other as the Colonel's Lady to Judy O'Grady. What looks like a bizarre delusion on the part of sophisticated thinkers may be an impression induced by their use of a double idiom, the verbal idiom of linguistic analysis and the ontological idiom of traditional philosophy. There is no question that the passage from statements about usage to statements about what is logically impossible and what is logically necessary, what 'really' is not and what 'really' is, creates the illusion of inferences being made from words to things: the passage, say, from 'The expression "did it of his own free will" has a correct use' to 'Free will does really exist' would certainly create such an illusion, *if* the inferred statement were an ontological reformulation of the verbal statement. And the work of Moore and Wittgenstein has shown that what seems obviously the case to philosophers, for example, that the philosophical sentence 'Free will exists' states the existence of a kind of action, may not be the case at all. It may well be that no philosopher, regardless of his creed and method, has ever *in fact* sought knowledge of things in philosophy, and that his appearing to do so has been a semantically generated illusion from which Moore's work has, in some measure, helped free us.

II

Moore, at least at times, accepted the interpretation of his defence of common sense as a defence of ordinary language against the attacks on it by metaphysical philosophers. It is perhaps not out of relation to this interpretation that Wittgenstein said, 'What *we* do is to bring words back from their metaphysical to their everyday usage'.[1] Moore's writings made many philosophical views an

---

[1] *Philosophical Investigations*, p. 48.

embarrassment to philosophy—such views as that we don't really know that anyone else has thoughts and feelings and that time is unreal; and placing a linguistic interpretation on them helped remove some of the strangeness that had settled over philosophy. But Broad's complaint that linguistic philosophers labour under the delusion that the scrutiny of verbal usage can yield ontological information carries with it the suggestion that *underneath* no philosopher gives up the idea (which he keeps at a distance from himself) that philosophical theories actually have the factual content they appear on the surface to have. If true, this would help us understand why philosophers who have taken refuge in the linguistic interpretation of the more bizarre utterances fail to see a comparable strangeness in the linguistic interpretations themselves, a strangeness which counts as much against them as the strangeness of the factual interpretations counts against the more natural readings. Construed as descriptions of the actual use of terminology, they are flagrant misdescriptions; and to attribute them to philosophers would, indeed, be nothing less than to suppose them to suffer from some sort of aberration. Moreover, the views have the mystifying feature of never intruding themselves into everyday talk, although they have been announced over and over again for centuries. This cannot be explained on the view that they are *mere* misdescriptions of everyday talk.

The linguistic construction placed on philosophical views which flout, in appearance at least, elementary common sense does offer a possible explanation of how philosophers can say the unbelievable things they seem to be saying. As has already been remarked, this is that they are not actually saying what they appear to be saying: their utterances are verbal, about the actual functioning of expressions in a language. But represented as having verbal content it is no less unbelievable to attribute them to philosophers than it is when they are represented as having factual, nonverbal content. The philosophical utterance, e.g. 'No one can know that anyone else exists' is no less wild when construed as having the verbal content that expressions like 'knows that there is someone else in the room' have no use to describe a circumstance, than it is when construed as having fact-claiming content. And the explanation again must be that the verbal content they appear to ordinary language philosophers to have is not their actual content. What the nature of their content is may be arrived at by looking again at the view which appears to be implied by a number of things Quine has said.

It goes without saying that no philosopher, regardless of any unconscious fantasies he may have about the magical power of words, consciously thinks that ontology, the contents of the cosmos, can be enlarged or diminished by grammatical gerrymandering with nomenclature. It would be unrealistic, to say the least, to disagree with Mill's words: 'The doctrine that we can discover facts, detect the hidden processes of nature, by an artful manipulation of language, is so contrary to common sense, that a person must have made some advances in philosophy to believe it; men fly to so paradoxical a belief to avoid, as they think, some even greater difficulty, which the vulgar do not see.'[1] And the belief that the world of things can be altered by altering grammatical categories is too absurd, too contrary to experience, to attribute to anyone who has not lost touch with reality, regardless of the extent of his 'advances in philosophy'. It is not a belief that anyone could fly to in order to avoid a difficulty, however great. When a philosopher uses language, in the expression of his position, which implies that objects can be created and destroyed by the manipulation of grammar, we are compelled to think that the 'objects' are of a very special kind: they are, we might say, philosophical entities and do not have the substantiality required to make them resistant to control by language. It would be the very height of absurdity to imagine that a philosopher, despite the suggestion of his language, might consciously believe that by reclassifying proper names like 'John' and 'Harry' with abstract nouns the nature of the bearers of the names would be changed. But it stretches the imagination not a whit to think that a philosopher has the idea that by grouping classes of terms in special ways he brings new entities into existence. And this is so because the 'entities' which are invoked by philosophical tinkering with grammatical categories are understood to be the kind that can be invoked in this way. The following passage helps us see what these are. In *Word and Object* Quine writes:

'This chapter has been centrally occupied with the question what objects to recognize. Yet it has treated of words as much as its predecessors. Part of our concern here has been with the question what a theory's commitments to objects consists in (§ 49), and of course this second-order question is about words. But what is noteworthy is that we have talked more of words than of objects

[1] J. S. Mill *A System of Logic*, Bk. II, Ch. VI.

even when most concerned to decide what there really is: what objects to admit on our own account.

'This would not have happened if and in so far as we had lingered over the question whether in particular there are wombats, or whether there are unicorns. Discourse about non-linguistic objects would have been an excellent medium in which to debate those issues. But when the debate shifts to whether there are points, miles, numbers, attributes, propositions, facts, or classes, it takes on an in some sense philosophical cast, and straightway we find ourselves talking of words almost to the exclusion of the non-linguistic objects under debate.'[1]

These words help us understand the nature of the mysterious entities which, unlike wombats and unicorns, are subject to control by the manipulation of grammar, and what it is about them that makes it possible to annihilate or create them by narrowing or widening grammatical categories. When the question regarding what a theory's commitment to objects *consists in* is a 'question about words' we are constrained to think that the theory is itself in some way about words. And when a philosopher perceives that his talk is more about words than about objects, even when his concern is to determine what there 'really' is, his question as to what there really is has to be understood in terms of his perception. And understood in this way, the *philosopher's* question about what there really is, unlike the corresponding questions of the explorer and the archaeologist, is in some way about language: the reality he is inquiring into, the 'ontology' which is the subject of his discourse, is linguistic in character. As against non-linguistic objects like wombats and unicorns, the 'objects' belonging to philosophical ontology are verbal, or, if not themselves verbal, are related to terminology more like the way in which a shadow is related to the thing that casts it than like the way in which the thing is related to its name. The 'entities' which come under discussion when there is, in Quine's words, a 'shift from talk of objects to talk of words as debate progresses from existence of wombats and unicorns to existence of points, classes, miles, and the rest'[2] are linguistically engineered illusions. What comes out clearly enough to be unmistakable is that the 'shift of talk of objects to talk of words' consists of an artificial grammatical manœuvre in which nouns like 'point', 'class', and 'mile', which are not names of things

[1] Pp. 270–1. [2] *Word and Object*, p. 271.

are assimilated into the class of nouns like 'wombat' and 'unicorn', which are names of things. The recategorization is a piece of holiday grammar. No corresponding semantic changes are made in the actual use of the words; they become names of things, not in fact, but only in name. And what creates the delusive idea that ontology is under discussion, that 'ontological slums'[1] are being cleared out or that a domain of reality is being added to the cosmos, is that the idle terminological classification is made in the ontological idiom, the form of speech in which language is used to refer to extra-linguistic objects.[2]

Wittgenstein has said that when we come upon a substantive we tend to look for a substance. These words do not describe what actually happens and were, perhaps, intended to call our attention, in a graphic way, to a tendency to classify all nouns with the special group of nouns which are names of things. This tendency, which no doubt has its roots in our earliest experience with language, may be an echo of the time when the words we learned were the names of things. John Stuart Mill's idea that all or nearly all words are names represents, at one level, a hidden reclassification of words under the term 'name', i.e., it represents an artificial use of the term stretched to cover words which do not normally count as names. At a deeper level of the mind it harks back to the first vocabulary in the history of our education. Be this as it may, the insight that Wittgenstein's words give us into the nature of the activity of philosophers who appear to look for, and to find, substances corresponding to substantives is that it is a creative, if semantically substanceless, manœuvre with category words. The stretched use of the expression 'name of a thing' creates the delusive impression that a realm of objects has come into existence; and if we consider the importance to philosophers of the idea that ontology is in dispute, the unavoidable conclusion is that the

---

[1] *Ibid.*, p. 275.

[2] It should be noted that Quine explicitly rejects the idea that 'the acceptance of abstract objects is a linguistic convention distinct somehow from serious views about reality'. (*Ibid.*, p. 275.) His notion is that 'The question what there is is a shared concern of philosophy and most other non-fiction genres'. (*Ibid.*) But what a philosopher *thinks* he is doing need not coincide with what he in fact is doing. Indeed, even the linguistic interpretation of Moore's defence of Common Sense implies that philosophers have always laboured under a false idea about the nature of their work. An observation of Wittgenstein's is worth repeating here. The confusion which pervades philosophy, he is reported to have said, consists of supposing that a philosophical problem 'concerns a fact of the world instead of a matter of expression'. (*The Yellow Book.*)

stretched use is introduced for the sake of the illusion it creates. The existence of the illusion is determined by the manipulation of grammatical classifications, and this is responsible for the idea, which caters to the wish for omnipotence of thought, that ontology is not merely discovered, but created, by doing things with language. Philosophical ontology is a recapitulation of, and indeed is created and annihilated by, academic moves with terminological categories. It is nothing more than a language game the moves of which are made in the ontological form of discourse. To put it aphoristically, the ontology of the philosopher is ontologically presented grammar.

This explanation of the position that the contents of the cosmos can be enlarged or diminished by a 'play of words', to use Hume's expression, or by manipulating the 'breadth of categories', to use Quine's expression,[1] affords us a possible explanation of the nature of philosophical claims which appear to be antithetical to ordinary language and which can be made by someone who does not give up everyday usage. This explanation Moore would not accept, but he would have wished to have it examined. The explanation is that the claims are not misdescriptions of ordinary language, but present in the ontological idiom make-believe changes in the use of everyday expressions. For example, the philosophical view that space is unreal presents different faces to different philosophers: to some it presents an ontological face and seems to make an incredible factual claim; to others it presents a verbal face and seems to make an equally incredible claim about that part of everyday language which employs space-indicating terminology. The invisible reality behind the visible faces is academically altered language presented in the ontological mode of discourse. It is this behind-the-scenes game with language which makes it possible for philosophers to say without embarrassment the strange things that they say. The game is the reality; the faces are appearance. Behind the game there undoubtedly lies a psychological reality, which gives the greatest importance to the game. For philosophy, like art, is an answer to the deep need of people 'to sugar the bitter pill of life with illusion'.[2]

[1] *Word and Object*, p. 275.
[2] Richard Sterba, *Remarks on Mystic States*, *American Imago*, Vol. 25, no. 1, p. 85.

REFLECTIONS ON SOME MAIN
PROBLEMS OF PHILOSOPHY[1]

by O. K. BOUWSMA

I should like in these pages to think about Moore's book in terms of the following passage from the first chapter. The first chapter is entitled 'What is Philosophy?' And the passage quoted is a part of Moore's answer to that question.

'To begin with, then, it seems to me that the most important and interesting thing which philosophers have tried to do is no less than this; namely: To give a general description of the *whole* of the universe, mentioning all the most important kinds of things which we know to be in it, considering how far it is likely that there are in it important kinds of things which we do not absolutely know to be in it, and also considering the most important ways in which these kinds of things are related to one another. I will call this, for short, "Giving a general description of the *whole* universe", and hence will say that the first and most important problem of philosophy is: To give a general description of the *whole* universe.'

I propose now to study these sentences both in order to grasp the conception of philosophy that determines the inquiry in this book and in order to understand how some parts of this book are related to the attempt described in this passage. First I want to study it in terms of a part of what Moore offers as such a description. My main interest will be in the phrase 'the most important kinds of things which we know to be in it', and of that phrase, especially the phrase 'kinds of things'.

So I want first to attend to the words, 'description' and 'the most important kinds of things'. Ordinarily a man describes what he has seen, for someone else who has not seen. And what in any place or time are 'the most important kinds of things' will depend upon a man's needs or interests. So, for instance, travellers and explorers when they return home tell their friends about what they

[1] Reprinted from *The Philosophical Review*, Vol.LXIV, 1955.

have seen. And they do not tell about everything but only about what excited their surprise and admiration. The following passage from *Robinson Crusoe* will illustrate this:

'It was on the 15th of July that I began to take a more particular survey of the island itself. I went up the creek first, where, as I hunted, I brought my rafts on shore. I found after I came about two miles up that the tide did not flow any higher, and that it was no more than a little brook of running water, very fresh and good: but this being the dry season, there was hardly any water in some parts of it—at least, not enough to run in any stream, so as it could be perceived. On the bank of this brook, I found many pleasant savannahs or meadows, plain, smooth, and covered with grass; and on the rising parts of them, next to the higher grounds, where the water, as might be supposed, never overflowed, I found a great deal of tobacco, green, and growing to a great and very strong stalk. There were divers other plants, which I had no notion of under-standing about, that might, perhaps, have virtues of their own, which I could not find out. I searched for the cassava root. . . . I saw large plants of aloes. . . . I saw several sugar canes. . . . [The next day I] found different fruits, and particularly I found melons upon the ground in great abundance and grapes upon the trees.'

It won't do, of course, to say that Robinson Crusoe *tried* to give a description of a part of the island. Perhaps he never tried at all. He just described. And he mentioned some at least of the most important kinds of things which he saw 'to be in it', running water, pleasant savannahs, tobacco, aloes, sugar-cane, melons, and grapes. As for the cassava root, he searched for that, and presumably thought it likely that there was some. Robinson Crusoe was, of course, a sailor and wrote down such notes as these for people who did not leave home.

Gulliver, such another sailor, on the sixteenth day of the pre-vious month, June, though not at all in that same year, also ventured forth upon a strange island. He observed 'the country all barren and rocky' and observed also 'a huge creature', and 'the length of grass, which in those grounds that seemed to be kept for hay, was about twenty-foot high'. As in the case of Robinson Crusoe, Gulliver too did not try to describe. He described. He was English, could write, and he had seen clearly what there was, or at least some of what there was, in the island. It perhaps never

occurred to him before he saw that 'huge creature' and that tall
grass that there were such things in the island. At any rate, that he
should tell about kinds of things so 'important' is not surprising.

Are Moore's philosophers, then, such men as Robinson Crusoe
and Gulliver? Are they men who have travelled far, and are their
eyes and hearts full of strange and new things, and are they eager
to tell the world? Are we perhaps to think of the philosopher as
like those who have penetrated the jungles and who have seen
what only those see who exercise themselves with 'deep penetra-
tion' of wilderness and swamps? For the moment I say, 'Well,
why not?' But before making up our minds about this, let us notice
Moore's explanation. Moore explains what it is that philosophers
try to do by an example, an example, that is, of a description, such
as a philosopher might give and, in part, such as Moore himself
does give. The description is introduced as 'certain views about
the universe, which are held nowadays by almost everybody'. This
description goes on, in part, as follows:

'To begin with, then, it seems to me we certainly believe that there
are in the universe enormous numbers of material objects of one
kind or another. . . . But now, . . . we believe also that there are
in the universe certain phenomena very different from material
objects. In short, we believe that we men, besides having bodies,
also have minds, and one of the chief things we mean by saying
we have minds, is, I think, this, namely, that we perform certain
mental acts of consciousness. . . . These things, these acts of
consciousness are certainly not themselves material objects. And
yet we are quite certain that there are immense numbers of them.'

You will notice at once that what is here called a description is
something quite different from those descriptions cited above from
Robinson Crusoe and Gulliver. If when they returned home, and
friends gathered at the harbour, eager to hear, if then, I say,
Robinson Crusoe or Gulliver had said, 'Well, there were enormous
numbers of material objects, and many acts of consciousness', it is
not unlikely that some of their eager friends would have gone
home disappointed. And if someone had shouted from the back
of the crowd, 'What! no tobacco, no melons, no grapes, no huge
creature, no grass twenty-foot high?' and Robinson Crusoe had
replied, 'Perhaps—we noticed material objects and those things
you mentioned are all material objects, so there might well have

been such things', would not that have been a strange thing to hear? And notice too how different is the idea of important kinds of things. Fresh water is important if you are thirsty. And fruit is important if you are hungry. And a huge creature is important if you do not want to be eaten or stepped on. But, in this instance, Moore shows no special interest in tobacco, nor in fruit, nor in huge creatures. There are material objects. But not as though he would say, 'Oh, what would we do without them!' In this book Moore seems much interested in the number of whatever the kind is that he is speaking of. There are 'enormous numbers of material objects', 'immense numbers' of acts of consciousness, 'an immense number of propositions', a 'number of truths . . . enormously greater', 'enormous numbers of universals', 'an immense number of different specks of pure white', 'tremendous numbers of them', 'many millions of the most obvious facts', and 'the number of spots in which no act of consciousness is taking place is immensely larger than that of those in which an act of consciousness is taking place'. But the number, of whatever it is, is very likely neither the measure of importance nor the importance itself.

I have been interested up to this point in a certain similarity and a certain contrast between what travellers do and what philosophers do. The similarity may be seen in comparing the following two sentences. What do travellers do? They give a general description of the lands they have visited (a part of the universe) mentioning all the most important kinds of things they have seen. What do philosophers do? They give a general description of the whole of the universe, mentioning all the most important kinds of things they know to be in it. Now one might suppose that philosophers do for the whole universe what each traveller does for some part. So a philosopher's book might include excerpts from the writings of travellers. His book might be a compendium of travel literature. We know, of course, that this is not the case. Or again one might suppose that what distinguishes the account of the traveller from that of the philosopher is a certain high degree of generality. It might be supposed that if a philosopher did not know that there are material objects then he might find this out by reading travel literature. For what are water, meadows, aloes, and sugar cane but material objects? And so too with acts of consciousness. For what are taking surveys and hunting and finding and perceiving and supposing and searching and understanding but acts of consciousness? This idea of what philosophers do might also seem to be confirmed by that part of the description which Moore cites as of the sort which philosophers have given. Nevertheless, this too would be a mistake. Who would listen to a traveller who talks like a philosopher? What is it that makes what the philosopher says alive when he says it? What is his interest?

In order to understand this I should like to revert to an aspect of what makes the traveller's account interesting. The traveller goes far away. He visits, and he tells about what others have not seen. He tells about what is covered by great distances, about what is hidden from eyes that stay at home. Let us say then that the traveller describes the hidden, and that this is also what the philosopher does. But the hidden is now obviously of a different sort; for whereas sailors sail the seas, the philosopher stays at home. I should like now to try to understand what it is that stirs the mind and heart of philosophers.

Before I go on to consider this, I should like to notice the role of what Moore calls 'common-sense views'. These are views 'which are held nowadays by almost everybody', and include that part which I quoted above. It is obvious that Moore does not consider that material objects and acts of consciousness are hidden. Concerning them no special investigation is required and there are no doubts. Those views, however, are only a part of that description which, according to Moore, philosophers have tried to give, and in Moore's book they serve as a starting point for the discovery of other 'important kinds of things'. This is especially true of material objects, and our knowledge of them. For they serve in much the way that a Chinese box serves, which, if you examine it carefully, reveals other boxes hidden within it. That our knowledge of material objects should serve in this way, is, I take it, no part of the 'common-sense' view. So we get in Moore's 'description . . . mentioning all the most important kinds of things', not only those recognized by almost everybody, but also those hidden from almost everybody. And among those hidden kinds of things are sense-data, 'material objects' (the hidden 'material objects' are not to be confused with the material objects almost everybody knows), propositions (which are, and later, in the book, cannot be) facts, truths, and universals. The interest in the hidden is common to children, to travellers, and to the philosopher. But the concept of the hidden which moves philosophers is nothing so simple as: 'What's in that box?' or 'Where are my spectacles?' or 'Are there zebras with stripes running the other way in Tasmania?' If we can understand this, I think, we may better understand what Moore also tried to do in these lectures.

I should like now to explain the idea of the hidden. A squirrel hides nuts. A thief hides loot. The cloud hides the sun. A cunning person hides his motives. The children hide behind the door. Nature hides secrets. We look for what is hidden. We dig in the sand. We lift the mattress. We look behind the door. We study a man's face. We peer through foliage. We use microscopes. What I want to notice especially is that when we look for what is hidden we must know first of all *that* something is hidden. We must know what to look for. Sometimes this is very simple. We may see the squirrel hide nuts. We may see the children run to hide behind the door. We may hear a rustling in the bushes. Sometimes the case is by no means so simple. A man may look into his microscope to discover a germ, a parasite, which he has never seen, but which he knows 'must' be there, just as an astronomer may look through his telescope to discover a planet, which he has never seen but which he knows 'must' be there. Now, then, if the excitement of the philosopher is that of search, of discovery, and if this is relative to the hidden, what is it that has led him to search and to discover? Has he seen the squirrel hiding something? Has he heard a noise in the chimney? Does he have a theory which, like the theory of the man with the microscope and like the theory of the astronomer, leads him too to probe? Has he come upon a knothole in the fences of this world through which he looks intently, distinguishing in an obscure plenum silver lightnings whose form and motion he can scarcely make out? Are there silken threads, which as by accident he has laid his hand on, and which lead his tugging grasp to 'things' on the other side to which the threads are attached? There are some things like knotholes in the fences of this world and some things like threads which lead the curious on and on. Beyond this, of course, looking intently through a knothole into a deep obscurity with flickerings of light, and tugging at a thread and hearing only the murmurs of the thread one tugs, may both be disappointing. It must be remembered that sometimes the hidden is not found. Among philosophers it sometimes happens that if one philosopher announces that he has discovered a new and 'important kind of thing', some other may announce that there has been only a new and important kind of mistake. And he may write an essay on how to look through a knothole.

In what follows I propose to study several cases in which Moore in effect says: Here is another 'important kind of thing'. There are sense-data. There are 'material objects'. There are universals. In each case there will be something which I propose to call a clue, and a discovery. I am using the word clue in this case in a broad sense, so that even such things as knot-holes and threads would be called clues. Anything is a clue, of course, only when taken in a certain way, and this is the conception I want to use. It is something which, taken in a certain way, leads to the discovery of sense-data, to the discovery of 'material objects', or to the discovery of universals. It is especially the nature of these clues which I want to explore.

Moore, in the course of trying to give 'a general description of the whole universe', mentions among 'the most important kinds of things', sense-data. Most people who look, for instance, at an envelope, are unaware of sense-data. Some people, expert, and, as it were, with practised eye, shall we say, discover them. Moore, of course, is such an expert. Now the case of sense-data is especially fascinating because though sense-data are to be discovered, yet they are represented as what one cannot help but see. How then can what one cannot help but see be hidden? Well, there are such things as the spectacles on your nose, cellophane, and the window you see through. For these too you may need a clue before you see them. Sense-data, like these, are hidden in full view, and yet not hidden like them. What then is the clue?

The clue to the presence of sense-data is a difference in the use of two such sentences as Moore cites in this 'exhibition' of sense-data. The sentences are these: 'The envelope is rectangular' and 'The envelope looks like a rhombus'. Moore, in the course of the exhibition, has held high in his right hand an envelope for all to see. Under these circumstances or similar ones these sentences and their uses are familiar to almost everybody. As Moore turns the envelope, though the envelope is rectangular, it now ceases to look rectangular. It looks like a rhombus. And isn't this now a strange thing, that when you keep your eye, as you suppose, fixed on the envelope, and you know very well that it does not change its shape, the envelope is not a caterpillar and is not a chamelion, nevertheless it now looks like a rhombus? What can have happened? What can have got in the way? This is the form of the question by which Moore introduces the conception of sense-data: 'What exactly is it that happens when (as we should say) we see a material object?' Is there from the point of view of some ideal perception a normal sort of eye trouble? If, for instance, the envelope looked rectangular from any point of view and no matter how it was turned, then we should never doubt that when we see the envelope we do see the envelope.

Consider this case. Someone holds up an envelope and asks you to look at it. You do so. Now he turns the envelope very slowly, and on the sly, invisibly, he slips between your eyes and the envelope, a piece of paper in the shape of a rhombus. He, then, asks you, 'What does the envelope look like?' And you say, 'It looks like a rhombus'. He smiles and says, 'No wonder!' and pulls out the piece of paper, and waves it before you. 'This is what you saw.' And he goes on to explain: 'This is what happened when (as you should say) you saw the envelope. I slipped this between your eyes and the envelope.' Now imagine, further, not that someone on the sly, invisibly, plays tricks on you whenever you look at an envelope, but imagine that your eyes, on the sly, invisibly, exude coloured shapes, and that these hang in the air between your eyes and the envelope, masking the envelope whenever you look. This would, as you can see, make seeing very interesting, but on the other hand, it might also make seeing very exasperating, supposing you wanted really to get a look at the envelope. How exasperating this might be, if you bother to think of it, would be clear if you thought, not of your eyes doing this, a fatality to which you might be resigned, but of that sly one's doing it, some pestering genius with pieces of paper whom you cannot shake off.

I have elaborated this point because of a common ambiguity in speaking of sense-data. Someone might say, 'Of course, there are sense-data', and he might go on to explain this as Moore did by holding up an envelope and saying, 'Now it looks different, doesn't it? And that's all there is to it.' What I intended to make clear in introducing the pieces of paper and the exudations is the conception of the sense-datum as a *thing*, and of the *intervention* of sense-data in perception. Sense-data are among those 'most important kinds of things which we know to be in it' (the universe).

Now, I think, I am prepared to explain in what sense sense-data are hidden and have been discovered. It is clear that when someone normally looks at an envelope when an envelope is held up for him to see, he does not have any of the feelings that go with being cheated, as though when he looks at an envelope something always intervenes to obstruct his view. If one ever did get a bare-faced look at the envelope, then, of course, when a sense-datum inter-

E

vened he might immediately sense the difference and realize that something had gotten in the way. As it is, he never suspects any interference. If you ask him what he sees, he says that he sees an envelope, and if you ask him what it looks like, he says that it looks like a rhombus. And he has an explanation for that too. It's the way you're holding it. Now, then, what is hidden from him is what Moore describes as 'What happens when' he sees an envelope. What happens when he sees an envelope is that he 'sees' something else.

The question is: How, then, are sense-data, in the same sense in which they are also hidden, discovered? Clearly not as one might detect the frayed edges of a piece of paper, or a tear in the rhombus, or a shape not quite in place. Sense-data always fit an envelope like a glove and are nearly always in place. How then? What is the clue? I am going to suggest one, which if it is not precisely the clue, will at any rate illustrate what I take the clue to be like. I suggested earlier that a clue is something which is taken in a certain way, and I also said that the clue in this instance is to be found in the difference in the use of two such sentences as 'The envelope is rectangular' and 'The envelope looks like a rhombus'. It is now the latter of these two sentences which when taken in a certain way is the clue. This sentence when interpreted by analogy with another sentence which is very much like it, will lead straight to the conception of the sense-datum as a 'thing' which intervenes in perception. Consider: If you put on the uniform of a policeman, then you will look like a policeman. Someone might even mistake you for a policeman and ask you the way to go home. And, then, of course, you would explain: 'Oh, I'm not a policeman. I only look like a policeman. I'm only wearing these clothes.' So you see, a man may look like a policeman, and an envelope may look like a rhombus. And how does a man come to look like a policeman? By wearing a policeman's clothes. And how does an envelope come to look like a rhombus? Well, by wearing, shall we say, the clothes of a rhombus? In any case, if in interpreting the sentence 'The envelope looks like a rhombus' you follow the pattern of 'He looks like a policeman', then the analogy will require a mask for the envelope. And how then could an envelope look like a rhombus? Naturally, by wearing the suitable mask. And this then is what it must do since it does look like a rhombus.

I was intent, you will remember, upon trying to understand the excitement of Moore's philosopher in terms of the conceptions of the hidden and the discovery of the hidden and the idea of the clue. The point of this was to understand also the use of the phrase, 'the most important kinds of things'. So I tried to identify the clue to the hidden and the now discovered sense-data, which are among 'the most important kinds of things'. Discovering sense-data is a little like discovering that what everyone, or 'almost everybody', takes to be a forest and a running brook is a theatre set; and wouldn't that be something to write home about? But discovering sense-data is also much more like discovering that what everyone, or 'almost everybody', takes to be the solid world, trees rooted in the earth and brooks running wet to the river, is an ever-shifting theatre set. And wouldn't that be something to cable home about? No wonder Moore's philosopher is excited. And the clue? It does not consist in anything like seams in the wallpaper, distinguished by looking closely. It consists rather in a peculiarity of certain sentences about what we see. Sentences similar to these and under other circumstances have other uses.

Moore also mentions 'material objects' among the most important kinds of things in the universe. It may seem odd that Moore should have made a point of this since 'almost everybody' would allow this, witness Robinson Crusoe and Gulliver. There would be some point in this if 'material objects' also were hidden, and if, accordingly, they too had to be discovered. What this suggests is that there is some considerable ambiguity in the use of the expression 'material objects', and there certainly is such ambiguity. Moore wrote: 'To begin with, then, it seems to me, we certainly believe that there are in the universe enormous numbers of material objects of one kind or another.' 'We' is 'almost everybody'. I think we can understand this. If Moore, for instance, had held up an envelope and asked, 'And what's this?' someone in the front row would have responded quite properly, 'An envelope'. And if he had gone on, smiling, 'And is it a material object?' meanwhile snapping it with a finger, then, if someone had responded with, 'Well, it isn't smoke. If you stick your finger through it, you'll tear it', Moore too, might have regarded that as a good answer.

We can, perhaps, even imagine a situation in a company of 'acts of consciousness' or 'spirits', in which it would come as a surprise and might occasion some excitement to discover that there are material objects, in the sense just noticed. Imagine, for this purpose, a small company of ghosts on a first visit to hard reality. Ghosts, of course, are well acquainted with space, but not with material objects. And now, for the first time, they observe human beings. They observe that human beings when they come to a tree walk around it. Human beings do not walk through walls. They climb over them. Human beings when they meet, step aside and pass. Ghosts, on the other hand, mingle their substance freely. They pass right through one another, like two plumes of smoke, but they are not scattered. 'Odd,' said one ghost, 'None of these things are in the same place with another.' 'That's right', said another. 'They seem to be limited to contiguity. That must be a great bother, always having to go around.' They noticed that human beings and trees and walls cast shadows, just as Dante once noticed that those damned souls in hell cast no shadows. 'Strange', said the tallest ghost, admiring a shadow. 'Like us, positively fascinating, but always on the ground.' A man passed by carrying a sack of potatoes, grunting, his back bent under his load. He walked right through one of the ghosts, expecting the ghost to step aside. He blinked and the ghost smiled. They noticed a child bouncing a ball against a wall and saw another child bump his head and run home crying with his feet on the ground, not skimming. The bouncing ball was a wonder to them.

When the ghosts got home they made their report to all the inhabitants of ghost town, and they had one of their writers, one who writes for others, keep the record. And for a long time these ghosts talked about the unghost objects which they had seen.

If now Moore had said that 'almost everybody' and, perhaps, even a few ghosts, believe that there are such things as trees, walls, human beings, potatoes, rubber balls, and that among human beings these are called material objects and among some ghosts these are perhaps called unghost objects, then there would have been no difficulty about this. Anyone who has tried to walk through somebody or who has carried a sack of potatoes or bounced a ball or even held a bottle, would recognize immediately what he was talking about. But, in this case, nothing is hidden and there seems no occasion for any human being, at least, to claim that he has discovered such things. A ghost, as we have seen, might do so, but this involves special circumstances.

In what sense, then, are we to understand 'material objects' in the required way that they be both hidden and discovered? It is obvious that this conception is relative to that of sense-data. We may understand this in terms of Moore's question: 'What exactly is it that happens when (as we should say) we see a material object?'

We know what happens. A sense-datum intervenes. The eye is represented, in this situation, as having something like a mysterious catalytic influence upon, let us say, an envelope, so that when the eye is turned upon it, the envelope emits something analogous to a smoke screen or better, camouflage, a camouflage so well adapted to deception, were this the purpose, that most people never do catch on. In any case the 'material object' due to what happens whenever we do perceive a 'material object' is completely covered, hidden, in the dark. Under these circumstances what is really amazing is that we should be aware that sense-data are hiding something. In this context Moore uses such expressions as 'an obscure belief', 'believe, however, obscurely', 'in this obscure way', which expressions show how hard it is to conceive of man getting a glimpse of what lies behind the sense-datum.

And now what about the clue? What has led to the discovery of what is hidden? We have already noticed the clue which leads to the discovery of sense-data, namely, such a sentence as 'The envelope looks like a rhombus', and now as the incidence of the expression 'material object' is intertwined with that of the expression 'sense-data' so the sentence 'The envelope is rectangular' is intertwined with the sentence 'The envelope looks like a rhombus'. As now the latter sentence, regarded in a certain way, has led to the discovery of sense-data, so the former sentence, regarded in a certain way, as contrasted with the looks-like sentence, leads to the discovery of something in the dark which has no looks at all. The situation is somewhat as follows: If you put on the policeman's clothes, then, of course you look like a policeman. But suppose I want to know who you really are. Then you put on a sailor's clothes, and so you look like a sailor. But, of course, you are neither policeman nor sailor. I complain and you try on other suits of clothes. Finally you appear before me naked, and I am still not satisfied. I say, 'That won't do. Those are the emperor's new clothes and you're not the emperor.' Or I say, 'Remove your skin. You can't fool me that way.' However you appear before me, I complain that I want to see *you*, and complain too that you are hiding from me. Your non-appearance is most phenomenal.

Is now the excitement of the philosopher in this case also intelligible? Well, suppose that you, at a certain stage in your philosophical development, unmindful of Descartes' instructions to get your feet well-planted somewhere before you set out, were now convinced that wherever you looked and whatever you heard, wherever and whatever were sense-data. You might, of course, have tried to turn the edge of a sense-datum, but in that case, there would only be another sense-datum. This would be like living in a dream. This would be frightening. And now imagine that in the midst of this dream you open your eyes, and look about you into the darkness, and find yourself believing 'however, obscurely', but most certainly, that there are material objects; would not that be a great relief? Well, this might be what the discovery of 'material objects' is like. Of course, the philosopher does not discover this by anything like waking from a dream. The clue does not consist in the perceived darkness into which one peers between dreams. It consists rather in a peculiarity of sentences of a certain kind. I have tried to indicate what that is.

I have noticed now two cases of the hidden and the nature of the clue in each case. The first is that of sense-data, and the clue in such a sentence as 'The envelope looks like a rhombus'. The second is that of the 'material object', and the clue is such a sentence as 'The envelope is rectangular'. I have also tried to indicate what it is that makes of such sentences clues. They must be taken in a certain way, interpreted, that is, in terms of the use of certain other sentences which are like them. In this way such sentences serve as chinks through which, as it were, one peers into the darkness, fascinated by the flickerings in that darkness, lights which enter through the chink one peers through, and from that side.

Now I should like to consider 'universals'. Universals are also among 'the most important kinds of things in the universe'. And are universals also hidden? Of course. Most people have never heard of them. And many people who are told about them and who are directed to discover them, never do discover them. Those, relatively few, who have discovered them have, however, established a definite technique for their discernment, and it is to this technique that we must attend in order to understand this discovery. In this case we begin, however, not with sentences, but with certain individual words. Words are the clue, and what, of course, is involved here is that they, words, have meaning. A word, it must be remembered, is usually, in a certain aspect, either a noise or a trail of ink. And yet such noises and such trails of ink have about them an atmosphere of mystery, almost as though they bore within them secret recesses of treasure and power. They are charmed noises, charmed trails of ink, which lead a borrowed life. They are like iron filings which dance and shimmy, at the behest of a magnet hidden, removed, invisible. Noises and trails of ink are alive, but the source of their life is not within them. It lies, of course, in their meanings. I should like to emphasize this point. Considering that words are mere noises and mere ink trails on a white surface, is not their behaviour amazing? Is it not clear that something else moves them? They are not self-moving, not animals.

The question is: What moves them? Consider, as Moore does, the word 'two'. This word, in all its variations in all languages, has been in the world a long time, and there has been, to use an expression of Moore's, 'an enormous number' of charmed occurrences of this noise, and, of course, of charmings. It was so from the beginning. There was the second day, one, two. 'And God made two great lights.' 'And the name of the second river is Gihon', one, two. And some years later: 'And of every living thing of all flesh, two of every sort, shalt thou bring into the ark.' Two has a long history. And the meaning of 'two' has been exercising its influence upon noises and trails of ink for a long, long, time. One thing is clear, and it shows in what I have just noted, and that is, that the meaning of 'two', namely two, has played in the background of our times from the beginning. If two is created, it must have been created before most things and perhaps after one. But most people say that two was not created at all. It was before the beginning, that is, before there were any words. Naturally this leaves open the question as to how two enlivens 'two'. Some people have spoken of 'two' as pregnant, and as wedded to two, that is, to its meaning. Some people have spoken of words as inspired, and that suggests two breathing the essence of its substance into 'two'. But some others who are less given to speculation say that the influence is electric and have their hopes set on advances in electronic studies for catching quiddity on a wire.

The point of what I have just written is to bring out that the meaning of 'two' is conceived as a thing, and this thing is intended or looked upon as explaining this remarkable difference between noises which are meaningless and those which have meaning. I want now to introduce a more sober figure which may once more show how the analogy through which one attempts to understand meaning leads to the conception of meaning as something hidden. Think of the word 'two' as bearing in the belly of its 'o' an arrow pointed in any direction you please. It bears such an arrow in every one of its billions of occurrences. Obviously, these billions of arrows point in all directions. Now, a word, in effect, directs you to its meaning as an arrow directs you to the town. So the meaning is something such that if you pursue the direction in which the arrow in the belly of the 'o' points, you will come upon the meaning of the word. But now we meet this puzzling situation. The meaning of 'two' in these billion occurrences is the same in all. Moore stresses this point in the following phrases, 'identical', 'identically the same', 'same', 'identically same'. The arrow, accordingly, in the belly of any 'o' of any 'two', points at the same two, that is, the same meaning as does the arrow in the belly of any other 'o' of any other 'two', rain or shine. But how can a billion arrows pointing in all directions all point at the same, identically same, thing? The answer is that this is just the sort of thing that two is.

I have introduced these analogies in order to show how in terms of them meaning may be revealed as something hidden. In relation to the quivering word, the meaning may be the disapparent father. In relation to the word with a referent, the referent is the village over the hill. In any case the meaning is regarded, as some people would say, as transcendental, over the hill and far away. And now I should like to notice the clue. Consider, as an ideal of explanation, the following. If someone asks, 'Who is Elizabeth?' then, if Elizabeth is in sight, and you, looking at Elizabeth, say, 'That is Elizabeth', this explanation should be effective. It is simple and easy to understand. There is the name 'Elizabeth' and there is Elizabeth and you, with your look and the formula 'That is Elizabeth', make the connection, lay the name on Elizabeth. All this happens in daylight and Elizabeth is in sight. Now consider: What is two? That is, what is 'two' the name of? If, now, two stood in the garden and it was daylight, see how simple this would be. You would look at two and say, 'That is two'. But two is not standing in the garden. If in this situation you ask the question 'What is two?' so that it now seems, at any rate, that you do not know, then though you may at the same time have a vague familiarity with two, still, as contrasted with Elizabeth, two is certainly hidden. And on the other hand, if in this situation you are asked the question 'What is two?' and it now seems to you that you certainly do know what two is, then, though you may at the same time suffer from baffling unfamiliarity with two, in any case, as contrasted with Elizabeth, two is certainly hidden. In any case, two is hidden. But at the same time two is; for otherwise, how should we speak of two bananas, two rivers, two days, two mosquitoes?

Now what precisely is the clue? The clue is such a question as 'What is two?' but it is a clue only as seen through such another question as 'Who is Elizabeth?' (or 'What is a chair?'). There is a form of explanation which goes with 'Who is Elizabeth?' which one now seeks to follow also in explaining 'What is two?' The bafflement which one meets in this attempt is explained by the hiddenness of two. Two is certainly a baffling kind of Elizabeth.

And now can you understand a philosopher's excitement about this? It is true, certainly, that there is nothing disquieting about this, as there might very well be in the discovery that there are sense-data. Nor again is there anything reassuring about this, as one's disquiet about sense-data has already been relieved by the discovery of 'material objects'. But there is other excitement. Columbus discovered a new world, and certainly that was exciting. And so it is with universals, 'the world of universals', otherwise hidden in the careless ignorance of people who do not notice that a word's having meaning is like an arrow pointing to the village over the hill. Imagine someone, for the first time, discovering the sky full of stars. For universals, too, are 'as the sand which is upon the sea shore'. The discovery of universals has stirred the imagination as no other discovery in philosophy has ever done. Silver statuettes shining like stars!

In these pages I have tried to understand Moore's philosopher. I have tried to do this hoping to see what that 'most important and interesting thing' is 'which philosophers have tried to do'. I wanted especially to see how it was 'important and interesting', in order to explain some of the excitement that goes into the writing of such a book as this. In order to do this I employed the figures of Robinson Crusoe and Gulliver. They, too, described, mentioning all sorts of most important kinds of things which they had seen. This helped me to see both how what Moore did was like what they did, and also how what he did was different from what they did. They were all discoverers, and they all wrote home about what they had discovered. There were 'melons and grapes' and 'sense-data', and 'material objects' and a 'huge creature', and 'pleasant savannahs and meadows' and 'universals'. The difference between these different sorts of things immediately suggests different means of discovery. Robinson Crusoe and Gulliver sailed, landed, and looked. But Moore stayed at home. So the question

E*

which I attempted also to answer was: How did Moore come upon the discovery of these things? Naturally I have given only a sketch of what, I take it, furnished Moore with means of discovery. It seemed to me, then, that just as there are chinks in walls and fences along which we pass each day and which chinks we miss seeing at all unless we look from a certain angle, so too there are chinks in the word, sentences, which when we look at them curiously from a certain angle, open out upon 'most important kinds of things'. I have tried to indicate what some of those chinks are.

In the writing of this paper I have been led especially to notice the ideas clustered about the idea of discovery, namely, the ideas of the hidden and the clue. In this way I came upon the idea of chinks. Among philosophers who have written during the last fifty years, there is none in whose writings the chinks are more clearly identified than they are in the writings of Moore. Moore has always found light by close scrutiny of phrases and sentences. And in telling us of what he saw, he has always respected fastidiously the confines of the chink. It may well be that Moore has in this way brought out into the open what philosophers have always tried to do, generally, of course, with more abandon, without Moore's severity, stretching the chink. All this has been very important in preparation for the question: But are phrases and sentences chinks? We can be grateful to Moore for our re-examination of this conception which, as I take it, Moore has employed with such uncommon skill and patience.

MOORE AND METAPHYSICS

by A. C. EWING

G. E. Moore has been associated with the enemies of metaphysics who have more or less dominated British thought in recent years. In fact however he was very far from either leading them in the attack or following in their wake. He never denied the possibility of metaphysics nor had he any general epistemological theory which would have required him to do so. He did not hold either the verification theory of meaning or the analytic theory of *a priori* propositions and inferences, the two foundations of the ruthless attack on metaphysics in the thirties. And although he gave the impetus which started the linguistic school of philosophy, he cannot himself be regarded as a typical linguist.

Here is the place for a word about his relation to Wittgenstein. Moore was a great admirer of the latter and was much too impressed by him to turn against him his devastating powers of criticism, as he did against certain other philosophers; but R. B. Braithwaite, who was well acquainted with both, says in his obituary notice on Moore that he can detect no positive influence of Wittgenstein in Moore's writings.[1] Moore himself said in 1942 that he could not tell how far Wittgenstein had influenced positively what he wrote, but added that 'he certainly has had the effect of making me very distrustful about many things which, but for him, I should have been inclined to assert positively. He has made me think that what is required for the solution of philosophical problems which baffle me, is a method quite different from any which I have ever used—a method which he himself uses successfully, but which I have never been able to understand clearly enough to use it myself'.[2]

For the emphasis which Moore laid on the importance of a study of language he had two reasons both of which would be quite compatible in themselves with even a far-reaching metaphysics. (*a*) Careful analysis of the meaning of words, on which Moore

[1] *Proceedings of British Academy*, Vol. 47, p. 304.
[2] *The Philosophy of G. E. Moore*, edited by P. A. Schilpp, The Library of Living Philosophers (Open Court Publishing Co.), Vol. IV, p. 33.

insisted so much, is an essential tool for the philosopher, whether he goes in for metaphysics or repudiates it completely. If anybody does not realize the urgent need for stressing the importance for philosophical work of this careful analysis of meaning, let him take a long course in either some of the idealist philosophers who preceded Moore or the works of modern 'existentialists'. Moore was right in insisting that a very common cause of error or confusion is that 'a philosophical question' is often really two or more questions jumbled together under the same words. For example Moore rightly complained very early in his career that when an idealist says that the universe is 'spiritual' he means to include under that term a number of different properties so that 'we are apt to overlook the number of *different* propositions which the idealist must prove' and so 'to assume that, if one or two points be made on either side, the whole case is won'.[1] And at the very beginning of the preface to *Principia Ethica* he says that in all philosophical studies 'the difficulties and disagreements are mainly due to the attempt to answer questions without first discovering precisely *what* question it is which you desire to answer'. Further, it is obvious that confusion as to the meaning of a word may lead one to commit the fallacy of ambiguous middle, or to accept as conclusion of an argument something which does not follow from the premises because, though the word used is the same, it has changed its meaning in the process. The conclusion may be interesting only if it assumes the second meaning but justified only if it retains the first.

But there was a second reason, peculiar to Moore's method of approach, which rendered the analysis of meanings specially important in his philosophy. The most important in many people's estimation and certainly the best known doctrine in Moore's philosophy outside ethics is to be found in his conviction that our 'common-sense propositions' are true, not 'partly' but completely true, and are known with certainty to be true, even by those philosophers who deny that we can attain certainty in these matters. Now if common-sense propositions are known to be true and must be accepted as primary data by the philosopher, it will be of great importance for philosophy to determine what the correct analysis of them is, and Moore sometimes gives the impression that this is the philosopher's main, he never suggested the only, task. A proposition is the meaning of a statement and

[1] *Philosophical Studies* (London: Routledge & Kegan Paul, 1922), p. 2.

therefore for this reason alone philosophy becomes to a very large extent the analysis of the meaning of words. It would not be at all fair however to say that this makes philosophy a mere branch of linguistics, for the analysis as practised by Moore is intended to give information not only about the use of words but about the reality to which the words refer. In almost his last important published contribution,[1] he criticizes somebody whom he thinks 'perhaps rather inclined to undervalue the importance of the analysis of propositions' by saying: 'If the propositions you choose to analyse are *true* contingent propositions, they can only be true because they tell you something about reality, and, if so, then I think the analysis of them will tell you something about reality too.' One can indeed go further and say that the analysis, if correct, will on Moore's assumption give information which falls within the sphere of metaphysics. For 'metaphysics', even in the older sense of the term, has been used to cover any very general propositions on topics such as matter, mind, time etc. which were of a kind that could not be established by the methods of natural science. Now if a common-sense proposition within these fields is known to be true and the philosophical analysis of it given is correct, the latter will obviously constitute a true general proposition about e.g. matter established not by scientific but by philosophical argument and so we shall have a metaphysical conclusion. It is interesting to recall that, when once in the thirties I asked Moore whether he admitted any metaphysical propositions he gave as an example the proposition that matter exists. I should have expected him rather to call it a common-sense proposition and a proposition which was reached by analysing this metaphysical, at least if the proposition did not merely affirm that so-and-so was the correct analysis but affirmed it thus analysed to be true of the real; but it might be argued that the two were really the same proposition since in a correct analysis the analysandum and the analysans are strictly equivalent, and so if one is metaphysical the other must be.

This is very different from admitting any sort of deductive transcendent metaphysics which goes quite beyond the realm of human experience. Moore does not produce any general argument to show this kind of metaphysics impossible, but he never attempts it himself except perhaps in the very early years just before the turn of the century when he was an idealist, and he was devastating in his criticism of those of the metaphysical arguments of this kind

[1] *The Philosophy of G. E. Moore*, p. 676.

which he selected for attack. In the first two decades of the century he made his fame outside ethics largely by his criticism of the arguments of the idealists. Further it would actually be difficult to put one's finger on any affirmative proposition that would usually be regarded as part of metaphysics which he considered to have been established, even if we do not use the term in a transcendent sense. I have said that to establish the correctness of a given mode of analysis of a particular kind of common-sense propositions is already to do metaphysics if we make Moore's assumption that common-sense propositions are known to be true, but while he has no hesitation in admitting that there are arguments for accepting one analysis of a common-sense proposition rather than another he hardly ever commits himself definitely to laying down which is correct. But this only amounts to saying that he regards the arguments in favour of those metaphysical conclusions to which he has some inclination as not conclusive while admitting that they are in some cases quite weighty, and it after all would be or at least certainly ought to be fairly hard to find a reputable philosopher today who thought he had conclusively proved the truth of his own metaphysical views. No doubt there remains a big difference of degree: Moore is much more cautious than most metaphysical or other philosophers and much less ready to find an argument convincing. And of course nobody would deny that he very decidedly belonged to the critical rather than to the speculative type.

But we shall now consider the one sphere (at any rate outside ethics) in which he did allow himself to be dogmatic, namely the sphere of common-sense propositions. That this topic is relevant to his attitude to metaphysics is clear both because metaphysical theories were often prefaced by a criticism of common-sense propositions purporting to show that the things to which they applied were not 'real' but mere appearances and also because if we accept common-sense propositions as true the question how they are to be analysed becomes a metaphysical one. The question whether 'idealism' is true is indeed more than a question as to the analysis of physical object propositions since 'idealism' as usually understood includes a theory about the 'spiritual nature' of reality as a whole, but certainly it is a major part of the issue between realism and idealism whether the physical objects of which both speak are to be regarded as independent things or mere appearances to human beings.

Regarding common-sense propositions Moore sets himself not against the dogmatism of metaphysicians so much as against their scepticism. It has been a favourite occupation of philosophers to produce arguments which, if valid, would show that a great number of propositions which everyone who is not a philosopher would say were true are really false; and a still greater number of philosophers have supported arguments to show that the propositions in question, though they might be true, were at any rate not known to be true but were at the best very probable. These arguments Moore treats like arguments to show that $2+2$ was not equal to 4 or that we did not know it to be so. I do not mean by this of course that Moore confused the logical certainty of the arithmetical proposition with the non-logical certainty of e.g. propositions about physical objects. Nobody is clearer than Moore as to the distinction between logical and non-logical certainty. What I mean is that just as everybody would say that we know that $2 + 2 = 4$ quite independently of any arguments by philosophers and if any argument produced by a philosopher contradicts this proposition we can dismiss the argument without even considering it, so Moore is saying of any argument which claims to prove that there are no material things or that all our common-sense propositions about them are false that it must be fallacious since its conclusion contradicts something we know to be true. He does indeed examine some of the arguments but then it may well be philosophically illuminating to examine an argument which would lead to a conclusion you know to be false and try to find out just where it has gone wrong. He makes a distinction however between the proposition that there are no material things and the proposition that nobody knows there are any material things in the Schilpp volume of 1942[1] (but not in 'A Defence of Common Sense' nor in 'Proof of an External World') and claims that he has rigorously proved the former but not the latter to be false, though he obviously thinks he has given a strong argument for the falsity of the latter also. He connects the difference between the status of the two with the fact that far more philosophers have held the latter than have held the former proposition to be true. I must add however that it seems to me Moore was inconsistent here. If Moore has a rigorous proof of the existence of material objects following from premises he knows to be true, he at any rate must have *known* that some material objects existed, and since

[1] p. 669.

according to his account at least corresponding premises must be known to a great many people and the conclusion from the premises is completely obvious, many other people must have known this too.

What is Moore's point here? I do not agree that he can be interpreted as using the paradigm argument or as merely recommending that one should not change one's way of using language in the manner suggested by the statements he was attacking.[1] The sceptics he was criticizing did not want to change ordinary language, nor did they wish in ordinary conversation never to commit themselves to statements about e.g. their hands or even to refrain from using the words 'certain' and 'know' about physical things in everyday speech. What they wanted to maintain was that such language, though correct in the sense of being in accord with ordinary usage was, strictly speaking, unjustified i.e. that it was not self-evident that material things existed and that there were no arguments sufficient to prove that they did or even that there were *a priori* arguments which proved that they did not. Such a view is not in itself self-contradictory, but it is very difficult to believe it true, so difficult that a person who holds the view is very liable to slip into saying things which imply the very commonsense views which he is attacking or others which would be subject to the same criticisms if these criticisms were valid at all, thus giving rise to the inconsistencies which Moore mentions. But in the last resort Moore's appeal is an appeal to a kind of self-evidence. I say 'a kind' because he certainly does not think of the propositions he is defending as having the kind of self-evidence which makes a proposition logically necessary. He either gives no proof of them at all or he gives an argument, as in 'Proof of an External World', which only proves their truth if we already assume that we know particular propositions about the kind of things he claimed to be proving existed and were known with certainty. Thus in the lecture just referred to he only proves the existence of external objects by pointing to an external object which it seemed quite obvious the audience knew existed, namely his hand. This looks like a vicious circle but it is not. He is saying that there is a certain kind or kinds of non-philosophical evidence which everyone must accept and which cannot be overthrown by philosophical argument. In ordinary life we all admit that such evidence is given by perception, and it is surely at least a strong

[1] *v. id.* p. 675.

objection against a philosophy if it leads to conclusions which we cannot possibly believe when we are not doing philosophy but leading a normal life. We may add that, since no system of epistemology can be built up purely *a priori*, the only ultimate way of determining the criteria of truth is to consider what circumstances make something appear clearly true to us in our ordinary life. Even Russell, certainly not an excessively credulous person about most subjects, said that 'all knowledge must be built up upon our instinctive beliefs, and if these are rejected, nothing is left'.[1]

It has been pointed out that a number of beliefs which would have certainly been included in common-sense knowledge at some earlier period are now rejected as false. An obvious example is the belief that the earth was flat. But there are obvious distinctions between these and the examples Moore gives of common-sense propositions. The reason which led people to say that the earth was flat is that it looks flat and it is by no means evident even to 'common sense' that whatever looks flat is flat. The belief is inconsistent with other beliefs which we have to accept if we use the ordinary common-sense perceptual criteria, such as that if we go on in a straight line we eventually come back to the same area from which we started, but in the absence of such inconsistencies with propositions which were only known late in human history, the fact that it appeared flat constituted a reasonable presumption in favour of its being flat. We can easily explain why men should have held the mistaken belief in question and the tendency to hold it commonly disappears when one is informed of the reasons against it, whereas the belief in the existence of some physical objects would be ever so much harder to eradicate. Further even the belief that the earth is flat has a certain partial truth, for it seems only reasonable to include in the meaning of physical object statements some reference to our experience of the objects, even if the statements are not merely statements about human experi-

---

[1] *The Problems of Philosophy* (Oxford University Press, 1912), p. 39. But there is this important difference between the position of Russell and the position of Moore that while Moore's common-sense propositions are held to be known with certainty and therefore never incompatible with each other, Russell admits that two instinctive beliefs can clash. He says that there can be no reason for rejecting an instinctive belief except that it clashes with others. His view is (or at the time he wrote the book was) that the fact that something is an instinctive belief is evidence though not conclusive evidence in its favour. I have been however unable to find anything about his concept of instinctive beliefs in his later works.

ence, and certainly our experience goes on in many respects as if the earth were flat. So one could defend Moore against this objection though he does not bother to defend himself.

Moore thus treats our ordinary perceptual knowledge of physical object propositions as a philosopher commonly treats mathematics, namely as something established with complete certainty by its own criteria which the philosopher may explain further but must not challenge. In view of the perpetual disputes between philosophers on the subject and the grave difficulties which arise on any view it is not possible indeed to maintain that we *know* how we know them i.e. whether directly or by inference and if by inference what is the exact nature of the latter, but I think Moore was right in claiming that we can know many things and yet not know how we know them. He must be because propositions about how we know things, if carried to the end beyond the obvious premises which raise further questions as to their own justification, fall within the subject of epistemology and, while all men know something, relatively few men have ever delved into epistemology. He may indeed well have been wrong in extending too far the field of absolutely certain knowledge and in common-sense statements we do often use the term 'know' in cases where we should not claim more than practical certainty, but it is hard indeed to credit the statement that I do not *know* that I existed five minutes ago or that I have a body.

Moore's doctrine of analysis was developed to reconcile the fact that there are grave philosophical difficulties about all these common-sense propositions with the claim that they are known with certainty to be true. The question of their truth is for him an easy one to be settled at the common-sense level, but that of their analysis a difficult and doubtful philosophical one. There is a real antinomy here. It is hardly possible to resist the conviction that we know with certainty at least some of the common-sense propositions mentioned by Moore e.g. I have a body. Yet on the other hand there are very serious and intractable philosophical difficulties about matter, mind, time, truth and indeed about every single general concept which we even at the common-sense level employ. But if philosophers are as divided as they are on such concepts, how can we expect common sense to be certainly right? This argument indeed seems to drive us to the conclusion put forward on rather different grounds by Bradley that all our ordinary judgements are partly false. Yet is this really credible?

Even Bradley seems to have been using 'false' in a rather different sense from the ordinary one when he put forward his view. It is tempting to meet the difficulty as Moore does by saying that we know our common-sense propositions to be true but do not know exactly what they assert. If we are to avoid having to admit that all our common-sense judgments are in all probability only partly true, we must exclude all debatable content from what we claim to know to be true. This Moore claimed to do by laying down the principle that we knew our common-sense propositions to be true but did not know how they were to be analysed.

Yet difficulties thicken. How can we really know a proposition to be true without knowing what it asserts, i.e. what its analysis is? We plainly do not know these propositions only in the sense of knowing that the words express something true. In this sense I can know a statement in Chinese to be true if it is made to me by someone who knows the language and in whom I have complete trust. But if our knowledge of the truth of common-sense propositions involves even a partial awareness of what is meant, then can we know them to be true without having at least a confused awareness of their analysis? It cannot be a fully clear one for even philosophers are without that, otherwise they would not have the disagreements and difficulties they do as things stand. Can we know any physical object propositions even at the common-sense level if we have not the slightest idea whether they are only propositions about actual and possible human experiences or whether they refer to strictly independent things? Is not the analysis of a common-sense proposition, if correct, just a making explicit of the elements in a concept of which we are indistinctly aware as a whole? But if our awareness of the concept at the common-sense level is somewhat confused, how can we say that we have *certain* knowledge of the common-sense propositions? Must not the certainty of the propositions be affected by any doubts about their analysis?

I think myself a distinction ought to be made here between the analysis of propositions and the analysis of that to which they refer. We must not assume that, if P is correctly analysed as Q + R, therefore the proposition S is P is necessarily the same as the proposition S is Q + R. For it may well be the case that, although the analysis of P as Q + R is correct, a person who asserts that S is P may strongly disagree with the analysis of P as Q + R. For instance Moore suggests as at least a possible analysis of 'This is a hand' that I have a sense-datum which is not part of the surface of the hand but is related to it by a certain relation which he regards as indefinable.[1] This was probably the kind of analysis of the proposition which he favoured most of the time. Now if what has been called the representative theory of perception is true, some analysis like this will be the correct analysis of what it is to perceive a physical object, but should we therefore say that a person to whom the representative theory has never occurred or who explicitly rejects it is when he talks about seeing physical things asserting a proposition which has to be analysed in this way? In that case if a certain theory as to what P is is true I am asserting this theory every time I assert P to exist, however completely I disagree with the theory in question. For this and other reasons philosophers who wrote about the topic later have commonly maintained that what we are doing when we analyse a proposition is not to give its exact equivalent but an account of what it entails, which of course the person who asserts it may fail to recognize. This is not however the view taken by Moore. In his last written important expression of his philosophical views, as opposed to publications of earlier works, namely his reply to questions and criticisms in the Schilpp volume, he says that he thinks he has always intended to use the word 'analysis' in such a way that for an analysis to be correct three conditions must be fulfilled '(a) nobody can know that the *analysandum* applies to an object without knowing that the *analysans* applies to it, (b) nobody can verify that the *analysandum* applies without verifying that the *analysans* applies, (c) any expression which expresses the *analysandum* must be synonymous with any expression which expresses the *analysans*'.[2] But in that case it would seem that a person could not know a common-sense proposition to be true unless he knew what the correct analysis was, at least if the first condition specified be taken seriously, and this would stultify Moore's whole discussion of the subject. On his view it is the business of the philosopher to analyse common-sense propositions but that a person cannot know common-sense propositions without doing philosophy is something that he would be the last person to assert. I do not know what the precise import is of Moore's distinction between 'knowing' and 'verifying' that the analysans and the analysandum

---

[1] 'A Defence of Common Sense' *ad fin.* in *Philosophical Papers* (London: George Allen & Unwin, 1959), p. 57.

[2] p. 663.

apply, but it does seem to me that I might correctly say that a man could verify that BC applied to something in cases where he verified that A did and A was really identical with BC, though he did not know it to be identical, but that we could not correctly say that somebody knew that BC applied to something because he knew that A applied and A was identical with BC unless he also knew that A and BC were identical.

There is indeed a possible line of escape from this difficulty compatible with Moore's wording. It might be the case that a person knew that the analysandum applied and the analysans applied without knowing that the analysans and the analysandum were the same concept. Suppose, for instance, the correct analysis of 'red' as applied to a physical object is 'having the property of appearing red to a normal observer in a normal light'. Now it might be the case that everybody who knew that a particular physical object was red knew that it had the property of appearing red to a normal observer in a normal light but yet that some people ('naïve realists') who knew this did not know that it constituted the correct analysis of red. But I do not think this can have been what Moore had in mind. In many cases where there is a dispute about rival modes of analysis many people deny not only that the analysans and the analysandum are the same concept but that they can always be applied to the same thing. Thus to take the analysis mentioned above of 'This is a hand' in terms of relation to a sense-datum, it is not merely the case that many people would deny that the analysans suggested and the analysandum were identical here but that many who would accept propositions like 'this is a hand' as true are very far from knowing that in such cases the percipient has a sense-datum which stands in a certain relation to the object. Very many people have never heard of sense-data and many who have deny that there are such things or at least that there is always a sense-datum present when we can say on the strength of present perception 'this is an x'. Yet such people would still make statements on the strength of present perception such as 'this is a hand'. No doubt the proposed analysis may be mistaken, but it could not be said that the fact that many people did not think there were sense-data logically proved it to be mistaken. Yet these people not merely do not know that the proposed analysans coincides with the analysandum but do not know that it even applies to all, if indeed any, of the things to which the analysandum applies. A person does not know what he emphatically disbelieves.

At the same time there no doubt are many cases where a person does say something without really knowing what he himself means, and I do not think that these are reducible to cases of not knowing its implications. Hosts of examples are provided by statements in philosophy made by people who are not very familiar with the subject (and, I am afraid, by a number of people who are). These can be described as cases where people are confused as to what they mean. This however hardly applies to the cases Moore has in mind, for it cannot be doubted and Moore had no wish to deny that in a quite ordinary sense of meaning people know what they mean without philosophical analysis when they make statements such as 'I see the cat'. It would not be said that they were confused; it would be said that they knew quite well what they meant by 'the cat' and 'see'. Yet unless we are to suppose that one side in this difficult philosophical controversy is quite certainly right, which would be a very bold thing to say, there is surely a doubt as to whether what they say ought to be analysed in a direct realist, a representative realist or a phenomenalist way. And it seems to be a question not merely about entailments but about what is actually meant by the statement itself. Surely the statement means something different according to whether it is merely a claim about actual and possible human experiences or a claim that a certain extended object exists quite independently of our experiences in a sense in which this cannot be reduced to statements about human experience. It seems to me quite obvious that it is the latter and if so it contradicts flatly statements which have been made by a very great number of philosophers. Yet it may well be contended that what is a person's meaning can only be judged by the kind of questions he intends his statement to answer and he is certainly not normally intending it to answer philosophical questions as to whether 'realism' or 'phenomenalism' is true. The question is therefore a very puzzling one; if Moore's account in the Schilpp volume of the relation between analysans and analysandum goes too far in one direction, the view of the 'analysis of common-sense propositions' as only concerned with what they entail goes too far in another. Men may well agree as to the meaning of a proposition and yet differ as to what it entails. But hard as it is to define what we are doing when we analyse common-sense propositions, there is no doubt that we are discussing something of importance, where the analysis is not merely verbal, as with the analysis of 'A is a father' as 'A has a child and is male', but something of a philosophical character. Moore's doctrine of analysis is an attempt to separate common-sense propositions from controversial metaphysics. I do not think he has solved the problem, but then nobody else has and unless it is soluble common-sense statements must be uncertain and indeed only partly true since it is unlikely in the extreme that common sense is just right on highly controversial philosophical issues. Common-sense propositions, as I have pointed out earlier, use concepts all the time the analysis of which is admittedly fraught with the gravest philosophical difficulties, e.g. matter, mind, number, time, ought etc. Yet how can we really know a proposition to be true when we do not know its analysis? Moore did not answer this question, but whatever he is defined as doing in his analysis he was doing something very important and did it with very great subtlety and skill. Further, the general principle on which Moore acted, namely that we must on the one hand separate common-sense propositions from philosophical ones and on the other that a consideration of our common-sense propositions is highly relevant to philosophy, because in that field we have means of cognition which yield us truth immune from philosophical criticism, is a sound one. Philosophy cannot create its epistemology *ex nihilo*, but must start with what we cannot help accepting as true at the level of common sense, asking what criteria we use there. Even if common sense should not give, as Moore thought, certainty, it can at least provide in regard to many matters good reason for belief; and even if we cannot give of any physical object proposition an analysis which is both precise and completely accurate, it is still a very important question whether physical object propositions are really only propositions about actual and possible human experiences, and a question on which Moore debated with great skill. Moore's 'common-sense philosophy' did not bind him to reject an analysis of such propositions just because it seemed quite obviously false when presented to most 'plain men', and he thought his acceptance of them quite compatible with phenomenalism. I have incidentally never heard a more persuasive criticism of a realist analysis of physical object propositions than that given in Moore's lectures in 1933, though Moore said to me many years later that he had always preferred a realist analysis of these propositions to a phenomenalist. Of the few things in philosophy of which Moore was sure he was very sure, and one of these was the certainty of common-sense propositions and another the distinction between knowing the meaning of common-sense statements as the man in the street does and knowing how the propositions they express are to be analysed, but he did not claim to be able to explain this distinction any more than he claimed to explain how we know the common-sense propositions to be true. But such omissions did not affect his ability to use his technique with devastating effect on the theories put forward by other philosophers.

So what can we say then about Moore's own metaphysics? We cannot say his views excluded metaphysics. He held we knew with certainty at the common-sense level propositions the analysis of which could give propositions of a general kind about mind and matter such as have figured in the metaphysics of other philosophers. Moore did not think that he could prove with certainty the correctness of any of these rival modes of analysis but he did think he could produce more or less weighty arguments on one side or the other. Thus some of the traditional arguments between realists and idealists reappeared as arguments concerning the analysis of common-sense propositions about material objects. But it may be replied that, when these arguments are treated as concerned with the analysis of propositions (the meaning of sentences) they become merely verbal and so really differ radically from the arguments of metaphysicians, properly speaking, and cannot answer the same questions, even if valid. About this there are two things to say. (1) Moore is quite sure that the common-sense propositions referred to are true, therefore for him a correct analysis of a common-sense proposition must itself give a truth about the real. Thus if we could show that, as he thought on the whole most likely most of the time, the correct analysis of perceptual statements was in terms of independent physical objects producing sense-data, realism of a representative kind would thereby be established for him, not merely as an analysis of physical object propositions but as a true theory of the real.

(2) The principal arguments for an analysis are simply arguments refuting alternative modes of analysis and while Moore nowhere, as far as I know, gave a list of the different kinds of argument employed in showing an analysis wrong, they seem generally to consist in showing that if you substitute the words expressing the analysans for the word expressing the analysandum in a sentence the resultant sentence sometimes has a property incompatible with a property that the original sentence had. Thus

you may get a case in which the second sentence is true and the former false, or the second sentence meaningful and the former meaningless, or the second sentence unjustifiable and the former justifiable, or vice versa. This may make it look as if it were just a matter of words, but this would be a misapprehension, for such arguments turn out to be only another way of putting arguments that the most objective of metaphysicians and the most non-linguistic of philosophers might employ. Idealists have argued that physical objects in the realist sense could not be admitted to exist because the supposition was meaningless on the ground either that it was self-contradictory or that there was nothing left of the content of physical object propositions if you eliminated the reference to experience. Such an argument would become in the context of Moore's thought the argument that our physical object propositions could not be analysed realistically because that would make the sentences which purport to express them meaningless whereas they are really meaningful. The idealist may also argue that if physical objects are conceived as the realist conceives them belief in their existence can never be justified. This now becomes the argument that the realist analysis is mistaken because if it were correct physical object statements would be unjustified whereas they are really justified. On the other hand realists have argued that realism must be true on the ground that unperceived physical objects are required to account causally for our experiences and that to act as cause something must exist in an actual and not merely a hypothetical sense. This now becomes the argument that an idealist analysis is wrong because the statement that an actually existing object caused so and so is true whereas on an idealist analysis it would be false. As put by the idealist or realist metaphysician these arguments do not look verbal, but the essence of the arguments is the same as expressed in the apparently verbal form involved in the method of analysis except that Moore starts with the assumption that we know with certainty some common-sense propositions asserting the existence of physical things. This assumption if once made might seem to beg the question completely in favour of the realist, but it does not do so since the assumption as made by Moore leaves it a quite open question whether these common-sense propositions are to be analysed in a realist or an idealist (as it would be usually called today phenomenalist) fashion.

Further, Moore's ethics in an important sense involves metaphysical statements about the real. It is true that he sharply opposes what most people would mean by 'metaphysical ethics', that is, a moral philosophy which seeks to deduce its fundamental principles from general propositions about reality such as that God exists. Moore actually defined a 'Metaphysical Ethics' as one which describes 'the Supreme Good in terms of a supersensible reality'.[1] But his objection is to defining the fundamental concepts of ethics in terms of supersensible existents and not in terms of supersensible qualities, for it is a fundamental feature of his ethics that good is a 'non-natural' quality. Good he holds is a very peculiar property but still a property which does belong to actual existents, if only (except for his dubious doctrine of the intrinsic value of beautiful things existing unperceived) states of mind or experiences. Further, he holds that all true propositions giving the intrinsic value (or disvalue) of something are necessary *a priori*. Where something is intrinsically good or bad in any respect its goodness or badness follows necessarily, its other characteristics being what they are. Ethics is thus full of *a priori* propositions ascribing qualities to things, and if so is it not metaphysical? And must not good be at any rate an existent property if it really qualifies something existent? Ought-propositions are indeed in a different position from propositions asserting intrinsic goodness or badness because they depend on causal properties, which Moore at any rate does not regard as logically necessary, but even so these causal properties would not make an act right or wrong if the effects produced in respect of them were not intrinsically good or bad. So it is the propositions asserting intrinsic goodness or badness which are ultimate. Moore certainly deals in metaphysical propositions when he talks about ethics, if one means by 'metaphysical propositions' general propositions about existing things reached *a priori* and ascribing non-sensible qualities to the things. Such statements as that pain is intrinsically evil or that the enjoyment of beautiful objects is among the greatest of intrinsic goods fall in this category according to Moore's account, though they are not reached by *a priori* reasoning but by *a priori* intuition.

It is this very reason which has made Moore's ethics very unpopular in recent years. The criticisms most commonly brought against it centre partly on its *a priori* intuitive character and partly on its treatment of moral and evaluative judgments as though they were a kind, though a very peculiar kind, of factual statements.

[1] *Principia Ethica* (Cambridge University Press, 1903), p. 113.

It has been objected that Moore commits the same kind of mistake as the naturalist in thinking of value judgments as ascribing qualities whereas they are really prescriptive in character. It is contended that an account like Moore's breaks down completely when we deal with obligation. According to *Principia Ethica* to say that I ought to do act A is just to say that of the acts possible to me at the time A is the one which will produce most good, but this makes obligation statements mere statements as to what will in fact happen, good being just one property among others to be found in the act's effects, but to state that someone is under a moral obligation is not just to say that something will happen. In *Ethics* Moore's view is indeed different because he now thinks of 'ought' as expressing an indefinable relation and not one analysable in terms of good. But if so he presumably regards it as just a unique relation which in fact exists quite objectively in the real world as good is a unique quality thus existing, and it may be doubted whether to say that I ought to do so-and-so is just to say that there is any sort of factual relation between the act and the situation (or would be if I performed the act). Moore is in fact criticized for having like the naturalist assumed that evaluative and presumably obligation judgments were descriptive in character. As a matter of fact Moore did feel that something was wrong there because he admitted that good was not part of the description of anything and even suggested that this was the differentiating ground between it and the ordinary sort of properties,[1] but he does not seem to have grasped the full implications of what he said. He seems, rightly or wrongly, to treat judgments in ethics as if they gave one information about something and did not rather signify the adoption of an attitude. His objection to the latter view is that it would make ethics subjective but he never discussed the more recent attempts to combine it with some sort of objectivity. However, this compromise view was little developed before about the time of his death except for forms of the view which make the objective element purely naturalist.

At the same time I think the sense in which Moore's ethics is metaphysical must be clearly differentiated from the sense of 'metaphysical' in which ethical theories are most commonly described as 'metaphysical'. What is usually meant by a metaphysical ethic is one in which the propounder of the theory bases it on propositions he believes to be established as regards the

[1] *Philosophical Studies*, p. 274.

nature of reality, i.e. propositions saying what sort of beings actually exist. Moore insists that the fact, if it is a fact, that something exists of a certain kind or even that that kind of thing preponderates in the universe is no ground for saying it is good. What is *a priori* for Moore and the basis of his ethics is that it follows from the qualities of certain things that if they exist they are good or bad respectively and that it is therefore our duty to produce, where possible, or avoid producing these things. But the fact that something is very rare or does not exist at all is no reason for saying that it would not be good if it did exist or did exist more frequently than it does. Nor even if a strict proof of the existence of God were available, could it without ethical propositions independently known give us ethical conclusions as to what was good or bad, right or wrong. I think Moore was right in rejecting at least that sort of metaphysical ethics. But there is a good sense in which a person who ascribes a whole set of properties to, I suppose, all minds at any rate, beyond those properties recognized by science is developing a different kind of metaphysical view of the world from somebody who does not.

There is a notion about that Moore later abandoned his characteristic ethical views, and in the Schilpp volume of 1942[1] he does say that he has an inclination to adopt a view according to which the judgment that an act is ethically right asserts nothing that could conceivably be true or false except perhaps that the act was done, adding that while he has some inclination to think that his former view is true he cannot say to which of these incompatible views he has the stronger inclination. However, many years later not very long before his death Moore told me in conversation that he still held to his old view and that he could not imagine whatever in the world had induced him to say that he was about equally inclined to hold the other view. He added that he thought and as far as he remembered always had thought that true judgments ascribing intrinsic value were all 'logically necessary', and he refused even to admit that there was a distinction between the sense in which they were logically necessary and the sense in which judgments of logic were logically necessary. He has made it quite clear that he did not think them analytic and that to do so would be quite inconsistent with his view that the fundamental ethical term was unanalysable, so this gives a whole host of what he held to be synthetic *a priori* judgments true of reality. I do not indeed

[1] pp. 544–5.

mean to imply that he thought all logically necessary propositions to be synthetic. I have no doubt he thought some analytic, so he must have held that the distinction between 'analytic' and 'synthetic' was not a distinction between different senses of 'logically necessary' but between different reasons which might make a proposition logically necessary. But he did hold that there were some necessary propositions outside the field of ethics too, the content of which was not included in the analysis of the terms to which they referred, e.g. the proposition that a cube has six sides. He never subscribed to the dogma that there could be no synthetic *a priori* propositions, even in metaphysics.

Moore originally gained fame, as much as anything, through his remarkable attacks on idealist metaphysicians. After a short period during which he was by his own confession an enthusiastic admirer of Bradley's philosophy[1] he became a pioneer of the realist reaction and was the author of several articles which became extremely well known as criticisms of favourite doctrines of idealists. Several of these have been reprinted in his *Philosophical Studies*. 'The Refutation of Idealism' is probably the best known, but much attention was also attracted by 'External and Internal Relations' and 'The Conception of Reality'. What I feel about these articles is that they expose in a very pointed and damaging fashion certain confusions which may have played a considerable part in making a number of people think leading idealist doctrines true, but that they do not do justice to the subtlety of the greater idealists, whose minds can hardly have worked in the ways suggested by Moore. 'The Refutation of Idealism' (1903) suggests that all idealism depends on confusing what is experienced with the experience of it but brushes aside the possibility of maintaining the view that though not identical they were necessarily connected. 'External and Internal Relations' (1919–20) attributes the idealist doctrine that all relations are internal or at least all things internally related largely to a confusion between the true proposition that, if A has a relation to B and C has not that relation to B, C is necessarily different from A and the false proposition that if A has a relation to B it would necessarily have had to be different in other respects if it had not had that relation, without producing much evidence that this is a fallacy which really deceived leading idealists. In 'The Conception of Reality' (1917–18) he contends that the contradiction in Bradley, which Moore thinks real and not merely

[1] *Schilpp Volume*, p. 22.

apparent, at least if Bradley 'means what he ought to mean' by his words,[1] between maintaining on the one hand that time is 'unreal' and on the other that change and so time is a fact and exists, is to be explained by the confused idea that, even if something is unreal, the mere fact that we think of it implies that it somehow is, because otherwise there would be nothing to think of. An idea which played a great part in his rejection of idealism is that knowledge essentially implies that the object known is independent of the knowing of it. In an article on 'The Character of Cognitive Acts' (1920–21) he argues that, if it can be shown in the case of cognition of sense-data that the object of the cognition is not identical with the cognitive act, *a fortiori* it will never be so since this is the only case where it seems on the face of it even plausible to suppose this. Moore then contends that they cannot be identical even in this case since to know a sense-datum is to know that a relation holds between it and a character that it appears to have, therefore to say that it is seen or known, because it involves this further term, cannot be the same as saying it exists.[2] One of his earliest articles (1903–4) is on 'Kant's Idealism',[3] attacking it on the grounds that (*a*) Kant's idealist principle is itself synthetic *a priori* and so cannot without a vicious circle be used to show how synthetic *a priori* propositions can be known to be true, (*b*) that a principle put forward as a presupposition of experience could at the best show that synthetic *a priori* propositions were true of some objects, i.e. those presented in experience, not those independent of it. While the article may show a certain misunderstanding of what Kant was driving at, it illustrates well Moore's basically realist standpoint. His more detailed discussions of sense-data and physical things constitute however a subject by themselves and there is no place to discuss them on their own merits in this article, though we have found earlier the nature of the method he uses in discussing them relevant to a consideration of his attitude to metaphysics.

What sort of metaphysics then had Moore? Certainly not a very comprehensive one. He believed in experiencing minds and independent physical objects and did not try to reduce either to the other. He did not believe that one could argue beyond these to a God or Absolute but did not produce any general arguments to

---

[1] *Philosophical Studies*, p. 218.
[2] *Proceedings of Aristotelian Society*, Vol. 21, pp. 132–40.
[3] *id.*, Vol. 4, pp. 129–40.

show on principle that that was impossible. He did not accept the verification principle, which had been used to rule out metaphysics, for he believed in non-natural properties at least in ethics and, I think, elsewhere. There is only one way in which causality can be made to conform to the verification principle and that is by reducing it to regular sequence, but he rejected this mode of analysis of causal propositions (though without putting another in its place). As I have said, he believed in synthetic *a priori* propositions,[1] and this involves the admission of some necessary connections not only in our language and thought but in the real world. He however revolted against the characteristic idealist view of the world as a rationally connected coherent system and Bradley's view of it as a unity so close that all our judgments are self-contradictory and partially false because they have to abstract. I do not think that Moore's criticisms demolish these opponents because their arguments function in the context of a different world-view based on intuitive assumptions or perhaps intuitive insights which Moore did not share. But Moore could show that they had not proved their cases, and he took a leading part in the philosophical revolution which seems to have ruled out their way of thinking altogether for good or for ill (though I think there is still more to be learnt from them than most modern thinkers admit). Without being dogmatic about it he had a view of the world which laid no stress on the element of order and system and regarded different existing things as only externally related. While he did not maintain the regularity theory of causation, he drew a sharp distinction between causal and logical necessity and did not think of the former as involving anything of the nature of *a priori* entailment. These statements do not amount to much of a positive metaphysics, but Moore's greatness does not lie in metaphysics, if indeed that is a subject in which one can still be great today, as I believe, but in his philosophical method and the ingenuity, thoroughness and integrity with which he carried it out. I think it was an evil day for philosophy when at least temporarily the method of Wittgenstein triumphed over the methods of Moore and Broad.

---

[1] It is interesting to see that in his early article on Kant Moore said that Kant's discovery that there were synthetic *a priori* propositions was perhaps sufficiently important even by itself to justify the rank in philosophy usually assigned to him (*Proceedings of Aristotelian Soc.*, Vol. 4, 1903–4, p. 130).

MOORE ON EXISTENCE AND PREDICATION

by W. E. KENNICK

'Je ne vois pas ici de quel genre de choses vous voulez que l'existence soit, ni pourquoi elle ne peut pas aussi bien être dite une propriété, comme la toute-puissance, prenant le nom de propriété pour toute sorte d'attribut ou pour tout ce qui peut être attribué a une chose, selon qu'en effet il doit ici être pris.'—Descartes to Gassendi.

Whether the so-called ontological argument for the existence of God proves what it purports to prove depends, it has often been said, on whether existence is a predicate. Since at least the time of Gassendi's objections to Descartes's version of the argument, many philosophers—perhaps even most philosophers—have held that existence is not a predicate; but others have continued to hold that it is, or that it is in at least the relevant sense of 'exists'; still others have been in doubt as to whether existence is, in any sense, a predicate. For over three hundred years, then, the question has continued to bedevil philosophers. The aim of this paper is not to attempt to answer this question—for, as will emerge, I do not think that the question, as a philosophical question, can be answered— but principally through an examination of G. E. Moore's well-known and widely respected contribution to the debate[1] to try to throw some light on the nature of that debate.

In the manner that many would regard as typical of his philosophizing, Moore begins by announcing that he is 'not at all clear as to the meaning of this question', i.e. the question 'Is existence a predicate?' What he has in mind is not what *sort* of question it is; whether, for example, it is a question logically analogous to the question 'Is sphericity a shape?', or to the question 'Is mercury a metal?', or to the question 'Is honesty always a virtue?', or to the question 'Is aspirin an analgesic?'—any one of which it might appear to resemble. What disturbs him is the fact that some

[1] G. E. Moore, 'Is Existence a Predicate?' originally appeared in the *Proceedings of the Aristotelian Society*, Supplementary Volume XV (1936) as the second paper in a symposium with W. Kneale. It is reprinted in Moore's *Philosophical Papers* (London and New York, 1959). All page references are to the reprinted text.

philosophers (Kneale in particular) have claimed that 'the word "predicate" has two different senses, a logical sense and a grammatical one'; and if so, then the question is ambiguous: it may mean either 'Is existence a predicate in the logical sense of "predicate"?' or 'Is existence a predicate in the grammatical sense of "predicate"?' Moore rightly notes that if the word 'predicate' is being used in the grammatical sense, then the question 'Is existence a predicate?' (or the corresponding affirmative or negative proposition) is clearly 'about certain *words*', about whether they are used in a certain way; not the word 'existence' itself, to be sure, but 'the word "exists" and other finite parts of the verb "to exist", such as "existed", "will exist" or "exist" (in the plural)'. But if the word 'predicate' is being used in the logical sense, then it is not clear, or not *as* clear, that the question 'Is existence a predicate?' is about the use of certain *words*; although as it turns out, Moore, following Kneale's lead, does take the question to be about words, for he takes it to be equivalent to the question whether 'exists', and other finite parts of the verb 'to exist', *stand for* a predicate in the logical sense of 'predicate'.

Whether because he took it to be a trivial or uninteresting question, or for some other reason, Moore does not discuss the question whether finite parts of the verb 'to exist' ever serve as the grammatical predicates of sentences in which they figure. It seems obvious that they do (e.g. in such sentences as 'Two-headed calves exist', 'Dinosaurs once existed', and 'In a few years manned rockets capable of reaching the moon will exist'), but, although an examination of grammar books does not show this impression to be mistaken, it does show that the question of grammar is not as simple as one might have supposed. Because of its close connection with the question 'Is existence a *logical* predicate?', I propose to take a brief look at the question of grammar.

Grammarians employ different criteria for identifying the subject and predicate of a declarative sentence. The following are representative:

A: A declarative sentence consists of two parts, the subject and the predicate. The subject denotes the person or thing spoken of. The predicate is that which is said of the person or thing denoted by the subject.[1]

---

[1] See, e.g., George R. Carpenter, *English Grammar* (New York, 1907), p. 5; R. W. Zandvoort, *A Handbook of English Grammar* (Englewood Cliffs, N.J., 1966), p. 196.

F

B: The subject of a declarative sentence is the person, place, or thing about which something is said. The predicate is the expression that tells what is said about the subject.[1]

C: Identify the main verb of a declarative sentence. When this has been done ask *Who?* or *What?* before the verb, and the word(s) used in answer will be the subject. All the sentence except the subject and its modifiers is the predicate.[2]

Now consider the simple sentence 'John smokes'. What is the subject of the sentence? According to (A) and (C) it is the name 'John', but according to (B) it is not the name 'John' but John, the bearer of the name. And what is the predicate of this sentence? According to all three it is '. . . smokes'.

But against grammarians who construe the notion *subject of a sentence* in the manner of (A) or (B) a proponent of (C) objects:

'A definition of subject which is sometimes found in grammars is "the thing concerning which the statement is made". This definition is inaccurate, showing a confusion between the grammatical and general meanings of the word *subject*.'[3]

She wishes to draw a distinction between the grammatical and what she calls the *notional* subject of a sentence, on the ground that in such a sentence as 'I hear that it was Henry who lost' the word 'I'—by her test—is the grammatical subject but the thing concerning which the statement is made is (or could be) Henry. For the same reason, and also because the notions of grammatical subject and predicate are not readily applicable, or are inapplicable, to some languages, e.g. Chinese,[4] many modern students of linguistics prefer to treat subject-predicate constructions as but one variety of what they call *topic-comment* constructions:

'the speaker announces a topic and then says something about it. . . . In English and the familiar languages of Europe, topics are usually also subjects, and comments are predicates.'[5]

[1] See, e.g., Thomas D. Pawley, *A Modern Advanced English Grammar for Secondary Schools and Colleges* (Baltimore, 1930), p. 1; George O. Curme, *The Grammar of the English Language*, Vol. III, *Syntax* (Boston, 1931), p. 1.

[2] See, e.g., Margaret M. Bryant, *A Functional English Grammar* (Boston, 1945), p. 8; Otto Jesperson, *Essentials of English Grammar* (New York, 1933), pp. 97–8.

[3] Margaret M. Bryant, *op. cit.*, p. 118.

[4] See Tsu-Lin Mei, 'Subject and Predicate, A Grammatical Preliminary', *The Philosophical Review*, LXX (1961), pp. 153–75.

[5] Charles F. Hockett, *A Course in Modern Linguistics* (New York, 1958), p. 201.

But in the sentence 'That new book by Thomas Guernsey/I haven't read yet' the phrase 'that new book by Thomas Guernsey' is said to be the topic, 'I' the subject.[1] A similar distinction is drawn by at least one philosopher between the grammatical and what he calls the *epistemological* subject of a sentence, and for the same reason:

'In epistemology the contrast between subject and predicate is a contrast between that part of a sentence which serves to identify or designate what is being discussed and that part which serves to describe or characterize the thing so identified.'[2]

In such sentences as 'Bats fly' and 'Fraser swims' the grammatical subject (identified by some such test as (C) but not (A) or (B)) identifies the subject of discourse, and here grammatical and epistemological subject coincide. But in such sentences as 'What is not pink is not a flamingo' and 'Andrew was hit by Bernard' they do not; for the first sentence is about flamingos, not non-pink things, and the second 'may be taken to be about' Andrew or Bernard or both depending on the context of the utterance.

'What counts as the epistemological subject of a statement may be determined in part by the context in which it is made. . . . The importance of context in determining what counts as a subject differentiates the epistemological conception of subject from all others.'[3]

That there is a point to drawing some such distinction as that between grammatical subject, on the one hand, and notional or epistemological subject or topic, on the other hand, cannot be gainsaid. Not only is every declarative sentence not obviously

---

[1] But is the topic of a sentence part of the sentence or is it what the sentence is about? Is the 'topic announced' by the speaker Thomas Guernsey's new book or 'that new book by Thomas Guernsey'? If the 'comment' says something about the 'topic', then it would appear that the topic is Thomas Guernsey's new book and not 'that new book by Thomas Guernsey', because nothing is said about the *phrase*, e.g. that it contains only six words.

[2] Newton Garver, 'Subject and Predicate', *The Encyclopedia of Philosophy*, ed. by P. Edwards (New York, 1967), Vol. 8, p. 33.

[3] 'Subject and Predicate', p. 34. Here the epistemological subject is said to be the subject of a statement. As opposed to a sentence?

about what would normally be identified as what the grammatical subject of the sentence designates (and here criterion (C), it seems to me, more adequately reflects such normal practice), but—a point not mentioned by the grammarians—it is questionable whether a sentence, *qua* sentence, is *about* anything at all. If I write or utter the English sentence 'The dog barks' simply to produce an example of a simple declarative sentence or of a sentence containing only three words, the sentence would normally be said to have a grammatical subject, viz. 'the dog', but it would not normally be thought to be about anything, because the question 'Which dog?' would not appropriately arise. However, if I write or utter the sentence by way of making a statement or assertion, the question 'Which dog?' could appropriately arise, and the *statement* or *assertion* in question would naturally be said to be about a certain dog. I propose, then, to say that statements or assertions expressible by sentences, but not the sentences themselves, are about something.

If the distinction at issue is to be used without confusion, however, an ambiguity that plagues it must be cleared up. It has often been pointed out that a sentence such as 'Socrates was wise' might express (be used to make) a statement about Socrates or a statement about wisdom, i.e. the statement that wisdom was a property of Socrates. On either reading of the sentence the name 'Socrates' is clearly the grammatical subject or subject-expression, a grammatical subject or subject-expression being part of a sentence identifiable by some such criterion as (C). But what is the notional or epistemological subject? Taking the statement expressed to be about Socrates, is it 'Socrates' or Socrates? Is it the thing—here, the person—designated, mentioned, denoted, or referred to by the grammatical subject or is it the same as the grammatical subject? Is it part of the sentence or not part of the sentence? It might seem to make little difference here which we answer, but if we take the sentence in question to express an assertion not about Socrates but about wisdom—a possibility that the notion of an epistemological or notional subject is introduced to account for—then we are not sure what to identify as that subject *unless* it is wisdom. For it can hardly be 'was wise', the only other part of the sentence besides the name 'Socrates', and the word 'wisdom', a word that might mention or designate what the assertion is about, does not appear in the sentence as the word 'flamingo'—but not 'flamingos'—does appear in 'What is not pink is not a flamingo' and as the names 'Andrew' and 'Bernard' do appear in 'Andrew was hit by Bernard'. I propose to say, then, that the subject of a statement or assertion is what the statement or assertion is about. The subject may, or may not, be designated or mentioned (as opposed to being indicated in some other way, such as by some feature of the context) by an element of the sentence, e.g. by the subject-expression.[1]

Let us return now to the question whether 'exists' or any other finite part of the verb 'to exist' ever figures as the grammatical predicate or predicate-expression of a sentence. Clearly, if we use some such criterion as (C) for identifying grammatical subject and predicate, the answer is that it does, e.g. in such sentences as 'Two-headed calves exist', 'Dinosaurs once existed', and 'In a few years manned rockets capable of reaching the moon will exist'. But if we use some such criterion as (B)—or even (A)—difficulties arise. What (B) identifies as the subject of a sentence is the same as what we have called the subject of a statement expressed by the sentence. The question is, then, 'Using some such criterion as (B), does any finite part of the verb "to exist" ever comment or predicate?'[2] If we look at sentences that contain some finite part of the verb 'to exist' as grammatical predicate and that express *true affirmative* statements—e.g. 'Spotted cows exist'—then the answer would appear to be that finite parts of the verb 'to exist' do (at least sometimes) express a comment, do predicate something of a subject. For it would be quite natural to say of the sentence 'Spotted cows exist' that the subject of the statement it expresses, what the statement is about, is spotted cows, and that what is said about them, the predicate of the statement, is that they exist. But if we look at similar sentences that express *true negative* or *false affirmative* statements, philosophical trouble at once ensues.

---

[1] The assertion expressed by 'It is raining' would naturally be said to be about the weather, although 'it', the subject expression, is not, of course, surrogate for 'the weather'. The weather, then, is the subject of the assertion, but the weather is not referred to by any element of the sentence in the way it is in 'The weather has been variable lately'.

[2] Or perhaps 'Does a speaker ever express a comment, ever predicate anything of a subject, by using some finite part of the verb "to exist"?'

The notion of an epistemological predicate or comment is as troubled by ambiguity as is that of an epistemological subject or topic. I propose to mean by 'predicate of a statement' what is said about the subject, where 'said' means 'stated' or 'asserted'. A predicate, then, as opposed to a predicate-expression, is not part of a *sentence* but is something expressible by part of a sentence, often the grammatical predicate. Thus if the subject of the statement expressed by the sentence 'Andrew was hit by Bernard' is Andrew, the predicate, what is said about Andrew, is that he was hit by Bernard, here expressed by '. . . was hit by Bernard'.

For by an ancient line of reasoning it may be argued that such statements make no comment about, predicate nothing of, a subject.

That line of reasoning may be expressed as follows: What a true negative existential statement is putatively about, its apparent subject does not exist. Therefore, a true negative existential statement is not about anything, has no subject. But subject and predicate are correlatives. Therefore, a true negative existential statement can have no predicate—any more than an unmarried woman can have a husband. But a true negative existential statement is equivalent to a false affirmative existential statement. Therefore, false affirmative existential statements have no predicate. Contrary to appearances, then, although 'purple cows' is the subject-expression of the sentence 'Purple cows exist' and 'exist' is its predicate-expression, the statement expressed has no subject and says nothing about purple cows.[1] The following contains an instance of this argument:

'This maxim ["Existence is not a predicate"] is often glibly and thoughtlessly used, but it has a serious use; it is an attempt to resolve the paradox of reference that arises over the denial of existence. For we *can* truly and significantly deny existence. . . . How is such a denial possible? It might look as though "A is not" or "A does not exist" were never true; for if it were, the subject-term "A" would fail to have reference, and so no statement would have been made at all, let alone a true statement.

'We can get out of this difficulty by denying that in "A is not" or "A does not exist" the verb "is" or "exists" is a logical predicate. For since "subject" and "predicate" are correlatives, this is tantamount to denying that the grammatical subject "A" is a logical subject. And from this again it follows that the statement "A does not exist" is not really about what the subject "A" ostensibly stands for; so in making the statement we do not fall into the

---

[1] This difficulty need not affect true negative and false *existential* assertions only. If we take a statement to be about a state of affairs, e.g. take the statement that Socrates was wise not to be about Socrates but to be about Socrates's being wise, then the argument given can be generalized to 'show' that false statements or thoughts and true negative statements or thoughts are impossible. See Plato's *Sophist* 236d–237e where the argument is so generalized—an argument that probably originated with Parmenides. Part of Plato's strategy in meeting this argument is to introduce the notions of subject and predicate, or ὄνομα and ῥῆμα (*Sophist* 257 f.).

absurdity of using "A" as though it stood for something and then in effect denying that it does so.'[1]

We can, of course, 'get out of this difficulty' in another way than by denying that we can truly or significantly deny existence (Russell) or by denying that a statement of the form 'A does not exist' has neither subject nor predicate (Geach); namely, by admitting that we can make statements *about* things that do not exist.

'I do not see why statements cannot be made about non-existents. We can dream about them, think about them, and describe them, just as we can wait for them, hope to have them and look for them. We can mention them, allude to or direct attention to them and make reference to them. One thing we cannot do, of course, is to *point* to them, and someone who thinks of mentioning, alluding or referring as a substitute for pointing will be puzzled as to how we can point to what does not exist. But if we have not fallen prey to this overly narrow conception of what it is to mention something, then we will not be puzzled about how we can mention something nonexistent.'[2]

Here we have an interesting philosophical issue that can be fairly represented, I think, in the following way, letting 'S' be a statement: Russell holds that if S is both negative and existential then it cannot be true. Geach holds that if S is both negative and existential then it can be true but it cannot have a subject and a predicate.[3] *Both* Russell and Geach assume that, as Russell put it,

[1] P. T. Geach, 'Form and Existence', *Proceedings of the Aristotelian Society*, LV (1954–55), pp. 262–3. Cf. Bertrand Russell, *The Principles of Mathematics*, 2nd ed. (London, 1937), p. 449, where it is argued that we *cannot* truly or significantly deny existence—or, as Russell would have it, being—because to do so leads to a paradox: '"*A* is not" must always be either false or meaningless. For if *A* were nothing, it could not be said not to be; "*A* is not" implies that there is a term *A* whose being is denied, and hence that *A* is. . . . Thus being is a general attribute of everything, and to mention anything is to show that it is.' That Russell later repudiated this view is of no philosophical significance whatever.

The line of reasoning here at issue does not alone touch true affirmative existential statements. Are we to say that they have subject and predicate? If so, then to know whether an existential statement does have subject and predicate we must first ascertain whether it is affirmative or negative, and then whether it is true or false.

[2] Jerome Shaffer, 'Existence, Predication and the Ontological Argument', *Mind*, LXXI (1962), p. 313.

[3] Geach does hold (*op. cit.*, p. 263 ff.) that there are different kinds of existential statements, at least one of which is in subject-predicate form; but that kind is not in question here.

'to mention anything is to show that it is', i.e. that 'S is about x' entails 'x is or exists'; and this assumption plays an important part in the argument each uses to arrive at his conclusion. Shaffer denies this assumption: S can be about something that does not exist ('S is about x' does not entail 'x exists'); and therefore, as far as the present issue is concerned and other things being equal, S can be both negative and existential and true and it can have a subject and a predicate. It would seem, then, that we must choose between Russell and Geach, on the one hand, and Shaffer, on the other hand, with respect to the question whether a statement can be about what does not exist; and, if we decide in favour of Russell and Geach on this issue, we must choose between them on the further question of whether a statement can be negative and existential and true. Only if we decide in Geach's favour on this issue are we committed to his claim that a statement cannot be negative and existential and true and have a subject and a predicate.

But how shall we decide? And what would our decision come to in any case? The answer, surely, depends on what view we take of the issue at hand.

Let us confine our attention to the question whether 'to mention anything is to show that it is'. I take this to be a putative analysis of the concept of *mentioning* or *being about*[1] and therefore to be logically analogous to the statement 'To verify a statement is to show that it is true'. The claim in question, in other words, is necessary or *a priori*; what it tells us is that it is logically or theoretically impossible to mention something and to fail to show that it is or exists, just as it is theoretically impossible to verify a statement and to fail to show that it is true. 'S mentions or is about x' entails 'x exists', just as 'A verified S' entails 'A showed or proved that S is true'. Now on one view of the nature of necessary or *a priori* statements—a view that cannot be defended here[2]— such statements are verbal in import in roughly the following way. Consider the two sentences:

S_1: 'To verify a statement is to show that it is true.'
S_2: 'The verb "to verify (a statement)" means to show or prove (it) to be true.'

[1] Also the concepts of referring to, denoting, standing for, designating, naming, and the like, in so far as these are purported to behave in the same way as those of mentioning and being about.

[2] For an extensive statement of this view, see Morris Lazerowitz, 'Methods of Philosophy', *Studies in Metaphilosophy* (London and New York, 1964), esp. secs. viii–x.

S_1 is typical of sentences that would be said to express conceptual analyses, to express necessary or *a priori* true statements. S_2, however, clearly expresses a statement about how a certain verb is in fact used and hence expresses a contingent statement; one which, in this case, is true but *could* be false. The statement expressed by S_1, therefore, is not logically equivalent to that expressed by S_2. But the statement expressed by S_1 may be said to be true by definition or true *ex vi terminorum*; which means that if I know that S_2 expresses a true contingent statement about the meaning of an expression, then I know *eo ipso* that S_1 expresses a true *a priori* or necessary statement; and conversely, if I know that S_1 expresses an *a priori* true statement, I know that S_2 expresses a true contingent statement. And the same holds, with the proper changes being made, for sentences that express necessarily false statements.

On this view of sentences expressing necessary statements the claim that to mention something is to show that it is or exists amounts to the claim that the expressions 'to mention' and 'to be about' are used in such a way that, like the phrase 'verified but false statement', the phrases 'mentions something that does not exist' and 'is about something that does not exist' express an absurdity and have no possible application in any conceivable situation. It is this that Shaffer apparently denies: the expressions in question are not used in the way indicated at all; 'is about something that does not exist' makes perfectly good sense and may be used in certain situations to say what is true. The issue between Russell and Geach, on the one hand, and Shaffer, on the other, then, would seem to be about how certain expressions are used and hence to have a fairly straightforward resolution.

If the question is about how the expressions 'to mention' and 'to be about' are used, then it is quite clear that Shaffer is right and Russell and Geach are wrong. 'So the gallant Odysseus crept out from under the bushes, after breaking off with his great hand a leafy bough from the thicket to conceal his naked manhood'[1]

---

[1] From *The Odyssey*, Book VI, E. V. Rieu's trans. Some philosophers might want to say that we can mention or make statements about legendary, mythological, or fictional persons, events, etc., because such persons, events, etc., do after all exist—*in* legend, *in* myth, *in* fiction. But that view is not pertinent here. The existence of Odysseus in *The Odyssey* may guarantee that *my* statement that (Homer's) Odysseus crept out from under the bushes has something to be about, but it does not guarantee that *Homer's* statement has something to be about; and it is Homer's statement that we are saying is about Odysseus.

F*

would normally be said to be about Odysseus, but this does not
commit us to saying that Odysseus exists, or even that he existed.
'The building that will stand on this site will be made of brick'
would normally be said to be about a building that has not yet
been built, hence about a building that does not exist.[1] The expressions 'to mention' and 'to be about' simply are not used in
everyday English in such a way that such phrases as 'mentioned
his funeral several times' and 'is about a merely imaginary animal'
express absurdities. But philosophers of Russell's and Geach's
persuasion surely know this as well as do philosophers of Shaffer's
persuasion; and if they do and if the issue *is* one of how certain
expressions are used, then we are confronted with the curious
anomaly that, as Moore put it, some philosophers 'have been able
to hold sincerely, as part of their philosophical creed, propositions
inconsistent with what they themselves *knew* to be true'.[2] We can
hardly believe, however, that Russell and Geach have advanced a
view so obviously inconsistent with what they know to be true.
Hence we are forced to suppose that the issue between them and
Shaffer is not merely one about how certain expressions are in fact
used.

The anomaly in question can be accounted for if we take
seriously a suggestion made by Shaffer himself, namely, that those
who hold that to mention something is to show that it exists have
artificially *narrowed* the use of 'to mention' or 'to be about' so that
its 'logic' or 'grammar' resembles or coincides with that of 'to
point to'. They know that 'to mention' and 'to be about' are not
actually used in everyday English in the way indicated by the
claim that to mention something is to show that it is (and hence
Shaffer himself cannot be telling them something they do not
know), but, for reasons unexpressed, they have revised the rules
normally governing the use of the expressions in question (a
revision that Shaffer sees no reason to accept). Of course, *if* 'to
mention' or 'to be about' were used in the way they suggest, then
a 'paradox of reference' would be involved in denials of existence,
assuming, as one normally would, that such denials mention or are

---

[1] An unnoted consequence of the principle that to mention something is to
show that it is is that future-tense statements—statements that would naturally
be said to be about the future in the same way that historical statements are said
to be about the past—either are not (cannot be) about anything, or they are
about something and the future already is or exists, i.e. there is no future—a
consequence that some philosophers (Parmenides) have not balked at accepting.

[2] 'A Defence of Common Sense,' *Philosophical Papers*, p. 41.

about what they say does not exist; and the only way to avoid the
paradox would be to hold either that denials of existence can never
be true or that, contrary to appearances, such denials are not
really about what they say does not exist. The decision we are
confronted with, then, is not one of who is right, Geach and
Russell or Shaffer, but whether to accept or reject what Wittgenstein might call a revised notation. Assuming that we reject the
suggested revision, we can continue to say with logical impunity
that such a statement as 'Purple cows do not exist' is about purple
cows and says that they do not exist; i.e. that purple cows are the
subject of the statement and that they do not exist is the predicate.

Let us turn now to the question whether existence is ever a
logical predicate.[1] This question is at least as unclear as the question whether any finite part of the verb 'to exist' is ever the
predicate of a sentence, i.e. is ever a grammatical predicate; for the
notion of a logical predicate as distinct from a grammatical
predicate is unclear. In one logic book we read:

(D): 'A term is a name or phrase denoting one or more objects.
. . . An ordinary proposition is made up of two terms joined by
the *copula*, which consists of some form of the verb "to be": the
first term is called the *subject term*, and the second is called the
predicate term, although in certain cases this order may be reversed.'[2]

And in another logic book we read, with respect to such a proposition as 'Theaetetus is sitting down':

(E): 'we might call "Theaetetus" the "subject" of the proposition and ". . . is sitting down" the "predicate", the subject being
definable as "what the proposition is about", or as the name of that,
and the predicate as "what is said about it".'[3]

(D) closely resembles (A) above, and (E) closely resembles (B), to
the point where we can see little or no difference between a proposition and a sentence, little or no difference between a grammatical

---

[1] I temporarily ignore the question of whether there are different senses of
'to exist' (as some philosophers maintain and others deny), and hence whether
there are different and distinguishable concepts of existence, some of which
may, while others may not, serve as the predicates of propositions. I restrict
my discussion to such propositions as 'Cows exist' and 'Black tigers do not
exist', which, if there are different concepts of existence, contain the concept
that is held not to be a predicate.

[2] John C. Cooley, *A Primer of Formal Logic* (New York, 1942), p. 296.

[3] A. N. Prior, *Formal Logic* (Oxford, 1955), p. 72.

subject and predicate and a logical subject and predicate. If we insist, however, partly for reasons already given,[1] on drawing a distinction between sentences on the one hand and propositions, assertions, or statements on the other, then (D) is obviously unsatisfactory as a criterion for identifying the subject and predicate of a *proposition*; while (E), slightly modified, becomes identical with our characterization of the subject and predicate of a statement. The author of (E), however, is not a 'traditional' logician and would not want to say that Atlantis is the subject ('what the proposition is about') of the proposition 'Atlantis does not exist', while the predicate ('what is said about it') is '. . . does not exist', i.e. that it does not exist. Traditional logic regarded existential propositions as being in subject-predicate form. Even Kant held that '. . . is' or '. . . exists' may be a logical *predicate*.[2] But modern logic generally rejects this view. It uses formulae composed of name-signs $(a, b, c, . . .)$, individual variables $(x, y, z, . . .)$, predicate-letters $(F, G, H . . .)$, quantifiers, and truth-functional operators to depict the logical form of propositions; and it tends to regard only singular statements, such as 'Theaetetus is sitting down', symbolized by 'Fa', as being in subject-predicate form. General statements, such as 'All men are mortal', symbolized by '$(x) Fx \supset Gx$', would not be so described; nor would existential statements, such as 'Cows exist', symbolized by '$(Ex) Fx$'—where, as A. N. Prior puts it, '". . . exist" has disappeared into the prefix, or "quantifier", "For some individual x, . . .".'[3]

One may be tempted to ask, with respect to the question whether existence (e.g. what is said by '. . . exist' in the proposition expressed by 'Cows exist') is a logical predicate: Who is right, the traditional Aristotelian logician or the modern symbolic logician? To which one reply might be, in effect, that neither is 'right':

'when [modern] logicians say that 'exists', or existence, is not a

---

[1] Another, perhaps the usual, reason is this: 'I have three children' and 'Ho tre figli' are clearly two different sentences, one English and one Italian, one containing four words and the other containing three. Yet they can be used to say the same thing, make one and the same statement or assertion, express one and the same proposition; as is clear if we regard one as the translation of the other.

[2] *Critique of Pure Reason*, A 598/B 626.

[3] 'Existence', *The Encyclopedia of Philosophy*, ed. by P. Edwards, Vol. 3, p. 144. If a man has disappeared into the woods, then (assuming that he has not come out again) he must still be there. As we shall see, one may suspect that the predicate *existence* is still there too.

logical predicate, what they mean is that it is not treated as one in first-order predicate logic. . . .'[1]

That is, the question 'Is existence a logical predicate?' is taken to mean 'Is existence treated as a predicate in logic?', and to this question the true answer is, 'In traditional or Aristotelian logic it is so treated, while in modern symbolic logic it is generally not so treated'.

Whether this reply will satisfy every logician, it will not satisfy every philosopher. Some philosophers clearly believe that modern logic is right and traditional logic wrong; that first-order predicate-logic's refusal to 'treat' existence as a logical predicate is justified, because existence is *not* a logical predicate and it can be *shown* that it is not. We have already considered one line of reasoning that may be used to 'show' this, but the most widely employed argument, what James Thomson calls 'the translation technique',[2] is brought out by Kneale in the following way:

'The word "existence" is not a symbol for anything which can be either a constituent or a component of a simple proposition. It is only a logically auxiliary symbol. The sentence "tame tigers exist" is just one way of expressing the proposition "for some x, x is tame and x is a tiger". Other ways of expressing the same proposition are "there are tame tigers", "some tigers are tame", "something is a tame tiger". The sentence "tame tigers exist" may mislead philosophers into thinking that existence is a predicate, because it is grammatically similar to such sentences as "tame tigers growl" and "Rajah growls".'[3]

The argument of the translation-technique may be represented as follows: Existence appears to be the predicate of propositions expressed by such sentences as 'Tigers exist'. But it is really not the predicate of these propositions. For the sentence 'Tigers exist' means the same as the sentence 'There are tigers' ('For some x, x is a tiger', 'There is (exists) an x such that x is a tiger', 'Something is a tiger', 'The propositional function "x is a tiger" is true

[1] James Thomson, 'Is Existence a Predicate?', *Philosophical Logic*, ed. by P. F. Strawson (London, 1967), p. 104.
[2] 'Is Existence a Predicate?', p. 106.
[3] William Kneale, 'Is Existence a Predicate?', *Proceedings of the Aristotelian Society*, Supplementary Volume XV (1938), p. 164. This line of reasoning does not depend on Kneale's view that a logical predicate is an attribute.

for at least one value of "*x*"'). Therefore, the proposition expressed by the first sentence is the same as, or is equivalent to, that expressed by the second. But existence is obviously not the predicate of the proposition expressed by the second sentence—even the verb 'to exist' does not appear in that sentence. Therefore, misleading appearances to the contrary, existence is not the predicate of the proposition expressed by the first sentence. Hence, existence is not a logical predicate.

Unfortunately, if this argument shows that existence is not the predicate of propositions expressed by such sentences as 'Tigers exist', it can be shown *by parity of reasoning* that existence *is* the predicate of propositions expressed by such sentences as 'There are tigers', despite the fact that the verb 'to exist' nowhere appears in these sentences. For the sentence 'There are tigers' means the same as the sentence 'Tigers exist'. Therefore, the proposition expressed by the first sentence is the same as, or is equivalent to, that expressed by the second. But existence is obviously the predicate of the proposition expressed by the first sentence. Therefore, misleading appearances to the contrary, existence is the logical predicate of the proposition expressed by the second sentence. Who, then, is being misled by grammar: the philosopher who thinks that existence is not the predicate of the proposition expressed by 'Tigers exist' or the philosopher who thinks that it is the predicate of the proposition expressed by 'There are tigers'?

Again we have a curious anomaly, the kind of anomaly that seems to occur only in philosophy, namely, that the same piece of evidence, viz., the synonymy of two sentences, can be used to show that existence is and is not the predicate of the same proposition or of logically equivalent propositions. What are we to make of this anomaly?

'Existence is a logical predicate', unlike 'Aspirin is an analgesic', is not an empirical proposition, one that some fact of observation or experiment could show to be true. If anything, it is a putative analysis of the concept of existence and thus logically resembles 'A square has four sides'. The linguistic fact that justifies our asserting 'A square has four sides' and makes it a correct analysis of the concept *square* or *being (a) square* is that 'has four sides' is used in such a way that it applies to whatever 'is (a) square' applies to, but not conversely. If 'Existence is a logical predicate' is an analysis of the concept *existence*, then, given that we mean by a 'logical subject' what a statement is about and by a 'logical predi-

cate' what it says about it, we would expect it to be the case that
'says that . . . exists' applies wherever 'uses ". . . exists" to make
a statement' applies, but not conversely. And surely this is in fact
the case as far as everyday English is concerned; in which case
'Existence is a logical predicate' is a correct analysis of the concept
existence—as far as everyday English is concerned.

But the notions of *logical* subject and *logical* predicate, like the
notion of a *proposition*, are not everyday notions. 'Logical subject',
'logical predicate', and 'proposition' are technical terms and may
be used by logicians in different ways. As generally used, however,
the notions that they express are parasitic on the notions of a
grammatical subject (subject of a sentence), grammatical predicate
(predicate of a sentence), and sentence respectively; in that
logicians usually introduce the technical notion of a proposition
by speaking of sentences or of using sentences to assert or say
something, the technical notions of logical subject and predicate
by speaking of the subjects and predicates of sentences. As is clear
from (D) above, 'logical subject', 'logical predicate', and 'proposition' are sometimes used in such a way that they are synonymous,
or almost synonymous, with 'grammatical subject' ('subject of a
sentence'), 'grammatical predicate' ('predicate of a sentence'), and
'sentence' respectively. This is the way in which they tend to be
used by traditional logicians; hence it is quite natural for a traditional logician to say that existence is a logical predicate, e.g. that
'. . . exist' is the logical predicate of the proposition 'Tigers exist'.
Still, the sentence 'Tigers exist', in at least one of its uses, is
synonymous with 'There are tigers'; and despite the fact that one
might naturally say that the statement 'Tigers exist' is about tigers
and says that they exist and 'There are tigers' is about tigers and
says that there are some, 'tigers' is the grammatical subject and
'exist' the grammatical predicate of the sentence 'Tigers exist'
while in 'There are tigers' 'tigers' figures as (or in) the grammatical
predicate and 'there' is what grammarians call a merely formal or
dummy subject.[1] Hence, depending on which member of this

---

[1] Prior, *Formal Logic*, p. 73, holds that in such a proposition as 'If Caesar was
a tyrant, Caesar deserved death', Caesar (or 'Caesar') is the subject and 'If . . .
was a tyrant, . . . deserved death' is the predicate. This is in keeping with his
definitions of 'subject' and 'predicate' ((E) above). But although it would be as
much in keeping with the same definitions to say that in 'There are tigers'
tigers are the subject, what the proposition is about, and 'There are . . .' is the
predicate, this Prior does not wish to do, apparently because he subscribes to the
view that '*S* is about *x*' entails '*x* exists' and also accepts the usual results of
the translation-technique.

pair of synonymous sentences one chooses to take as paradigmatic or to use for the purposes of introducing or illustrating the notion of a logical predicate (and he can choose *either*, because they *are* synonymous), he will tend to say either that existence is, or that existence is not, a logical predicate. And if he is impressed by the fact that 'There are tigers' (or some other favoured sentence) is synonymous with 'Tigers exist' but that in saying 'There are tigers' the word 'exist' has disappeared—or has 'disappeared into' 'There are . . .'—he might be even more strongly inclined, other things being equal, to say that existence is not a logical predicate. One can, then, 'play it either way', and this is all that the translation-technique shows, if it shows anything.

This is not to say that there may not be reasons having nothing to do with the philosophical question of whether existence is a logical predicate for preferring to symbolize 'Tigers exist' as '(Ex) Fx' rather than in some other way, and therefore, perhaps, for preferring 'There are tigers' or 'Something is a tiger' to 'Tigers exist'. But surely such preferences *prove* nothing.[1]

In examining the question whether existence is a logical predicate, we have so far meant by 'logical predicate' merely 'predicate of a proposition, assertion, or statement' where this is defined in some such way as (E). But this is not all that has been meant by 'logical predicate'. By 'logical predicate' some philosophers have meant a property, trait, feature, characteristic, or attribute (what Kant apparently meant by a 'real' or 'determining' predicate); so that the question whether existence is a logical predicate becomes the same as the question whether existence is an attribute. This is the question Moore confronts in 'Is Existence a Predicate?'

To say that existence is not an attribute may be taken to be the same as saying that finite parts of the verb 'to exist' do not stand for an attribute in the sentences in which they are used; that is, that whereas in such sentences as 'Apples are red' and 'Tame tigers growl' the words 'red' (or 'are red') and 'growl' do stand for attributes, in such sentences as 'Red apples exist' and 'Tame tigers exist' the word 'exist' does not stand for an attribute. This way of

[1] James Thomson, *op. cit.*, p. 106.' The logical relations of the assertion that unicorns do not exist are probably better grasped through the sentence "No animal is a unicorn" than they are through the sentence "Unicorns do not exist." But it remains the case that we could not hope to show by this kind of method that "exists" isn't a predicate. The translation-technique could only seem to show such a thing if it were thought that some special status could be claimed for predicate-logic.'

putting the issue, as Moore notes, apparently points to a difference between the way in which finite parts of the verb 'to exist' are used and the way in which such expressions as 'are red' and 'growl' are used in sentences of the kind given. Hence, says Moore (p. 116), 'if we can find what differences there are between the use of finite parts of the verb "to exist", and the use of "is red", "growl" and "growls", we may perhaps find what the difference is' that is expressed by saying that 'growl' stands for an attribute whereas 'exist' does not. Moore claims to find *two* differences between the use of 'growl' in 'Tame tigers growl' and the use of 'exist' in 'Tame tigers exist' that might be taken to show that 'exist' does not stand for an attribute.

(1) Moore notes that 'Tame tigers growl' is 'ambiguous' or indefinite; it may mean any of the following (that is, if it expresses a proposition it will express the proposition expressed by one of the following), $A_1 - A_3$, the corresponding natural negatives (but not corresponding logical negations) of which are marked $\bar{A}_1 - \bar{A}_3$:

A_1: 'All tame tigers growl' $\bar{A}_1$: 'No tame tigers growl'
A_2: 'Most tame tigers growl' $\bar{A}_2$: 'Most tame tigers do not growl'
A_3: 'Some tame tigers growl' $\bar{A}_3$: 'Some tame tigers do not growl'

Although Moore holds that no similar ambiguity attends 'Tame tigers exist'—'It always means just "Some tame tigers exist", and nothing else whatever' (p. 117)—we can construct a table similar to the one above but based on 'Tame tigers exist':

B_1: 'All tame tigers exist' $\bar{B}_1$: 'No tame tigers exist'
B_2: 'Most tame tigers exist' $\bar{B}_2$: 'Most tame tigers do not exist'
B_3: 'Some tame tigers exist' $\bar{B}_3$: Some tame tigers do not exist'

Now while every sentence in the A-table is clearly meaningful or significant and may be used to express a proposition, whether true or false, this is not the case with every sentence in the B-table. B_1 and B_2 are 'puzzling expressions, which certainly do not carry their meaning, if they have any, on the face of them'; which points to an important difference between the use of 'exist' and the use of 'growl', although 'it does not make clear just what the difference is' (p. 118). The difference can be made clear, however, by considering A_3 and $\bar{A}_3$ together with their analogues B_3 and $\bar{B}_3$. $\bar{A}_3$ 'has a perfectly clear meaning'—just as clear a meaning as has A_3, and the propositions expressed by both could be true together. But whereas B_3 also has a perfectly clear meaning ('it just means "There are some tame tigers"'), $\bar{B}_3$ is 'another queer and puzzling expression'. Either it has no meaning or else it means the same as 'There are some tame tigers, which don't exist'. But this 'has no meaning at all—it is pure nonsense';[1] hence $\bar{B}_3$ also has no meaning at all.

From this it follows that B_1 and B_2 also 'have no meaning at all'. For the logical analogue of the proposition expressed by B_1 is that expressed by A_1, which is equivalent to the proposition expressed by A_3 together with that expressed by 'There is no tame tiger which does not growl' $(\sim (Ex)\ Tx\ \&\ \sim Gx)$.[2] This last sentence has a meaning because the sentence 'There is at least one tame tiger which does not growl' $((Ex)\ Tx\ \&\ \sim Gx)$ has a meaning; or, in other words, if 'There is at least one tame tiger which does not growl' has no meaning (expresses no proposition) then 'There is no tame tiger which does not growl' has no meaning, in which case the sentence putatively expressing the conjunction has no meaning, and hence A_1 has no meaning. By parity of reasoning, if 'There is at least one tame tiger that does not exist' has no meaning, then B_1 has no meaning; but 'There is at least one tame tiger that does not exist' has no meaning. (A parallel line of reasoning will show that B_2 also has no meaning.)

'I think, therefore, we can say that one important difference between the use of growl in "Some tame tigers growl" and the use of "exist" in "Some tame tigers exist" is that if in the former case we insert "do not" before "growl", without changing the meaning of "growl", we get a sentence which is significant, whereas if, in the latter, we insert "do not" before "exist" without changing the

---

[1] Moore does allow that 'There are some tame tigers that don't exist' might after all have a meaning, but not with the use of 'exist' that is here at issue. I return to this question below.

[2] Moore apparently does not take 'All tame tigers growl' to mean $(x)\ x$ is a tame tiger $\supset x$ growls. For he says of the sentences I have labelled A_1–A_3: 'Of each of them . . . it is true that the proposition which it expresses is one which cannot possibly be true, unless some tame tigers growl' (p. 117). That is $\sim I \supset \sim A$: or $A \supset I$.

meaning of "exist", we get a sentence which has no meaning whatever.'

And this 'explains why' A_1 and A_2 are 'both significant' while B_1 and B_2 are 'utterly meaningless'.

'And if by the statement that "growl", in this usage, "stands for an attribute", whereas "exist", in this usage, does not, part of what is meant is that there is this difference between them, then I should agree that "exist", in this usage, does not "stand for an attribute" (p. 119).

To this line of reasoning it has been objected[1] that although it may be persuasive, given some examples, such as 'Tame tigers growl' and 'Tame tigers exist', it is not persuasive, given other examples; in short, a counter example can be produced. Consider the edition of a book published in 1849. About the copies constituting this edition we can significantly say 'All copies are bound in red', 'Most copies are bound in red', and so on; in short, we can construct a table of sentences analogous to the A-table above. But we can also construct a table analogous to the B-table above, which, unlike the B-table, contains no meaningless utterances:

C_1: 'All copies still exist' $\bar{C}_1$: 'No copies still exist'
C_2: 'Most copies still exist' $\bar{C}_2$: 'Most copies no longer exist'
C_3: 'Some copies still exist' $\bar{C}_3$: 'Some copies no longer exist'

Here $\bar{C}_3$ has a perfectly clear meaning, and (hence) so have C_1 and C_2.

Moore does allow (pp. 119–20) that there are sentences of the form 'Some . . .'s don't exist' or 'There are some . . .'s that don't exist' which make perfectly good sense, but only because 'exist' in such sentences is being used in a way different from the way it is used in 'Tame tigers exist', where this is used simply to assert that there are some tame tigers. (Cf. 'There are some primes between 2 and 20, but there are no primes between 24 and 28'.) Moore points out that 'There are some tame tigers that don't exist' might mean 'There are some tame tigers that are not real, e.g. that are merely imaginary'. It might also mean (although

[1] Frank B. Ebersole, *Things We Know, Fourteen Essays on Problems of Knowledge* (Eugene, Ore., 1967), p. 246.

Moore does not note it) 'There are some tame tigers that no longer exist, i.e. that are no longer alive'. And surely Moore is right in saying that in these cases 'exist' is being used in a way different from the way it is used in 'Tame tigers exist'. For consider the negatives. If B_3 means the same as 'There are some tame tigers' and the proposition expressed by B_3 is logically analogous to that expressed by A_3, then $\bar{B}_3$ must mean 'There are some tame tigers that don't exist' where *this* means 'There are some tame tigers but there are none'. This last sentence clearly expresses a contradiction, which is probably why Moore says that $\bar{B}_3$ is 'pure nonsense'.[1] But if $\bar{B}_3$ means the same as 'There are some tame tigers that don't exist' and this now means the same as 'There are some tame tigers that are no longer alive' or '. . . are merely imaginary', then, since this last sentence does not express a contradiction, $\bar{B}_3$ does not express a contradiction. $\bar{B}_3$ must, therefore, have at least two senses. But since there is no difference in the way 'some tame tigers' is used, the difference must lie in the way 'exist' is used.

If we now look at the sentences of the C-table, we can see that in them 'exist' is being used in a way different from the way it is used in the examples of Moore's argument; that in them 'exist' is being used in a way analogous to the way it is used in 'Some tame tigers no longer exist, i.e. are no longer alive'. For 'All copies of the book still exist' means something like 'All copies of the book are still extant', and so for the other items of table-C. Now 'Tame tigers exist' *could* mean something like 'Tame tigers are still extant; that is, they have not all died off' but 'Tame tigers exist', *as contrasted with*, say, 'Black tigers do not exist' (where this does *not* mean 'Black tigers are merely imaginary' or anything like it), does not mean 'Tame tigers are still extant', because 'Black tigers do not exist' does not mean 'Black tigers are no longer extant'. And if this is so, then the sentences of table-C do not constitute a counter-example to Moore's argument, any more than does 'All tame tigers are merely imaginary'.[2]

---

[1] Moore appears to use such expressions as 'is significant' and 'has a meaning' (of sentences) to mean the same as 'expresses a proposition' or 'does not express a contradiction'.

[2] It was apparently the use of 'exist' involved in 'Most copies still exist, i.e. are still extant', 'Some tame tigers no longer exist, i.e. are dead', etc. that Aristotle had in mind when he observed (*De Anima* 415 b 13) that 'for living things, to be (or to exist) is to be alive', and generally when he remarked that 'to be' or 'to exist' (εἶναι) has many uses or senses. See G. E. L. Owen, 'Aristotle on the Snares of Ontology', *New Essays on Plato and Aristotle*, ed. by Renford Bambrough (London and New York, 1965).

(2) Moore's second argument has to do not with the meaninglessness of $\bar{B}_3$ but with the meaning of B_3. He adopts a modified version of Russell's theory of descriptions according to which 'Some men are Greeks' means 'The propositional function "x is a man and x is a Greek" is true in at least two instances' or '. . . is true for at least two values of the function'. But Moore says (p. 121) that he 'cannot imagine what sort of propositions would be "values" of "x is a man and a Greek", except . . . propositions which we express by pointing at (or indicating in some other way) an object which we are seeing (or perceiving in some other way) and uttering the words 'This is a so and so (or equivalent words in some other language)'.[1] Now that the use of 'growl' in A_3 can be seen to differ from the use of 'exist' in B_3 'in the respect that, while the first asserts that more than one value of "x is a tame tiger *and growls*" is true, the second asserts, *not* that more than one value of "x is a tame tiger and *exists*" is true, but merely that more than one value of "x is a tame tiger" is true' (p. 123). 'The further and more important difference' that explains 'why' B_3 means merely that more than one value of 'x is a tame tiger' is true is that, although 'This is a tame tiger'— a value of 'x is a tame tiger'—is significant, 'This exists'—a value of 'x exists'—'does not express a proposition at all', is 'absolutely meaningless'. Hence 'This is a tame tiger, *and exists*' is 'not tautologous but meaningless' (p. 124).

According to some philosophers—Moore himself in the last section of 'Is Existence a Predicate?'—'This exists' is not meaningless; it does express a proposition, albeit one that is always true. D. F. Pears, for example,[2] holds that 'This room exists' expresses 'a referential tautology', while 'This room does not exist' expresses 'a referential contradiction':

'we get a referential tautology when the statement refers to the thing that it is about in such a way that it implies its existence, so that the verb "exists" adds nothing new. Conversely, if the verb were "does not exist" it would be trying to subtract what had already been referentially implied, and this would produce a referential contradiction.'

[1] Here Moore apparently goes along with Russell's view that only demonstratives can serve as genuine proper names, although he rejects calling 'this' a proper name (p. 126). At any rate, 'King Constantine is a man and a Greek' is rejected as a value of the function 'x is a man and a Greek'. This view is closely tied to the view that to mention (name) something is to show that it is.

[2] 'Is Existence a Predicate?', *Philosophical Logic*, ed. by P. F. Strawson, p. 98.

In either case, however, it is admitted (assuming a propositional-function analysis of such sentences as A_3) that there is an important difference between sentences like A_3 and sentences like B_3. For if A_3 means 'At least one [Russell], or more than one [Moore], value of the propositional function "x is a tame tiger and x growls" is true', and B_3 analogously means 'At least one, or more than one, value of the propositional function "x is a tame tiger and x exists" is true', it remains the case that the values of the second conjunct of A_3 are significant and express contingent propositions, whereas the values of the second conjunct of B_3 are either meaningless or referentially tautologous.

We have now to ask ourselves whether Moore has shown that existence is not an attribute; that words like 'growl' in such sentences as A_3 do stand for an attribute, while the word 'exist' in such sentences as B_3 does not stand for an attribute. Of course, if all one means by saying that existence is not an attribute is that sentences such as those of table-A differ from sentences such as those of table-B in the ways specified, then he must admit that Moore has shown that existence is not an attribute, if he concedes that the differences Moore has pointed out do obtain. But one can easily imagine a philosopher agreeing that A-sentences differ from B-sentences in the ways specified and denying that Moore has shown that existence is not an attribute. He would, of course, have to mean by 'Existence is an attribute' something other than that A-sentences do not differ from B-sentences in the ways specified (either that, or contradict himself), and Moore might like to know what it is, then, that he *does* mean; but he can still claim either that Moore has failed to show that existence is not an attribute or that Moore has shown only that existence is a peculiar kind of attribute,[1] an attribute different from such attributes as growling and being red.

Moore, note, takes the claim that existence is not an attribute to be verbal in import—which he can justifiably do only if something like the view of sentences expressing necessary propositions sketched out above is true. He takes it to mean that finite parts of the verb 'to exist' (in at least one sense of 'to exist') do not stand for an attribute; and he takes this to mean that 'exist' in such sentences as 'Tame tigers exist' behaves or is used in a way different from such grammatical predicates as '. . . growl' and '. . . are red' in such sentences as 'Tame tigers growl' and 'Apples are red'.

[1] Cf. Pears, *ibid.*, p. 100.

He then searches for differences and claims to find at least two that the philosopher who says 'Existence is not an attribute' might have in mind when he says this. In short, Moore represents the dispute between the philosopher who says that existence is an attribute and the philosopher who says that it isn't as an empirical dispute about the meaning of certain sentences or the use of certain expressions: Is '. . . exist' in fact used in sentences in the same way as '. . . growl', or are they used in different ways?; do the two verbs significantly take exactly the same grammatical antecedents, or don't they? That Moore may be right in so representing the issue as far as *some* philosophers are concerned, I do not dispute. But in suggesting that a philosopher might continue to hold that existence is an attribute, perhaps a peculiar kind of attribute, while admitting the verbal differences Moore has pointed to, I have suggested that there might be more to the philosophical dispute about the nature of existence than simply an empirical disagreement about the behaviour of certain bits of English, or of languages into which English is translatable. Still, 'Existence is (is not) an attribute', unlike 'Aspirin is (is not) an analgesic', purportedly expresses an analysis of the concept of existence, and as such it purportedly expresses a necessary or *a priori* proposition; and if the view of sentences expressing necessary propositions sketched out above is accepted, the claim that existence is (is not) an attribute *is* verbal in import. But it does not follow that the issue is one of the actual use of certain English expressions, or their equivalents in other languages.

The verbal import of 'Existence is not an attribute' would seem to be that 'exist', in such sentences as 'Tame tigers exist' or 'Spotted cows exist', does not stand for an attribute; and it would therefore seem to be on all fours with the claim, say, that words such as 'the', 'a', 'of', and 'because' do not stand for attributes. The latter claim is clearly correct, and so is the former. The word 'attribute'—and this goes for the kindred words 'quality', 'feature', 'property', 'trait', and 'characteristic'—is used in such a way that to list the attributes of a thing (or of a kind of things) is to say what it is like, to describe it. An expression having no use to say what a thing is like does not stand for a property, i.e. does not have an attributive use. To tell someone that tame tigers growl is to tell him what tame tigers are like, to describe them; to tell him that all (most, some) tame tigers growl is to tell him what all (most, some) tame tigers are like. Hence, 'growl' in 'All (most, some) tame tigers growl' does have an attributive use. But 'exist' in 'Tame tigers exist' does not have an attributive use; it does not tell anyone what all, most, or some tame tigers are like, how they differ from what they would be like if they did not exist. A person who said of a tiger at the zoo 'It's tame; it growls' would properly be said to be describing the tiger or to be attributing certain traits or characteristics to it; but if he should say 'It exists' (where this does not mean something like '. . . is alive') he would not properly be said to be describing it or attributing any trait or characteristic to it. This is a linguistic point that may be made by means of the translation-technique, i.e. by calling attention to the fact that 'Tame tigers exist' is synonymous with 'There are tame tigers' or 'Some tigers are tame'; for in 'There are tame tigers' and 'Some tigers are tame', There are . . .' and 'Some . . . are . . .' are no more used attributively than is 'the' in 'The dog barks at strangers'.

This is a fact of language that no philosopher can reasonably be supposed to be unaware of; hence, in pointing it out we are not telling him something he does not already know. But in the face of this fact he can hold that existence is after all an attribute, perhaps a peculiar kind of attribute. We are forced, therefore, to conclude that in so doing he is not disagreeing with anyone about how certain expressions are actually used. That is, the import of his claim that existence is an attribute is *not* that 'exist' (in the sense at issue) is used attributively in English in such sentences as 'Tame tigers exist'—for this he knows is false. Still, the import of his claim is linguistic, but since it is not about how English (or any other language) is commonly used, it must reflect an implicit rule of a new or revised notation, one in which the meaning of 'stands for an attribute' or 'has an attributive use' is extended to cover 'exist' in such sentences as 'Tame tigers exist'. What obviously makes it relatively easy to do this for 'exist' and difficult to do it for 'the' is that the use of 'exist' does, after all, bear some similarity to the use of such verbs as 'growl', as the fact that we can construct the parallel well-formed sentences 'Tame tigers exist' and 'Tame tigers growl' shows. In the revised notation, then, 'Existence is an attribute' is just as much expressive of a necessary or *a priori* truth as is 'Red is a colour' in everyday English. But since in that notation 'Tame tigers exist' can continue to be synonymous with 'There are tame tigers' and 'Some tigers are tame', 'There are . . .' and 'Some . . . are . . .' can be 'shown' by what might be called a reverse use of the translation technique to have an attributive use.

If this is correct, then there is no *disagreeing* with a philosopher who holds that existence is an attribute and who dismisses discussion of common linguistic usage as 'a mere matter of words', 'mere lexicography'. Nor is there any *showing* him, in the manner of Moore, that he is mistaken. *His* 'Existence is an attribute', which figures only in philosophy, is logically compatible not only with the true empirical proposition that 'exist' (in the sense at issue) is not used attributively in everyday English but also with the corresponding *a priori* proposition that existence is not an attribute; which explains how he can consistently assert as a philosopher that existence is an attribute without denying linguistic facts with which he is obviously as well acquainted as is any other sophisticated speaker of the language. Hence, one can only go along, or refuse to go along, with him in his 'holiday' manner of speaking, and those who think they are *refuting* him by pointing to facts of common usage must be presumed to be expressing a refusal to go along.

Russell, as is well known, often insisted that existence is not a genuine predicate; that 'exists' when attached to a genuine proper name (e.g. 'This') expresses no proposition, is nonsense:

'there is a vast amount of philosophy that rests upon the notion that existence is, so to speak, a property that you can attribute to things, and that the things that exist have the property of existence and the things that do not exist do not. This is rubbish. . . . It is only where a propositional function comes in that existence may be significantly asserted. You can assert "The so-and-so exists", meaning that there is just one *c* which has those properties, but when you get hold of a *c* that has them, you cannot say of this *c* that it exists, because that is nonsense: it is not false, but it has no meaning at all.[1]

Why is this?

'As regards the actual things there are in the world, there is nothing at all you can say about them that in any way corresponds to this notion of existence. It is a sheer mistake to say that there is anything analogous to existence that you can say about them. You get into confusion through language, because it is a perfectly correct

[1] 'The Philosophy of Logical Atomism', *Logic and Knowledge: Essays 1901–1950*, ed. by R. C. Marsh (London, 1956), p. 252.

thing to say "All the things in the world exist", and it is easy to pass from this to "This exists because it is a thing in the world". There is no point in a predicate which could not conceivably be false . . . if there were such a thing as this existence of individuals that we talk of, it would be absolutely impossible for it not to apply, and that is the characteristic of a mistake."[1]

Russell's argument, spelled out, goes something like this: Consider a clear case of predication (p) 'This is red', said of an object of direct acquaintance. Here we attribute a property, redness, to a subject, the object designated or named by 'This'. Although 'This is not red' ($\sim p$) might be false, it implies no contradiction and theoretically could be true. In short, p is a contingent proposition. But suppose that existence is a property like redness. Then 'This exists' (q) attributes the property existence to the object signified by the demonstrative, and its denial ($\sim q$) is 'This does not exist'. But $\sim q$ implies a contradiction. For it tautologously implies itself; but it also implies its denial, in virtue of the fact that it contains a genuine proper name, in this case a demonstrative. In short, $\sim q \supset (q \& \sim q)$. Hence, if existence is a property, it follows that 'This exists' is always or necessarily true. For if $\sim q \supset (q \& \sim q)$, then $\sim M \sim q$.[2] But this is absurd: 'there is no point in a predicate which could not conceivably be false'. Therefore, existence is not a property or predicate. And if this is the case, then 'This exists' cannot express a proposition in subject-predicate form; and, since there is no other kind of proposition it could plausibly express, it must be meaningless.

In the last section of 'Is Existence a Predicate?' Moore gives an argument that stands to Russell's as the second member of an antinomy. Moore does not look upon it as showing that existence is not an attribute or predicate—although placed against Russell's argument this is what it must show—but only as showing that 'This exists' is significant, does express a proposition.[3] Moore's

---

[1] 'The Philosophy of Logical Atomism', p. 241.

[2] I owe this way of putting the argument to M. Lazerowitz.

[3] In section I of his paper Moore denies that 'This exists', the second conjunct of 'This is a tame tiger and exists', makes sense; in section II he asserts that 'This exists' said of an object of present acquaintance, e.g. an after-image, does make sense.

I here ignore what Moore says about sense-data in the last part of his paper. His argument about the meaningfulness of 'This exists', except for part of what he says on p. 125, has nothing inherently to do with the sense-datum theory.

argument is: Wherever we can significantly say of an object of present acquaintance 'This is (an) F', e.g. 'This is a book' or 'This is red', we can also say significantly of the same object 'This exists'. For of any such object one can 'say *with truth*', and therefore significantly, 'This might not have existed', 'It is logically possible that this should not have existed'. But if 'This might not have existed' expresses a true proposition, then 'This does not exist' must express a false proposition; in which case, 'This exists' must express a true proposition. In short, 'This might not have existed' entails 'This exists'. Therefore, 'This exists' is significant.

But Moore suggests a reason for saying that, although 'This exists' is significant, 'exists' here does not stand for an attribute.

'It seems to me that "This exists" (in this usage) always forms part of what is asserted by "This is a book", "This is red", etc., etc., where "this" is used in the manner with which we are now concerned; and possibly part of what is meant by saying that "is a book", "is red", etc. "stand for attributes", is that *part but not the whole* of what is asserted by any "value" of "x is a book", "x is red", etc., is "This exists". In that case "exists" in "This exists" would not "stand for an attribute", solely because the whole of what it asserts, and not merely a part, is "This exists" (p. 126).'

Now by saying that part but not the whole of what p asserts is q Moore *may* mean only that p entails but is not equivalent to q. If this is what he does mean, then his reason for saying that 'exists' does not stand for an attribute reduces to this: 'This is red' entails but is not equivalent to 'This exists', whereas 'This exists' not only entails but is equivalent to 'This exists'. But surely this is a singularly weak reason for saying that 'exists' does not stand for an attribute. For by parity of reasoning it can be shown that 'is coloured' does not stand for an attribute: 'This is red' entails but is not equivalent to 'This is coloured', whereas 'This is coloured' not only entails but is equivalent to 'This is coloured'; therefore, 'is coloured' does not stand for an attribute. But if 'is coloured' does not stand for an attribute, then surely neither does 'is red'; and if 'is red' does not stand for an attribute, then no expression stands for an attribute.

Of more interest than this is 'the curious consequence' that Moore feels 'bound to admit' stems from his view that 'This exists' is significant; namely, 'that "This exists", when used in this way, is always true, and "This does not exist" always false'—the very 'absurdity' that led Russell to say that existence is not an attribute and therefore 'This exists' is senseless. That this is a consequence of Moore's argument seems clear. For if one can 'say *with truth*' of any object of present acquaintance, e.g. an after-image, 'This might not have existed', and if 'This might not have existed' entails 'This exists', then one can say with truth of any object of present acquaintance 'This exists', which means that he cannot say with truth of such an object 'This does not exist'. But now an odd, indeed a paradoxical, feature of Moore's argument appears to emerge. For if 'This might not have existed' is true, then 'This exists', it seems, must be contingent, which means that it must be possible that 'This exists' is false. Thus A. N. Prior has observed of Moore's argument:

'The suggestion is that "This might not have existed" is analysable as "It might have been the case that (it is not the case that (this exists))", and this could have no meaning if its innermost component did not. The odd thing, however, is that when it is thus analysed, the statement does not appear to be true. "It is not the case that this exists" is just "This does not exist", but under what circumstances might this have been true, if "this" is being used as a genuine proper name?'[1]

Clearly, under none.

The first step towards understanding the present predicament is to ask ourselves what it means to assert that such-and-such

[1] A. N. Prior, 'Existence', *op. cit.*, p. 145. Prior's 'solution' is to analyse 'This might not have existed' as 'This need not have existed', meaning 'It is not the case that (it is necessary that (this exists))'. The 'verification' of this 'does not require that there be states of affairs in which we could truly say of the object in question "This does not exist"; it is enough that there are states of affairs in which nothing can be said of the object in question at all (for then not all states of affairs will be ones in which we can say of it "This exists", that is, "This exists" will not be a necessary truth' (*ibid.*). Prior admits that this solution requires that $M\sim p$ and $\sim Np$, which in most logical systems are equivalent, not be equivalent.

But what does the *verification* of 'This does not exist' have to do with the matter? To be sure, if there were no creatures capable of speaking (clearly a theoretical possibility) or if nothing at all existed (a dubious possibility), then there would be no one who could truly *say* 'This exists' or 'This does not exist'. But it would still be *possible* for there to be such creatures or for there to be something, and therefore it would have to be *possible* that 'This does not exist' should express a true proposition. But this, Moore claims, it cannot do.

might not have been the case, e.g. 'This might not have been red'—which implies 'This is red' just as much as 'This might not have existed' implies 'This exists'. Prior's way of putting it—either 'It might have been the case that (it is not the case that (this . . .))' or 'It is not the case that (It is necessary that (this . . .))'—suggests that what is being asserted is 'It is possible that (it is not the case that (this . . .))', or generally, $M(\sim(p))$, i.e. $M \sim p$. This brings out the suggested contingency of p, but it does not give the requisite implication that p. That is, $M \sim p$ does not imply p. If it did, then a proposition's being contingent would be a sufficient condition of its truth; which is absurd. And since $(M \sim p) \supset p$ is equivalent to $\sim p \supset \sim (M \sim p)$, a proposition's being false would be a sufficient condition of its being necessarily true; which is absurd. A more plausible analysis of 'It might not have been the case that p' is 'p but it is possible that not-p'. This tautologously gives the implication that p—that is, $(p \,\&\, M \sim p) \supset p$—and it also implies the contingency of p—that is, $(p \,\&\, M \supset p) \supset (Mp \,\&\, M \sim p)$.

This mode of analysis will clearly work for such propositions as 'This might not have been red'; for that simply becomes 'This is red but it is logically possible that this is not red', which is logically acceptable. It will even work for such propositions as 'The object I am now pointing at might not have existed' and 'The after-image I am now experiencing might not have existed'. For these become respectively 'I am now pointing at an object but it is logically possible that I am not now pointing at an object' and 'I am now experiencing an after-image but it is logically possible that I am not now experiencing an after-image'. But what are we to say of 'This might not have existed'? In the suggested mode of analysis this would become 'This exists but it is possible that this does not exist'; in which case it cannot be true that the proposition expressed by 'This exists' must always be true. For to say that it must always be true simply means that there is no theoretically conceivable situation in which it could be false.

The trouble obviously stems from the pairing of a demonstrative or Russellian proper name, not with just any verb, but with the verb 'exists'. How are we to account for this fact? How are we to account for the fact that we can apparently say with truth of any object of present acquaintance 'This might not have existed', which implies that 'This exists' is always true and yet seems to imply that 'This exists' might be false?

Let us consider first Moore's claim that 'This exists', when said of an object of present acquaintance, is always true. This is reminiscent of a very similar claim made by Descartes in the second of his *Meditations on First Philosophy*: 'this proposition "I am", "I exist", whenever I utter it or conceive it in my mind, is necessarily true'. 'This exists', like 'I exist', appears to express a statement of fact, a statement about the world or what there is in the world; like 'Tame tigers exist' or 'A man named "Bertrand Russell" exists'. But if 'This exists', like 'I exist', expresses a proposition that must always be true, then it cannot express a factual proposition, one that gives information about the world or what's in it, any more than 'Either this apple is entirely red or this apple is not entirely red' can give information about the colour of the apple.[1] 'This exists', unlike 'Tame tigers exist' (which it nevertheless resembles), merely gives the illusion of giving information about the world; which *may* be why Moore was inclined to say that it is senseless, although he knew that 'This exists', unlike a bit of gibberish, is not senseless. If the view of propositions that are always or necessarily true, which we adopted above, is correct, then 'This exists' and 'I exist', must have, so to speak, a verbal sense, must be verbal in import. Morris Lazerowitz brings out the verbal import of 'I exist' in the following way:

'if "I exist" does express a logically necessary truth, then understanding it comes to knowing a convention of language. As in the case of "I think", a feature of the use of "I" is being called to our attention, and what this is can be seen without much difficulty, once we disperse the ontological mists created by the mode of speech in which the sentence is formulated. The term "I" is not only a singular first person pronoun, it also has a function like that of a demonstrative, which has a use only in the presence of what it refers to. . . . It is this feature of the use of "I" which Descartes brings before us by means of his statement that *I exist* is an *a priori* truth. What understanding the words "I exist" amounts to is knowing that the sentence, " 'I' has a demonstrative function", states a true grammatical proposition.'[2]

---

[1] I ignore the question whether such a statement as 'Either this apple is entirely red or this apple is not entirely red' is *about* this apple at all. Some philosophers would want to say with Wittgenstein that all necessary statements are about the same thing, namely, nothing; others, like Moore, would want to say that they are about what they appear to be about, e.g. 'Either it's raining or it's not raining' is about the weather.

[2] Lazerowitz, *op. cit.*, pp. 59–60.

Similarly, if 'This exists' must always express a true proposition, what Pears calls 'a referential tautology', or, what comes to the same thing, if 'This does not exist' must always express a false proposition, 'a referential contradiction', then understanding this amounts to knowing a rule or convention of language, namely, that 'this' is a demonstrative, 'an adjective or pronoun having the function of pointing out the particular thing referred to' (O.E.D.). This information, and this information alone, is indirectly apprehended through the apprehension that 'This exists' has no true or significant negative. That is, if (S_1), 'This exists', expresses a proposition that must always be true, then (S_2), '"This" is a demonstrative' expresses a true contingent proposition; and conversely. And if this is the case, then it is also easy to see that 'This exists' does not attribute a property to the referent of the demonstrative, any more than 'This is either entirely red or not entirely red' ascribes a colour to the referent of its demonstrative.

We come finally to Moore's claim that one can say with truth of any object of present acquaintance 'This might not have existed'. This, as we noted, appears to imply that the proposition expressed by 'This exists' is contingent, i.e. could be false, and at the same time to imply that 'This exists' is always true.

Two features of 'This might not have existed', said of an object of present acquaintance, are worthy of note. (*a*) This sentence uses but does not mention the demonstrative 'this'; therefore, if it is to express a proposition at all, the demonstrative must have an object. That is the point of saying that 'This might not have existed' implies 'This exists'. But (*b*) 'This might not have existed' can be said with truth only of objects that do not, so to speak, exist necessarily. 'This might not have existed' can be said with truth of any object of present acquaintance such as an apple or an after-image; but it makes no sense to say, for example, 'There might have been no prime between 2 and 20', for that means 'There is a prime between 2 and 20 but it is possible that there is no prime between 2 and 20', and since the second conjunct is necessarily false, the whole is necessarily false. We are now in a position to understand the verbal import of the claim that 'This might not have existed' can be said with truth of any object of present acquaintance, namely, 'The demonstrative "this" does denote an object, but it is logically possible that that object does not exist'. The first conjunct is implied by the use of the demonstrative and thereby excludes 'This does not exist' from making sense; the second reflects the condition that 'This might not have existed' can be said with truth only of a contingent being.

Many philosophers, Moore among them, have had the idea that important philosophical truths can be shown by analysis or that equally important philosophical mistakes can be refuted by analysis, but if the dispute over whether existence is a predicate is typical of philosophical disputes generally, this would appear not to be the case. The correct analysis of a concept is one supported by a linguistic convention, either a general convention covering some item of common speech or a special convention covering a technical expression. Philosophical 'theories' generally appear to have the form of a conceptual analysis, but they are independent of linguistic convention, in that a philosopher can, with a show of reason, maintain and argue for a view that patently runs counter to the linguistic convention appropriate to that view, *if* it is a genuine conceptual analysis. Philosophy, in short, is not lexicography. This is most obvious in the case of such views as that motion is impossible, time and space are unreal, and existence is an attribute. But if views such as these are independent of linguistic convention, in that they cannot be shown to be false by an appeal to facts of usage (facts that the philosopher who holds such views knows just as well as does his opponent), then the denials of such views are, *as* their denials, equally independent of linguistic convention, even when, as in the case of 'Existence is a predicate but not an attribute', they happen to coincide with correct analyses. If no *philosophical* analysis can be *in*correct, then none can be correct either.

PHILOSOPHY AND 'COMMON-SENSE'[1]

by C. D. BROAD

I propose to consider in some little detail a view of the nature of
philosophy which has been accepted in recent years by a number
of very able thinkers in England and the USA. It may be formulated
roughly as follows. The sole or the main business of philosophy is
to analyse the various kinds of proposition which constitute the
common-sense view of the world. For many philosophers this line
of thought originates in the paper 'A Defence of Common Sense',
which was G. E. Moore's contribution to the collection of essays
published in 1925 under the title *Contemporary British Philosophy*.
It will be well worth while to devote some careful attention to this
famous and very influential essay of Moore's.

Moore does not attempt to define the word 'common-sense' or
the phrase 'a common-sense proposition'. Instead, he begins by
enumerating a long list of propositions, each of which would, he
thinks (and I would agree), readily be admitted to be a common-
sense proposition. In order to classify them briefly and intelligibly
I will begin by introducing a few simple technical terms.

Let us call a proposition 'epistemic' if and only if it asserts that
a certain individual, or some one or other, or everyone, *knows* a
certain proposition, or *knows* propositions of a certain class. Thus,
the following propositions would be epistemic: Jones knows that
the angles at the base of an isosceles triangle are equal; Everyone
knows that twice two is four; Some people know all the propositions in the First Book of Euclid. On the other hand, the proposition: Twice two is four, would be non-epistemic. An epistemic
proposition may be of the first, or the second, or of a still higher
'order'. The examples which I have given above are all of the
first *order*, since what each asserts to be known is a *non*-epistemic
proposition. But the proposition: I know that Jones knows that
twice two is four, is an epistemic proposition of the *second* order.

Now the first point to be noted is that Moore's propositions fall
into two primary groups. The first consists of a large number of

---

[1] Extracted by C. D. Broad from papers published in *Inquiry*, Vol. I, no. 2,
1958.

G

non-epistemic propositions. The second consists of a single *epistemic* proposition of the *first order*, concerning the members of the first group.

The non-epistemic propositions, which constitute the first primary group, may themselves be subdivided into *physical* and *psychological* propositions. The physical propositions may then be subdivided into *autobiographical, heterobiographical,* and *non-biographical*. The autobiographical physical propositions are assertions *by Moore himself* of the existence, and certain spatial and other relationships, *of Moore's own body* during a certain period. The heterobiographical ones are similar assertions made by Moore about *other* living human bodies and the same or earlier periods. The non-biographical ones are similar assertions made by Moore about certain ostensibly non-living bodies, e.g. the earth and the sun, and the same or earlier periods.

Finally, the psychological non-epistemic propositions may be subdivided into a number of *autobiographical* ones, and a single *heterobiographical* one. The autobiographical ones are assertions by Moore himself that *he* has had from time to time experiences of each of certain specific kinds. The single heterobiographical one is an assertion by Moore, with regard to the human bodies *other than his own* whose existence he asserted in the heterobiographical physical propositions. It is that many of these have been the bodies of *persons*, who have had, during the life-times of their several bodies, experiences of the various kinds which Moore himself has had during the lifetime of his own present body.

So much for the first primary group, i.e. the *non*-epistemic propositions. We come now to the second primary group, which, as I have said, consists of a single *epistemic* proposition of the *first order*. This may be stated as follows. It is true of many of the persons other than Moore himself, whose existence is implied by the heterobiographical psychological proposition stated in the immediately previous paragraph, that *they* have often, during the life-time of *their* present bodies, *known* propositions corresponding *mutatis mutandis* to each of those enunciated in the first primary group. The *mutanda* here are, of course, such terms as the person denoted by the proper name 'Moore', the date at which Moore was born, the date at which he wrote the essay, and so on, in the *auto*biographical propositions.

Now Moore claimed to *know* many propositions in each subdivision of the first group. Since this is an assertion of knowledge, it is an *epistemic* proposition. Since all the propositions in the first group are *non*-epistemic, it is an epistemic proposition of the *first order*. But Moore also claimed to *know* the one proposition in the second group. Since that is itself an *epistemic* proposition of the *first order*, the assertion that Moore knows it is an epistemic proposition of the *second order*.

We can now sum up this complicated business as follows: (1) Moore claims to *know* that he has a *body* of a certain kind, viz. a living human body, and that he has had *experiences* of certain specified kinds. He claims to *know* that there are *other living human bodies beside his*, and also that there are *bodies of other kinds*, e.g. trees, chairs, etc. He claims to *know*, with regard to each living human body, that it is the body of a *person* who has had experiences of the same kinds as he himself has had. (All this is a conjunction of many epistemic propositions, all of the first order.) (2) Moore claims to *know*, with regard to each such person, that *that person* knows facts corresponding *mutatis mutandis* to each of the kinds of fact enumerated above which Moore himself claims to know. (This is an epistemic proposition of the second order.)

The next point to be noted is this. The word 'know' is commonly used in English in such a way that it would be nonsensical to say of a proposition that it is known by someone but may yet be false. Therefore anyone who admits Moore's claims, and abides by ordinary English usage, must admit that there are true propositions in all the subdivisions of Group I. He must admit also that the proposition which is the only member of Group II is true. There are, indeed, two ways in which he might seek to whittle down these admissions. One is to say that in each of the final subdivisions enumerated above there are propositions which are at any rate *partly* true, though everyone of them is also partly false. The other is to say that, for the propositions in each of these final subdivisions, it is possible to find an *interpretation* in which some or all of them are *wholly true*, though in their ordinary sense they are all false. We must note that Moore explicitly rejects both these expedients. He is committed to holding that in each of the final subdivisions there are propositions which, when taken in their *ordinary sense*, are *wholly true*.

This last point deserves further consideration. Moore asserts that each of the common-sense propositions which he has taken as examples, and which he claims to know, has *one and only one meaning*, and that everyone who understands English understands that meaning. Take, e.g. the proposition: There is a penny on the table before me now. Moore would say that this has one and the same *meaning* (allowing for the systematic and understood ambiguity of the words 'I' and 'now') for everyone who understands English. But he says that there might be, and in fact are, great differences of opinion as to the *right analysis* of this and similar propositions. He does not claim to know the right analysis of them. Unfortunately, he does not further discuss these two vitally important notions of the 'meaning' and the 'correct analysis' of a proposition, nor does he explain in any detail how he supposes the two to be connected. All that he says on that point is this. It is impossible to raise the question: What is the correct analysis of such and such a proposition?, unless one understands the meaning of the proposition.

On all this I would make the following comments: (1) Surely it is not propositions, but *sentences*, which can significantly be said to have a meaning. A proposition is what a sentence means, or, more accurately, it is the common meaning of a whole multitude of equivalent sentences, spoken or written, in English or in German, and so on. If that be so, we must begin by substituting for Moore's original assertion some such statement as follows. Any person who understands English will think of one and the same proposition whenever he sees or hears or utters or images an instance of the type-sentence 'There is a penny on the table before me now'. Now that seems to me to be an empirical assertion about the experiences or the behaviour of members of a certain class of men when placed in situations of a certain kind. I do not see how Moore, or anyone else, can be justified in affirming it with complete confidence. On general grounds it seems to me highly doubtful. The utmost that I could admit is that one could describe fairly accurately the kind of circumstances which would be *necessary*, though not sufficient, conditions for a sane waking adult Englishman to utter or write (as distinct from babbling or scribbling) an instance of this type-sentence. We could also describe fairly accurately the sort of circumstances which would be held to be relevant for testing the truth or the falsity of such an utterance.

(2) Since a *proposition* cannot significantly be said to have a 'meaning', we cannot significantly contrast the 'meaning of a proposition' with its 'analysis'. We must substitute for this the contrast between a *proposition itself* and that set of interconnected propositions which together constitute the correct analysis of it.

For Moore's assertion about 'meaning' and 'correct analysis' we could then substitute the following assertion. Although everyone who understands English would think of one and the same proposition whenever he sees or hears or utters or images an instance of the type-sentence 'There is a penny on the table before me now', yet there is no general agreement as to the set of interconnected propositions which together constitute the correct analysis of that proposition. I have already commented adversely upon the first part of this assertion. Let us, however, waive these objections and consider the second part of it.

(3) I suppose it would be generally admitted that, in order for a conjunction of propositions p_1 & p_2 & . . . p_n to count as the correct analysis of a proposition p, the following conditions are *necessary*. (i) That, if p is true, then p_1 & p_2 & . . . p_n is true, and conversely. (ii) That this equivalence is not merely contingent, like the equivalence between being a ruminant and having cloven hoofs, but is in some sense *necessary*. (iii) That this equivalence, though necessary, is *not merely linguistic*. By this I mean that it really is a case of two different *propositions*, viz., p, on the one hand, and p_1 & p_2 & . . . p_n, on the other, and not merely a case of two different *sentences*, e.g., 'This is a negro' and 'This is a black man', which in a certain language stand for one and the same proposition.

Now, although these conditions are severally necessary for a set of propositions to count as the correct analysis of a given proposition, I think it is certain that they are not jointly sufficient. Some further condition seems to be needed, and I do not know what it is. I think that this can be made obvious by the following example.

Take the sentence 'n is a prime number'. Here I think it is probably true that everyone who understands English and has learned elementary mathematics does attach one and the same meaning to it, viz. that n is an integer which is not exactly divisible by any other integer. Now consider the following sentence: 'The immediate successor of the product of all the integers less than n is divisible by n'. I think it is plain that this really does mean a different proposition from that which is meant by the sentence 'n is a prime number'. So our third condition is fulfilled. And it can be proved that the proposition which is meant by this sentence entails and is entailed by the proposition which is meant by the sentence 'n is a prime number'. (This mutual entailment is known as Wilson's Theorem.) So the first and the second of our conditions are also fulfilled. But, although all the three conditions are thus fulfilled, would anyone be prepared to say that this complicated proposition is 'the correct analysis' of the proposition that n is a prime number? I should hardly think that anyone would.

If, however, anyone did, he might be invited to consider the following questions. There are plenty of other complicated propositions which can be shown to entail and be entailed by the proposition that n is a prime number. Are *all* of them to be counted as 'correct analyses' of the proposition that n is a prime number? If so, the phrase '*the* correct analysis' has no application here. If, on the other hand, a certain one of them is to be singled out as '*the* correct analysis', whilst the rest are to count only as various logical equivalents and not as analyses, on what principle is the distinction to be drawn?

The only suggestion that I can offer here is the following. It might be said that the proposition that n is a prime number does not *by itself* entail the proposition that the immediate successor of the product of all the integers less than n is divisible by n. The latter proposition, it might be said, is entailed only by the *conjunction* of the former with the axioms of arithmetic. Similarly, it might be said, the former proposition is entailed, not by the latter *alone*, but only the *conjunction* of the latter with the axioms of arithmetic. We are inclined to overlook this because these axioms are themselves necessary propositions, which are the common premisses or principles of all deductions within pure arithmetic.

Perhaps, then, we ought to add the following as a fourth condition which is necessary if a conjunction of propositions p_1 & p_2 & ... p_n is to count as an *analysis* of a given proposition p. The proposition p must *suffice by itself* to entail the conjunctive proposition p_1 & p_2 & ... p_n, and similarly the latter must suffice by itself to entail the former. Whether these four conditions are jointly sufficient as well as severally necessary to mark out a 'correct analysis', I do not know. Nor is it obvious that, if they are, there would be *only one* such analysis, and therefore something which could be called '*the* correct analysis'. And, finally, I do not feel any confidence that the fourth condition is compatible with the third, viz., that the analysandum and the analysis shall be two *propositions* and not just two different *sentences* which in a certain language mean one and the same proposition.

(4) I think that I can sometimes say with confidence that a certain set of propositions is *not* an analysis at all (and therefore

not the correct analysis) of what I understand by a certain sentence. (I have given an example above in connexion with the proposition that n is a prime number.) But I cannot state any satisfactory general criterion by which I would decide this. Still less could I state any criterion by which I could recognize that a certain set of propositions *is* the correct analysis of what I understand by a certain sentence, if and when that is in fact the case. In view of all this, I do not find it particularly illuminating to say that what is *meant* by such a sentence as 'There is a penny on the table before me now', when understood in its ordinary sense, is and is known to be wholly true; and that the business of philosophy is to seek for the *correct analysis* of the propositions meant by such sentences, and not to question their truth.

It should be noted that Moore himself never alleged that this is the *only* business of philosophy. Still less did he claim that the philosophical analysis of common-sense propositions must itself be expressed in the language of common-sense. Some philosophers in recent years seem to me to have written as if they held the latter view, but perhaps I do them an injustice. If anyone really does hold it, I can only say that it seems to me completely unjustifiable. The philosophical analysis of common-sense propositions, whatever it may really consist in, is obviously a reflective activity carried out by certain specialists upon materials provided by common-sense. It is no part of the business of common-sense itself. There is, therefore, not the least reason to expect that the language of common-sense would contain a suitable terminology for expressing the results of philosophical reflexion even on nothing but common-sense propositions. So it is no *prima facie* objection to a proposed philosophical analysis that it is expressed in technical terms, e.g. 'sensation', 'sense-datum', 'perceptual acceptance', etc., which either do not occur at all in common-sense language or occur there in a different and non-technical sense. One might as well object to a theoretical physicist because he uses the word 'entropy', to which no word in everyday speech corresponds, or because he uses the word 'energy' in a specialized technical sense which is very different from that which it has in daily life.

There are, indeed, two things which can be said in favour of the line taken by Moore in this essay and in some of his other writings. In the first place, it is certainly most desirable to bring high-sounding technical terminology to the test of concrete situations, as Moore has so often done with such devastating effect. Secondly, it is true and important to note that a technical term may, and often does, tacitly presuppose a certain theory, and that those who habitually use it are in danger of unwittingly assuming and expecting their readers to accept that theory without question, when it is in fact open to doubts and objections. (I think that this is true, e.g. of the word 'sensum' in the writings of many who have used it.) But, provided that a philosopher takes care to bear such facts in mind, he need not reproach himself if he sometimes expresses the results of his reflexions on common-sense propositions in terms which would be unintelligible to his bedmaker or unfamiliar to his bookmaker.

Subject to the above qualifications, I think that *one* very important part of philosophy *is* something which it is convenient to call the 'analysis' of various types of proposition, though I must confess that I cannot give a satisfactory definition of 'philosophical analysis', or a criterion for deciding whether a certain set of propositions is or is not 'a' or 'the' correct analysis of what is meant by a certain sentence. (Perhaps, the phrase 'philosophical analysis' is itself one that tacitly presupposes a certain type of philosophical theory as to the nature of propositions.) I also think that *one* very important class of propositions to be subjected to philosophical analysis are those which plain men and philosophers alike express by the sentences which they utter, and understand by those which they hear or read, in the most ordinary business of their everyday life.

I would point out, however, that, in my opinion, the importance of these latter propositions, and therefore the importance of a correct analysis of them, would be very little diminished if one rejected (as I do) Moore's claims, on behalf of himself and the rest of us, to *knowledge* here. Suppose I were content to say that in my unreflective moments I *unhesitatingly believe* such non-epistemic propositions as Moore claims that he and I *know*, including propositions that there are other living human bodies, and that many of them are the bodies of persons who have experiences of similar kinds to those which I *unhesitatingly believe* myself to have had. Suppose, further, I were content to say that in my unreflective moments I *unhesitatingly believe* that these other persons, whom I unhesitatingly believe to exist and to have experiences like mine, *unhesitatingly believe* in *their* unreflective moments propositions similar *mutatis mutandis* to those which *I* unhesitatingly believe *in* mine. Then the importance to *me* of these propositions, and therefore of a correct analysis of them, would still be very great. And presumably the importance of similar propositions *mutatis mutandis* to another person would be no less great, if, as I unhesitatingly believe, there are other persons like myself.

Even if all this were granted, it would still seem to me that the analysis of such propositions would constitute only a part, and not the most important part, of the philosophy of sense-perception. I will conclude by developing this contention very briefly.

We commonly think of a material thing as something which has all the following characteristics. It is something which has at each moment a certain shape, size, and position in a common three-dimensional space; which has at each moment various qualities, such as colour and temperature, in certain determinate forms; which has various causal properties, such as inertia, impenetrability, elasticity, etc.; and which persists, moves or rests, retains or alters its determinate shape, size, qualities, and causal properties, and interacts with other material things through impact, gravitation, radiation, chemical action, etc. We commonly think that our senses reveal to us the presence, and certain of the qualities, mutual relations, changes, and causal properties of certain bodies. We assume that these bodies would have existed; would have had the same qualities, mutual relations, and causal properties; and would have undergone much the same changes; even if they had never been perceived by anyone, human or non-human. Again, we take for granted that when a person sees a certain object, e.g. a star, that object exists and is in the state and at the place in which it then visually appears to him to be. We think that the same person can perceive the same part of the same body at the same time by different senses, e.g. sight and touch; and that different persons can perceive the same part of the same body at the same time by the same sense, e.g. sight.

Now there is a philosophical problem about sense-perception for the following reasons. (1) If we attend carefully, we note such facts as these. (i) Of two persons, who would be said to be seeing the same part of the same thing at the same time, e.g. the top of a penny, one may see it, e.g. as round and the other as elliptical. (ii) One and the same person, who would be said to be seeing and feeling the same part of the same thing at the same time, may, e.g. see it as elliptical and feel it as round. (iii) One and the same person, who would be said to have been seeing the same *unchanged* part of the same thing at different times from different positions, may, e.g. see it on one occasion as round and on the other as

G*

elliptical. Common-sense is more or less aware of such minor and systematic variations in normal sensible appearances, and it has certain modes of expression for describing them, but in the main it ignores them. Certain sciences and arts, e.g. geometrical optics and perspective drawing, deal explicitly and systematically with some of them.

(2) There are visual perceptual experiences which are abnormal in various ways and degrees, but are similar to and continuous with normal visual perceptions. They range, e.g. from mirror-images and sticks which feel straight but look bent when half immersed in water, through 'seeing double' when one eyeball is pressed aside or the percipient is giddy or drunk, to dreams and full-blown waking visual hallucinations. Now those which come at the latter end of this scale cannot plausibly be interpreted in the naïvely realistic way which ordinary language inevitably suggests for normal sense-perceptions, and yet qualitatively the series is continuous from one end to the other.

(3) There are certain highly relevant facts which are still quite unknown except to a minority of grown-up educated persons. They must have been completely hidden from everyone at the time when the language in which we express our perceptual experiences was first formed, and for thousands of years afterwards. One of these is the *physical* fact that light takes time to travel, and that a visual experience referring to an event in a remote object does not begin until light which left that object simultaneously with that event reaches the percipient's eye. A consequence is that an experience, which would naturally be described as 'seeing a certain remote object in a certain state at a certain moment', does not guarantee the existence of any such object at *that* moment, nor does it reveal the *contemporary* shape, size, position, colour, etc., of such an object if it does still exist. At the best such an experience guarantees only the existence of such an object in the more or less remote *past*, and reveals only the shape, size, position, colour, etc., which it *then* had. To this physical fact we must add the *physiological* fact that visual appearances vary with certain differences in the percipient's eyes, optic nerves, and brain, even when the retinal stimulus is the same. And, finally, we must add the *psychological* fact that visual perceptions are determined to some considerable extent by the percipient's past experiences and present mental attitude and expectations.

Now there is a philosophical problem of sense-perception for those and only for those who try to envisage all these facts together, and to give an account of sense-perception and its objects which fits them all into a coherent pattern. The language in which we express our sense-perceptions and talk about material things and events was formed unwittingly in prehistoric times to deal in a practical way with a kind of normalized extract from our total perceptual experience. It was formed in utter ignorance of a whole range of relevant physical, physiological, and psychological facts. It would surely be nothing short of a miracle if it were theoretically adequate, and if it were not positively misleading in some of its implications. If an adequate philosophy of sense-perception is to be constructed, this must be done by persons of philosophic interest and training, who are adequately informed of these and other relevant facts, beside the beliefs and the linguistic usages of common-sense.

For the reasons which I have given, it seems to me that Moore's essay 'A Defence of Common Sense' is not one of his happier efforts. It has, however, had a very great influence, and this seems to me to have been in the main an unfortunate one. It has led many able men, who might have contributed to solving the real problems of the philosophy of sense-perception, to waste time and labour and ingenuity in semi-linguistic studies of the usages of ordinary speech in the language with which they happen to be familiar. To imagine that a careful study of the usages, the implications, the suggestions, and the *nuances* of the ordinary speech of contemporary Englishmen could be a substitute for, or a valuable contribution towards, the solution of the philosophical problems of sense-perception, seems to me one of the strangest delusions which has ever flourished in academic circles.

MOORE ON PROPOSITIONS
AND FACTS

by A. J. AYER

In the third chapter of *Some Main Problems of Philosophy*, Moore sets out to explain what he means by a proposition. His method is to mention a couple of sentences and inform his audience that when they understood these sentences they were directly apprehending propositions. They were, of course, in Moore's view, also directly apprehending the sense-data which were conveyed to them by his utterance of the sentences; but he makes it clear that his use of the word 'proposition', unlike that of some other philosophers, is such that a proposition is not to be identified with any collection of words, whether the words be regarded as tokens or types, but only with the meaning of the words, with what a sentence is used to express. He does not attempt to define the relation of direct apprehension, beyond saying that it is the relation that one has to a proposition when one understands a sentence, and he confesses himself unable to decide, whether in speaking of directly apprehending propositions, as well as of directly apprehending sense-data, he is using the term 'directly apprehending' in the same or in a different sense.

Having given this account of what he means by a proposition, Moore goes on to list some of the most important characteristics which he thinks that propositions have. The first of these is that, in addition to being apprehended, a proposition may also be the object of the mental attitudes of belief or disbelief, in any of their various degrees. Secondly, he says that while the most common way of apprehending a proposition is to understand some sentence which expresses it, we also often apprehend propositions without seeing or hearing or even having in mind any sentences which express them. Presumably he is referring here to the cases in which we cannot, or cannot immediately, find the words to express exactly what we are thinking. He notes also that even when propositions are verbally expressed, they need not always be expressed by whole sentences; for example, a man who calls out 'Fire' may be expressing a proposition. Conversely, he says that he is not sure that all whole sentences express propositions; for example, imperatives may not. His third point is that whenever we apprehend a proposition 'we always also apprehend things which are *not* propositions: namely, things which would be expressed by *some* of the words, of which the whole sentence, which would express the proposition, is composed'.[1] In the case where these words designate a concrete particular, other than a present sense-datum, Moore seems to have held that the relation was only one of what he calls indirect apprehension. We are said by him to apprehend a particular indirectly when we do not directly apprehend it but do directly apprehend a proposition which is about it. On the other hand, every sentence which expresses a proposition must also contain at least one word, or set of words, which stands for what Moore calls a general idea or universal: and he appears to have held that universals were directly apprehended. Finally, he remarks that propositions are 'a sort of thing which can properly be said to be true or false'.[1] They are not the only sort of things of which this can properly be said. For instance, it is also correct to say it of acts of belief. Moore says that the sense in which propositions are true or false is different from that in which acts of belief are, but that the two senses are inter-definable. We can equally well say that an act of belief is true when it has for its object a true proposition or that a proposition is true when it is the object of a true act of belief.

The lectures of which *Some Main Problems of Philosophy* is composed were delivered in the winter of 1910–11, though the book was not published until 1953. Except for one important point, to which I shall come in a moment, Moore seems to have adhered pretty closely to the conception of a proposition which I have just set out. One very slight difference is that in his later writings he definitely commits himself to the view that the only sentences which are capable of expressing propositions are what he calls declarative sentences: and in an entry in the note-book which he began at the end of the year 1947, he defines a declarative sentence in the following way: 'An English sentence is "declarative" if and only if *both* it makes sense, when the words and syntax are used in accordance with good English usage, and also *either* (1) begins with "I know that", "I think that", "I feel sure that", "It's certain that" or any other of the English phrases which mean the same as one of these *or* (2) is such that the sentence formed by adding

[1] *Some Main Problems of Philosophy*, p. 62.

one of these before it makes sense.'[1] He does not comment on the fact that if we accept this definition we may be put into the position of having to say either that not every declarative sentence expresses a proposition or that not every proposition is either true or false. For instance, it is clear that both sentences which are used to express moral judgments and sentences like 'The present King of France is bald' which refer to non-existent individuals satisfy Moore's definition: yet with regard to sentences of each of these kinds some philosophers have held that what they express is neither true nor false. In the case of sentences which refer to non-existent individuals Moore himself accepted Russell's theory of descriptions, which does assign a truth-value to what they express. On the other hand, in his reply to his critics in *The Philosophy of G. E. Moore*, he admits to being half-inclined to accept Professor Stevenson's 'emotive' theory of ethics, from which it would follow that sentences which expressed moral judgments were not used to assert anything of which truth or falsehood could be predicated.[2]

The distinction between propositions and sentences is maintained throughout Moore's writings on the topic. It is always clear to him that a proposition, in his usage, is not identical either with any token-expression or with any type-expression. There is, however, one passage in the printed selections from a course of lectures which he gave in the years 1925–26, in which he allows there to be a sense in which it might be true that some propositions, in his usage, were token-expressions. He explains that the sense in which this might be true is not one which would imply that any token-expression was identical with a proposition. In saying of some token-expression that it was a proposition, what one would mean would be that it had a certain predicate. The suggestion is 'that just as in "*S* made use of ⟨uttered⟩ the *expression*: It will be dark soon", what we are saying is *quite certainly* of the form "*S* made use of *some* token having this predicate"; so in "*S* was believing the proposition: it will be dark soon", what we are saying is of the form "*S* was believing *some* token which had this predicate"'.[3] In short, it is suggested that token-expressions may bear to propositions a relation analogous to that which they bear to the type-expressions of which they are tokens. Moore rather strangely speaks of this theory as one that might be expressed by

[1] *Commonplace Book* (George Allen & Unwin, 1962), pp. 357–8.
[2] *The Philosophy of G. E. Moore* (1942), p. 545.
[3] *Lectures on Philosophy* (George Allen & Unwin, 1966), p. 139.

saying that there are token-propositions. He does not say what predicate he thinks a token-expression would need to have in order to be a proposition in this sense, but appears at least to leave the possibility open that it could be described in some more illuminating way than simply by saying, as he does, that for someone to stand to something which has this predicate in some unspecified relation is on this theory a necessary condition of his believing a proposition. Neither does he commit himself as to the truth or falsehood of this theory. He says that he sees nothing against it, but also nothing for it. He does, however, add that if it were true it would point the way to the analysis of 'is believing the proposition that': and from this it might be inferred that he had given up the view that one can believe propositions which one cannot find words to express. His saying that it is only of some propositions that it might be true that they are token-expressions could still be accounted for by the fact that not all propositions are either believed or disbelieved.

Assuming that what he means by a proposition is made sufficiently clear by the explanation which he gives in the third chapter of *Some Main Problems of Philosophy*, Moore declares it to be certain that propositions are among the things that there are in the Universe. It may, therefore, come as something of a shock to find that when he devotes himself to the analysis of belief in Chapter Fourteen of the very same book, he reaches a conclusion which he expresses by saying that there simply are no such things as propositions, and that when, in the seventeenth chapter, he attacks the view that truths are to be identified with true propositions, he speaks of propositions as imaginary. Moore does not seem to have noticed this discrepancy at the time, but later, when he wrote the preface to the book, he remarked that there was at least a possibility that he had not contradicted himself, since it might be that when he said that there certainly were propositions he was using the sentence 'there are such things as propositions' in a different sense from that in which he was using it when he said that there were no such things. His point was that in the second case he was making the reality of propositions depend upon the correctness of a particular analysis of such sentences as 'I believe the proposition that the sun is larger than the moon', whereas in the passage in which he said that there certainly were propositions he thought it possible that he was 'using it in such a sense that the truth of what it expresses would follow from the mere fact that such expressions as "I believe the *proposition* that the sun is larger than the moon" are perfectly correct ways of expressing something which is often true'.[1]

But what exactly is this sense in which there being propositions is supposed to follow from the mere fact that sentences of the form 'I believe the proposition that so and so' can correctly be used to say something true? Moore can hardly be assuming that to receive a mention in a sentence which is used to express a truth is a sufficient title to reality. It is no doubt true that the average man does not believe in leprechauns; but Moore would surely not have held that it followed from this that there are leprechauns or that there is such an entity as the average man. Indeed, he himself remarks in his essay on 'The Conception of Reality'[2] that whereas from the proposition that lions are hunted it follows that there are lions, from the proposition that unicorns are thought of it does not follow that there are unicorns. The example is unfortunate in that hunting does not necessarily entail the existence of what is hunted; in reporting that an expedition had been organized to hunt abominable snowmen, I should not be committing myself to the assertion that there were such things; it would be enough that the members of the expedition should believe that there were, even if their belief were false. Nevertheless the point which the example is intended to make is sound. In some cases one can legitimately infer from the truth of what is expressed by a sentence of the subject-predicate form that there are things of the sort of which the subject is, in other cases one cannot.

But how are these two types of case to be distinguished? Could there be any means of deciding, otherwise than by a process of trial and error, whether a given predicate belongs to one class or the other? I do not know the answer to this question. I have not been able to discover any general criterion by which it can be satisfactorily determined in all instances whether a predicate admits of existential generalization or not. One point, however, which does seem clear is that the existential inference is never valid with respect to anything which is referred to by a proposition which is said to be believed. From the truth of 'A believes that S is P' it never follows that there is such a thing as S. So, in the sense in which S, in this example, can be said to be an object of A's belief, the fact that something is an object of a belief is certainly not

---

[1] *Some Main Problems of Philosophy*, p. xii.

[2] *Philosophical Studies*, p. 216.

sufficient to prove that there is any such thing. The question is whether the position changes when the object of a belief is taken to be not something to which the proposition which is expressed by the subordinate clause refers but the proposition itself.

This question is difficult to answer, if only because it is not clear what is involved in casting propositions as the objects of beliefs. If the assumption is that a reference to propositions is required for the analysis of belief, we shall see in a moment that Moore himself gives a very good reason for holding that this is false. If all that is meant is that it is grammatically respectable to speak of believing propositions, it is hard to see why this fact about English philosophical usage should be thought to license any inference about what there is in the Universe, apart from the existence of some philosophers and the signs which they employ. What I think most likely is that Moore was making the assumption that something must be in order to be believed, but this assumption, in so far as it is intelligible at all, appears to presuppose the sort of analysis of belief that he himself was shortly to reject.

Another possibility is that Moore was led to the conclusion that there must be propositions not so much by any views that he held about the nature of belief as by his theory of meaning. From the innocent premiss that to understand a sentence is to apprehend its meaning, he inferred that there is something, the meaning of a sentence, in short a proposition, which one apprehends. But here again, if the conclusion of this inference is to be anything more than a mere repetition of the premiss, it must be interpreted as implying the correctness of a certain analytical position. The underlying assumption is that in order to give an analysis of what it is for a sentence to have a meaning, it is sufficient to postulate an abstract object which the sentence can be taken to signify. But once this assumption is brought to light, it becomes clear that what we are being given is not an analysis of meaning, but rather the result of a decision that no analysis is possible. To say that sentences signify propositions, and that is all there is to it, is merely a way of saying that the notion of signifying, as applied to sentences, and the notion of what is signified, are not further analysable. Now I do not know that any of the numerous attempts that have been made to give a further analysis of these notions has been entirely successful, but the difficulties are not such as to make it seem likely that success is unobtainable. I think, therefore, that Moore may simply have been mistaken in saying that propositions are directly apprehended, in so far as this is not merely a restatement of the fact that sentences are understood, but would also commit us to treating the meanings of sentences as objects. Not only is this an unwarranted denial of the possibility of a more informative analysis of meaning but in suggesting, as it does, that what happens when one understands a sentence is that one contemplates an abstract entity, it is at least seriously misleading. I shall say a little more about this when I come to Moore's reasons for not treating propositions as the objects of beliefs.

In his paper on 'Facts and Propositions' which appeared as the second part of a symposium with F. P. Ramsey in the *Supplementary Proceedings of the Aristotelian Society* for 1927, and is reprinted in his *Philosophical Papers*, Moore remarks that he has not come across any argument which seemed to him to show conclusively that propositions were not genuine entities.[1] He did not say what sort of argument he would regard as conclusive, neither did he say what the assertion that propositions were genuine entities would be understood by him to mean. An indication of what he took it to mean may, however, be found in his treatment of the very similar question whether there are classes. He discusses this question in the 1925–26 course of lectures, and there makes the point that the proposition that there are classes can be taken in two different senses. The first of these senses is characterized by him as one in which the proposition that there are classes is not a proposition about symbols, the second as one in which it is. Of 'there are classes', in the first sense, he says that it seems to him 'something which is *logically equivalent* to saying that there are more than one proposition of a certain sort that are true: viz. "My fingers are a class", "The hairs of my head are a class". *If* there are classes, at least two different propositions of this sort must be true; and if *one* proposition of this sort is true then there is at least one class'.[2] Moore goes on to suggest that this can serve as a general explanation of this sort of existential statement. Whether, to use his own examples, it is a matter of there being men, or lions, or relations, or qualities, to say that there are things of the kind in question is to say that at least two propositions of the form '*x* is a so and so' are true. In other words, the question of existence, in this sense, is settled by giving instances.

There is, however, still a difficulty about deciding when an existential statement comes into this category. If 'there are men'

---

[1] *Philosophical Papers*, p. 76.   [2] *Lectures on Philosophy*, p. 122.

follows from the fact that the propositional function 'x is a man' is satisfied in at least two different instances, then, as Moore remarks, 'you might think similarly that (1) "There are imaginary beings" will follow from "Ariel is an imaginary being" and "Oberon is an imaginary being"; and that (2) "There are fairies" will follow from "Oberon is a fairy" and "Titania is a fairy"'.[1] His answer is that you would be wrong in thinking this because 'x is an imaginary being' or 'x is a fairy' is not a function of the same sort as 'x is a man' or 'x is a class'. To say that Oberon is an imaginary being, if it is not to be taken as expressing the self-contradictory proposition that a certain set of predicates both belongs to one individual and to nothing at all, must be interpreted as saying that a certain set of predicates has been imagined as belonging to one individual, without in fact being attributed to anyone. To say that Oberon is a fairy is to say that the attribute of being a fairy is one of those that have been attributed to a particular imaginary character. Moore sees, however, that this gives no rule for determining when the existential inference is legitimate. You have first to decide whether the subject exists before you can decide whether the expression which appears to attribute a predicate to it is to be interpreted according to the model of 'Shakespeare is a man' or according to the model of 'Oberon is a fairy'.

In the case of propositions, it is safe to assume that Moore did consider the existential inference to be legitimate. If 'There are classes' is allowed to follow from 'My fingers are a class' and 'The hairs of my head are a class', and if 'There are qualities' is allowed to follow from 'Red is a quality' and 'Blue is a quality', then there is no reason why 'There are propositions' should not be allowed to follow from '"Shakespeare wrote Hamlet" is a proposition' and '"Queen Anne is dead" is a proposition' or from any other pair of different propositions that one cares to mention. The only thing that might make one hesitate to attribute this view to Moore is that he seems, in the paper on 'Facts and Propositions', at least to admit the possibility that propositions are not genuine entities, though he certainly cannot have been in any doubt concerning the fact that at least two propositions of the form '"p" is a proposition' were true. But the probable explanation of this is that when Moore considered the possibility of its being demonstrated that propositions are not genuine entities, he was interpreting the expression

[1] *Op. cit.*, p. 123.

'there are propositions' not in a sense corresponding to his first sense of 'there are classes' but in a sense corresponding to his second sense, the one in which 'there are classes' is construed as expressing a proposition about symbols.

But what exactly is this second sense? The account which we are given of it in Moore's lecture notes is somewhat compressed and not at all points easy to follow, but its outline is reasonably clear. It is closely based on the treatment of classes which Russell adopts in *Principia Mathematica* and elsewhere. Russell used the word 'class' in such a way that every predicate can be said to determine a class. If nothing satisfies the predicate, it determines the null-class: if only one thing satisfies it, it determines a unit-class: and in general, for any number n a predicate determines a class with n members if it is satisfied by just n things. In this usage, the concept of class is an extensional concept: if two predicates are co-extensive in their application, they determine the same class. So the class of unicorns is identical with the class of centaurs, the class whose only member is the author of *Hamlet* is identical with the class whose only member is the author of *Macbeth*. Moore regards this as a queer usage, not because of the extensionality, to which he has no objection, but because he thinks that, in ordinary language, it is contradictory to speak of a class with less than two members. We shall see in a moment that this is a point of more consequence to Moore than might at first appear.

To understand the next step, it is necessary to know the construction which Moore puts upon Russell's notion of an incomplete symbol. In *Principia Mathematica* Russell said that what he meant by an incomplete symbol was a symbol which was definable in use but had no meaning in isolation. So, according to his theory of descriptions, definite descriptive phrases are incomplete symbols. This definition does not satisfy Moore, both because he thinks it a mistake to say that expressions like 'the author of *Waverley*' have no meaning in isolation, and because he thinks that it fails to bring out the most important features of Russell's procedure. He first points out that what needs to be defined is not just 'x is an incomplete symbol' but rather 'x *in this usage* is an incomplete symbol' and then offers the following definition of Russell's use of this expression, 'In the case of *every* sentence, p, in which x occurs *with this meaning*, there can be formed another sentence, q, for which p is short, such that neither x itself nor any expression for which x is short occurs in q, and p always *looks as if* the rest of it expressed a propositional function, such that the proposition expressed by p is a value of that function, whereas in fact it never does'.[1]

This may sound a little obscure, but it becomes clear enough when applied to Russell's theory of descriptions. Thus 'The author of *Waverley* went bankrupt' is taken in this theory to be equivalent to 'At most one person wrote *Waverley*, at least one person wrote *Waverley*, and it is not the case that anyone both wrote *Waverley* and did not go bankrupt'. The second sentence is more complex than the first: it does not contain the expression 'the author of *Waverley*'; the first sentence is so constructed that it looks as if it supplies a value for the function 'x went bankrupt'; the translation shows, however, that this is not so; the descriptive phrase does not supply a value for the function but conjoins another predicate to it. This can all be summarized, for our purpose, by saying that what makes a symbol incomplete, in this sense, is that there is a special sort of way of translating it out.

Russell goes so far as to say that if anything is designated by an incomplete symbol, it follows that it is a logical fiction, but, as Moore points out, this cannot be correct, if only because it would have the unacceptable consequence that genuine entities could only be named and never described. For it to be true that there are no classes, in the sense in which this is a proposition about symbols, it is, indeed, necessary that symbols for classes should be incomplete, but it is not sufficient: a further condition is required, which is, according to Moore, that symbols for classes should not be descriptions. But now we run into the same difficulty as before. It seems that in order to decide whether symbols for classes are descriptions, one has first to decide whether classes are genuine entities. If symbols for classes are not descriptions, then, as Moore puts it, the expression 'determined by', in the sense in which classes are said to be determined by predicates, 'does not express any relation';[2] if there are, it does. Surprisingly Moore says that, in the sense in which Russell speaks of classes, 'hardly anyone would be disposed to question' that 'determined by' does not express a relation.[3] On the other hand, when it comes to classes in what he takes to be the ordinary sense of the term, he is disposed to go the other way; he inclines towards the view that 'having x for a member' is an ultimate relation in which classes stand to their elements. But, so far as I can see, his only reason for adopting this position is that he just cannot bring himself to believe that there is such a thing as the null-class, or that there is an entity distinct from Scott, namely the class of which Scott is the only member, which is determined by the predicate 'wrote *Waverley*'; whereas he has no difficulty in believing that there are such entities as the classes constituted by the fingers on his right hand, or the pennies in his pocket. He fails, however, to explain what he thinks is meant by saying that these classes exist, over and above the fact that the predicates 'being a finger on Moore's right hand' or 'being a penny in Moore's pocket' at a given date are satisfied by such and such particulars.

All this applies *mutatis mutandis* to the question whether there are propositions. In this case also, the only substantial point at issue would seem to be whether propositions are designated by incomplete symbols. If it could be shown that in all cases in which we ostensibly referred to a proposition, the reference could be eliminated either by translation or at least by an adequate paraphrase, then it is not clear what motive anyone could have for continuing to assert that there were propositions; it is not clear even what his assertion could, at this stage, be taken to mean. I shall, therefore, assume that if we can find a way of eliminating propositions, in this sense, we shall have demonstrated that they are not genuine entities. What we are required to show is that the reference to propositions is not necessary for explaining how sentences have meaning, or for the analysis of belief, or for the theory of truth.

I shall begin with the analysis of belief, both because Moore devoted more attention to it than he did to the topic of meaning, and because the little more that I have to say about meaning arises out of it. As we have already remarked, it was Moore's rejection of his previous assumption that belief consists in having a proposition before the mind in a special sort of way that led him, in *Some Main Problems of Philosophy*, to conclude that there were no such things as propositions. His argument, though his exposition of it is elaborate, is essentially quite simple. I shall try to set it out as clearly as I can.

Moore takes as an example the false belief that anyone would be having if he believed that Moore and his audience were currently hearing the noise of a brass band. What would make this belief false, he says, would be the fact that they were not hearing any such noise, or to put it another way, the absence from the Universe of the fact which would make the belief true. He then points out that this conclusion can be generalized. What makes a belief true is the presence in the Universe of the fact to which it refers: what makes a belief false is the absence of the fact from the Universe. If we now ask what the fact is to which a given belief refers, the answer is that it is '*the* fact which has the *same name* as that which we have to use in naming the belief'.[1] To name a belief is to say that it is the belief that so and so, the belief that my scissors are lying on the table, the belief that unicorns exist, or whatever it may be, and the same verbal clause is used to name the fact, the fact that my scissors are lying on the table, the fact that unicorns exist, or whatever, the being or non-being of which renders the belief true or false. Moore makes it clear that he is not putting this forward as a definition of what is meant by the fact to which a belief refers: he is not suggesting that what we mean by saying that a belief is true is that the Universe contains a fact which has the same name. The identity of name expresses another relation which needs to be brought to light. But for this we require an analysis of belief.

Now the analysis which Moore had hitherto accepted was, as we have seen, that belief was a special act of mind which was directed towards an objective entity, a proposition; and the proposition was supposed to exist, or perhaps we should say, to subsist, whether the belief was true or false. It follows, as Moore now remarks, that in the case of a true belief there are two objective entities to be reckoned with: the proposition which is the object of the belief and the fact which makes it true. Though they are both named by the same name as the belief, these entities are identical neither with it nor with each other: the proof that they are not identical with each other is that the proposition is present in the Universe whether the belief is true or false, whereas the fact is present only if the belief is true.

This reduplication of entities is not regarded by Moore as a fatal objection to the theory, though he allows that it casts a suspicion against it. He thinks that the best line for an advocate of the theory to take would be to maintain that truth and falsehood were unanalysable properties of propositions and that the fact which made a given belief true simply consisted in the possession by the corresponding proposition of the property of truth. This would not be inconsistent with the definition of truth, according

[1] *Some Main Problems of Philosophy*, p. 256.

to which 'to say that a belief is true is to say that there *is* in the Universe *the fact* to which it refers'.[1] The sense of 'truth' in which propositions are true would, on this theory, be fundamental; and talking of the being of the fact to which a belief referred would come down to defining the truth of a belief in terms of the truth of the proposition which was its object.

Moore has two objections to this theory. He does not think that either of them is conclusive, but they are enough to make him give the theory up. The first, which is an objection only to the proposed analysis of the fact to which a true belief refers, is that he no longer finds it credible that such a fact can consist merely in the possession of some simple property by a proposition. Even if it be granted that there are propositions, their relation to facts must surely be something different from this. The second objection is more general; it puts in question the basic assumption that propositions are the objects of beliefs. In Moore's own words, 'it is that, if you consider what happens when a man entertains a false belief, it doesn't seem as if his belief consisted merely in his having a relation to some object which certainly *is*. It seems rather as if the thing he was believing, the *object* of his belief, were just *the* fact which certainly is *not*—which certainly is not, because his belief is false.'[2] But to say that the fact is not is only a clumsy way of saying that there is no such fact: and if there is no such fact, then no belief can have it for an object. Moore is therefore led to the conclusion that beliefs do not, in this sense, have any objects at all.

To develop this argument, Moore returns to his original example. He points out that the difficulty to which he is trying to draw attention does not arise only in the case of false belief. It is enough for his purpose that his audience should be able to conceive such a hypothesis as that they are now hearing the noise of a brass band. Here again it might be suggested that what they were conceiving was a proposition, and that this proposition had being, even though the fact which there would have been, if the proposition had been true, did not. But then, he goes on, in order to distinguish the proposition which is from the fact which is not, it is surely necessary to conceive both; and what can the object of the conception be in the case of the non-existent fact? It cannot be the proposition that they are not now hearing the noise of a brass band, for that has the same status as its contradictory: and anyhow what

[1] *Op. cit.*, p. 262.   [2] *Op. cit.*, p. 263.

they need to distinguish is not a proposition from its contradictory but a proposition from the fact, the non-being of which makes it false. The only possible answer is that when they conceive of this non-existent fact, their conception has no object at all. But once it is admitted that there can be conceptions without objects, the motive for bringing in propositions disappears. In Moore's own words, 'if, in some cases, when we conceive or believe a thing, there really *is* no such thing as that which we *are said* to believe or conceive—if sometimes the words which we seem to use to denote the thing believed or conceived, are[1] not really a *name* of anything at all, I think there is no reason why we should not admit that this is *always* the case in false belief, or in conception of what is purely imaginary. We should then have to say that expressions of the form "I believe so and so", "I conceive so and so", though they do undoubtedly express *some* fact, do *not* express any relation between *me* . . . and an object of which the name is the words we use to say *what* we believe or conceive. And since there seems plainly no difference, in mere analysis, between false belief and true belief, we should have to say of all beliefs and suppositions gener-ally, that they *never* consist in a relation between the believer and something else which *is* what is believed.'[2]

What emerges from this argument is that propositions have no part to play in the analysis of belief. If they are treated as symbols, they gratuitously reduplicate the sentences which are used to state what is believed. It is, however, only if they are treated as symbols that it makes any sense to predicate truth and falsehood of them. To treat them as objects, on to which beliefs are directed, is to make it impossible to explain how anything comes to be true or false. Since an object, in this sense, does not refer beyond itself, the propositions simply cut off the beliefs from the actual course of events by which they are verified or falsified.

An objection of the same kind holds against the attempt to cast propositions in the role of the meanings of sentences. There is, indeed, no harm in talking of propositions, so long as it is under-stood that this is just a convenient device for referring to what is true not only of a given sentence but of any other sentence which has the same meaning. But to conceive of the meaning of a sen-tence as an abstract object is, as I said earlier, not only to fail to explain how sentences are endowed with meaning, but also to

---

[1] The 'is' which occurs here in the text is presumably a misprint.
[2] *Op. cit.*, pp. 264–5.

misrepresent the way in which they are understood. If one supposes that understanding a sentence simply consists in apprehending an abstract entity, one will be at a loss to explain how one ever succeeds in communicating any valid information about matters of empirical fact. Once again, if the proposition is not itself a symbol, it acts not as a bridge but as a barrier between words and things. If it is a symbol, it gratuitously reduplicates the words.

This argument does perhaps afford a sufficient justification for saying that there are no such things as propositions. We should, however, note that in saying this we shall be giving yet another sense to this existential negation. What we shall in effect be saying is that propositions need not be taken seriously, that they are incompetent to do the work to which they have been assigned. But clearly this is not the same as saying that propositions are designated by incomplete symbols. It leaves it an open question whether all the apparent references that we make to propositions can be translated out. I am in fact of the opinion that they can at least be paraphrased out and I have tried elsewhere[1] to sketch a theory of meaning which could secure this result. I have, however, to admit that in common with all the other attempts that I know of to achieve anything like a formal elimination of propositions, my theory encounters difficulties which I cannot claim to have entirely removed.

Moore himself seems not to have been altogether satisfied with his proof that propositions are not the objects of beliefs. At least I can find no evidence that he ever subsequently relied on the argument which I have just been summarizing, and in his essay on 'Facts and Propositions', which appeared sixteen years after he delivered the lecture in which this argument is set out, he still wrote as if he thought it possible that a proposition should be what he calls 'the objective factor' in a fact of a certain sort. Since he explains that one condition for anything A to be an objective factor in a fact of the kind in question is that the fact should entail both that A is being believed and that if anything else is being believed it is contained in A, and since he goes on to say that only a proposition can satisfy the condition, and then only if it is a 'genuine entity', it is clear that in allowing this possibility he has gone back on his earlier position. To see how far he has gone back it will be necessary to examine his essay in some detail.

[1] *Vide The Origins of Pragmatism* (Macmillan and Co. Ltd., 1968), 173–9. (Freeman Cooper & Co.), 162–8.

The first point to remark is that the facts with regard to which Moore says that he thinks it possible that they contain propositions as objective factors are facts of a peculiar sort. He defines them as facts which correspond in a certain way to another class of facts which he defines, as so often, by means of an example. The example is the fact which someone, who was at a given moment judging that Caesar was murdered would express if he at that moment uttered the English words 'I am now judging that Caesar was murdered'. The class of facts which Moore uses this example to define consists of all those which resemble it in being correctly expressible by an English sentence of the form 'I am now judging that p'. Moore has no doubt that there are facts of this kind and he also has no doubt that they are all what he calls general facts. What he appears to mean by saying that they are general facts is that they are in some degree indeterminate. Thus, in the case of his example, he assumes that someone who judges that Caesar was murdered must be judging with regard to some description such as 'the author of *De Bello Gallico*' or 'the conqueror of Pompey' that the person who answers to this description was murdered: but certainly this information is not conveyed merely by saying 'I am now judging that Caesar was murdered'. The answer to this might appear to be that if the description in question were substituted for the word 'Caesar', as it evidently could be, the resulting sentence would still express a fact which answered to Moore's definition; but I suppose he would have replied that even this would not remove the element of generality, on the ground that there were different ways in which the description might be thought to be satisfied. Again, he assumes that when one makes a judgment one must make it with a definite amount of precision, with a particular degree of conviction and so forth; yet none of this is stated in merely saying that one makes the judgment. Finally, he thinks it possible, in a fashion which he does not explain, that the use of the word 'I' in this context imparts a further element of generality.

Now it is Moore's contention that to every general fact of this kind there corresponds one and only one non-general fact. The way in which it corresponds is that every one of the general facts 'is, or is equivalent to, a fact, with regard to a certain description, to the effect that there is one and only one non-general fact answering to that description';[1] the non-general fact in question is then the one which does so answer. It would seem that in order

[1] *Philosophical Papers*, p. 69.

to express such a non-general fact, one would have to state, in a completely determinate way, exactly what happened on the relevant occasion to make it true that someone was then judging that Caesar was murdered or whatever it might be. Moore is, however, of the opinion that none of these non-general facts 'could possibly be expressed in any actual language', presumably on the ground that none of the sentences of any actual language which one might try to employ for the purpose would be sufficiently determinate; and he adds that 'perhaps even none could be expressed in any possible language'.[1] It is then with these inexpressible non-general facts that Moore believed that his co-symposiast, Ramsey, was really concerned when he wrote in his paper about analysing judgments; and it is of these that he asserts that they may contain propositions as their objective factors.

There is a good deal here that is puzzling. If we consider not the fact which someone might express by saying that he believed that Caesar was murdered, but simply the fact that Caesar was murdered, then I suppose that a case could be made out for saying that this was a general fact to which just one non-general fact corresponded. What might be meant by saying that it was a general fact would be that there were a number of different possible concrete states of affairs which would make what is expressed by the sentence 'Caesar was murdered' true; and what might be meant by saying that just one non-general fact corresponded to it would be that there was just one state of affairs which did make it true, a state of affairs which consisted in a particular man's being killed at a particular time and place by such and such other men in such and such a particular way. But if this is an example of what Moore meant by a non-general fact, I do not find it at all obvious that non-general facts are inexpressible. To avoid any difficulties that there might be in pinning down their subjects, we could attempt to cast them in such a form that the only referential expressions of which we needed to make use in stating them were expressions which referred to places and times: and it would appear possible to make these references completely precise. In order to state what occurred at the place and time, we should then need only to use predicates; and these, I take it, would be qualitative predicates standing for observable properties: they might, for example, be predicates of colour or shape. But then, in view of the fact that there are limits to our powers of sensory discrimination,

---

[1] *Philosophical Papers*, p. 69.

there would appear to be no reason in principle why these predicates should not be wholly determinate, in the sense that all the
instances in which they were satisfied were qualitatively indistinguishable in the relevant respect. In the case of sentences
which were designed to express the non-general facts which verified propositions about human actions there would, indeed, be
special difficulties, since we might have to bring in predicates
which were satisfied by mental images or by unspoken thoughts:
but here again I see no reason in principle why a mental image
should not be described with complete precision, or even an unspoken thought, to the extent that it consists not merely in the
subject's having certain propensities to speak or act in certain ways,
but in some actual state of his consciousness. Of course, no series
of sentences of this kind would express anything equivalent to
what is expressed by such a sentence as 'Caesar was murdered';
for one thing, they would not rise to the level at which causal
relations can be formulated. Nevertheless they could still constitute
a completely accurate record of the particular stretch of history
in virtue of which the sentence with the greater generality of
meaning could be held to express a fact.

This is, however, a simpler problem than the one with which
Moore presents us. As we have seen, his example of a general fact
is not the fact that Caesar was murdered, but rather the fact which
someone would express by saying truly with reference to a particular time that he judged at that time that Caesar was murdered;
and it is in the non-general facts which correspond to general facts
of this sort that he thinks himself able to distinguish objective and
non-objective or at least 'not merely objective' factors. We have
seen that one sufficient condition which Moore lays down for
anything to be an objective factor in a fact of his sort is that it be
the one and only proposition which in asserting the fact in question one is asserting to be believed. A second sufficient condition
is that it be something about which the fact entails that something
is being believed, in 'some sense of the word "about"'.[1] A not
merely objective factor is one that may or may not satisfy one of
these conditions, but in any case also enters into the fact in some
other way. Thus, in Moore's view, the time at which the judgment
is made is an objective factor in the non-general fact corresponding
to the fact of someone's judging that Caesar was murdered, since
he assumes that anyone who made such a judgment would be

[1] *Op. cit.*, p. 70.

judging with regard to the time at which he made it that the event of Caesar's murder occurred before that time. On the other hand, the time at which the subject made the judgment would also enter into the fact in another way 'since it would also be the time, with regard to which the fact in question would be a fact to the effect that he was making that judgment *at* that time'.[1] After the same fashion, the word 'I' might refer to a factor which enters into a fact of this kind in two different ways, if the judgment is one that the subject makes about himself. Because of this, Moore thinks it advisable to define what Ramsey calls a 'mental factor', in a fact of the kind in question, in such a way that for something to be a mental factor is not inconsistent with its also being an objective factor. His proposal, given that F is a fact of the appropriate sort and B a factor in F, is that 'B will be a "mental" factor in F, if and only if both (1) B is not *merely* an "objective" factor in F and also (2) B is not the time or (whatever "factor" in F corresponds to this time) *about* which F is a fact to the effect that a certain judgment is being made at that time'.[2]

Having defined mental and objective factors in this way, Moore takes it for granted that every fact of the sort he is concerned with contains mental factors and he also thinks it unquestionable that every such fact contains more than one objective factor. Unfortunately, he does not say how factors are to be individuated. Thus, if we consider such a fact as that lions exist, we do not know whether to take lions and existence as factors, or the property of being a lion and the fact that it is satisfied, or some set of properties which together make up the property of being a lion and the fact that they are conjointly satisfied. Since the judgment that lions exist could, in some sense or other of the word 'about', be said to be about any of these things, it would seem that we have a pretty free choice.

There is, however, some indication that Moore held this choice to be subject to at least one serious restriction. From what he says about propositions, in this context, it may be inferred that he was not prepared to count anything as an objective factor unless it was a genuine entity. But, in that case, so far from its being certain that the facts of which Moore is speaking always contain a plurality of objective factors, it may very well be doubted whether they need contain any objective factors at all. The sort of counter-example which I have in mind would be one in which the judgment in

[1] *Op. cit.*, p. 71.   [2] *Op. cit.*, p. 73.

question did not refer to any particular period of time or to any existent things. The most obvious instance would be judgments about mythical entities, like centaurs or unicorns. It might be argued that what such judgments were really about were the stories in which these imaginary creatures figured: but the answer to this would be that one can ascribe characteristics to such things as unicorns or centaurs, without knowing them to be imaginary. In face of this difficulty, the easiest line for Moore to have taken would have been to say that the objective factors, in such instances, were the properties in terms of which these imaginary creatures were defined. But then what ground would he have had for saying that properties were genuine entities? Here again, Moore's failure to supply any criterion for what is to count as a genuine entity makes this question impossible to answer. All that I can say is that just as one does not explain how sentences have meaning by saying that they stand for propositions, so one does not explain how adjectival expressions have meaning by saying that they stand for properties.

Having admitted, for whatever reason, that every fact of the sort he is concerned with has more than one objective factor, Moore considers whether this admission precludes him from holding that propositions are ever the objective factors in such facts. He thinks that it would so preclude him if the principle, which he attributes to Ramsey, that there cannot be two different facts, each of which entails the other, were true: but he says that he can find no reason for believing this principle to be true, and some reason for believing it to be false. Accordingly, his tentative conclusion appears to be that in the case of any general fact which consists in someone's making a judgment, there are two corresponding non-general facts. One of them consists in the holding of some relation or relations between some not merely objective factors and a plurality of objective factors and the other consists in the holding of some relation or relations between some not merely objective factors and a proposition. In the second case, the constituents of the proposition are also objective factors which are contained in the fact, but the fact does not, as in the first case, consist in their standing in any relation to the not merely objective factor, but only in the proposition's doing so. These two non-general facts are equivalent, in the sense that they mutually entail each other, but they are not identical.

Apart from the unclarity of the notion of an objective factor, there are two further difficulties here. The first is that Moore does not attempt to explain, still less to justify, his mysterious distinction between what a fact consists in and what it contains. The second and more serious difficulty is that he fails to give any rules for individuating facts. He seems to have had no doubt that facts, both general and non-general, were genuine entities, but at the same time no very clear idea how one fact was to be distinguished from another.

One thing which we do know is that Moore was not willing to identify facts with true propositions. His proof that they are not identical is given in an entry in the first of his note-books, which was written in the year 1919 or thereabouts. It is shown, he says, 'by showing that "This is scarlet" is equivalent to "That this is scarlet is a fact" but is *not* equivalent to "The proposition that this is scarlet is a fact". "The proposition that this is scarlet is a fact" is nonsense, which shows that "is a fact" and "is true" are not interchangeable, although the sentences "That this is scarlet is a fact" and "That this is scarlet is true" have the same meaning.'[1] In short, the argument is that since the expressions 'is a true proposition' and 'is a fact' are not universally interchangeable, facts and true propositions cannot be identical. This would be a valid argument if its premiss were true, but the trouble is that the example, which is meant to show that the premiss is true, itself relies on the truth of the conclusion. If someone were convinced that facts were identical with true propositions, he would presumably not admit that the sentence 'The proposition that this is scarlet is a fact' was a piece of nonsense: he would accept it as an inelegant way of stating that the proposition that this is scarlet was true.

Moore's claim that his facts are not identical with true propositions might carry more conviction if he had been able to show how they could be separately identified. I shall suggest in a moment that this can be achieved in the case of Moore's non-general facts. On the other hand, when it comes to his general facts, I am unable to see any way of identifying them except through the true propositions which they gratuitously mirror, and ultimately, therefore, through the sentences by which these propositions are expressed. To the non-general fact to which the general fact that Caesar was murdered corresponds, there also correspond, if one is to believe Moore, the general fact that the author of *De Bello*

[1] *Commonplace Book*, p. 3.

Gallico was murdered, the general fact that Caesar did not die a natural death, the general fact that a great-uncle of Augustus did not die a natural death, the general fact that either Caesar or Napoleon was murdered, the general fact that either Caesar was murdered or Napoleon was an Irishman, and countless others of similar types. What distinguishes these facts from one another is just the differences in content of the propositions with which they are severally paired and the only purpose that is served by speaking of them is to make the point that these propositions are true. We have already had enough difficulty in attaching meaning to the thesis that propositions are real constituents of the Universe; there seems even less excuse for talking as if, corresponding to every true proposition, the Universe contained yet another sort of abstract entity, in the form of a general fact.

The case of non-general facts is different because here we are justified in thinking of facts, not as true propositions masquerading under a different title, but as the concrete states of affairs which make propositions true. Thus all the propositions corresponding to the so-called general facts which I have just listed are made true by the non-general fact of Caesar's dying at the particular time and place and in the particular way he did. Even here, however, Moore shows his lack of concern for Ockham's razor. He distinguishes the fact that Caesar died from the event of Caesar's death, with the implication that they are both constituents of the Universe. But while it is true that facts are not identical with events, in the sense that we can say of one what we cannot significantly say of the other, the difference is no more than a difference of grammar: whichever way of speaking we find it convenient to employ, there is a sense in which the phenomena to which we are referring are the same. There is just one stretch of the world's history which Caesar's murder occupies, and whether we refer to it in terms of facts, or events, or states of affairs, or things and their attributes, or the instantiation of properties, or the satisfaction of predicates is a matter for our convenience. There is no reason indeed why we should not draw on all these forms of vocabulary: but it is neither necessary nor profitable to reify all the entities which figure in them.

One motive which Moore may have had for upholding the reality of facts was that he thought that this was required for his correspondence theory of truth. The relation of correspondence on which this theory depends is one which is supposed to hold

H

between a fact of the form 'A judges that p' and the fact which the p in question expresses, if it does express a fact. Moore maintains that in some uses of the word 'true', the meaning of this word can be defined by reference to this relation, and that '*all* our usages of "true" are such that a proposition expressed by the help of that word is *equivalent* to some proposition in which this relation occurs'.[1] For instance, he thinks that, in one of its meanings, '"It is true that p" means the same as "If anyone were to believe that p, then the fact which consisted in his believing that p would correspond to a fact"'.

This theory is not objectionable in itself. It avoids the mistake into which some other correspondence theories fall of trying to cash 'correspondence' in terms of resemblance or structural similarity. All the same it achieves nothing that is not achieved more clearly and simply by the semantic schema 'S is true in L if and only if p', where it is understood that the expression which is put in the place of 'S' designates a sentence of the language L which has the same meaning as the sentence which is put in the place of 'p'. In both cases, the interesting philosophical problems still remain to be tackled. We need an informative account of meaning; we need a clear specification of the forms of sentences which are used to record the empirical states of affairs which finally determine the truth or falsity of everything that we say about the world; and we need an exact analysis of the ways in which the truth or falsity of what is expressed by sentences of other types depends upon the truth or falsity of what is expressed by sentences of this basic sort. If we had satisfactory answers to all these questions, we should, I think, be left with only a stylistic motive for speaking of propositions or of any but what Moore calls non-general facts.

In a recent review of Moore's *Commonplace Book* and his *Lectures on Philosophy*, Mr. G. J. Warnock has remarked on the lack of sophistication which went with Moore's extraordinary critical acumen.[2] I think that this remark is just and that it particularly applies to most of Moore's writing on the topic of facts and propositions. The lack of sophistication is shown in his approach to the question whether these are genuine entities. He treats it as a much more straightforward question than it turns out to be. Only in the chapter on 'Beliefs and Propositions' in *Some Main*

---

[1] *Op. cit.*, p. 83.
[2] *Vide Mind*, Vol. LXXVII, no. 307, pp. 431–6.

Problems of Philosophy does he bring out the connection between the belief in the reality of propositions and the acceptance of a particular, unsatisfactory, theory of meaning and truth. It is strange that having had this insight he never again attempted to develop it.

PROPOSITIONS AND TIME

by WILLIAM AND MARTHA KNEALE

I

Almost all logicians who use the word 'proposition' agree in holding that propositions are the basic subjects of truth and falsity. But they do not all agree in the rest of what they say about the meaning of the word. There are some, for example, who would have us use it, as *propositio* was used in the Middle Ages, with the sense of 'propositional sign', that is either for a complete sentence or for a clause which signifies in the same way as a complete sentence except for not having declarative, interrogative, imperative, or optative power. It is probably safe, however, to say that most of those who favour the word follow Moore in wishing to reserve it for what is or may be expressed by use of a propositional sign, e.g. what is stated by a person uttering a declarative sentence. This usage is quite common in mathematical and legal contexts, and there are anticipations of it already in medieval philosophy. It is clear, for example, that, when John of Cornwall (or whoever wrote the *Quaestiones Exactissimae* on Aristotle's *Prior Analytics* which were wrongly attributed to Duns Scotus) said that a *propositio impossibilis* entailed everything, he was not interested in impossible sentences (whatever they might be) but in impossible theses expressible by actual sentences such as 'A man is an ass'. Sometimes a proposition in Moore's sense is said to be the meaning of a sentence, but this attempt at explanation is unfortunate for two reasons. In the first place the meaning of a sentence may reasonably be held to include its declarative, interrogative, imperative, or optative power, which is not relevant to the discussion of propositions. And secondly, even when we abstract from the functions of sentences in manifesting attitudes, we commonly think of them as patterns of words that may be uttered on various occasions to express different propositions. Thus the phrase 'It is raining here' is a type sentence such as might be considered in a textbook of English grammar, and it has a meaning which is the same as that of the French sentence *Il pleut ici*, but that meaning is not to be identified with any of the different propositions expressible in particular utterances of the sentence. If we overlook the distinction, like persons who identify propositions with sentences we shall be committed to saying that propositions may change their truth-values not only from time to time (which some philosophers find acceptable) but also from place to place and even from mouth to mouth. For when Tom and Dick both say 'I am hungry' at the same time and in approximately the same place, their statements may still have different truth-values.

In what follows we shall use the word 'proposition' as we think it was used by Moore, and say nothing further about rival accounts of what may be true or false, but try to deal with a special form of the problem of propositional identity. The general difficulty of determining what is to count as one and the same proposition has been presented by some critics as a serious objection to Moore's view, but it is one which should interest all friends of propositions even if they are firmly convinced of the hopelessness of giving any satisfactory account of thought and language without reference to those abstract entities. It can be formulated briefly as follows.

If propositions are to be useful for explanation of the direction of our thought on objects and of the way in which we make communications by utterance of sentences, it seems plausible to say that they must be independent not only of all actual utterances but also of all possible utterances. In particular, talk of a proposition can scarcely be equated with talk of all the utterances there might be of a certain kind, since it will not be possible to specify the relevant kind without a new reference to the proposition. No doubt impossible propositions such as we mentioned in our first paragraph must be allowed to be in some sense creatures of language, but it seems natural to say of other propositions that they are objective possibilities, and among objective possibilities the simplest may be thought to be an individual's having a certain character. In the artificial language of *Principia Mathematica* such a basic possibility is supposed to be represented by a complex sign of the form '$F(X)$' where 'X' is a logically proper name, that is to say a sign whose sole contribution to the meaning of the complex in which it occurs is its denotation of an individual. But as Russell himself argues, ordinary proper names such as 'Socrates' are never logically proper in his sense, because each has a connotation of some sort without any sure guarantee of a denotation. How, then, can we ever succeed in expressing a basic proposition? We may, it is true, be able to select an individual as subject of discourse by use of a definite description such as 'the Greek philosopher who first sought definitions of the virtues', but only at the expense of introducing a new complication. For though Russell was mistaken in the pattern of translation he offered for sentences containing definite descriptions, he was right in thinking that such sentences cannot be used to express propositions of the kind considered basic. This is clear enough from the simple consideration that replacement of one definite description by another with the same denotation is not enough to preserve the sense of the whole sentence in which the first occurred. To say 'The Greek philosopher who first sought definitions of the virtues was accused of corrupting the youth' is certainly not the same as to say 'The Greek philosopher who was accused of corrupting the youth was accused of corrupting the youth', though the subject phrase of the first sentence denotes the same individual as the subject phrase of the second. In practice Russell falls back on use of a demonstrative or a personal pronoun as grammatical subject when he wishes to express a proposition that he can plausibly call basic. But there is no place in his original scheme for such token-reflexive signs, which may designate different things on different occasions of utterance. And when we examine carefully the way in which they work, we find that an utterance of such a sentence as 'I am hungry' seems to be directly about itself and only indirectly about its speaker inasmuch as it signifies that it comes from a person who is hungry. That, of course, is why Reichenbach called it token-reflexive. If, however, his analysis is right, the singular proposition which such an utterance expresses can never be expressed again by any other utterance, though general propositions which are very closely related to that singular proposition may no doubt be expressed at any time by mention of the original utterance in sentences involving definite descriptions.

This conclusion is not obviously absurd, but it is certainly surprising. Our purpose is to investigate it further with special reference to a temporal example that interested Moore.

II

In the year 1926 or thereabouts Moore wrote several short notes on the meaning of the present tense.[1] His favourite example is the sentence '*A* is happening', where '*A*', it seems, may be either an abbreviation of a definite description such as 'the battle of Arma-

---

[1] G. E. Moore, *The Commonplace Book*, pp. 87–9, 97–101.

geddon' or an abbreviation of an indefinite description such as 'an awful attack'. In the first paper he says that he thinks a use of the sentence cannot *assert* that A is simultaneous with that use. But his reason for making this remark seems to be no more than a feeling that it is strange to speak of an assertion about a particular (in this case a particular use of his sentence) where there is no explicit mention of that particular. For he says in the same paragraph that a use of his sentence *implies* that A is simultaneous with that use, and goes on to declare several times that it cannot be a correct expression of anything true unless A is simultaneous with that use. From this it seems to follow that each distinct use of the sentence expresses a proposition that A is simultaneous with that use, and there can be no doubt that Moore accepts this conclusion, since he ends his first note by saying that each one expresses a different proposition:

'It seems at first sight obvious that, if you have a number of judgements with the same content, if one is true the rest must be. But if you take a set of judgements with regard to a given event A, either that it is happening, or that it is past, or that it is future, some of each set will be true and some false, which are true and which false depending on the time when the judgement is made. It seems a sufficient answer to say that a judgement "A is happening" made at one time never has the same content as the judgement "A is happening" made at another.'

A similar contention is to be found in a paper on Propositions and Facts which Moore wrote about the same time for a symposium with F. P. Ramsey:

'If I say twice over "Caesar was murdered" the proposition which I express on each occasion is a different one.'[1]

It is easy to see why Moore said what he did, but it should be noticed nevertheless that there is something odd in his conclusion. Although utterances of the sentence 'It is raining' would naturally be taken to express different propositions if they were made on different days or so far apart on the same day that the second might have been supplemented by 'still' or 'again', two closely consecutive utterances would ordinarily be taken to express the same proposition. If this were not so, we could not speak, as we do, of

[1] *Philosophical Papers*, p. 71.

one man's confirming another man's statement or answering another's question about the weather. For when one man asks 'Is it raining?' and another says 'Yes, it is', the second must be supposed to assert the proposition about which the first manifested curiosity. Similarly when a modern historian says 'Caesar was murdered', he may be said to adopt as his own the account of Caesar's death which Suetonius gave by use of the Latin perfect passive *transfossus est*. Although it is often said that each generation must rewrite the history of the past for its own benefit, this dictum is certainly not to be understood as implying that it is impossible for an historian to repeat any statement of a predecessor, and Moore's common sense was so strong that he would never have maintained such an absurdity. How then are we to reconcile what he wrote with what we all believe about the possibility of expressing the same proposition on different occasions by repetition of a sentence in which the tense is to be taken seriously?

There cannot be raining which does not last for a period, and to say that it is raining is, no doubt, to say that the time of speech falls within such a period. But when we trouble to say that it is raining we are not ordinarily interested in the time of speech as opposed to other moments falling within a small interval of that time, and we are therefore content to ignore any differences there may be between propositions expressible by utterances of 'It is raining' within that interval. Similarly when we consider how Caesar died, we are interested primarily in the course of events at a time before our consideration, rather than in the relation of those events to the speech or writing of various historians; for we assume already that, however Caesar died, he died before the work of all historians who profess to record his death. And so we are content to ignore any differences there may be between propositions expressible by utterances of 'Caesar was murdered' after the time we suppose him to have died. In either case, however, it is possible to conceive circumstances in which we should insist on interpreting a tensed utterance strictly as expressing a proposition different from any expressible by another utterance of the same sentence. Thus after a long drought the first cry of 'It's raining' may have the precise sense of 'It is raining even as I speak'. And in the same way an utterance of *Caesar interfectus est* by one conspirator to another immediately after the stabbing in the senate house would be understood in the sense of '*Now* it's done!', something not to be conveyed by the reports of historians in later ages. For the simple preterite of the English 'Caesar was murdered' it is rather more difficult to find a use that involves special attention to the moment of speaking, but there is a narrowing of attention when we say 'Caesar was murdered just two thousand and twelve years ago', and at the limit of precision in the specification of the interval since the murder what we state by utterance of such a sentence will be a proposition that cannot be stated either truly or falsely by any other utterance of the same sentence.

We should not be surprised by these facts; for it is a general rule that men consider only what is relevant to their present interests when they decide whether two utterances express the same proposition or, as we often put it more loosely, come to the same thing. There are, of course, some sentences so different that they can never be used to express the same proposition, but in other cases differences of various kinds may be ignored when they are irrelevant to our purposes. So long as Sir Walter Scott did not acknowledge his authorship of *Waverley* talk which referred to him by name was different in a very important way from talk which referred to him as the author of *Waverley*, and in certain contexts we must still preserve the distinction with care. In other contexts, however, substitution of 'the author of *Waverley*' for 'Scott' may be thought no more than a stylistic variation which leaves the gist of the remark unaltered. Here the utterances which we compare differ only in using different designations for the same individual, but we proceed in the same way when we have to do with utterances that differ in using different but connected predicates. Thus in geometry the statement that a certain triangle is equilateral must be distinguished carefully from the statement that it is equiangular, but in engineering such statements about triangular frames may be treated as equivalent in a strong sense, i.e. as expressing the same proposition, because the difference between them has no importance for practice. Nor is this the end of the complications to be found in the way men talk of propositions. To logicians who are interested in logical relations for their own sake, it seems clear that sentences which differ only in respect of transformations such as double negation may nevertheless be used to express distinguishable propositions. But to other scientists, including geometers and number theorists, it never occurs to make such a distinction during their professional hours, because the differences which interest logicians have no consequences for their own study. When Moore said that different propositions were

H*

expressed by all the different utterances of 'Caesar was murdered',
he was trying to make the finest possible discrimination among
temporal propositions. This is a reasonable ambition for a philosopher, since the ignoring of distinctions which prove over-subtle
for various parts of practical life can safely be left to ordinary
human instinct. But it should be noticed that when carried out in
full, the programme of maximum discrimination leads beyond the
distinction of objective possibilities which we mentioned at the
beginning of this paper. The propositions which we express by
different utterances of 'Caesar was murdered' are distinguishable
because each may properly be said to be about the utterance that
expresses it. But we have seen that the propositions distinguished
by mathematicians and logicians for the special purposes of their
studies may not all be states of affairs distinguishable from each
other. Or to put the matter in another way, formulae which
mathematicians and logicians treat as expressions of different
propositions may not have separable truth conditions. Indeed it is
only by drawing a distinction between propositions and possible
states of affairs that we can allow for the varieties of necessary and
impossible propositions. For in a theory of propositions dominated
exclusively by the notion of truth-conditions there is just one
truism expressed by all statements of necessary truth and nothing
at all expressed by the negations of such statements. If we find this
paradoxical, the reason must be that we do not think of utterances
as propounding the same proposition unless they seem to us to
express the same situation in the same way, though perhaps with
different words. Obviously the possibility of our saying anything
at all with meaning depends on our ability to conceive various
alternative states of affairs. Without this there could be no language and no superstructure of *a priori* science. But even where
there is no distinction of truth-conditions for two utterances there
may nevertheless be a distinction of meaning because they are
utterances of complex signs formed in different ways. Thus an
English speaker who says '*ABC* is an equilateral triangle' conveys
something different from what he might have conveyed by saying
'*ABC* is an equiangular triangle', because the words 'equilateral'
and 'equiangular' may have different ranges of application outside
the context of talk about triangles. On the other hand he conveys
the same as a German speaker would convey by saying *ABC ist ein
gleichseitiges Dreieck*, because his sentence is built on the same
semantic plan though all his words are different. Admittedly the

account of propositions to which we are led by these reflections will be more complicated than others which have been offered, but we cannot do justice to our ordinary notion of identity in statements, beliefs, wishes, suggestions, etc. if we ignore either (*a*) the differences there may be between utterances of the same sentence on different occasions or (*b*) the differences there may be between utterances that have the same truth-condition but use different semantic structures.

III

Although Moore insisted on the token-reflexive character of tenses some twenty years before Reichenbach invented a convenient terminology for talking about it, he did not (as we might perhaps expect) go on to say that the proposition expressed by utterance of a tensed sentence such as 'A is happening' could never be expressed again in any way. On the contrary, considering the case where the proposition is true, he wrote in his notebook:

'The fact expressed . . . could theoretically be expressed by an expression such that that expression could be truly used if the use of the expression was not simultaneous with the fact in question. No such expression is at our command in English. But suppose we agree to use the expression "is timelessly" in such a way that the expression "*A* is timelessly *P*" can be truly said where *A*'s possession of *P* is not simultaneous with the use of the expression. We can then say that the fact . . . is a fact of the form "*A* is timelessly simultaneous with *C*" where *C* is an event.'

It should be noticed that in saying that the fact expressed by an utterance of 'A is happening' could theoretically be expressed again by utterance of a new untensed sentence he is no longer demanding the finest possible discrimination of propositions but siding for the moment with the vulgar. For obviously the nearest we could get to expressing the original proposition again in the conditions Moore has indicated would be to replace '*C*' in his formula by some designation of the original utterance such as 'Moore's production of his example of the present tense'. And although the new utterance which arose in this way might be good enough for many practical purposes, it would not satisfy the high standards Moore set up a few pages earlier, since it would differ from the original in somewhat the same way as our saying 'The author of *Principia Ethica* read many novels when he was not philosophizing' would differ from Moore's saying 'I read many novels when I was not philosophizing'. Perhaps it is also worth noticing that in the passage quoted Moore has slipped into talking of a *fact* as though it were something with which an utterance might be simultaneous. This is not a usage he would normally approve. But it is interesting to go on to ask whether even by the looser standards of practical life it would be possible to replace all token-reflexive talk of past, present, and future with 'timeless' statements of temporal relations between events. Probably Moore had McTaggart's work in mind when he wrote. Many years later it was still a favourite topic of reflection for him, not because he had any inclination to accept McTaggart's metaphysics, but because he found it interesting to consider why a person so intelligent said what he did.

The example of Chinese is enough to show that men can say all they want to say without tensed verbs. But this is not enough to answer our question. For Chinese, like other languages, has token-reflexive words for indicating times, and it is evident that all we now express by means of tenses could be expressed equally well by relational signs such as 'before' and 'after' provided only there were available a token-reflexive sign that could be used, as 'this expression' may be used in English, for the purpose of referring to one of its own instances. Instead of 'Caesar was murdered' we might say, for example, 'Some fellow kill Caesar before this utterance'. Our question then reduces to this: 'Could there be an equally good pidgin without the phase "this utterance" or any other phrase that would allow for its introduction?'

Following the suggestion of Moore, we might relate all events temporally to other events, including acts of speech, without labelling any as past, present, or future, but so that they held together in a tight web. Or better still, we might organize our speech in such a way as to place them all within a single chronological scheme so that their temporal relations could be read off from a comparison of their dates. This is the programme suggested by some logicians who recognize the impossibility of applying their science directly to the sentences of ordinary language but dislike talk of propositions and hope to avoid it by showing how token-reflexive utterances can be translated into formulae which resemble those of mathematics in not being subject to changes of truth-value from one use to another. Such formulae have been described by Quine as eternal sentences,[1] and the name is appropriate for a reason he does not consider. To try to describe the world in this way is to think of oneself as Boethius thought of God when he said in the last chapter of his book *De Consolatione Philosophiae* that the eternal creator sees all temporal parts of his creation at once much as an observer on a hilltop may see men at various places on a road which runs from left to right across the plain below him. Because he is not in the world, such a god cannot talk to himself of its contents by means of token-reflexive utterances, whose working depends essentially upon their position in the whole. In short, his eternal, i.e. timeless, monologues must consist solely of eternal sentences. More recently the God's eye view of nature has been adopted by some idealist philosophers and by some theoretical physicists who take very seriously Minkowski's suggestion that the universe should be considered as a four-dimensional continuum. Einstein himself, for example, has published a statement to this effect:

'The world of events can be described dynamically by a picture changing in time and thrown onto the background of the three-dimensional space. But it can be described also by a static picture thrown onto the background of the four-dimensional time-space continuum. From the point of view of classical physics the two pictures, the dynamic and the static, are equivalent. But from the point of view of the relativity theory the static picture is the more convenient and the more objective.'[2]

It is therefore not surprising that a philosopher who is much impressed by such remarks should argue for the elimination of tenses from philosophical discourse on the ground that use of them fosters the illusion of something absolute in our anthropocentric, perspectival distinction of past, present, and future and so makes it more difficult to see the world *sub specie aeternitatis*.[3]

After quoting Moore's remarks on the possibility of introducing a tenseless idiom to express what is expressed in ordinary English by an utterance of '*A* is happening' we noticed that '*A* is

[1] W. V. Quine, *Word and Object* (Cambridge: M.I.T. Press, 1960), p. 193.

[2] A. Einstein and L. Infold, *The Evolution of Physics* (New York: Simon and Schuster, 1938), p. 220.

[3] J. J. C. Smart, *Philosophy and Scientific Realism* (London: Routledge & Kegan Paul, 1963), pp. 132–142.

timelessly simultaneous with C' could be no more than an approximation in sense to the original, even if 'C' was supposed to be a designation of the original. Let us now suppose that instead of an utterance of 'A is happening' we take for our example an utterance of 'A is timelessly simultaneous with this utterance', where 'this utterance' is supposed to refer to the very utterance we take for our example or, more narrowly, to its last two words. This is not an instance of the form of words Moore considered but a parallel production in a tenseless idiom. If, however, we ask whether it has the peculiarity which Moore supposed to go with use of that idiom, we see immediately that it does not. For it must be wrong to assume that the proposition which it expresses is expressed also by all other utterances of the same sentence. In order to produce an utterance satisfying that condition we must avoid use of any token-reflexive phrase. Now it may be that in place of 'this utterance' we can use some designation, say 'D', which does in fact single out the original utterance but by a method independent of its own occurrence in an utterance. If so every utterance of the sentence 'A is timelessly simultaneous with D' will express the same proposition and that proposition will be true if and only if a true proposition is expressed by our original utterance of 'A is timelessly simultaneous with this utterance'. But we are not entitled on that account to say that the proposition expressible by utterances of this new sentence is the same as that expressed by our original utterance. On the contrary, it is clear that, unlike our original utterance, utterances of the new sentence give no absolute indication of the time of A. Just because the sentence is eternal in Quine's sense, it might have been used to express a true proposition even before the occurrence of D. If in practice we assume that any utterance of the eternal sentence must be later than D, that is only because of beliefs we hold about the working of human minds. Furthermore to assume on hearing an utterance of the new sentence that D was earlier than that utterance would be to use 'that utterance' as a token-reflexive sign, at least in our thinking.

It may perhaps be thought curious to say that an utterance of 'A is timelessly simultaneous with this utterance' would give an *absolute* indication of time, since sentences of that kind have been recommended for use as paraphrases of tensed statements on the ground that they reveal in a clear way the relativity of our distinction of past, present, and future. What we have in mind can best be explained by consideration of what is involved in establishment of a single chronological scheme of the kind favoured by the friends of eternal sentences. Instead of treating all events alike, we give primacy of honour to some one event of great importance (say the foundation of Rome, the birth of Christ, or the flight of Mohammed from Mecca to Medina) and date all other events, including the events of our own lives, by reference to it. The event which we take as origin in the mathematical sense must of course be one which we believe to have occurred at some determinate interval before our establishment of the system, and the system will remain fully usable, i.e. allow for the dating of further events, only so long as we are able to say at any moment what time has elapsed since the event chosen as origin, or in other words what the date is in the system at any moment when we want to use the system. It is conceivable, of course, that we should be able to make some use of the chronological system of an extinct civilization even when we were unable to connect the system precisely with our own, but even then we should at least assume that the event which served as origin for the old system and most of the other events recorded in it were earlier than the time of our investigation. If for the sake of a thought-experiment we try to go even farther and suppose a chronological system in which it can never be possible to give any indication of the date of our own activity, we find that we have ceased to think of the events in the system as historical rather than fictional. For to treat an event as historical is precisely to assume that it is past, present, or future, even if we cannot at the moment tell which. It seems clear therefore that in serious use of a chronological system there must be a possibility of dating the time of use within the system, and that a tenseless pidgin without 'this utterance' or some equivalent phrase would allow only for relative dating and so not be a full language. In short, tenses may be dispensable, but what we express in ordinary English by use of tenses is essential to the concept of time and not something that might conceivably be excised in the interests of relativity theory or 'sentence' logic.

IV

It appears, then, that Moore was right when he said that, for certain purposes at least, different utterances of the sentence '*A* is happening' must be held to express different propositions but wrong when he said, or implied, that for all purposes a single utterance of the token-reflexive sentence could be held to express the same proposition as might be expressed at any time by use of an eternal sentence. And from these two conclusions there follows a third, namely that at least for certain purposes each utterance of the sentence '*A* is happening' must be held to express a proposition expressible by no other utterance whatsoever. For if there is some purpose for which the proposition expressed by a single utterance is not expressible by use of an eternal sentence, *a fortiori* there will be some purpose for which that proposition is not expressible by utterance of another token-reflexive sentence. Thus a man does not necessarily repeat himself if he says first '*A* is happening' and then a moment later '*A* was happening when I said "*A* is happening"'.

These considerations about the identity of propositions can be used for solution of a problem much discussed by medieval philosophers. In his *Sentences* Peter Lombard declared that what the prophets proclaimed in the words 'Christ will be born' is affirmed by Christians in the words 'Christ has been born'. This thesis seems to be connected with a God's eye view of history according to which our need to use tenses arises solely from our location inside the sequence of events, but it was rejected by many later theologians, including St Thomas Aquinas, on the ground that it presupposed the doctrine 'Once true, always true' which did not hold for propositions in their sense, i.e. sentences.[1] Applying our principles, we must distinguish various degrees of strictness with which men may speak of affirming the same proposition.

1. Peter Lombard holds in effect that the doctrine in which a Christian agrees with an Old Testament prophet is the thesis that Christ's birth is (timelessly) real, i.e. has a place in the order of events. In further explanation of his position he might say that the different tenses used by the prophet and the Christian serve only to *show* their different temporal relations to the event of which they speak.

2. There is something strange, however, in saying that an utterance in the perfect tense can express the same proposition as an utterance in the future tense, even when it is clear that they are made at different times, and so it may perhaps be suggested that the proper way for a modern Christian to confirm what a prophet proclaimed is to say 'Christ has indeed to be born after the

[1] W. and M. Kneale, *The Development of Logic* (Oxford: The Clarendon Press, 1962), pp. 238–41.

prophet's utterance of the sentence "Christ will be born"'. Anyone who takes this line holds in effect that the doctrine in which the Christian and the prophet agree is the thesis that Christ's birth comes (timelessly) after the prophet's utterance. If questioned, he may say that the difference of the Christian's phraseology from that of the prophet is necessary because of the difference of his relation to the prophet's utterance which both take as a point of reference, and he may add that the additional complexity of the Christian's utterance serves to *show* something with which the prophet was not concerned at all, namely the relation of the Christian's utterance to the other two events under consideration.

3. Some persons may perhaps object that even the form of words considered in the last paragraph cannot properly be said to express exactly the same proposition as a prophet expressed by saying 'Christ will be born', and they may go on to argue that the proposition expressed by the utterance of the prophet could only be expressed again by a similar utterance in the future tense at some time before the birth of Christ. Anyone who takes this line sets up a stricter requirement for the identity of propositions expressed, and he will probably find no need for the notion of *showing* that we have attributed to the holders of the two first views.

4. In certain circumstances we may find ourselves disposed to insist upon a requirement for identity which is still stricter since it does not allow for the possibility of expressing again at any time the proposition expressed by use of a token-reflexive sentence. This was the position towards which Moore was attracted when he said that he expressed a different proposition by each utterance of the sentence 'Caesar was murdered'.

All these different views seem to us defensible. That is to say, we think that for each of the four different standards of propositional identity there are circumstances in which it might reasonably be adopted, and that when this relativity of usage has been accepted there is no further problem about which we need be seriously worried. If some philosophers are puzzled a little by talk of propositions that become inexpressible, their mystification should disappear when they realize that such propositions do not become inaccessible to thought but may on the contrary be discussed as often as men choose. For while it may be impossible to *express* again precisely that proposition which Moore expressed when he said for the first time 'Caesar was murdered', it is easy to *designate* it. In fact we have just done so.

MOORE AND ANALYSIS[1]

by GORDON GREIG

In 1942 in his article 'Moore's Notion of Analysis'[2] Langford remarked that Moore had not attempted to apply his method of analysis to the notion of analysis itself, and he believed that Moore had not 'attempted to examine systematically the question what relation it is that must hold between an analysandum and an analysans in order that the latter should correctly analyse the former'.[3] Since that date, however, the situation has radically altered; with the publication of the reply to Langford,[4] the article 'Russell's "Theory of Descriptions"',[5] the *Commonplace Book*,[6] and, most importantly, the *Lectures on Philosophy*,[7] we are now in a very much better position to state Moore's views as to the nature of analysis. Having said this, I must immediately add a qualification. Strictly it *might* be more correct to say that we are now in a very much better position to comment on Moore's use of the *word* 'analysis'; certainly, there is some evidence to suggest that Moore would have preferred this amended description. For example, when Langford said[8] that he wished to 'induce Professor Moore to state more explicitly his own position regarding the nature of analysis' Moore replied 'I think that what Mr Langford must primarily want is a statement as to how I myself have intended to use, and, so far as I know, actually used, the word "analysis". Other people may have used it in different senses, but I do not

---

[1] This essay is intended as little more than a series of remarks; despairing of producing anything like an adequate account of Moore's views on the nature of analysis within the scope of a single article, I have elected to discuss only a limited number of topics suggested by Moore's most lately published writings on analysis.

[2] *The Philosophy of G. E. Moore*, The Library of Living Philosophers, Vol. IV (ed. P. A. Schilpp), pp. 321–42, 1942.

[3] *Ibid.*, p. 323.

[4] *Ibid.*, p. 660–7.

[5] *The Philosophy of Bertrand Russell*, The Library of Living Philosophers, Vol. V (ed. P. A. Schilpp), pp. 177–225, 1944.

[6] *Commonplace Book 1919–1953* (ed. Casimir Lewy), 1962.

[7] *Lectures on Philosophy* (ed. Casimir Lewy), 1966.

[8] *The Philosophy of G. E. Moore*, p. 323.

think that he wants me to state my position with regard to what they may have meant by it'.[1]

I wish initially to attempt to elucidate the implications of Moore's somewhat cryptic reply. Is Moore here intending to suggest that it may be improper to speak of (the nature of) analysis and only proper to speak of particular uses of the word 'analysis'? Is this what Langford *'must'* have wanted, because, logically, he could not have wanted what he could not have? (*I* am not suggesting that, logically, one cannot want what one cannot have—I am merely suggesting that Moore might have thought this.) The suggestion that questions concerning the real nature of analysis are bogus and that the only proper questions are questions concerning 'analysis' gains support from the following. 'Analysis', as Moore and others have used the term, is a technical innovation of philosophers; it is not of 'the very type of an unambiguous expression, the meaning of which we all understand'.[2] This being so, one is at liberty, within limits, to confer a meaning on, give a sense to, the word, and different people may confer differently with the result that there is no one ordinary, established, correct use for the word 'analysis'. This in turn being so, one cannot properly speak of *the* correct (established etc.) use of the word 'analysis', and if *this* is so, one cannot then speak of analysis, for to speak of analysis, to say what it is, just is to speak of how the word 'analysis' is correctly or properly used. (As will become apparent very shortly, I think that this last premise should be questioned, whether or not it is questionable.) One should, therefore, confine one's self to autobiographical remarks merely stating, hopefully within consistency confines, that one has in fact conferred such or such a sense upon the word 'analysis', implying that others are at liberty, logic permitting, to indulge their linguistic predilections in parallel fashion.

If Moore's remarks in reply to Langford were to be interpreted in this way, i.e. in such a way that the above argument would support his view, then its consequences for my study would be considerable. Owing to its putatively programatic character we should, I suppose, take it as applying to the interpretation of his later work on analysis and, retroactively, to his *Lectures on Philosophy*. This then would mean that Moore, in the sources I cited,

[1] *The Philosophy of G. E. Moore*, p. 660.
[2] *Contemporary British Philosophy* (2nd Series) (ed. Muirhead), 1925, 'A Defence of Common Sense', p. 198.

would be giving us no more than autobiographical comments on how *he* used the word 'analysis'—it would give us no doctrine as to the correct use of 'analysis', nor therefore (?) any theory as to the nature of analysis.

I do not, however, wish to accept this line of argument and the accompanying suggestion of triviality. Moore's reply to Langford is, I think, slightly disingenuous; he seems to suggest that rather than set himself to answer a profound question concerning 'the nature of analysis', he will assume the more modest task of commenting merely upon his own use of the word 'analysis'. As a matter of fact, in commenting upon his own use of the word 'analysis' he comments also on that of others; further, in his comments on his own use and that of others, he says that both they, and possibly he himself, have used the word 'analysis' *improperly*. Thus Moore writes: 'Mr Langford seems to imply (p. 336) that he thinks that to make the statement: " '*X* is a small *Y*' means what is meant by '*X* is a *Y* and is smaller than most *Y*'s' ", could properly be called giving an analysis of the verbal expression "*X* is a small *Y*". I do not think it could. But I wish to make it plain that I never intended so to use the word "analysis", that by making a statement of this sort you would be *giving an analysis* at all. I think many philosophers (e.g. Mr W. E. Johnson) have supposed that by making this statement you would be giving an analysis, not indeed of the verbal expression "*X* is a small *Y*", but of the *concept* "is a small *Y*". And I may, perhaps (I do not know), sometimes have talked as if, by making a statement of this sort you were giving an analysis of some *concept* expressed by the verbal expression which appears between inverted commas: as if, e.g. by saying " '*X* is a brother' means the same as '*X* is male and is a sibling'", I were giving an analysis of the *concept* "being a brother". But, if I have done so, it was merely through a confusion, which I shared with others, as to what you are doing when you make such a statement; had I seen what you *are* doing, I should never have called making such a statement "giving an analysis".'[1]

The situation in brief is this. Langford had proposed what he called 'two views as to the nature of analysis'.[2] For this last expression Moore prefers to substitute 'two different ways in which the word "analysis" might be used'.[3] The ensuing discussion makes

---

[1] *The Philosophy of G. E. Moore*, pp. 661–2.
[2] *Ibid.*, p. 323.   [3] *Ibid.*, p. 661.

Moore's motive evident. He does not regard these 'views' as competing rival accounts of the true nature of analysis because in stating these views Langford, in Moore's opinion, uses the term 'analysis' in two completely distinct and different senses, and seems by implication, to be unaware that these are different senses. According to Moore, we can speak of the analysis either of a verbal expression (or sentence) or, alternatively, of a concept (or proposition), but the corresponding activities of 'giving an analysis' are utterly different. There is a correct use, or more strictly, a not incorrect use of the word 'analysis' according to which we can speak of the analysis of a verbal expression, and there is another quite distinct use of 'analysis' according to which we can speak of the analysis of a concept (or proposition). Moore makes it unambiguously clear what *he* means by the analysis of a verbal expression—'To take an example from Mr Langford: Consider the verbal expression "*x* is a small *y*". I should say that you could quite properly be said to be analysing this expression if you said of it: "It contains the letter '*x*', the word 'is', the word 'a', the word 'small', and the letter '*y*'; and it begins with '*x*', 'is' comes next to it, then 'a', then 'small', and then '*y*'." It seems to me that nothing but making some such statement as this could properly be called "giving an analysis of a verbal expression". And I, when I talked of "giving an analysis", have never meant anything at all like this.'[1]

Moore, therefore, is making the following claims: (1) that we may speak, not incorrectly, of giving an *analysis* either of a concept (or proposition) or of a word (or verbal expression or sentence), (2) that the activities of giving such analyses are utterly distinct, (3) that he has been concerned solely with the former (analysis of concept or proposition), and (4) that it is a definite mistake to say that to give a (philosophical) analysis[2] is to give an analysis of a verbal expression. Of these claims (3) alone is merely autobiographical, hence my claim that Moore's comment is slightly disingenuous. From the foregoing quotations we can *at least* conclude that Moore is *laying down some of the conditions which must, in his view, be satisfied in order that one could correctly be said to be* 'giving an analysis' (A), and how this could differ from *giving a list of some of the necessary conditions for the giving of an analysis* (B),

---

[1] *The Philosophy of G. E. Moore*, p. 661.
[2] *Ibid.*, p. 662. Cp. *The Philosophy of Bertrand Russell*, pp. 199–200, and also *Lectures on Philosophy*, pp. 157–8.

is a matter for conjecture; and how this last could differ from *supplying some one partial account as to the nature of analysis* (C), is a further matter for conjecture.

It seems to me that in this context (B) and (C) are merely unimportant stylistic variants. (B) and (C) are not equivalent, for we may, of course, speak of the nature of analysis and not speak specifically concerning what conditions must necessarily be satisfied for any statement to be a statement of analysis; however, if one does speak of those conditions (or rather, some of them) that must be satisfied for any statement to be a statement of analysis, then, perforce, one is giving some partial account of analysis—trivially one is saying that the nature of analysis is such that if you want to produce a statement which is properly a statement of analysis, then necessarily etc. . . . (B), therefore, in my view implies (C) and the main question is as to whether (A) implies (B); if (A) implies (B) and therefore (C) then the depressing implications of Moore's original remark[1] need not be taken too seriously and we can attend to those things he says concerning 'analysis' and therefore the nature of analysis, and disregard what he says about what he says (or, perhaps more correctly, disregard what he implies about what he says).

There are in fact three main questions here: (1) did Moore think that A-type talk was importantly different from B-type talk, (2) did he intend deliberately to exclude B-type talk by indulging in A-type talk, and (3) is A-type talk really different from B-type talk? With regard to (1) it is alleged by some commentators, for example A. R. White,[2] that there is ample evidence that Moore did generally regard A-type talk as being radically different from B-type talk. Perhaps the quotation that most explicitly points in this direction is the following: 'Of course, a man may be using a sentence perfectly correctly, even when what he means by it is *false*, either because he is lying or because he is making a mistake; and, similarly, a man may be using a sentence in such a way that what he means by it is *true*, even when he is not using it correctly, as, for instance, when he uses the wrong word for what he means, by a slip or because he has made a mistake as to what the correct usage is. Thus using a sentence *correctly*—in the sense explained[3] —and using it in such a way that what you mean by it is *true*, are

---

[1] *The Philosophy of G. E. Moore*, p. 660.
[2] *G. E. Moore: A Critical Exposition* (Basil Blackwell & Mott, 1958), pp. 8–9.
[3] i.e. 'in accordance with the best English usage'.

two things which are completely logically independent of one another: either may occur without the other.'[1]

The problem however is more complex than White seems to imply and I shall deal with it in greater detail later. For the present, and for the sake of convenience, let us take as simpler analogues of (A) and (B), (D) and (E), where (D) is 'it is correct to say "P"', and (E) is 'it is correct to say that P' (where we might substitute for 'P' in (D) 'an analysis has been given', and for 'P' in (E) 'an analysis has been given'). As I shall argue later, Moore is much concerned with the distinction between D-type and E-type talk and what implications such a distinction would have for any adequate account as to the nature of analysis, and he became increasingly more concerned when, after 1942, he devoted more attention to talk about analysis (or 'analysis'). In brief, Moore would argue that there is a not incorrect use (let us call it use (i)) of the sentence (D) according to which the sentence (D) could be used to make a claim concerning the use of a particular expression (or sentence) 'P', in a particular language (where, as he puts it, in 1944,[2] we should be using 'P' merely as a name for itself'). In using the sentence (D) in this sense we would mention 'P' whereas in using the sentence (E) in *any* correct use of (E) we would never mention 'P' but use 'P'.

When the use of the *sentences* (D) and (E) differ as described, Moore would say of the resulting propositions (D) and (E) that (D) never could entail (E), nor (E) entail (D).[3] It would however be over-hasty to conclude on these grounds alone that Moore would reject the assimilation of D-type and E-type talk, for as yet we lack a criterion for what it is to be committed to either type of talk. As Moore notes[4] the sentence '(D)' may be used in another way which is as correct as that already described. We may use '(D)' in such a way (let us call this use (ii)) that '(D)' expresses what '(E)' expresses; that is, 'it is correct to say "P"' may be synonymous with 'it is correct to say that P'. Thus we cannot infer merely from the fact that Moore employs a D (or an A)-type idiom that he would not equally and as readily employ an E (or a B)-type idiom. In his reply to Langford Moore moves easily from the

---

[1] *The Philosophy of G. E. Moore*, p. 548.
[2] 'Russell's "Theory of Descriptions",' *The Philosophy of Bertrand Russell*, p. 198.
[3] Cp. *Commonplace Book*, p. 312.
[4] 'Russell's "Theory of Descriptions",' *The Philosophy of Bertrand Russell*, p. 198.

idiom of 'the conditions for *calling* something "an analysis"' to the idiom of 'something's being an analysis', without adducing any argument, on the presumption that no logical hiatus would be involved nor any essential transitional step omitted.[1]

This immediately gives us an answer to question (2) posed above: we cannot assume merely because Moore is talking about what may properly be called 'analysis' that he is not talking about the conditions under which something is an analysis. In fact we may assume the converse and argue as follows: if Moore speaks indifferently of analysis and of 'analysis', then when he speaks of 'analysis' he must be indulging in D-type talk as a permitted variant of E-type talk; that is, he is using a D-type sentence, the use of which is analogous to our use (ii) and not to our use (i).

Summarizing my conclusions to this point: I think we may regard Moore, in his reply to Langford and in the other sources cited, as having in part at least talked of analysis and not as having commented merely on his own putatively idiosyncratic use or uses of the word 'analysis'. Some uses proposed or employed by others certainly imply a mistaken conception of analysis. It would be a definite mistake ('. . . a *confusion* which I shared with others . . .')[2] to endorse Langford's proposal and to say that to give a (philosophical) analysis is to give an analysis of a verbal expression. Others are free to use the expression 'analysis of a verbal expression' but are not free to use it as a synonym for the expression 'analysis of a concept (or proposition)'. Stating the import of this in the material mode we could say that for Moore, and in his view for others, philosophical analysis necessarily is the analysis of concepts or propositions—and this is as explicit a statement about the nature of analysis as any could be. My interpretation of the force of Moore's original remark[3] comes to this: he is neither proposing *systematically* to substitute the formal mode of speech for the material mode, nor is he implying that since the word 'analysis' is a philosophers' innovation, idiosyncratic rules for its use may be generated by individual philosophers; rather he is listing some of the necessary conditions that must be satisfied for a statement to be a statement of analysis. Others may attempt to produce rival sets of conditions (both necessary and sufficient) with the proviso that their sets of necessary conditions may not be inconsistent with Moore's own. If, for example, they do not regard

---

[1] *The Philosophy of G. E. Moore*, p. 662.
[2] *Ibid.*   [3] *Ibid.*, p. 660.

his necessary condition that the *analysandum* and the *analysans* be a concept or proposition as necessary, then they are mistaken.[1] They are either using the word 'analysis' in some totally different sense, or are failing to see that what is a necessary condition is a necessary condition. He is comparatively modest in that he does not propose to list *all* the necessary and sufficient conditions for a statement to be a statement of analysis, let alone for a statement to be a true, correct statement of analysis (in fact both in his reply to Langford[2] and in 'Russell's "Theory of Descriptions"'[3] he despairs of producing such a list, largely because of the so-called Paradox of Analysis). Others presumably may add to the list of necessary conditions and revise the list of the sufficient, and to this extent Moore has given merely a partial account of what he takes to be the nature of analysis.

Questions (1) and (2) remain as yet unanswered. In my review of what Moore has to say as to the nature of analysis and in my criticism of it, I shall attempt answers to these questions. Undoubtedly for Moore the viability of the propositional idiom and the contrast between proposition-talk and sentence-talk is central to his discussion of analysis. Even those, for example, such as A. R. White,[4] who have thought that Moore's account of analysis was, in its main features, almost entirely mistaken have not denied this, but have, in fact, been quick to point out that some of the shortcomings of Moore's account largely stem from commitment to the essential non-redundancy of the propositional idiom. In White's view, to be committed to the essential non-redundancy of propositional or concept talk is to be committed to the so-called 'concept theory of meaning' (a mistaken 'theory') and commitment to this theory is alleged to bedevil Moore's meta-talk. Thus White writes: '. . . Moore's worries about analysis are largely due to his mistaken theory of meaning . . .',[5] and again: 'Central to Moore's view of analysis is his careful and important distinction between questions about the meaning of an expression and questions about

---

[1] 'In G. E. M. I give 5 conditions, each of which I take to be a *necessary* condition if a man is to be said to have given an analysis of a given concept.

'I *think* it is true that not only I, but everybody else, when speaking correctly, only says that a person has given an *analysis* of a concept when these 5 conditions are fulfilled.' ('. . . I do not say these conditions are sufficient . . .') *Commonplace Book 1919–1953*, p. 256.

[2] *The Philosophy of G. E. Moore*, p. 667.

[3] *The Philosophy of Bertrand Russell*, p. 212.

[4] *G. E. Moore: A Critical Exposition*, especially Chaps. IV–V–VI.

[5] *Ibid.*, p. 111.

the analysis of that meaning, between a definition of an expression and a definition of a concept or proposition, between a philological and philosophical interest in language. But largely on account of the concept theory of meaning, he draws conclusions from this distinction which I shall argue are mistaken.'[1] White, having produced his argument, concludes: 'the true position on this matter is easily summarized by omitting any reference to propositions'.[2]

By way of an apology for what may appear to be a somewhat lengthy digression on issues peripheral to analysis, I should like to note the following: the question of the viability and essential non-redundancy of the propositional idiom is important not only for Moore's account of analysis but for other aspects of his work also. Some critics and commentators when adjudicating on interpretative issues concerning a particular Moorean doctrine seem to pay attention solely to Moore's specific remarks on that doctrine and to disregard significant clues occurring elsewhere. To give one example—there have been vexed disputes concerning the nature of Moore's 'appeals to Common Sense and Ordinary Language'. How, if at all, should we distinguish these appeals? Is it, as White claims, a mistake to confuse and assimilate the two appeals?[3] Or should we agree with Malcolm that these are not distinct and viable appeals but that the former should either be discarded as philosophically irrelevent, or be re-labelled and assimilated to the latter?[4] According to White (who wishes to claim not merely that Moore *should have* distinguished the two appeals, but that he *did* so, and that a correct reading of his work would show this[5]) the 'appeal to ordinary language is, for him, mainly subsidiary to the appeal to common sense. Malcolm and those who agree with him have reversed the correct relative positions of the two.'[6] In making his plea for deprecating and redescribing the so-called appeal to common sense, Malcolm claims that 'the essence of Moore's technique of refuting philosophical statements consists in pointing out that these statements *go against ordinary language*'.[7]

---

[1] *G. E. Moore: A Critical Exposition*, pp. 98–9.   [2] *Ibid.*, p. 100.

[3] *Ibid.*, p. 5.'. . . there is one enormous howler which, in my opinion, some of Moore's supporters have committed, namely to confuse or assimilate these two quite distinct appeals.'

[4] *Knowledge and Certainty*, N. Malcolm (Prentice-Hall, 1963), pp. 180–1.

[5] *G. E. Moore: A Critical Exposition*, p. 7.

[6] *Ibid.*, p. 7.

[7] *The Philosophy of G. E. Moore*, p. 349.

One immediately striking fact about this interpretative dispute seems to me to be this. Malcolm made this last remark in a context where Moore in his 'A Reply to My Critics'[1] had ample opportunity to refer to Malcolm's 'enormous howler'. Yet not only does he not point to the 'howler', Moore accepts Malcolm's account of his method of refuting 'philosophical statements'.[2] The question now is—did Moore inexplicably fail to see the howler (which, if White is right, is not only a howler in its own right but is inconsistent with some of Moore's most insistently stated doctrines), or was Malcolm's text actually howler-free? Let us consider a specimen sample Malcolm gives of a typical Moorean refutation of a philosophical statement (a refutation which proceeds by 'appealing to ordinary language').

'(1) Philosopher: "There are no material things."
    Moore: "You are certainly wrong, for here's one hand and here's another; and so there are at least two material things".'[3]

Malcolm makes his 'Moore' adopt the material mode of speech; despite this he interprets 'Moore's' reply as constituting an appeal to ordinary language, so clearly Malcolm believes that one could correctly be said to be appealing to ordinary language without having, in making this appeal, to *mention* any particular expression or expressions. One can thus appeal to ordinary language by *exhibiting* a correct (or ordinary[4]) use for an expression without specifically *mentioning* that expression in order to talk about its correct use.[5]

Unfortunately it is not *unambiguously* clear that White would accept this. Perhaps he weakly implies that he would not. In arguing for the distinction of the two appeals he remarks: 'To say that "it is correct to say so and so" may mean either that "it is true to say so and so" or that "it is good (or idiomatic, standard, correct, linguistically permissible) English to say so and so". If anyone ever did argue from "it is correct, i.e. good English" to "it is correct, i.e. true" to say so and so, he would indeed deserve

---

[1] *The Philosophy of G. E. Moore*, pp. 668–9.   [2] *Ibid.*, p. 668.
[3] *Ibid.*, p. 346.
[4] It is, of course, irrelevant to my present point whether *ordinary* language is *correct* or not.
[5] Possibly White concedes this when he says that an appeal to ordinary language is an appeal to *what most of us say*. *G. E. Moore: A Critical Exposition*, p. 32.

the rebuke that "vulgarity of speech is no guarantee of truth. How absurd that anyone should have thought it was!"[1] We might make what is possibly White's point and unpack some of the implications of his remark. We cannot intend to use the expression 'it is correct, i.e. good English to say so and so' as a synonym for 'it is correct, i.e. good English to say *that* so and so', because the idioms 'it is correct to say that . . .' and 'it is true to say that . . .' are intersubstitutable, and it makes no sense, is not good English, to say 'it is *true, i.e. good English* to say that . . .'. The parenthetical 'i.e.' can here have no characteristic appositive rôle—for 'good English' cannot be itself true, it can only be true *that* something is good English. Further, 'it is good English that (e.g.) the moon is round' is not good English and is just as deviant as is its transform 'the moon's being round is good English'. (Cp. 'It is a fact that the moon is round' and its transform 'the moon's being round is a fact'.) Phrases such as 'it is good English . . .' do not admit of being followed by those propositional constructions introduced by a 'that' (conjunctival) but require, rather, to be followed by a quotation where we mention, and not merely use, some expression.

If, however, this is part of what White wishes to say, or imply, then his summary of the dispute between himself and Malcolm is decidedly odd. For now White is implying that in appealing to Common Sense we would typically be appealing to statements of the form 'it is correct to say that . . .' while in appealing to Ordinary Language we would typically be appealing to statements of the form 'it is correct to say ". . ."' (where the occurrence of quotation is essential). Malcolm, however, and also, I think, Moore, employ the former idiom from which it would seem to follow that White and Malcolm must be using the expression 'appeal to ordinary language' in two different senses, and that White should be aware that this is so. White, therefore, should, in my view, be saying not that Malcolm has confused the two appeals, but that he is misusing the expression 'appeal to ordinary language' and is in fact appealing to Common Sense and not Ordinary Language and is thereby misdescribing his own procedure. As long as Malcolm sticks to the material mode Moore certainly has no quarrel with him. Moore's most explicit statement occurs in the *Commonplace Book* (1946–47, p. 312) when he asks the question: 'If the moon can't be properly said to be round does it follow that it's not round?' In answer to this he claims that 'from (*a*) "the

[1] *G. E. Moore: A Critical Exposition*, p. 8.

moon can properly be said to be round" it seems to follow that
(b) the moon is round. (b) does follow from (a) but (a) does not
follow from (b)'. Moore here gives no argument for his claim that
(b) follows from (a) (nor has he, to the best of my knowledge, *ever*
given one) and perhaps this is an indication of its, for him, truistic
character. The proper procedure for White is to ask whether in
employing the appeal to ordinary language (a) is typical of the
type of statement to which we ought to appeal. If it is, then
Malcolm is right in his reportage of Moore. If it is not, then White
has to square Moore's acceptance of Malcolm and has in turn to
produce evidence that Moore intended (weakly, should have
intended) to appeal to another type of statement which explicitly
mentions some expression or other.

One further shortcoming of White's account is indicated by the
Commonplace Book entry.[1] White contrasts and compares the *two*
idioms—'it is correct to say " . . . " ' and 'it is correct (true) to say
that . . .'. To these we ought to add Moore's idiom '. . . can be
properly said to be . . .'. This idiom is ambivalent in similar
fashion: we would, for example, distinguish between ' "the moon"
can be properly said to be an expression of English' and 'the moon
can be properly said to be round'. Let us call the proposition
expressed by this latter sentence (A).[2] Now, does sentence (a)
have the same meaning as 'it is correct (true) to say that the
moon is round' (e), or does it have the same meaning as 'it is
correct to say "the moon is round" ' (d)? Moore has said that
the proposition (A) is not logically equivalent to the proposition
(B) 'the moon is round', for (B) might be true and (A) be false.
Now, will (E) and (B) be, for Moore, logically equivalent? If (E)
were equivalent to 'it is true that the moon is round' (F), then (E)
and (B) would be equivalent.[3] The difficulty is that neither Moore
nor White does explicitly say whether (E) and (F), and therefore
(B), are equivalent.

I think the truth of the matter may be this, that White has
unconsciously assimilated (d) to (e) rather than to (a)—my warrant
for this is White's presumption of the *relevance* of the Moore
quotation he cites above.[4] Despite this he emerges with an
apparently clear-cut dichotomy between 'it is correct to say

[1] p. 312.
[2] I shall use letter abbreviations to permit easy mention of both propositions
and sentences, reserving capitals for the former.
[3] *Lectures on Philosophy*, p. 143.
[4] *The Philosophy of G. E. Moore*, p. 548.

"..."' and 'it is true to say that ...'. The former is clearly concerned with the appropriateness of our sayings and the latter with the truth of our sayings. But if we are tempted to assimilate (d) to (e) we may forget that the latter is concerned with the *truth of our sayings* and not just with *truth*. I think White succumbs to this temptation—viz. he concludes his argument by stating 'Certainly Moore did not confuse the appeal to common sense and that to ordinary language in this way any more than Berkeley confused his *similar* [my italics] appeals to "the truth of things" and to "propriety of language"'.[1]

(B) clearly does not entail anything about our *sayings*; thus, Moore quite unequivocally writes: 'From the prop. that the moon is round, it does not follow that the sentence "the moon is round" expresses *any* true prop.; *nothing* follows about the *sentence* "the moon is round" or about any word or sentence whatever.'[2] (It might possibly, however, be thought to entail something about what we *could* say. Consider for example the proposition 'the moon is round' (B) and the proposition 'if anyone were to say that the moon is round, then what he would be saying would be true' (F).[3] If we wish to say that (B) and (F) are in some sense logically equivalent we *may* feel tempted to say that those things we can say of (F) may also be said of (B), so that if (F) is concerned with the truth of what we might say, then so, perforce, is (B) whether the *form of words* makes this explicit or not.)

(A) does not entail anything concerning any specific sentence (for example 'the moon is round'); however Moore must regard (A) as being in some sense about what we say, for (A) would not be true if there was nothing (for example no sentence) of which it would be true to say that that sentence expressed the proposition that the moon was round. 'It is certain that the moon might have been round, and that yet there might have been *no proper way of saying* that it was; that therefore the sentence "the moon is round" might not have been a proper way of saying so'.[2] We have, in Moore's opinion, explicitly to add that (C) *the sentence* 'the moon is round' means that the moon is round; ((B) and (C)) will entail (A). The significance of this statement is that in order that (B) should entail (A), we require to add the, for Moore, non-

[1] G. E. Moore: A Critical Exposition, p. 8.
[2] Commonplace Book: 1919–1953, p. 312.
[3] Cf. The Philosophy of Bertrand Russell, p. 196, and 'Equivalence and Identity', C. Lewy, Mind, Vol. LV, 1946.

redundant premise (C), and (C) must be a proposition which mentions a sentence while (A) does not. This conclusion cuts across what was, I think, one of White's guiding assumptions (as indicated in the discussion in pp. 7–8 of his book), viz. that to talk of the appropriateness of our saying something was to talk of what might be properly said. In order to say that a form of words is permissible, idiomatic, etc., we must mention the form of words, but in order to say what it is proper, correct to say, we need not.

There is one point of minor interest. If White accepts that ((B) and (C)) entail (A) and does not accept the non-redundancy of (C) on the grounds that (C) is a tautology, then he must accept that (B) entails (A). But White would wish to say that (C) was a tautology.[1] Therefore he would have to accept that (B) entails (A) although whether he *would* wish to accept this I do not know. It largely depends on whether he thinks that an appeal to (A) is an appeal to ordinary language or to common sense. The situation is worse confounded when White writes (*op. cit.*, p. 32) that *one* of the ways in which we appeal to ordinary language is to appeal to what *most of us say* (relevant to what is commonly accepted as being true), another is to appeal to how *most of us speak*. Here he seems to be agreeing with me that the distinction must be drawn but does not agree with my description of the distinction. Much may hang on the use of the word 'relevant'. It may be that our diction *is just* our manner of speaking while what is commonly accepted as true *is just indicated* by what most of us say.

To conclude this somewhat lengthy discussion—in discussing some of Moore's doctrines we often employ as meta-theoretic terms, terms which stand in need of further clarification. Further clarity can sometimes be achieved by considering evidence from other sources. Moore, in his accounts as to the nature of analysis from 1933 to 1953, frequently has occasion to explain the, to him, fundamentally important distinction between proposition-talk and sentence-talk. In the course of elaborating this distinction he raises issues directly relevant, to, for example, the Malcolm–White controversy. Sometimes, as in the 'Sentences and Propositions' *Commonplace Book* entry, which I have been discussing, the positions stated, and even the examples cited, decide in part the interpretative issues.

In this second section I wish to raise issues crucially relevant to

[1] *G. E. Moore: A Critical Exposition*, pp. 102–6 (where he argues for the tautological status of ' "Z" means that Z').

the adequacy of Moore's conditions for saying of something that it is an analysis and, further, a correct analysis.

The condition that Moore first lists as necessary is that 'both *analysandum* and *analysans* must be *concepts*,[1] and, if the analysis is a *correct* one, must, in some sense, be *the same concept*'.[2] Langford introduced the terminology of 'analysandum/analysans'; Moore adopted it in his reply to Langford, but only on rare occasions thereafter (although he adopts an analogous terminology 'definiendum/definiens' in 1944[3]). Neither, however, has, to the best of my knowledge, claimed any special advantages for this terminology, and this seems a serious omission for there are definite advantages in adopting these locutions. The introduction of the word 'analysans' helps to resolve a crucial ambiguity latent in Moore's use of the term 'analysis'. Moore frequently uses the term 'analysis' in such a way that indifferently it may refer both to the statement that the analysandum is equivalent to the analysans, and to the analysans itself. Thus, when you give an *analysis*, in one sense, you may be making a statement concerning the relation of the analysandum to the analysans, and in the other, when you say of some proposition, or concept, that it is the analysis of another you may be speaking of the analysans itself. Sometimes the ambivalent uses, when happily juxtaposed with revealing locutions, can be easily distinguished in the text, sometimes not. When they are not the results may be serious. Max Black, not noting the ambiguity, seems to exploit it and mount a strong attack on Moore when he writes '. . . attention to what Moore says brings formidable difficulties to light. Consider, for instance, what is said about the proposition, P, say, expressed by the words "This is a hand", when uttered in the appropriate circumstances. Moore thinks there are "three, and only three alternative types of answer possible". Let us suppose that three different propositions, A_1, A_2, and A_3, are offered as possible analyses of P. Now if one of them is the *correct* analysis of P, it must, according to Moore, be identically the same proposition as P. So we must have either $P = A_1$, or $P = A_2$, or $P = A_3$ (where "$=$" means *identically the same as*). Since we know P to be certainly true, we must, therefore, know either A_1 or A_2 or A_3 to be certainly true. How is it, then, that Moore can say that none of the possible analyses of P "comes

---

[1] It is immaterial here whether Moore talks of 'concepts' or 'propositions', vide *The Philosophy of G. E. Moore*, p. 664.   [2] *Ibid.*, p. 666.

[3] *The Philosophy of Bertrand Russell*, pp. 196 *et seq.*

anywhere near being certainly true" without at once using this as a conclusive ground for rejecting all of them?"[1]

There seems to be one and only one way for Moore to escape Black's criticism—to avoid the more serious charge of inconsistency he must plead guilty to equivocating on the word 'analysis'. Construing 'analysis' as other than 'analysans', he must claim that he may know P (to be true) and know A_1 (to be true) while not knowing the truth of the *analysis* $P = A_1$. (I shall hereafter use '$P = A_1$' as an abbreviation of 'the analysis $P = A_1$'. I think this proposal is of some importance; presumably Black would not resist it, for he implies that to speak of A_1 as the analysis of P yields us $P = A$.[2] My intent is this: if we forget how '$P = A_1$' was introduced, we may easily be deceived into thinking that '$P = A_1$' just expresses the claim that P and A_1 are one and the same (identical) proposition. However, for '$P = A_1$' to express an *analysis*, this is merely a necessary and not a sufficient condition. To say, therefore, that $P = A_1$, is not merely to say that P and A_1 are the same proposition (whatever that may turn out to mean), it is to say rather, that further conditions are satisfied such that A_1 can correctly be said to *analyse P*.) That is, he may know the analysandum P and the analysans A_1 to be true without thereby knowing that the *analysis* $P = A_1$ is true. Further, in accordance with his own explicit criteria[3] he may even know P and A_1, and know, in proffering $P = A_1$ as his statement of analysis, that if he knows P then he knows A_1, without knowing *that* $P = A_1$. If this claim seems implausible an example may help: let us take as our analysandum 'Q' and as our analysans 'It is true that Q' (R); Moore would say that we could consistently affirm the set: 'He knows Q, knows R, and knows R if he knows Q,[4] and deny 'he knows $Q = R$'. Moore

---

[1] *Philosophical Analysis* (ed. M. Black), Cornell University Press, 1950, pp. 8-9. Black's quotation of Moore refers to 'A Defence of Common Sense'— *Contemporary British Philosophy* (Second Series), 1925, p. 219. Black indulges in otiose paraphrase here: a more directly relevant and from his point of view equally damning quotation is to be found on page 216.

[2] *Philosophical Analysis*, p. 9.

[3] *Vide* 'Nobody can know that the *analysandum* applies to an object without knowing that the *analysans* applies to it', *The Philosophy of G. E. Moore*, p. 663. (The shift to 'know' (from 'The Defence of Common Sense' quotation) to 'know for certain to be true' is immaterial as far as Moore is concerned.) Cp. *Philosophical Papers*, 'Certainty', p. 236.

[4] This requires further qualification—a full discussion should take account of Moore's implied distinction between 'he knows Q' and 'he knows that he knows Q'. Cp. Moore's remark on Langford's 'cube' example. Cf. *The Philosophy of G. E. Moore*, p. 663.

I

would deny[1] 'he knows $Q = R$' because no one *could* know that $Q = R$, because, in his view, $Q = R$ is false.[2]

Moore would certainly agree that, as described, P is known (for certain) to be true; he would certainly agree that if P is known to be true, and if the statement $P = A_1$ is a statement of analysis, then A_1 must also be known to be true. So, where we construe 'analysis' as 'analysans' I should agree[3] with Black that according to Moore's criteria 'It would seem that since the correct analysis must be identically the same as a proposition known to be certainly true, any proposition *not* known to be certainly true must be eliminated as a possible answer: there seems no room for hesitation or doubt'.[4] This seems a very much stronger version of the claim more typically made by (rather than foisted on) Moore— when for example he claims that if A_1 (a putative analysans) is inconsistent with P, and P is certainly true (most usually when P is known to be a common-sense claim), then there is sufficient reason for rejecting the analysis, $P = A_1$.[5]

The former claim is the stronger in that it requires a weaker claim to disconfirm $P = A_1$; in the former case we require only that A_1 be not known for certain to be true, whereas in the latter case, we require that A_1 be known for certain to be false (because it is inconsistent with P, which is, by hypothesis, known to be true). This seems to force a dilemma—do we opt for Black's interpretation, take the consequences of Moore's talk on analysis seriously, and as a consequence, enlarge the relevant field for the disconfirmation of philosophical analyses (and thus inflate the role of the appeal to Common Sense and/or Ordinary Language)—or do we discount Moore's implicit claim stemming from his talk of analysis? The question in this—has Moore, unwittingly, committed himself, in his talk about analysis, to a certain position concerning the disconfirmation of philosophical theories, or analyses, but

[1] *Commonplace Book: 1919–1953*, p. 256.

[2] Moore is not denying Ramsey's claim (cp. *The Foundations of Mathematics*, F. P. Ramsey, p. 142, 'Facts and Propositions', 1927) that Q is logically equivalent to R; he is merely denying that '$Q = R$' expresses an analysis.

[3] I agree that Moore (on this interpretation) is thus committed (as Black suggests) but I would prefer to reject the commitment and thereby reject the assumption (*The Philosophy of G. E. Moore*, p. 663) that yielded that commitment.   [4] *Philosophical Analysis*, p. 9.

[5] 'I actually know that this is a thumb, and if the proposition that "This is a thumb" could be shown to be inconsistent with the Sensum Theory, I should say the Sensum Theory was *certainly* false.' 'The Nature of Sensible Appearances' (*Proceedings. Aristotelian Society*, Supp. Vol. VI, p. 186).

declined to accept the consequences of his own talk when he explicitly speaks of *disconfirming* such analyses?

Moore's original claim[1] and the revised claim suggested by Black's interpretation involve parallel paraphrases of Moore's procedures. The first (Black's) goes: 'A_1 is known' follows from the conjunction, '$P = A_1$' and 'P is known';[2] but 'A_1 is known' is not true, while 'P is known' is, therefore, 'not$-(P = A_1)$'. The second goes: 'Not$-P$' follows from '$P = A_1$' but 'P', therefore, 'Not$-(P = A_1)$'. In neither case does it follow that A_1 (Black's unique candidate for 'analysis' status) is false, merely that $P = A_1$ is false, that is, that A_1 does not analyse P; A_1 may well be true and not an analysis of P—it may for example be a partial analysis (cf. 'A Defence of Common Sense' in *Contemporary British Philosophy*: Second Series, pp. 218–19).

My compromise suggestion goes thus: 'A_1 is known' follows from the conjunction 'P is known' and '$P = A_1$ is known'. But 'A_1 is known' is not true, while 'P is known', is; therefore '$P = A_1$ is not known', and this, of course, is compatible both with 'A_1' is true and '$P = A_1$' is true. (My suggestion could be legislated out only if Moore had claimed, which I believe he did not, that a statement of analysis, if true, must be known to be true). I think also my suggestion that Moore's real premise is '$P = A_1$ is known' and not '$P = A_1$' may do more justice to what Moore says and intends. He writes that no analysis 'comes anywhere near to being *certainly* true'[3] (my italics). This last expression, as we have seen, reduces, in Moore's view, to 'comes anywhere near being known for certain to be true'.

To reject my interpretation out of hand on the ground that 'analysis' always, for Moore, is synonymous with 'analysans' is, in my view, to beg the question. I have been concerned to make two claims: that the 'analysandum/analysans' idiom has the merit of relative precision and, more importantly, that one fundamental objection to the basic soundness of Moore's account of analysis

---

[1] 'A Defence of Common Sense', pp. 216 and 219.

[2] It may be thought that here is an illicit move from Black's 'is certainly true' to my 'is known'. If we are worried about the interpretation of Moore, this paraphrase is admissible: on the connection between '. . . is certain . . .' and '. . . is known . . .' Moore writes as follows (*Philosophical Papers*, p. 240): 'It is indeed, obvious, I think, that a thing can't be certain, unless it is *known*; this is one obvious point that distinguishes the use of the word "certain" from that of the word "true"; a thing that nobody knows may quite well be true, but cannot possibly be certain.'

[3] 'A Defence of Common Sense' in *Contemporary British Philosophy*, p. 216.

need not stand if we look more closely at the possibilities of a revised terminology.

Moore's requirement that the analysandum and the analysans be a concept or a proposition invites the attacks of those who reject the propositional idiom, either strongly, as non-viable, or weakly, as redundant. His further use of the propositional idiom to formulate his remaining conditions[1] is even more vulnerable to such attacks. In formulating his remaining conditions he employs such locutions as 'is the *same* proposition (or concept)', '*mentions* a concept', 'explicitly mentions *more* concepts and the *method of their combination*', etc.: if talk of propositions/concepts is obscurantist, then so, *a fortiori*, is talk of the same proposition/concept, more concepts, etc. Others, less independently committed to the non-viability of the propositional idiom, may eventually argue *to* it from their difficulties with 'same proposition' etc. That is, lacking, for example, a criterion for the *individuation of propositions* they may reject the idiom. My own position is somewhat different. I am impressed with the arguments[2] for the essential non-redundancy of the propositional idiom, and hence for its viability: I do also, however, have reservations concerning the use of the words 'concept' or 'proposition' as they occur in certain relevant and crucial locutions. (For example, it is not only not clear to me whether the sentence 'it is true that P' *explicitly mentions more concepts than* the sentence 'P', it is also not clear what is here at stake.) While it is, as I shall argue, perhaps possible to introduce the term 'proposition' relatively aseptically, and thereby in a sense make the idiom viable, there is also a danger that, forgetting the manner of its introduction, we may proceed to employ it with less than proper discretion.

Following the lines of a suggestion made by Moore[3] we might introduce propositions via noun clause structures and oblique contexts, arguing, for example, 'I believe (that) P' is equivalent to 'I believe the proposition (that) P' and that, if we understand the former, then we understand the latter. Thus, if we understand the function of the conjunctival 'that' then we understand the word 'proposition' (though as yet, and perhaps always, we understand

---

[1] *The Philosophy of G. E. Moore*, pp. 663 and 666.

[2] Alonzo Church, 'On Carnap's Analysis of Statements of Assertion and Belief', in *Analysis*, Vol. 10, no. 5, 1950. Cf. G. E. Moore, *Lectures on Philosophy*, pp. 133–6. *Commonplace Book: 1919–1953*, pp. 374–6.

[3] *Lectures on Philosophy*, pp. 135–42; also *Commonplace Book: 1919–1953*, p. 374.

it only *as introduced and used in this way*). When we say that 'I believe that *P*' is equivalent to 'I believe the proposition that *P*' we are implying that the expression 'the proposition' is in this context redundant, but this does not in my opinion imply that the *propositional idiom* is redundant. Much depends on what we take as a criterion for '*being committed to the propositional idiom*'. I am in effect proposing that to be committed to the essential non-redundancy of this idiom is to be committed to the view that the indirect mode of speech in reportatively used noun clauses, is not eliminable in favour of purely sentence mentioning direct contexts; so that to be committed to 'the propositional idiom' is to follow Church[1] and refuse, for example, to translate 'Seneca asserted that man was a rational animal' along the lines of (the *purely* sentence mentioning) 'Seneca uttered/wrote with assertive intent some sentence *S*' . . .'of some language such that . . .'. The point being that the former is less committal than the latter in that what is true or false of '*S*' is relevant to the confirmation of that expressed by the latter but not to that expressed by the former; and that the former is also more committal than the latter in that we use the former to say *what* Seneca asserted and use the latter merely to say what sentence Seneca might have used without saying that this sentence was used to say *what* Seneca asserted (to add *that* it was so used just is to resurrect the propositional idiom). By specifying in detail why any proposed sentence-mentioning translation fails, we exhibit what it is to employ the propositional idiom, and this idiom is no more obscurantist than the 'what', 'that', 'that which' locutions which it replaces, given that we strictly observe rules for the correct generation of propositional locutions from the 'what', 'that', 'that which' idiom. The question which most immediately concerns me is: does Moore strictly observe such rules, or does he transgress them and thus sanction impermissible locutions?

Perhaps I should add a brief note on 'impermissible locution'. I have used 'impermissible locution' in a restricted sense to refer to a locution that is not generated by legitimate transforms from ordinary, non-deviant uses of 'that', 'what' etc. To say that a locution is permissible is to imply a respectable certificate of origin; to say that a locution is impermissible is to say that no such certificate *has* been supplied, it is not to say that no equally re-

---

[1] 'On Carnap's Analysis of Statements of Assertion and Belief,' *Analysis*, Vol. 10, no. 5, 1950.

spectable certificate *could* not be supplied. Rival accounts of proposition-talk might well produce recipes for generating permissible propositional locutions, for I have not been making the strong claim that proposition-talk can be vindicated *only* along the lines suggested by Moore and Church, just that it *can* be vindicated in this way. Let me cite, as a sample, one locution which may well, according to my line of argument above, be, on *one interpretation*, impermissible. Consider Lewy's use[1] of the expression 'entailment proposition'. It is consistent with Lewy's[2] (and Moore's) general position to claim that to speak of a proposition is not to speak of any sentence used to express that proposition, and presumably, unless any rider is added to the contrary, we should be justified in taking this to apply also to any 'entailment proposition'. It would seem, therefore, that Lewy could not consistently explain his use of 'entailment proposition' by claiming that all and only entailment propositions were propositions not incorrectly expressed by sentences containing the word 'entails', where 'entails' was so used . . . etc. Of the 'two' propositions, 'there is nobody who is a brother and is not male' and 'the proposition that somebody is a brother entails the proposition that that person is male', the latter seems, to Lewy, unquestionably to be an *entailment* proposition, while the former does not. Is it merely coincidental that the sentence used to express the latter contains the word 'entails', while the sentence used to express the former does not? Or is this an indication of an unacknowledged criterion for thus distinguishing them (for he gives no other)? *If* it is, in fact, his criterion, then he seems committed to the claim that a proposition may be classified as a function of a sentence that may properly express it.[3] The expression 'entailment proposition' would then seem to behave deviantly[4]—its use would be at variance with the 'general position' outlined above, and also with other

[1] Cf. *Philosophical Analysis* (ed. Max Black), 'Entailment and Necessary Propositions', p. 204.   [2] *Ibid.*, p. 199.

[3] Moore comes near to this. (Cf. *The Philosophy of G. E. Moore*, p. 666) when he says that statements may be both 'about concepts and verbal expressions'.

[4] If we can argue that a proposition does not state an entailment because the sentence we employ to express it does not use the word 'entails' (or a synonym?), we might as well argue that to assert the proposition that the moon is round is not assert 'the true proposition' (expressed by 'it is true that the moon is round') since we have not used the word 'true'. Therefore just as Lewy's 'There is nobody who is a brother and is not a male' does not state an entailment, so, for us, to assert that the moon is round is not to assert the proposition correctly expressed by 'it is true that the moon is round'.

grammatically similar expressions, e.g. 'necessary proposition'. (Lewy devotes some time to *proving* that the proposition 'the proposition that there is nobody who is a brother and who is not male is necessary' is necessary, and is content to *assume* that the proposition 'there is nobody who is a brother and who is not male' is necessary, making it clear, not only that the absence of the word 'necessary' does not show that the sentence in question does not express a necessary proposition, but that the presence of the word 'necessary' (with suitable restrictions) does not, by itself, guarantee the contrary).

We could of course legitimize the expression 'entailment proposition' by supplying, in a context, a suitable transform, e.g. 'He asserted an entailment proposition' = 'He asserted that some one thing (or some one thing's being so) entailed some one other thing (or some one other thing's being so)'. For the point I am making, it is very important to understand that I am not at all suggesting that this transformation is illuminating except in one especial regard. The transaction that gives us the vagueness of 'thing' for the alleged obscurity of 'proposition' *may* be no great bargain. Much depends on our motives for making the transaction. *My* motive is of course this: the transformation shows that in this use, the word 'proposition' can, in a context, be eliminated in favour of familiar words of everyday discourse. If this is so, and if, in every case, we run a precautionary check on the availability of a transform, then no more systematic obscurity (of the 'boojum', 'snark' variety) attaches to the *word* 'proposition' than to the *words* 'that', 'what', 'thing' etc. We do, of course, understand the words 'that', 'what', 'thing', etc. in that we are not ignorant of their meaning as a foreigner might be.[1] So, if the transformation does not enlighten us, then our worry was not with the *word* 'proposition', and this is *all* that I wanted to show. We may find the transformation unhelpful even to the extent that our doubts with regard to 'propositions' now attaches also to 'things', but these doubts do not mean that we do not understand the meaning of the word 'things'. 'Anyone who takes a contrary view must, I suppose, be confusing the question whether we understand its meaning (which we all certainly do) with the entirely different question whether we *know what it means*, in the sense that we are able to *give a correct analysis* of its meaning.' (G. E. Moore, 'A Defence of Common Sense', p. 198, in *Contemporary British Philosophy*.) That is,

[1] Cp. G. E. Moore, *Some Main Problems of Philosophy*, p. 216.

philosophical issues can be raised by, and stated in everyday
ordinary discourse and merely to cite a chunk of idiomatic, non-
technical English as a transform of some allegedly more obscure
locution is no guarantee of philosophical progress. Moore's talk of
analysis in terms of concepts and propositions is not *necessarily*
trouble-free if the viability of proposition-concept-talk is vindicated, but it is certainly trouble-laden if such talk is not vindicated.

I have been claiming that, according to Moore's prescription,
proposition-concept-talk can be viable. ('What it does is to connect the meaning of '*prop.*' in a definite manner with something
which we all are familiar with, i.e. what is meant by believing *that*
so-&-so or conceiving *that* so-&-so: but it doesn't say anything as
to the *analysis* of this pred. The question *what* a prop. is, in this
sense, can only be answered by an analysis of this kind of expression & I don't think anyone knows what the analysis is.' (G. E.
Moore, *Lectures on Philosophy*, p. 134.)) My remaining concern is
with his consistency. He has introduced the sentence-proposition
distinction via indirect contexts, where to mention a proposition
P is not to mention any sentence S which may express P,[1] and to
mention S is not to mention proposition P which S may express,
nor to say that S expresses any proposition whatsoever. My
problem is: does this hold for all P and thus crucially when P is
the proposition that A_1 analyses P_1 (in our former use $P_1 = A_1$).
That is, does the proposition that Moore stated that $P_1 = A_1$
entail that Moore stated anything with regard to the sentence
'$P_1 = A_1$', even where '$P_1 = A_1$' is *in fact* used to express the
proposition '$P_1 = A_1$', and anything thereby with regard to the
sub-sentences 'P_1' and 'A_1', where these *in fact* express propositions 'P_1' and 'A_1'? Consistency would *seem* to require that it
should not. Moore, however, lists three conditions which he
regards as necessary for a statement to be a statement of analysis
and his listing of these conditions might suggest the contrary.
(I say 'might suggest' because Moore is here talking of statements,
and the introduction of the word 'statement' may constitute a
'give-away' or a 'get-out' depending on how we look on the matter

---

[1] G. E. Moore, *The Commonplace Book: 1919–1953*, pp. 360–1.
'But what *is* a prop.?
'We have only said that "He asserted the prop. '*p*'" does not mean the same
as "He uttered (or wrote) the sentence '*p*' or some equivalent", & that it means
in addition "he uttered a sentence which means *p*". That sentence "*p*" means *p*
is an empirical proposition. But of course a man who says that the sun is larger
than the moon is not saying anything about the sentence "*p*".'

—it certainly adds complications.)[1] The three conditions are (i) 'that the *expression* used for the *analysandum* must be a different *expression* from that used for the *analysans*'; (ii) that 'the expression used for the *analysans* must explicitly *mention* concepts which are not explicitly mentioned by the expression used for the analysandum'; (iii) that 'the *method of combination* should be explicitly mentioned by the expression used for the *analysans*'.[2]

Does 'Moore stated that $P_1 = A_1$' entail anything about the expressions 'P_1' and 'A_1'? It would seem utterly inconsistent with our previous line of argument to say that it does—further, to say that it does would be to vitiate the distinction we have drawn between proposition-talk and sentence-talk, for propositions and sentences have been *distinguished in, and solely by recourse to, indirect contexts*. However, Moore would, I think, having listed the above conditions as necessary, have to take the contrary view and claim (1) that, in one sense, and for some examples, a proposition '$P_1 = A_1$' could entail something about the verbal expressions which are used to express that proposition (perhaps not necessarily anything about any *particular* verbal expression, but perhaps necessarily something about some *type* of verbal expressions), and claim in consequence (2) that were we to employ a form of words purporting to cite the analysis Moore stated, where Moore would deny that this form of words could properly state any analysis at all, then Moore would say that he had been misreported. For example, were we to say 'Moore stated that the proposition "The male sovereign is dead" is analysed by the proposition "the male monarch is dead"' Moore would say that he had been falsely reported; whereas if we had said 'Moore stated that the proposition "The king is dead" is analysed by the proposition "The male monarch is dead"' Moore would not have described this as false reportage; and this despite the fact that, for him, the propositions 'The king is dead' and 'the male sovereign is dead' would be 'logically equivalent' ('in some sense the same proposition'). That this is not simply a matter of not allowing synonym substitutes to occur in indirect contexts is shown by the following: Moore would

---

[1] He lists the conditions which are necessary 'if in making a given statement one is to be properly said to be "giving an analysis"'. (*The Philosophy of G. E. Moore*, p. 666.) Is he here stating what conditions must be satisfied in order that one correctly states an analysis, or what conditions must be satisfied in order that something be an analysis? The problems raised in attempting to distinguish 'he correctly states *a* ...' from 'he correctly states *that* ...' would require a lengthy and separate discussion.   [2] *The Philosophy of G. E. Moore*, p. 666.

I*

not have objected had we, in reporting what Moore stated, used 'The king is deceased' rather than 'The king is dead' (for the former presumably does not 'explicitly mention more concepts' than the latter, though it is otherwise with 'male monarch' and 'king'.[1]

The simple rebuttal of this is that if it is true that Moore stated that the *proposition* 'the king is dead' is analysed by the *proposition* 'the male monarch is dead', then so is the proposition 'the male sovereign is dead' analysed by the proposition 'the male monarch is dead', for the proposition the 'king is dead' and the proposition 'the male sovereign is dead' are the same proposition,[2] because if we were to state that the male sovereign is dead we would be stating that the king is dead. That is, we have not *yet* had a legitimate introduction to the notion that propositions may be individuated as a function of the sentences which may correctly express them. The essence of the resort to the propositional idiom, as explained and justified so far, is that it should permit us to report *what* is said without committing us to quoting what words were used to say what was said. It would, therefore, be a definite mistake, at this stage in our understanding of the word 'proposition', to claim for example, that when *the proposition* to be analysed is 'the king is dead' we could *not* express this proposition by the sentence 'the male sovereign is dead'. What could this (mistaken) claim amount to? By using the words 'when the proposition to be analysed is "the king is dead"' we imply some degree of individuation, and by adding that we could not express that proposition by the sentence 'the male sovereign is dead' we imply some further degree of individuation. We imply also, else the presumption of conformity with Moore's conditions is not satisfied, that the sentence 'the king is dead' expresses the proposition that the king is dead.[3] By a parallel procedure we could assume that the sentence 'the male sovereign is dead' expresses the proposition that the male sovereign is dead. Hence we seem to be saying that the proposition to be analysed is the proposition that the king is dead and *not* the proposition that the male sovereign is dead. In terms

[1] A borderline case can be posed by 'one and only one' and 'uniquely one'. Does the first expression 'mention' more concepts? Does 'and' denote a concept? Moore says that 'the' does not. *Vide Lectures on Philosophy*, p. 161.

[2] The propriety of 'same proposition' is given by such transforms as, e.g.— he asserted the same proposition at T_1 as at T_2 = what he asserted at T_1 was the same as that which he asserted at T_2.

[3] This is an *argumentum ad hominem*; *I* am not committed to giving an interpretation of the sentence 'the sentence "the king is dead" expresses the proposition that the king is dead'.

of *our* understanding of the *word* 'proposition' how could we say this? This degree of individuation of the 'two' propositions, granted that the two sentences which express 'them' are equi-significant, goes beyond what our understanding of the term 'proposition' warrants. The whole question of misreportage depends on the accuracy and intelligibility of the claim 'Moore spoke of the proposition "the king is dead" rather than of the proposition "the male sovereign is dead".' What is it to speak *of* a proposition and *of* one proposition *rather than another*? 'He spoke *of* the proposition that . . .' does not of course conform to my paradigm[1] —'the proposition' is not redundant in that 'he spoke of that . . .' is not syntactically proper. 'He spoke of the proposition that the king is dead' must be rendered in some such fashion as 'He spoke of what is said when it is said that the king is dead'; and 'He spoke of the proposition that the king is dead and not of the proposition that the male sovereign is dead' must be rendered as 'He spoke of what is said when it is said that the king is dead and did not speak of what is said when it is said that the male sovereign is dead'.[2] But if the expressions which we use to report what he said, and what allegedly he did not say, are synonyms, then we must be forever puzzled as to what he did or did not say. In a similar fashion we *should* be puzzled by the following claim—'he spoke of the proposition that the king was dead and *not* of the proposition that the male sovereign was dead because it was required that he should speak of a proposition which was analysed by the proposition that the male monarch was dead'.[3]

[1] Some of the propositional locutions *I* have employed equally fail to match exactly the 'paradigm', but this does not, I hope, make them deviant. I have employed principally three locutions, (i) 'the proposition ". . ." entails the proposition ". . ."'; for this I provided an explicit transform (see page 263); (ii) 'the proposition ". . ." is the same as proposition ". . ."'; for this I have provided an explicit transform (see page 266, note 2), and (iii) 'the sentence *S* ". . ." expresses the proposition *P* ". . ."'; for this last, although transforms have already been implied, I might explicitly supply the following as a sample: 'He used the sentence *S* ". . ."' = 'He used the proposition that *P*' = 'He used the sentence *S* ". . ." to say what is said by saying that *P*'.

[2] To say this is as absurd as to say 'He said *that* Russell was a brother but did not say *that* he was a male sibling'.

[3] Since concept-talk parallels proposition-talk, parallel difficulties attach to the condition that the sentence used to express the analysans should *explicitly mention more concepts* than the sentence used to express the analysandum. Even if we were to amend the unfortunate locution *'mention of a concept'* we are still left with the puzzle: why does the sentence 'the male monarch is dead' mention more concepts than the sentence 'The king is dead' while the sentence 'It is true that the king is dead' does not?

To summarize my argument: Moore has, in my opinion, legitimized talk of propositions in introducing the word 'proposition' by recourse to indirect contexts. When he comes to talk *of* propositions (in listing the conditions necessary for an analysis) and, thereby, mentions them in indirect contexts, he lacks the means for individuating them, when his conditions for analysis require that he *does* individuate them. In these indirect contexts we fail to individuate them, to refer to one proposition rather than another, just as in other indirect contexts we did not, *for the very same reason*, succeed in referring to one sentence rather than another. Moore, therefore, would have, either to introduce some further equally aseptic rule of use for the word 'proposition' which would permit requisite individuation, or he would have to revise his list of conditions that must be satisfied for 'a giving of an analysis'.

MOORE ON FREE WILL

by THEODORE REDPATH

Moore seems to have spent less time on Free Will than on a number of other leading philosophical problems; but what he did write about it is clearly the fruit of much thought, and is characteristically acute. Moreover, the relations between what he wrote on the topic at different times seem to me of considerable philosophical interest.

There is a quite long early paper by Moore called 'Freedom',[1] which was read to the Aristotelian Society in 1897, and published in *Mind* in 1898.[1] It was written when Moore was very much and very sympathetically preoccupied with Kant's ethics, and it was indeed part of a much longer essay on Kant's idea of Freedom, which Moore at the time intended to rearrange and enlarge into a treatise on the whole of Kant's ethical philosophy. The paper comprises three sections. In the first section Moore emphasizes that Kant was a Determinist in the ordinary sense of the term; in the second he defends Kant's Determinism, and 'disposes' of the theory of 'Liberty of Indifference'; and in the third he attacks certain parts of Kant's doctrine of Freedom, where Kant seems to come nearest to upholding 'Liberty of Indifference'. For the modern reader concerned with Free Will, and not especially inclined to enter into the intricacies of Kant's doctrine of Freedom, the most important part of Moore's paper is the second section (pp. 185–94), in which he defends Kant's Determinism, and 'disposes' of the theory of 'Liberty of Indifference'. Moore's discussion is of particular interest in relation to his later treatment of Free Will in *Ethics*, since in the early paper he maintains positions which seem to be presupposed in *Ethics*, but are not there argued for or discussed, and he also says a number of things which contrast markedly with some of the statements in *Ethics* and are, in my view, nearer the truth. I shall mainly mention points Moore makes in this second section, though I shall not confine myself to it.

Moore shows himself to be a convinced Determinist, not only

[1] *Mind*, VII (1898), pp. 179–204.

about physical but also about mental events. He quotes[1] a contemporary statement[2] of 'the doctrine of Free Will, as commonly understood':

'Whenever a man exercises his will, and makes a voluntary choice of one out of various possible courses, an event occurs, whose relation to contiguous events cannot be included in a general statement applicable to all similar cases. There is something wholly capricious and arbitrary, belonging to that moment only; and *we have no right to conclude that if circumstances were exactly repeated, and the man himself absolutely unaltered, he would choose the same course.*'

Moore comments forcefully: 'Now this doctrine Kant would absolutely condemn'; and he makes it clear later in the paper that he could concur with Kant.[3] It is also worth noting, however, especially in view of Moore's later treatment of Free Will in *Ethics*, what Moore here takes as 'the doctrine of Free Will, as commonly understood'.[4]

In the second section Moore considers the common idea of 'freedom', and sees its most universal characteristic as 'absence of external constraint'. Where the proximate cause of a motion or change seems to lie in the thing which moves or changes, we normally call the thing 'free'. Moore points out that this is clearly not limited to human actions. Moreover, the idea itself is fraught with difficulties. The spatial or temporal limits of a 'thing' are more or less arbitrary; and why should the 'proximate' cause be considered pre-eminent (in any case, how far back does a cause cease to be 'proximate'?)? Moore suggests that such difficulties seem to have caused people gradually to restrict the idea of freedom to man, because the distinction between the self and other things is the most striking and the most practically important to people. Moore sees 'the vulgar doctrine of Free Will, as "Liberty of Indifference"', as chiefly an attempt to make this distinction between the self and everything else a non-arbitrary one—the self

---

[1] *Art. cit.*, p. 181.
[2] By W. K. Clifford in his essay on 'Right and Wrong' in *Lectures and Essays*, London, 1886, p. 318.
[3] *Art. cit.*, pp. 185–94, especially p. 188.
[4] Cf. the description on p. 182 of the dispute between Libertarians and Determinists.

being thought of as an agent undetermined by previous events in time, i.e. as an uncaused cause.[1] This idea derived plausibility from the lack of progress in psychology as compared with physical science. 'And the region of the incompletely known is the favourite abode of a metaphysical monstrosity', is Moore's tart comment. Moore also asserts that the results of human volition, alone among causes, must *of necessity* remain incapable of complete prediction,[2] and this fact had combined with the greater empirical difficulty of predicting mental events, to strengthen belief in uncaused volition. Recent advances in empirical psychology had, however, made it more and more difficult to doubt that this belief in uncaused volition was illusory. Yet that would not, Moore recognizes, refute the doctrine of Free Will. This could be refuted only by recourse to the *a priori* necessity that every event must have a cause. That *a priori* necessity had, however, to Moore's satisfaction, been established by Kant in the Analytic, and therefore the common doctrine of Free Will could not stand.[3] Moore's analysis of the process leading to the formation of the doctrine of 'Liberty of Indifference' is stimulating, and his account of the reasons for its plausibility carries conviction; but the validity of his final refutation does, of course, depend on whether the proposition that every event must have a cause is true.

Moore also considers in the second section of his paper[4] the argument for Free Will from 'the immediate affirmation of consciousness in the moment of deliberate action'.[5] Here Moore points out that to be relevant to the Free Will controversy, this 'affirmation of consciousness' must be not that it is possible for me to *do* what I choose, but that it is possible for me to *choose*.[6] The question whether a choice 'will produce in any degree the effect chosen' Moore thinks to be irrelevant to the Free Will controversy, 'if the issue of that controversy be clearly stated'.[7] This seems to me to be absolutely right, but it is, as will be seen, entirely at variance with what Moore comes to say, fifteen years later, in *Ethics*. In this connexion, moreover, Moore goes on, in the paper on 'Freedom', to castigate Locke and Hume (very justly, in my opinion) for their

---

[1] *Art. cit.*, p. 186.
[2] I am omitting Moore's subtle argument (pp. 186–7) for this point because I want to keep clearly in view the main lines of his discussion.
[3] *Art. cit.*, p. 188.   [4] At pp. 188–91.
[5] Henry Sidgwick, *Methods of Ethics*, 7th edn., London, 1907, p. 65.
[6] *Art. cit.*, p. 188.   [7] *Ibid.*, pp. 188–9.

cavalier treatment of the Free Will controversy, which they were only able to dismiss with contempt because they had taken Liberty to mean simply 'a power to act as we choose'.[1] Moore rightly concedes that Locke does at one stage[2] see that the point in dispute is 'Are we free to choose?', but Moore also acutely points out that Locke had no right to assume that 'Are we free to choose?' means 'Can a man will, what he wills?', since it would only have that meaning if Locke's definition of freedom, as power to do what one chooses, were already acceptable. Moore goes on:

'It would indeed be absurd to ask "Can I choose to choose?" in the sense "Am I free to choose which of two alternatives I will choose?". But Locke had no right to assume that this is meant by the question "Am I free to choose?". That question may mean "Am I the original cause of my choice?" and this he leaves undiscussed. Both Locke and Hume therefore neglect the point of the controversy by their definition of freedom. They have, however, done some service to the question, inasmuch as their treatment of it is a protest against the confusion of freedom "to do, if I choose", with "freedom to choose". Their defect is that they assume that it was an answer to the first question only, which was really wanted; and hence their contempt of the dispute.'[3]

In this brilliant passage Moore seems to me to have fired very effectively against Locke and Hume; but we shall see that he comes to write quite differently, and, I think, by no means so validly, in *Ethics*. In the early paper, however, Moore, keeping to the right central issue, raises the question what evidence consciousness offers about it: 'Does consciousness affirm, when alternatives are presented, that I can choose any of them that I think either good or bad?'.[4] He considers a possible answer to an objection urged by Clifford[5] that the affirmation by consciousness, to be 'of any use in the controversy' must be 'competent to assure me of the nonexistence of something which by hypothesis is not in my consciousness'. Moore holds that it would be enough if consciousness could affirm what *is* the cause of the choice, without requiring it

[1] *Art. cit.*, p. 189.
[2] Locke, *An Essay concerning Human Understanding*, Book II, s. 27.
[3] *Art. cit.*, pp. 189–90.   [4] *Art. cit.*, p. 190
[5] W. K. Clifford, *op. cit.*, p. 327.

to prove that nothing else in the world can be (otherwise no scientist could ever establish a law of nature). If consciousness were to affirm that 'I' am the cause of the choice, that would be sufficient. But Moore goes on to question whether consciousness actually does affirm more than that 'it is possible that such a choice will take place in my mind'.[1] Such an affirmation, Moore points out, would be compatible with Determinism. And it seems quite uncertain that consciousness does affirm more. These are the main lines of Moore's argument. I have not space to do full justice to its admirable details; but even without these the argument seems to me both clear and cogent. Its conclusion could perhaps be expressed by saying that consciousness makes no certain affirmation inconsistent with Determinism. And with that conclusion I, for one, would firmly agree.

The main positions on the Free Will controversy, that Moore holds in this early paper, therefore, are (1) that Determinism holds both for physical and for mental events, and is an *a priori* necessary principle; (2) that the Free Will controversy as ordinarily understood concerns freedom to choose, not freedom to act as one chooses; (3) that, with regard to freedom to choose, consciousness makes no certain affirmation contrary to Determinism.

In *Principia Ethica* (1903) Moore says little about Free Will, and even that little only in relation to Kant's assertion of 'the Autonomy of the Practical Reason'.

It is in Chapter VI of *Ethics* (1912)[2] that Moore again intensively addresses his mind to the problem. In the earlier chapters of that book Moore had advanced an ethical theory which implied that people very often act wrongly. Now Moore saw that philosophers who (1) deny that anyone ever *could* have done anything other than what he actually did do; and who (2) hold that right and wrong depend upon what the agent *absolutely can* do (not merely *can do if he so chooses*), are logically bound to hold that no human action is ever right or wrong. He also saw (and this was a subtler insight) that philosophers who, on the contrary, hold (1) that we *absolutely can* do things which we do not do, and who also hold (2) that right and wrong depend upon what we thus *can* do, also contradict the ethical theory which he had put forward. For the ethical theory held that we are fully entitled to say that a person acted rightly or wrongly, if that person could, on the occasion concerned, have done something else, *if he had chosen.*

---

[1] *Art. cit.*, p. 190.   [2] *Ethics*, pp. 196–222.

Moore roundly admits that it seems to him (1) very difficult to be sure that right and wrong do not really depend upon what we *absolutely can* do, and not merely on what we can do, *if we choose*; and (2) also very difficult to be sure in what sense it is true that we ever *could* have done anything different from what we actually did do.[1] He then concentrates attention on the second of these difficulties.

Actually, Moore's formulation of the second difficulty is not entirely satisfactory. For he proceeds to indicate very soon afterwards[2] a sense in which people quite certainly *can* do what they do not do. His subsequent discussion, indeed, makes it clear that the difficulty which really baffled Moore was not that it is hard to be sure *in what sense* it is true that we ever *could* have done anything different from what we actually did do; but rather that he found it very hard to be sure whether there is a sense of 'could', other than the *absolute sense* of 'could', but *relevant to the Free Will problem*, in which we ever *could* have done (or chosen) anything different from what we actually did do (or choose).

I shall return to this point later, and add to it; but meanwhile let us follow the lines of Moore's discussion. He rightly repudiates as 'a mere abuse of language' the view that our wills can properly be said to be free if we *never* 'can', in any sense at all, do anything but what, in the end, we actually do.[3] He also easily disposes of the unqualified assertion that 'nothing ever *could* have happened, except what actually did happen', by indicating, with examples, that one of the commonest and most legitimate uses of the terms 'could' and 'could not' is to express a difference between two things *neither* of which did actually happen (e.g. 'I *could* have walked a mile in 20 minutes this morning, but I certainly *could not* have run 2 miles in 5 minutes', when I actually did neither).[4]

Moore's next move is to consider the relation of this legitimate use of 'could' to the familiar determinist argument from p 'every event has a cause' to q 'nothing ever could have happened except what did happen'.[5] Moore holds that all that would follow from p would be that in *one* sense of 'could' q would be true. Moreover, if the word 'could' is ambiguous, it is clearly quite possible that in *another* sense of 'could' some things which did not happen *could* have happened. And if 'could' is *not* ambiguous, Moore boldly and

---

[1] *Ethics*, pp. 201–2.
[2] *Ibid.*, pp. 205–8.
[3] *Ibid.*, p. 203.
[4] *Ibid.*, pp. 204–8.
[5] *Ibid.*, pp. 208 ff.

interestingly contends, then, since, in one sense of 'could' (that sense already indicated with examples), some things which did not happen *could* have happened, and since that would, if 'could' is unambiguous, be the only sense, we should have to give up the principle that everything has a cause.[1] Now Moore rightly points out that many people had rashly assumed that 'could' is un-ambiguous; and so, in the Free Will controversy, had taken for granted that the question at issue was solely whether everything is caused, or whether acts of will are sometimes uncaused. Moore contends that the truth is that it is extremely doubtful whether Free Will is inconsistent with the principle that everything is caused; and he says that this all depends 'on a very difficult question as to the meaning of the word "could"'. He maintains that all that is certain is (1) that if we have Free Will, it must be true, *in some sense*, that we sometimes *could* have done what we did not do; (2) that, if everything is caused, it must be true, *in some sense*, that we *never could* have done what we did not do. And he adds that what is very *un*certain, and needs to be investigated, is whether these two meanings of the word 'could' are the same. Moore's way of putting the question is not only very typical of him, but must have appeared novel at the time, and, *methodologically*, seems to me to be an early example of linguistic philosophy at its best.

Let us, however, follow Moore's investigation. He starts by asking what sense the word 'could' has when I say that I *could* have walked a mile in 20 minutes this morning, though I did not.[2] He considers the suggestion, often made, that what is meant is that 'I *should* have walked . . . if I had chosen' (personally I think a slightly better formulation would have been 'I *would* have walked . . . chosen', avoiding the overtones of obligation in 'should', and I see that Moore himself actually changes to this formulation on the next page,[3] though he later uses the terms interchangeably). Moore says that 'there are very good reasons for thinking' that we *very often* do mean by 'X could have . . .' merely 'X would have . . . if he had chosen'. In point of fact, though, Moore does not specify his 'reasons' at all. Yet he is surely right in believing that 'could have' very often means just that. And he is also surely right in holding that the fact that, in this sense of 'could', we often *could* have done what we did not do is perfectly compatible with the principle that everything has a cause. Moore goes on, however, to offer what he calls 'an additional reason' for supposing that this

---

[1] *Ethics*, p. 210.   [2] *Ibid.*, p. 211.   [3] *Ibid.*, p. 212.

is what we often mean by 'could'.[1] It was, in my view, a misnomer to speak of this as 'an additional reason', since Moore had not yet specified any reason at all. What Moore *had* done, I suggest, was simply to realize and point out that that was a correct and very common use of the word 'could' in English. Moore's insight was unerring; yet he misdescribed it. But let us move on. Moore's 'additional reason' is that people who denied that we ever *could* have done anything which we did not do, often thought and stated that it followed that we never *would* have acted differently, *even if* we had chosen differently. Those whom Moore calls 'Fatalists' (people who believed that *whatever we willed* the result would be the same) held such a view; and so did those who thought that moral praise and blame were never justified. Moore firmly and rightly asserts that neither view follows from the principle that everything has a cause.[2] With regard to Fatalism he also stoutly and rightly states that it is often true that if we choose C_1 the result will *always* be different in some respect from what it would have been if we had chosen C_2, and that *sometimes* the difference will be that we achieve our objective. As to the view that moral praise and blame are never justified, Moore stresses the point that the fact that an individual A would have avoided committing a crime, *if* he had chosen, whereas B would *not* have succeeded in avoiding a disease, *even if* he had chosen, affords ample justification for regarding and treating the two cases differently, because by blame or punishment we often have a reasonable chance of preventing crimes like A's in the future, whereas where the will is not involved we have no such chance.[3] Here again we may, I think, properly concur with Moore, provided that we regard moral praise and blame, reward and punishment, simply as useful tools for producing socially desirable consequences. The question on which I wish to focus, however, is whether this 'additional reason' of Moore's for holding that we very often mean by 'X could have' simply 'X would have, if he had chosen', is valid. Now, I believe that very often people do say, in contradiction to what Moore calls 'Fatalism', 'X could have done a' (which he did not do), meaning by this that X would have done a if he had chosen to. I also believe that what they say is often true; though this does not matter for the present purpose, since all that we are now concerned with is usage. Again, I believe that very often people do say, in considering a case of crime, that X 'could have avoided

[1] *Ethics*, p. 212.   [2] *Ibid.*, p. 213.   [3] *Ibid.*, pp. 215–16.

committing it', and that, as Moore says, they very often mean by this that X would have avoided committing the crime if he had so chosen. I also believe that what such people say is often true; but common usage is our only concern at present. Once again, however, in both cases these are *insights* into the use of the English language, rather than 'reasons' for believing that this is a common meaning of the term in question.

But now we come to the crunch; and it is faced by Moore with his habitual care and tentativeness:

'And for my part I must confess that I cannot feel certain that this may not be *all* that we usually mean and understand by the assertion that we have Free Will; so that those who deny that we have it are really denying (though, no doubt, often unconsciously) that we ever *should* have acted differently, even if we had willed differently. It has been sometimes held that this *is* what we mean; and I cannot find any conclusive argument to the contrary. And if it is what we mean, then it absolutely follows that we really *have* Free Will, and also that this fact is quite consistent with the principle that everything has a cause; and it follows also that our theory will be perfectly right, when it makes right and wrong depend on what we *could* have done, *if* we had chosen.'[1]

This passage deserves as close attention as that with which it was undoubtedly written. Moore says at the beginning that he cannot feel certain that the given analysis may not be *all* that we *usually* (my italics) mean and understand by the assertion that we have Free Will. Now this leaves open (and rightly leaves open) the question whether the term 'Free Will' is not itself ambiguous, at least in the sense that it is used with different meanings, however legitimately, by different people. But later in the passage Moore seems inclined to discard the ambiguity, when he writes 'It has sometimes been held that this *is* what we mean; and I cannot find any conclusive argument to the contrary'. Here Moore is implicitly admitting that 'Free Will' may well be an *un*ambiguous term. This is curious. For he certainly goes on to assert that there are many people who would not admit that this is what 'Free Will' means.[1] It is surely, then, at least possible that the term is used in different senses by different people. A further question would, of course, be whether there is one correct sense, or more than one correct

[1] *Ethics*, p. 217.

sense, or whether the term really has no clear sense at all. It is worth remembering at this point, in any case, however, that in his article on 'Freedom' Moore had, indeed, recognized only one ordinary sense of 'Free Will', but that that sense was quite different from that which he is here considering.

Now, early in his discussion in Chapter VI of *Ethics*[1] Moore pointed out that he had all along in his book been using the word 'could' *in a special sense*, and this 'special sense' he had described in Chapter I,[2] and again described early in Chapter VI,[3] as equivalent to 'could . . . if X had chosen' (he later replaces that formula by 'should . . .' and by 'would . . .', as we have seen). And Moore went on to distinguish this 'special sense' from the absolute sense.[3] Not only, then, did Moore recognize, as we have seen, the absolute sense of 'could', but he evidently regarded it as primary, and his own sense as special. However this may be, though, my suggestion is that many people who assert the existence of Free Will would quite certainly wish to assert that we 'could', in an absolute sense, do many things that we do not do.[4] Indeed, once having recognized the absolute sense of 'could', had Moore any good ground for withholding recognition to an absolute sense of the term 'Free Will' corresponding to it? It is interesting that he should not readily allow the possibility that, although there may be some 'special sense' of the term 'Free Will' (corresponding to his 'special sense' of 'could'), there is also an absolute sense of the term 'Free Will', corresponding to the absolute sense of the term 'could', whose existence he has taken for granted. He writes that he 'cannot find any conclusive argument' against the view that the term 'Free Will' has no other sense than that in terms of the hypothetical analysis of 'could'; yet he recognizes that many people would not accept that use of the term 'Free Will', and he has also admitted that the hypothetical sense of 'could' was a 'special sense'. Those two points could surely have impressed him as conclusive *argumenta ad hominem* against his own position? Exactly why Moore does not seem to have adverted to them would be an interesting question; but I want to pass now to the final phases of his discussion.

Moore considers a reason (which he holds to be plausible but not conclusive) which many people would have for denying the

---

[1] pp. 197–8.   [2] *Ibid.*, pp. 29–30.   [3] *Ibid.*, p. 198.
[4] This would not, however, be their formulation of the doctrine of Free Will itself, as I shall indicate later.

hypothetical analysis of the term 'Free Will'.[1] This reason is that for us to have Free Will it would also need *often* to be true that we *could* have *chosen* differently. In answer Moore indicates two senses in which we often *could* have chosen what we did not choose, pointing out that in neither sense would that fact contradict the principle of causality.[2] The first of the two senses which Moore indicates is just the old sense again, in which '*X could* have *chosen* differently' means '*X would* have chosen differently *if* he had chosen *to make the choice*'. Now Moore seems quite sure that this is a perfectly sensible thing to say, and that it is quite often true. Yet this time he gives no example, and it is legitimate to wonder whether such a statement has much application in concrete cases, even if it makes good sense at all. I believe it does, in fact, make good sense, but that its field of application is a fairly narrow one. It will apply, for instance, I think, to such cases as that in which X, a habitual gambler, drinker, or chain-smoker, decides to try to break himself of the habit, and to do so by refraining, first of all, say, every Tuesday and Thursday. He may choose beforehand to make specific choices on those days. The statement also, no doubt, covers some other kinds of case, but I do not wish to spend further time on it, since, besides its having a somewhat unnatural and tortuous character, it would certainly not satisfy a great number of those 'many people' who would be dissatisfied with the original, simpler hypothetical analysis of Free Will. Let us now examine, then, the second of the two senses which Moore indicates as senses in which we often *could* have chosen what, in fact, we did not choose. This is, that we *could* have so chosen, in the sense that no one could *know for certain* that we would not do so. Now, with regard to this sense, Moore candidly admits that it may go no way to justify us in saying that we have Free Will;[3] and I believe not only that he was right to admit this, but that the sense has no bearing whatever on the question of 'Free Will' in what is probably the most important, if not the only legitimate, sense of that term. Yet when Moore sums up his discussion, this sense of '*could* have chosen' figures, and figures importantly, among the propositions which he enumerates as possibly highly relevant to the whole problem.

It is again worth quoting the passage, both for its admirable clarity and vigour, and to facilitate effective critical discussion: 'It is, therefore, quite certain (1) that we often *should* have *acted*

---

[1] *Ethics*, pp. 217–18.   [2] *Ibid.*, pp. 218–20.   [3] *Ibid.*, p. 219.

differently, if we had chosen to; (2) that similarly we often should have *chosen* differently, *if* we had chosen so to choose; and (3) that it was almost always *possible* that we should have chosen differently, in the sense that no man could know for certain that we should *not* so choose. All these three things are facts, and all of them are quite consistent with the principle of causality. Can anybody undertake to say for certain that none of these three facts and *no* combination of them will justify us in saying that we have Free Will? Or, suppose it granted that we have not Free Will, unless it is often true that we *could* have chosen, what did not choose: Can any defender of Free Will, or any opponent of it, show conclusively that what he means by "*could* have chosen" in this proposition, is anything different from the two certain facts, which I have numbered (2) and (3), or some combination of the two? Many people, no doubt, will still insist that these two facts alone are by no means sufficient to entitle us to say that we have Free Will: that it must be that we were *able* to choose, in some quite other sense. But nobody, so far as I know, has ever been able to tell us exactly what that sense is. For my part, I can find no conclusive argument to show either that some such other sense of "can" is necessary, or that it is not. And, therefore, this chapter must conclude with a doubt.'[1]

Much could be said about this passage, but I only want to make one or two points. First, then, Moore seems to think that the onus is on the defender (or opponent) of Free Will to 'show conclusively' that what he means by '*could* have chosen' is different from Moore's (2) and (3). Yet Moore himself, as we have seen, has admitted the existence of an absolute sense of 'could', so why should he require anyone to *prove* its existence? Can it not be *seen* to exist by anyone who knows English usage, just as Moore himself quite clearly saw that it existed? Again, in his challenge: 'Can any defender of Free Will, or any opponent of it, show conclusively . . .?', what exactly was Moore requiring for conclusive proof? Suppose a Libertarian and a Determinist agreed together that what they meant by '*could* have chosen' in that proposition was '*could* have chosen, even if all things in the universe up till that moment, including our own dispositions, had been exactly what they were'. Would Moore then have taken that as conclusive proof that this was what both parties did mean by the words '*could* have chosen'? Quite possibly not (though he would clearly have

[1] *Ethics.*, pp. 220–2.

taken the expression just in that sense in the article written fifteen years before).[1] But is there any good reason to suppose that this was not what they meant? I suggest that there is no good reason. In my view, Moore was interestingly misguided in asking for conclusive proof if he wanted anything more than can be seen by inspecting the clause '*could* have chosen, even if everything in the universe up till that moment, including our dispositions, had been exactly what they were', and *seeing* (as one easily can) that this does not mean the same as his (2) or (3) or 'any combination' of them.

Now it does seem to be this, or something very like it, that many philosophers have meant when they have asserted or denied the existence of Free Will. There have, no doubt, been other philosophers on both sides who have used the term in an attenuated sense, and Moore's suggested analysis of at least one such attenuated sense (in terms of his (2) and (3), his (1) being really irrelevant) is certainly of interest. Yet whether any such attenuated sense of the term is really legitimate, is a question to which Moore would pretty certainly have answered 'No' at the time when he wrote the article on 'Freedom'. Moreover, we may, I think, justifiably regard such attenuated senses, even if legitimate, as probably a good deal less important than the absolute sense.

Again, towards the end of the passage I have quoted, Moore says that he 'can find no conclusive argument to show either that some such sense of "can" is necessary, or that it is not'. Here he means, of course, 'necessary' for us to be able to affirm (or to deny) the existence of Free Will. Now there are two points to be made here: First, there may be more than one sense of the term 'Free Will', and, if so, then one of these senses may be more important than another, and, possibly, one more important than *any* other. Personally I believe that one of the most important senses, and probably, indeed, the most important, if not the only legitimate, sense requires more than Moore's (2) or (3) or 'any combination' of them. Secondly, if an absolute sense of 'can' exists, then Moore's difficulty may perhaps be seen not as a difficulty as to what the required sense of 'can' is, but as a difficulty as to what the term 'Free Will' means. Yet Moore makes the difficulty seem to be that of seeing exactly what the sense of 'can' is, that the defenders and opponents of Free Will have in mind. For many, if not most, of those defenders and opponents that sense was, I suggest, that which he had clearly recognized as the absolute sense.

---

[1] *Art. cit.*, p. 190.

I want now to leave for a moment Moore's discussion in *Ethics*, and to mention briefly a note which he seems to have made about forty years later.[1]

This note of Moore's begins with the statement that my will is free if and only if both (1) *if* I had *chosen* (or *decided*) to make a 'voluntary movement' which I did not make, I should have made it; and (2) I *could* have *chosen* (or *decided*) to make it. The whole note depends on this basic position, and I shall therefore confine myself to a few comments on the two parts of the position. Now, at the outset, we may, I think, justifiably deny that (1) is relevant to Free Will at all. This corresponds to a point I have already made in discussing Chapter VI of *Ethics*, and which Moore himself had already made in the 1898 article. (1) concerns Freedom of Action according to Choice, rather than Free Will. The vital question for Free Will in the most important sense or senses is whether I could ever have made a different choice or decision or effort from that which I did make. Moreover, this choice or decision or effort may not concern a 'voluntary movement' at all. It may, for instance, be to think about something rather than about something else. Moore's (2), however, suitably modified so as not to be restricted to cases of 'voluntary movements', does seem to face the crucial point. But Moore's note does not analyse or examine the proposition, and it does not offer any advance on his earlier discussion in *Ethics*.

We are left, then, substantially, with the discussions in the early article on 'Freedom' and in Chapter VI of *Ethics* as Moore's contributions to the problem. I propose now to make some general comments on the discussion in *Ethics*, then to compare this briefly with that in the 1898 article, trying to account for the difference. Then I want to mention Moore's reconsideration in 1942 of certain points in Chapter VI of *Ethics*, and finally to make some concluding observations on the whole matter.

One special feature of Moore's treatment in *Ethics* is that he does not discuss in any detail the principle of causality. He enunciates it, and then assumes, *for the purposes of his argument*, that it is true. He regards the relation of cause and effect as *necessary*; and assuming the principle, which he enunciates as 'absolutely everything that happens has a *cause* in what precedes', he admits that it follows that, in one sense of 'could', nothing ever

[1] G. E. Moore, *Commonplace Book: 1919–1953*, ed. C. Lewy, London and New York, 1962, pp. 409–10.

could have happened, except what did happen. (Interestingly enough, here again Moore seems to recognize that sense of 'could' without demur.) Now, many of the discussions of Free Will both before and since 1912 *do* consider in some detail the principle of causality. Why did not Moore do so? Did he believe that the principle of causality as enunciated by him was so clearly true as not to deserve discussion? Or did he think that his own suggested analysis of Free Will might well be true, and, since Free Will, in that sense, did not infringe the principle of causality, a detailed discussion of that principle was not required? Either or both of these factors may have operated. In connexion with the latter Moore may well, indeed, have felt pretty strongly that no one would be able to meet his challenge, and to show conclusively that another sense of 'could' was required for Free Will besides those which he had himself described. There is also the possibility that he may have thought that a thorough discussion of causality would be out of place in a short book on ethics. Whatever Moore's reasons for not discussing causality, however, I believe that this must be considered a gap of some importance.

A second interesting feature of Moore's discussion in *Ethics* is connected with his concern to maintain that moral blame and punishment are amply justified whenever X *would* have succeeded in avoiding a crime, *if* he had chosen. Moore clearly inclines to regard Free Will as necessary for the validity of moral praise and blame, reward and punishment, and he takes what I have called 'Freedom of Action according to Choice' as quite possibly *all* that we usually mean and understand by 'Free Will'. He evidently does not, on the other hand, believe that, for moral praise or blame, reward or punishment, there is required absolute freedom of choice or decision, in the sense that we could, on some occasions at least, have chosen (or decided) otherwise than we did, everything up till then being exactly as it was; though he does admit (at the foot of page 201) that it is 'very difficult' to be sure about this. The view Moore inclined to was, in one way, a hard-headed view. Moore did not feel convinced, as some people have been, that if X really *could* not (in an absolute sense) have chosen otherwise, he would not deserve moral *blame* at all, and would only deserve *punishment* on social grounds. On the other hand, in another way, Moore's view was far from being hard-headed, in that he required 'Free Will', in some sense, as a necessary condition of the validity of moral praise and blame, and of reward and punishment. He did not hold the view, which many people have held (especially in ages and countries when the rule of absolute liability has predominated),[1] that people deserve moral praise and blame, and reward and punishment, in virtue of their acts, irrespective of their intentions or motives. Nor did he hold the view, also often held, that people deserve moral praise and blame and reward and punishment for their acts, if intended, and if motivated in certain ways, even though the intentions and motives were such that, given the agents' own history and that of the world at large up to that point, their intentions and motives *could* not have been other than they were. Moore's disinclination to dispense with 'Free Will', in some sense of the expression, leads him to try to define it in terms of Freedom of Action according to Choice; and later, when that does not entirely satisfy him, and in view of the fact that many people would *certainly* not be satisfied with it, to have recourse to the tortuous and ineffective expedient of a 'choice of choice', and also to unpredictability, as possible elements in the idea of Free Will; which, in the absolute and probably most important (if not the only legitimate) sense of that term, they certainly are not. Before leaving this topic it is, I think, worth calling attention to a little touch by Moore when he switches from discussing the analysis 'X would have done Y, *if* he had chosen'. At that point he outlines the view of the 'many people' who would be likely to reject the analysis:

They will say, namely: Granted that we often *should* have acted differently, *if* we had chosen differently, yet it is not true that we have Free Will, unless it is *also* often true in such cases that we *could* have *chosen* differently. The question of Free Will has been thus represented as being merely the question whether we ever *could* have chosen, what we did not choose, or ever *can* choose, what, in fact, we shall not choose.'[2]

It is intensely interesting to find Moore here alleging that the question of Free Will has thus been represented as being '*merely*'

---

[1] Readers interested in this matter may be referred to the articles by Nathan Isaacs, 'Fault and Liability', 31 *Harvard Law Review*, pp. 954 ff., *Harvard Essays*, pp. 235 ff., and by P. H. Winfield, 'The Myth of Absolute Liability', 42 *Law Quarterly Review*, pp. 37 ff., and also to such standard works as Holdsworth's *History of English Law*, Bohlen's *Studies in Jurisprudence*, Holmes's *Common Law*, Pollock's *Torts*, Salmond's *Torts* and Winfield's *Tort*.

[2] *Ethics*, p. 218. This is, as may be remembered, the very way in which Moore had himself 'represented' the question of Free Will in the article on 'Freedom'.

that, when surely that *is* probably the most important question, and is certainly the question which very many philosophers, both in previous centuries and in our own, have thought they were discussing when they considered the problem of Free Will.[1] It is strange that Moore should evidently at that point have thought that his hypothetical analysis '*X* would have done *Y*, *if* he had chosen' was far nearer to the heart of the matter than what those philosophers (including himself in 1897) have had in mind. It is hard to speculate with any confidence on why Moore apparently thought this. I wonder whether it may have been because he felt the strength of the principle of causality, wanted to retain Free Will, in some sense, but was as puzzled as Locke how to give any clear and satisfactory account of it consistent with the principle of causality, and so at that point regarded the whole venture beyond this hypothetical analysis (the first part of which closely resembles Locke's) with mistrust.

A third important feature of Moore's treatment is that he takes little or no account of what is often called 'the sense of freedom', the sense which many people have said they have, through introspection, that their wills 'are free'. This sense is apparently often pretty vague, and perhaps comparatively few philosophers, even if pressed hard, would say that what they sense is that they often could make any one of a number of choices or decisions, including those they do not make, even if everything up till that moment were the same; and that they could often have done the same kind of thing in the past. Indeed, it may well be that quite a number of people would be satisfied with some analysis of their 'sense of freedom' short of strong Libertarianism. If so, this would seem to chime in with the suggestion I made earlier, that the term 'Free Will' has been used in a number of different senses. Moreover, I think we could reasonably add that the sense in which it is being used on any occasion would be indicated by the criteria which would be accepted by its user for its application. Yet, whatever anyone means by saying that he feels (or knows by introspection) that his will is free, I do not think that this can be counted as substantial evidence for his will really *being* free, in any proper sense;[2] and I believe that Moore was quite right to leave such

---

[1] E.g. in this century, C. D. Broad, *Five Types of Ethical Theory*, London, 1930, p. 193; W. D. Ross, *Foundations of Ethics*, Oxford, 1939, p. 234.

[2] Cf. W. D. Ross, *Foundations of Ethics*, Oxford, 1939, pp. 223–46; and D. J. O'Connor, 'Possibility and Choice', *Aristotelian Society Supplementary Volume XXXIV* (1960), pp. 21–4.

purported evidence out of account. I do not wish to argue this point; but to pass to a still more important feature of Moore's discussion.

It will be remembered that, in his final summary, Moore stated that many people would no doubt insist that to entitle us to say that we have Free Will it must be true, in some cases at least, that we were *able* to choose, in some quite other sense than any he had indicated in his analysis; but that nobody, so far as he knew, had ever been able to tell us exactly what that sense is.[1] I have already suggested two *argumenta ad hominem* against Moore on this point, which seem to me to be conclusive. But one had better also face the question, at least briefly, on its merits. Was Moore himself right to admit, as he did at several points in *Ethics*, an absolute sense of 'can' and 'could'? The question whether such an absolute sense exists has received a fair deal of consideration by philosophers in recent years, notably by the late Professor Austin,[2] who held that there is such a sense, and by Professor D. J. O'Connor,[3] who has maintained that there is no good evidence that there is or is not such a sense. How are we to decide whether there is such a sense or not? Presumably by considering plausible instances of such a use, and seeing whether they after all turn out to be disguised hypotheticals. With respect to Moore's challenge, however, I presume that if we were to find instances of an absolute use it would not then be fair to ask us, in addition, to say what that use was, other than to call it an 'absolute' or 'unconditional' or 'categorical', as contrasted with a 'hypothetical' or 'conditional' use. The fact that it could not be analysed further would, indeed, constitute its absoluteness. Now, if I say 'I could have chosen X at t_1, but I chose Y' it is not yet clear whether I am using 'could' in an absolute sense, though I may well be. If what I mean by the statement is S: 'I could have chosen X at t_1, even if everything in the universe up to t_1 had been exactly the same, but I chose Y', then, it seems to me, I could reasonably be said to be using 'could' in an absolute sense, since I have expressly excluded any condition. If it were objected that so far from *excluding* conditions

---

[1] *Ethics*, p. 221.

[2] 'Ifs and Can's, *Proceedings of the British Academy*, XLII (1956), pp. 109–32.

[3] 'Possibility and Choice', *Aristotelian Society Supplementary Volume XXXIV* (1960), pp. 15–24. It is interesting to find Professor O'Connor, who doubts the existence of an absolute sense, writing of 'the generally recognized', *conditional* or *hypothetical* sense of 'can if . . .', which Moore designated as a 'special' sense. *Tempora mutantur!*

I have *specified* them (namely, as all the conditions which were in fact fulfilled), then, though I should regard the objection as a quibble (for the 'even if' is concessive = 'even though', not conditional = 'provided that'), I would assert that it is, in any case, in *that* sense of 'could have', *whatever we call it*, that many defenders of Free Will would use 'could have' in this connexion. Moreover, I should want to maintain that such an assertion as *S* is perfectly intelligible, though whether it is ever true is an entirely different matter, which I am deliberately regarding as outside the scope of the present article.

I want to pass now to another interesting feature of Moore's discussion: his use of the notion of 'choice'. Up till this point I have not thought it necessary to make much fuss about the appropriateness of this term in Moore's analysis. I have mentioned the inadequacy of the concept of 'choosing to choose'; but there are other difficulties involved, some of which have been pointed out by philosophers in recent years. One difficulty is that in the statement 'I would have done X, if I had chosen', the condition seems to be a necessary precondition[1] of my doing X, whereas, it has been urged, choice is sometimes continuous with and indeed part of the action itself.[2] I believe that Moore could properly have answered this objection, however, by making the point that the condition is, indeed, a necessary condition, but not a necessary precondition in a sense involving *temporal* priority. But there is another difficulty which might seem more serious, namely that the word 'choice' suggests that the agent faces two or more alternative possibilities, and *picks* one of them. Now, it could be said, it might well be possible for me to do X without any of this taking place, and therefore 'I could have done X' does not mean the same as 'I would have done X, if I had chosen'. This objection can also, however, be answered. The word 'choose' may, indeed, *suggest* picking one of several alternative possibilities; but the word has a range which passes well beyond such cases, so that Moore's proposed analysis might well still hold. Yet it might also be objected that the word 'choose' does, at least, suggest a deliberate process of some kind, and that there are certainly cases where I could have done X (which I did not do), and yet not deliberated at all. Does the range of the word 'choose' really stretch beyond even that?

---

[1] I believe, in any case, that Austin, who took it to be a *sufficient* condition, misunderstood Moore here.

[2] See e.g. P. H. Nowell-Smith, *Ethics*, London, 1954, p. 101.

Suppose I am sight-reading at the piano, and play a particular note with my first finger instead of with my second, I 'could' certainly, in some sense short of an absolute sense, have played the note with my second finger: but if I gave the matter no thought, and mechanically played the note with my first finger, would we really want to say that if I had done the same thing with my second finger I would have *chosen* to do so? If we say that it would *not* have been a 'choice', then we should have to admit that Moore's equivalence does not hold. On the other hand, if we say that it *would* have been a 'choice', not only do we seem to be stretching the term 'choice' unwarrantably, but it is even very hard to see what actions would be left for us to call '*not* chosen'. Whichever nomenclature we adopt, therefore, Moore's analysis of 'could have done *X*' in terms of 'would have done *X*, if I had chosen' is unsatisfactory. Moreover, in any case, it will be remembered, that analysis does not, if I am right, concern the matter of Free Will.

Moore's attempt in *Ethics* to suggest a means of reconciling the Principle of Causality with Free Will and Moral Responsibility must be regarded as a brilliant failure. Moore tells us[1] that he was not himself satisfied with it then, and that he had become still less so by 1942. It may well be that Moore was attempting an impossible feat. Why he attempted it is probably a question worth asking, and I shall suggest an answer to that question a little later, after I have taken a further look at the 1898 article and compared it briefly with Chapter VI of *Ethics*.

The 1898 article contrasts sharply with Chapter VI of *Ethics* in several respects; while some of their basic positions are identical. The 1898 article contains detailed discussion of causality, and argues to a determinist conclusion for both physical and mental events. This position is not simply taken over, or even presupposed as true, in *Ethics*, but it is there clearly regarded as a position to be reckoned with, and so it is assumed to be true *for purposes of argument*, and a suggestion is made there as to how Free Will might be reconciled with it. No such suggestion was even adumbrated in the earlier paper; and, indeed, there Moore held that Free Will, in the ordinary sense of the term, was incompatible with Determinism, and impossible. Moreover, in the earlier paper Moore expressly repudiated the idea that Free Will consists in

[1] *The Philosophy of G. E. Moore*, ed. P. A. Schilpp, Evanston & Chicago, 1942, p. 626.

the power to act as one chooses, which is one of the parts of his suggested analysis of Free Will in *Ethics*. In the earlier paper, indeed, he took 'can' and 'could', quite simply, without making any difficulties, in an absolute sense. On the other hand, there is no reason to believe that when he wrote *Ethics* Moore would have repudiated his close refutation, in the earlier article, of the claim that consciousness affirms, against Determinism, that the self is an uncaused cause. Furthermore, in both treatments, Moore clearly recognizes that neither human actions nor human choices can be predicted with certainty.

Why does *Ethics*, though sharing or recognizing the force of some of the earlier article's basic positions, differ so sharply in the other respects? I suggest that this is because in the intervening period (during which Moore had written *Principia Ethica* (1903)) Moore had come to evolve an ethical theory which required Free Will in some sense, though not in an absolute sense. In the earlier article Moore had not dealt with moral responsibility, and was clearly more concerned with causality. I suggest also that in the early article Moore had described the Free Will controversy, in its most important, if not, indeed, in its only legitimate sense, correctly. Since, however, he had been convinced of the *a priori* necessity of Determinism, and remained at least highly respectful of it at the date when he wrote *Ethics*, he was obliged to look round for some other sense of 'Free Will' than that which he had unhesitatingly recognized as the ordinary sense in the early article. The sense he now required could not, of course, be an absolute sense, nor could the senses of 'can' and 'could' corresponding to it, be absolute senses. As we have seen, his search led him, interestingly enough, to incline, first of all, to adopt as the analysis of 'Free Will' the very kind of hypothetical account in terms of action, which he had repudiated in his attack on Locke and Hume in the early article. Rightly not satisfied with this, however, he then tried the translation of 'X could have chosen Y' into 'X would have chosen Y, if he had chosen to choose Y'; then had recourse to the idea of uncertainty as to future choice; and finally suggested one or more of the three analyses as affording a true account of Free Will. He tells us later that he was not satisfied, even at the time, with his suggestions, and he was quite right not to be.

In later years Moore evidently went on hoping that it might be possible to find some sense of 'Free Will' which would be compatible with Determinism. This comes out clearly in his reply in

K

The Philosophy of G. E. Moore (1942) to some criticisms by Professor A. Campbell Garnett. There[1] Moore sticks firmly to the statement he had made in *Ethics* that 'If every event is caused, it must be true, in *some* sense, that we *never could* have done what we did not do'.[2] Moore does not in his reply, any more than in *Ethics*, actually assert the principle of causality, but he is far from jettisoning it, and, indeed, is evidently very concerned to find another sense of 'could', distinct from that sense of 'could' in which, if the principle of causality holds, 'we *never could* have done, what we did not do'. Moore actually writes that there is 'nothing that he would like better than a *clear* answer' to the question what the sense of 'could' is in which we sometimes could have done what we did not do.[3] It will be noticed, however, that here again, Moore is couching the question in terms of *doing*, not of *choosing*. Now he had certainly found in *Ethics* a reasonable analysis of '*X* could have done *Y*' as '*X* would have done *Y*, if he had chosen'; but this, as he had clearly seen in 1897, does not concern Free Will. I do not, however, attach much importance to Moore's slipping back here into the language of action instead of choice, since earlier on the same page he had stated the entailment as being from the principle of causality to the impossibility, in some sense, of freedom of *choice*. Moreover, two pages earlier, in the reply to Professor Garnett, Moore also couches the problem in terms of *choice*. Moore is there withdrawing from one of the positions advanced in *Ethics*. He writes as follows:

'In *Ethics* I thought that the mere fact that another action, which an agent *would* have done *if* he had chosen, would have had better total results than the action which he actually did do, was *perhaps* sufficient to entitle us to say that the action which he did do was morally wrong. I now think it is *certainly* not sufficient; and that one reason why it is not is that a *necessary* condition for its being true that his action was morally wrong is, that he should have been *able to choose* some other action instead. If he *could not* have chosen any other action than the one he did choose, then his action cannot have been morally wrong. I think now that this is *certainly* true, for *some* sense of "*could* have chosen". There is *some* sense of "could have chosen", and that *the* sense in which we naturally use it in this context, in which the proposition that an action was

---

[1] *Op. cit.*, p. 625.   [2] *Ethics*, p. 190.
[3] *The Philosophy of G. E. Moore*, p. 626.

morally wrong, and, more generally, the proposition that the
agent was morally responsible for it, certainly *entails* that the
agent *could* have made a different choice from the one he did make.
In *Ethics* I thought, and implied, that this was not certain."[1]

It will be seen from this passage that Moore is quite convinced
that there is *some* sense of 'could have chosen' in which moral
responsibility entails that X could have chosen what he did not
choose. Moore is therefore here recognizing two entailments: (1)
Moral Responsibility entails Freedom of Choice in some sense;
(2) the Principle of Causality entails the impossibility of Freedom
of Choice in some sense. As in *Ethics*, however, there is still an
asymmetry. Moore states categorically that some choices are
morally wrong,[2] whereas he does not state that the Principle of
Causality is certainly true. There were, therefore, only two
alternatives open to him: (1) to jettison the Principle of Causality,
or (2) to find a sense of 'can' and 'could' in which 'X can choose Y,
though he will not do so' and 'X could have chosen Y, though he
did not do so'. Moore is here still less satisfied with his two
suggestions in *Ethics* than he was when he wrote that book; but
he does not offer any new suggestion. Nor does he jettison the
Principle of Causality. As to his omission to offer any new suggestion as to the required sense of 'can' and 'could' perhaps, in
point of fact, no satisfactory suggestion could be offered. Perhaps
the true solution is that the absolute senses of 'can' and 'could'
which Moore had taken for granted in the 1898 article, and still
recognized both explicitly and implicitly, in *Ethics* and in his 1942
'Reply', were the only senses relevant to 'Free Will' in its most
important, and perhaps only legitimate, sense; so that even Moore,
with all his ingenuity, could never have found a sense of 'can'
or 'could', other than the absolute sense, which was really relevant
to the problem. Nevertheless Moore's bid was worth making. It
was a distinguished attempt to reconcile beliefs (in Determinism,
in Free Will, in Moral Responsibility, and the Justification of
Moral Praise and Blame, Reward and Punishment) all of whose
claims Moore had come to recognize as strong, and the relations
between which have caused a great deal of philosophical perplexity
to the many people over the centuries who have thought about
them seriously.

---

[1] *The Philosophy of G. E. Moore*, p. 624.
[2] *Ibid.*, p. 626.

G. E. MOORE ON THE NATURALISTIC FALLACY[1]

by C. LEWY

G. E. Moore's literary remains contain very little concerning ethics; but they include an unfinished draft (in manuscript) of what was intended to be a preface to the second edition of *Principia Ethica*. For various reasons it seems to me highly probable that this was written in 1920 or 1921; but in the end Moore abandoned the idea of a second edition, and in 1922 *Principia* was reprinted without any alterations, except for the correction of a few misprints and grammatical mistakes and the inclusion of a prefatory note of seven lines.

Owing to the fact that the draft is unfinished and in parts very fragmentary, the task of preparing it for publication would be a very difficult one, though I may possibly attempt it in the future. What I want to do today is first to give a synopsis, or rather a reconstruction, of what seem to me to be the main points of the unpublished preface (which from now on I shall simply call 'the Preface'), and secondly to discuss independently one particular aspect of the subject.

I

Moore begins by pointing out that there are several senses of the word 'good', and that in *Principia* he was concerned with only one of them. He does not now think, however, that this sense can be called *the* ordinary sense of the word, even if any one sense of it is commoner than any other. But he thinks that the sense in question can be specified by saying that it is *the* sense which has a unique and fundamentally important relation to the conceptions of right and wrong. *What* the relation in question *is*, he proposes, he says, to discuss later; but in fact no such discussion is included in the Preface.

He goes on to ask, however, what are the main things that he

[1] Reprinted from *The Proceedings of the British Academy*, Vol. L, 1964 (Oxford University Press).

wished to say in *Principia* about the concept which is expressed by the word 'good', when the word is used in this sense. The first thing he wished to say, he continues, is that Good[1] is simple in the sense of being indefinable or unanalysable. Is this proposition true?, he asks. He still thinks it is probably true, but he is not certain, for it seems to him that possibly 'right' is unanalysable, and Good is to be analysed partly in terms of 'right'. But whether Good is analysable or not does not seem to him now nearly as important as it did when he wrote *Principia*. If Good *were* unanalysable, it would follow that it could not be identical with any such property as 'is desired' or 'is a state of pleasure', since these *are* analysable; but it would be a great mistake to suppose that, as he implied in *Principia*, the fact that Good is not identical with any such property *rests* on the contention that Good is unanalysable.

He says that in the passage in *Principia* (§§ 6–14) in which he asserted that Good was unanalysable, he made another assertion which must not be confused with it, though he did so confuse it, namely, the assertion '. . . good is good, and that is the end of the matter' (*Principia*, p. 6). What, he asks, did he mean by this? Clearly, he meant to assert about Good what Bishop Butler, in the passage which Moore quoted on his title-page, asserted to be true of everything, namely, that it is what it is, and not another thing. In other words, he meant to assert that Good is Good, and nothing else whatever.

But this, Moore now says, may mean *either* 'Good is different from everything other than Good' *or* 'Good is different from everything which we express by any word or phrase other than the word "good"'. The first is wholly trivial and unimportant; and that Good is unanalysable cannot possibly follow from it, since the property of being different from every property that is different from it, is a property which must belong to every property without exception, analysable and unanalysable alike. And for the same reason it cannot possibly follow from it that certain particular properties such as 'is a state of pleasure' or 'is desired' are different from Good. For even if Good were identical with, say, 'is desired', Good would still be different from every property which was different from it.

---

[1] As Moore himself does in the Preface, I shall write *Good*, with a capital *G* but without quotes, when I talk about the concept, and not the word. But (again like Moore) I shall not adopt this device in connexion with other concepts.

The second assertion, however—that Good is different from everything which we express by any word or phrase other than the word 'good'—is far from being trivial. If it were true, it would really follow that Good was different from any such property as 'is a state of pleasure' or 'is desired'. And also, if it were true, it would afford at least a strong presumption that Good was unanalysable. For 'where a word expresses an *analysable* property, that property is generally also sometimes expressed by a phrase, made up of several words, which point out elements which enter into its analysis, and, in that sense, "contain an analysis" of it'. So that if Good were analysable, it would probably be sometimes expressed by some such complex phrase—a phrase, therefore, different from the mere word 'good'. Indeed Moore thinks that this fact probably partly explains how he was led to identify such obviously different propositions as 'Good is Good, and nothing else whatever' and 'Good is unanalysable'. For we have just seen that if the former proposition be understood as asserting that Good is different from any property expressed by any phrase other than the word 'good', this proposition, if true, would at least afford a strong presumption that Good was unanalysable. And he may have supposed—he continues—that, conversely, from the fact that Good was unanalysable, it would follow that it could not be expressed by any phrase other than 'good'. He may have supposed so owing to his perceiving that if Good were unanalysable, it could not be expressed by any phrase which *contained an analysis* of it, but failing to perceive the distinction between expressing the meaning of a word in other words which *contain an analysis* of it, and expressing its meaning by giving a synonym.

But the fact that there is this distinction is fatal to the truth of the proposition we are now considering. It may be true that Good is unanalysable, and therefore cannot be expressed by other words which contain an analysis of it: but it is certainly not true that it cannot be expressed by any other words at all. For instance (quite apart from the obvious fact that there are languages other than English), the word 'desirable' is sometimes used as a synonym for 'good'.

Moore therefore concludes that the assertion 'Good is Good, and nothing else whatever' is either merely trivial or else obviously false.

But this is not the end of the matter. For Moore also thinks that the examples which he gave in *Principia* do suggest to most people's minds that what he really meant to assert was that Good was not identical with any property belonging to a *particular class*; and *this* assertion still seems to him both true and important. But what is the class in question? Moore says in effect that he can only describe this class by saying that it is the class of all those properties which are either natural or metaphysical; and what he really wanted to assert, he says, was that Good was not identical with any natural or metaphysical property.

He admits that in *Principia* he confused natural objects (or events) with a certain kind of property which may belong to them. He actually confused a particular event, which consists in somebody's being pleased, with the property which we ascribe to it when we say that it is 'a state of pleasure'—just as he confused a particular patch of yellow with the property of being yellow. And he also admits that he confused *parts* of natural objects with *properties* of such objects.

For these and other reasons his attempts to define a 'natural property' were, he says, hopelessly confused. The nearest he came to suggesting a correct definition in *Principia* was on p. 40, where he said that to identify Good with any natural property resulted in replacing ethics by one of the natural sciences (including psychology). This now suggests to him the following definitions. A 'natural' property is a property with which it is the business of the natural sciences or of psychology to deal, or which can be completely defined in terms of such. A 'metaphysical' property is a property which stands to some super-sensible object in the same relation in which natural properties stand to natural objects.

Moore now points out that the proposition that Good is not identical with any natural or metaphysical property (as now defined)—which is what he really wished to assert in *Principia*—neither implies nor is implied by the proposition that Good is unanalysable. For it might plainly be true, even if Good *were* analysable; and, on the other hand, even if Good were *un*analysable, Good might still be identical with some natural property, since many such properties may be unanalysable. At the same time, he says, if Good is not identical with any natural or metaphysical property, it does follow that, if it is analysable at all, it involves in its analysis *some* unanalysable notion which is not natural or metaphysical. That some unanalysable notion of this sort, he says, is involved in ethics was certainly a part of what he wished to assert when he asserted that Good was unanalysable.

Only he did not see that this was a far more important and less doubtful assertion than that Good itself was the unanalysable notion in question.

Of course Moore realizes that his new definitions—and it would perhaps be better to call them 'explanations' rather than 'definitions'—are still not fully satisfactory. It is clear that he intended to return to the topic in a later part of the Preface; but he never in fact came to write it.

There are, however, still some pages of the Preface which are of considerable interest, and of special relevance to our subject. It will have been noticed that so far the expression 'the naturalistic fallacy' has not been introduced, although it is obvious that what Moore meant by it is very closely connected with the propositions we have been considering. But he now explicitly raises the question: What *is* 'the naturalistic fallacy'? And he says that the most important mistake which he made in his discussion of the matter in *Principia* was exactly analogous to the chief of those which he made in his assertions about Good. In the latter case, as we have seen, he confused the three entirely different propositions 'Good is not identical with any property other than itself'; 'Good is not identical with any analysable property'; and 'Good is not identical with any natural or metaphysical property'. In the case of the naturalistic fallacy, he goes on, he similarly confused the three entirely different propositions (1) 'So-and-so is identifying Good with some property other than Good'; (2) 'So-and-so is identifying Good with some *analysable* property'; and (3) 'So-and-so is identifying Good with some *natural or metaphysical* property'.

He points out that he sometimes implies that to say of a man that he is committing the naturalistic fallacy is to say (1) of him; sometimes that it is to say (2) of him; and sometimes that it is to say (3) of him.

But in addition to this, his main mistake, he also made, he says, two further mistakes. First, he sometimes talked (*Principia*, p. 14) as if to commit the naturalistic fallacy was to suppose that in, for example, 'This is good', the word 'is' always expresses identity between the thing called 'this' and Good. And secondly, he confused (A) 'To say that so-and-so is committing the naturalistic fallacy is to say that he is holding, with respect to some property of a certain kind, the *view* that that property is identical with Good', and (B) 'To say that so-and-so is committing the naturalistic fallacy is to say that he is *confusing* some property of a certain kind with Good'. But the operation mentioned in (A) is quite different from that mentioned in (B).

Finally, Moore admits that he feels doubtful whether either of these two operations could properly be called the commission of a fallacy, for the simple reason that to commit a fallacy seems properly to mean to make a certain kind of *inference*; whereas the mere confusion of two properties, or the holding of a view with regard to them, seems not to be a process of inference at all.

Moore ends this part of the Preface by saying that if he still wished to use the term 'naturalistic fallacy', he would define it as follows: 'So-and-so is committing the naturalistic fallacy' means 'He is *either* confusing Good with a natural or metaphysical property *or* holding it to be identical with such a property *or* making an inference *based* upon such a confusion'. And he would also expressly point out that in so using the term 'fallacy' he was using it in an extended, and perhaps improper, sense.

This concludes my synopsis, or reconstruction, of the Preface, or rather of that part of it which it is possible to reconstruct, for the rest is in a very incomplete state indeed. And it will, I think, have been seen that many of the criticisms made of Moore's treatment of the naturalistic fallacy and related topics in the 1930's and 1940's were fully anticipated by him many years earlier.

II

I now wish to discuss independently one particular aspect of the subject. In the Preface, it will be recalled, Moore says that he still believes it to be true and important to assert that Good is not identical with any natural or metaphysical property. But he neither produces any new arguments for this assertion nor makes any comments on the arguments which he gave in *Principia*. I wish now to examine in some detail two passages in the book which contain such arguments. The first occurs in § 13 (pp. 15–16), and runs as follows:

'The hypothesis that disagreement about the meaning of good is disagreement with regard to the correct analysis of a given whole, may be most plainly seen to be incorrect by consideration of the fact that, whatever definition be offered, it may be always asked, with significance, of the complex so defined, whether it is itself good. To take, for instance, one of the more plausible, because

K*

one of the more complicated of such proposed definitions, it may easily be thought, at first sight, that to be good may mean to be that which we desire to desire. Thus if we apply this definition to a particular instance and say "When we think that A is good, we are thinking that A is one of the things which we desire to desire", our proposition may seem quite plausible. But, if we carry the investigation further, and ask ourselves 'Is it good to desire to desire A?" it is apparent, on a little reflection, that this question is itself as intelligible, as the original question "Is A good?"— that we are, in fact, now asking for exactly the same information about the desire to desire A, for which we formerly asked with regard to A itself. But it is also apparent that the meaning of this second question cannot be correctly analysed into "Is the desire to desire A one of the things which we desire to desire?": we have not before our minds anything so complicated as the question "Do we desire to desire to desire to desire A?" Moreover anyone can easily convince himself by inspection that the predicate of this proposition—"good"—is positively different from the notion of "desiring to desire" which enters into its subject: "That we should desire to desire A is good" is *not* merely equivalent to "That A should be good is good". It may indeed be true that what we desire to desire is always also good; perhaps, even the converse may be true: but it is very doubtful whether this is the case, and the mere fact that we understand very well what is meant by doubting it, shews clearly that we have two different notions before our minds.'

The second passage occurs a little later (p. 38). Moore there says that he will discuss certain theories which claim that only a single kind of thing is good. He thinks that such theories rest on the naturalistic fallacy, and goes on as follows:

'That a thing should be good, it has been thought, *means* that it possesses this single property: and hence (it is thought) only what possesses this property is good. The inference seems very natural; and yet what is meant by it is self-contradictory. For those who make it fail to perceive that their conclusion "what possesses this property is good" is a significant proposition: that it does not mean either "what possesses this property, possesses this property" or "the word 'good' denotes that a thing possesses this property". And yet, if it does *not* mean one or other of these two things, the inference contradicts its own premise.'

It will have been noticed that Moore speaks in these passages as if he were showing that Good is not analysable at all; but what I chiefly wish to discuss is the question whether he has shown that Good is not identical with the property of being one of the things which we desire to desire—that is, with the property which he takes as an example in the first passage. Moreover, I cannot hope to say here all that ought to be said about these passages. In particular, I cannot consider all the different arguments which they contain and which are not clearly distinguished from each other. All I can do is to try to reformulate and discuss what seems to me to be the chief of these arguments.

I think I can do this most clearly with the help of an analogy. Let us suppose that we are concerned, not with Good, but with the concept of being a brother. Suppose that someone asserts that to be a brother is to be a male sibling—or, to use the terminology that Moore himself often used in later life—that the concept of being a brother is identical with the concept of being a male sibling. Now what follows from this proposition? So far as I can see, one thing which certainly follows from it is that the proposition 'John is a brother' is identical with the proposition 'John is a male sibling'. Similarly, in Moore's case, if to be good is to be one of the things which we desire to desire, it follows that any proposition of the form '*x* is good' is identical with the corresponding proposition of the form '*x* is one of the things which we desire to desire'. It follows, for instance, that the proposition 'A is good' (and we must now assume that 'A' is a name or description of a thing or state of things) is identical with the proposition 'A is one of the things which we desire to desire'.

Consequently, Moore could have argued against the identification of Good with the property of being one of the things which we desire to desire, by pointing out that even if at first it may seem plausible to suppose that these two propositions are identical, yet further reflection makes it apparent that they are *not* identical.

But this is not what he does. He obviously thought that he had a more complicated but more convincing argument. For what he asks us to consider are not the two propositions I have just mentioned, but the completely different propositions 'It is good to desire to desire A' and 'The desire to desire A is one of the things which we desire to desire'. And he says that it is apparent on reflection that *these* propositions are not identical.

Let me put the matter in terms of questions rather than propositions. Moore could have argued that the question (1) 'Is A good?' is quite different from the question (2) 'Is A one of the things which we desire to desire?'. Yet if to be good is to be one of the things which we desire to desire, these questions are identical. But what he in fact says is that the question (3) 'Is it good to desire to desire A?' is quite different from the question (4) 'Is the desire to desire A one of the things which we desire to desire?'.

But though the latter questions are more complicated than the former, they are no better. For on the view he is discussing, just as (1) and (2) are identical, so are (3) and (4). And it is no plainer that (3) and (4) are *not* identical than it is that (1) and (2) are not identical. Similarly, on the view in question, the proposition (3A) 'It is good that we desire to desire A' *is* identical with the proposition (3B) 'It is good that A is good' (and each of them is identical with the proposition 'We desire to desire to desire to desire A'). And again, it is no plainer that (3A) and (3B) are *not* identical than it is that 'A is good' and 'A is one of the things which we desire to desire' are not identical.

Did Moore, then, have at the back of his mind some other questions, even more complicated? I think that the second passage which I have quoted makes it fairly clear that he did, and that they were (5) 'Is A, which is one of things which we desire to desire, good?', and (6) 'Is A, which is one of the things which we desire to desire, one of the things which we desire to desire?'. And I think that he confused (5) with (3), and (6) with (4).

Unfortunately, each of these last two questions—(5) and (6)—is capable of at least two totally different interpretations. Question (5) may mean *either* 'Is it the case that A is good if and only if it is one of the things which we desire to desire?'—where the expression 'if and only if' is used truth-functionally;[1] *or* 'Is it the case that to say that A is good is the same thing as to say that A is one of the things which we desire to desire?'. More generally, the question of which (5) is merely a particular example may mean *either* 'Is it the case that a thing is good if and only if it is one of the things which we desire to desire?' (where the expression 'if and only if' is used truth-functionally); *or* 'Is it the case that to be good is to be one of the things which we desire to desire?'. An affirmative answer

---

[1] That is to say, in such a way that the question can also be expressed by asking 'Are the two propositions "A is good" and "A is one of the things which we desire to desire" either *both* true or *both* false?'.

to the *first* question would be given by the proposition 'It *is* the case that a thing is good if and only if it is one of the things which we desire to desire', which is logically equivalent to the proposition (α) 'A thing is good if and only if it is one of the things which we desire to desire'. An affirmative answer to the *second* question would be given by the proposition 'It *is* the case that to be good is to be one of the things which we desire to desire', which is logically equivalent to the proposition (β) 'To be good is to be one of the things which we desire to desire'.

Similarly, the question of which (6) is merely a particular example may mean *either* 'Is it the case that a thing is one of the things which we desire to desire if and only if it is one of the things which we desire to desire?' (where 'if and only if' is used truth-functionally); *or* 'Is it the case that to be one of the things which we desire to desire is to be one of the things which we desire to desire?'. An affirmative answer to the *first* question would be given by the proposition 'It *is* the case that a thing is one of the things which we desire to desire if and only if it is one of the things which we desire to desire', which is logically equivalent to (γ) 'A thing is one of the things which we desire to desire if and only if it is one of the things which we desire to desire'. On the other hand, an affirmative answer to the *second* question would be given by the proposition 'It *is* the case that to be one of the things which we desire to desire is to be one of the things which we desire to desire', which is logically equivalent to the proposition (δ) 'To be one of the things which we desire to desire is to be one of the things which we desire to desire'.

For the sake of simplicity, I will now again speak in terms of propositions rather than questions. The main point I now wish to make is that there is a fundamental difference between (α) and (γ) on the one hand, and (β) and (δ) on the other. For the truth-value (that is, the truth or falsity) of (α) would not be altered if we substituted for any expression which occurs in the sentence which I have used to express (α), another expression with the same extension (that is, another expression which applies to exactly the same things); and the same is true of (γ). But this is not true either of (β) or of (δ). In current logical terminology, whilst the setences which I have used to express (α) and (γ) are *extensional*, those I have used to express (β) and (δ) are *not* extensional.

It is clear that at the time Moore wrote *Principia* (1903), he did not see this distinction; and he therefore failed to distinguish

(α) from (β), and (γ) from (δ). But (α) *is* quite different from (β), and (γ) *is* quite different from (δ). Consequently, we get two different interpretations of Moore's argument.

First, we can interpret him as arguing that to be good is not the same as to be one of the things which we desire to desire, because, if it were, then (β) would be identical with (δ); and maintaining, further, that it is apparent on reflection that (β) is *not* identical with (δ). If interpreted in this way, the argument seems to me to be completely invalid. For in the same kind of way it would be possible to show with regard to any concept whatever that it is unanalysable—in other words, that it is simple. For instance, we could show that to be a brother is not the same thing as to be a male sibling, because, if it were, then the proposition 'To be a brother is to be a male sibling' would be identical with the proposition 'To be a male sibling is to be a male sibling'. Yet it is clear on reflection that these propositions are *not* identical.

In other words, Moore's argument, in this interpretation, would be a particular instance of what he himself later in life called the 'Paradox of Analysis'. He was never fully satisfied with any solution of it, and said different things about it at different times. But I have no doubt at all, on the basis of a large number of discussions which I have had with him on the subject over a period of many years, that his considered view was that whatever may be the *complete* solution, it was essential to hold that (in the example I have just given) to be a brother *is* to be a male sibling, and that yet the proposition 'To be a brother is to be a male sibling' is *not* identical with the proposition 'To be a male sibling is to be a male sibling'. And he therefore held that from 'To be a brother is to be a male sibling', the identity of these propositions does *not* follow. I think that this is right; and if so, then his *Principia* argument, in the interpretation I am now considering, is clearly invalid.

We must now, however, discuss my second interpretation. Here we should interpret Moore as arguing that to be good is not the same as to be one of the things which we desire to desire, because, if it were, then (α) would be identical with (γ); and maintaining, further, that it is apparent on reflection that (α) is *not* identical with (γ). Now *this* argument seems to me to be perfectly valid. For, although I once succeeded in so confusing myself as to deny it, I now think it undeniable that *if* to be good is to be one of the things which we desire to desire, then (α) *is* identical with (γ). Yet it is absolutely clear that (α) is *not* identical with (γ). And that (α)

is not identical with (γ) follows from something which is also absolutely clear, namely, that it is logically possible to doubt (α) *without* doubting (γ); and each of these things follows from something which is also absolutely clear, namely, that whilst (γ) is a necessary proposition, (α) is a contingent proposition.

Moreover, it is *not* possible to use this kind of argument to show with regard to any concept whatever, that it is unanalysable. Indeed, if to be a brother is to be a male sibling, then the proposition 'A creature is a brother if and only if it is a male sibling' is identical with the proposition 'A creature is a male sibling if and only if it is a male sibling' (where in both sentences 'if and only if' is used truth-functionally). But *these* propositions *are* identical.

Of course, Moore's argument, in the present interpretation, may be said to be 'begging the question'. For a person who holds that to be good is to be one of the things which we desire to desire, may admit that if this is so, then (α) is identical with (γ); and he may then go on to assert that (α) *is* identical with (γ). This is true: but I think we can all see that a person who asserted *this*, would be mistaken.

It seems to me obvious that any theory which identifies Good with a concept which is not itself at least partly ethical, can be refuted in an analogous way. I think therefore that for all his mistakes, Moore can fairly be said to have found a means of refuting any such theory.

INTRINSIC VALUE: SOME COMMENTS ON THE WORK OF G. E. MOORE[1]

by AUSTIN DUNCAN-JONES

The object of this paper is to review and examine some of the things which G. E. Moore says about the nature of intrinsic value, about the sort of objects which possess it, and about the method of ascertaining the intrinsic values of things. Most of the discussion will be based on *Principia Ethica* (1903): for in that work Moore stated the substance of his ethical theories once and for all. He explicitly changed his mind later on a few specific issues, which will be noted when they are relevant: and I shall argue in my fourth section that he also changed his mind in one matter without acknowledging that he was doing so. With those exceptions, it seems to me that his later writings differ from *Principia* chiefly by their style of presentation and by the introduction of some new distinctions, and I shall think myself justified, on most points, in treating them as an aid to amplifying or refining the position which Moore adopted in *Principia*. The other works to be referred to are *Ethics* (1912); 'The Conception of Intrinsic Value', written about forty years ago and published in *Philosophical Studies*: 'Is Goodness a Quality?' in *Aristotelian Society Proceedings*, Supp. Vol. (1932); and 'A Reply to My Critics' in *The Philosophy of G. E. Moore*, edited by P. A. Schilpp (1942). The last work will be cited as *Reply*.

I am going to assume without argument that when Moore uses the words 'good' or 'goodness', unless the context indicates some non-intrinsic kind of goodness, and when he uses such phrases as 'good in itself', 'good as an end', 'intrinsically good', 'intrinsic goodness', 'intrinsic worth', he is always concerned with the same concept. He is also, I assume, concerned with the same concept when he uses the phrase 'intrinsic value'. That phrase is used interchangeably with the phrase 'intrinsic goodness' in *Principia* § 13 and in many subsequent passages. In a wider sense, in which Moore uses the phrase less frequently, both

[1] Reprinted from *Philosophy*, Vol. XXXIII 1958.

intrinsic goodness and intrinsic badness are kinds of intrinsic value. For example, in *Principia* § 129 Moore refers to wholes whose parts have 'a great intrinsic value, positive or negative'.

It is, as I shall show, an essential part of Moore's position that the intrinsically good and the intrinsically bad are, so to speak, commensurable in a single dimension. A general term is needed for the single quasi-quantity of which good and evil are the positive and negative, whereas a synonym for 'intrinsic goodness' is superfluous. Henceforth, therefore, I shall adhere to Moore's wider usage. And I shall copy Moore's practice of omitting the word 'intrinsic' when the context makes it superfluous.

1. *The Logical Form of Judgements of Value*

Moore has often discussed the particular force of the word 'intrinsic' and its synonyms. The reason for its importance may perhaps be seen in the statement (*Principia* § 18) that 'all judgements of intrinsic value are . . . universal', in a sense which Moore explains as follows: 'a judgement which asserts that a thing is good in itself . . . if true of one instance of the thing in question, is necessarily true of all'. On the other hand, judgements concerned with non-intrinsic value are not in that sense universal. In order to penetrate what Moore is saying we have to understand what would count as two instances of the same thing.

There seem to be two extremes between which our interpretation might move. (*a*) The claim might be merely that, if X is good, and if Y is exactly like X in every way, then necessarily Y is also good. (*b*) A much wider claim would be that, if X is good, and if Y resembles X in one respect, or shares one characteristic with X, then necessarily Y is also good. Either of those extreme positions has its own difficulties. Position (*a*) requires us to determine the boundary between the essential and the inessential characteristics of X and Y: to determine, for example, whether X and Y are to be regarded as exactly alike if they differ *only* in existing at different places, or at different times. That metaphysical question may be soluble: but however it might be solved we should have a futile notion of universality on our hands; for no solution of it would allow of our ascertaining in practice that two things were exactly alike. It follows that, having judged a particular thing to be good in itself, we should never be able to ascertain to what judgements about the goodness of other things we were thereby committed. But another, more disabling consequence would surely follow. Suppose X were something I judged to be good in itself, I could not entertain the proposition that Y was also an 'instance of the thing in question', because I could neither know nor suppose myself to know the characteristics of Y fully enough to ascertain that Y was exactly like X. But in order to extend my judgement from X to Y I cannot be required to know the characteristics of Y more fully than I am required to know those of X. Therefore, in order to judge that X is intrinsically good I must know, or suppose myself to know, the characteristics of X more fully than I can possibly know them; and it follows that I can never make a judgement of intrinsic value at all, unless under the delusion that I know something's characteristics with impossible exactness.

Interpretation (a) makes the conditions under which two things are to be 'instances of the same thing' so stringent that we could never have adequate grounds for supposing them to be fulfilled. Interpretation (b) makes them so lax that they would be fulfilled much too easily. For whatever X may be there are likely to be innumerable heterogeneous things which have, or appear to me to have, one characteristic or another in common with X. And nothing which was so widely extensible as that interpretation would allow could generate the limited number of classes of intrinsically good or bad things which Moore and other moral philosophers hope to arrive at.

Between these two extremes, the medium suggests itself that a thing is always judged to be intrinsically good or bad *sub quadam specie*, as being of a certain kind. That this is Moore's position might be shown in various ways; the clearest indication is perhaps in *Principia* § 70, where Moore is discussing 'Metaphysical ethics'. He draws attention to an ambiguity in the question 'what is good?', which, he says, may mean either 'which among existing things are good?' or 'what *sort of* things are good?': he adds that to know the answer to the former question we must know the answer to the latter. I think it is implied here that answering the latter question is a necessary precondition, not only of giving, as Moore puts it, 'a catalogue of all the good things in the universe', but of ascertaining that any particular existing thing is good. Any judgement of the goodness of an existing thing must, then, embrace or presuppose at least these two elements: the judgement that the thing is of a certain sort, and the judgement that anything whatever of that sort would be good. A judgement of intrinsic value is universal in the sense that it consists of, or embraces, or presupposes, the latter of those elements. Henceforth I shall use the phrase 'value generalization' to refer to judgements to the effect that anything of a certain sort would have a certain intrinsic value, and to the propositions or truths which form the content of such judgements. The qualities or sorts referred to by the subject term of a true value generalization may be called 'value-implying'.

Moore seems to treat 'this is good' as equivalent to 'this would be good, if it existed' (*Principia* § 73). He also speaks of the *existence* of something as being good, or of its being good that something should exist: for example, in §§ 19, 50, 113. I venture the opinion that, when Moore presents for discussion statements of the type 'so and so is good', they are always short for, or are assumed to include, statements of the type 'such and such a kind of thing is good'; and that those in turn are short for statements of the type 'the existence of a thing of such and such a kind' or 'that a thing of such and such a kind should exist would be good (in itself)'. The point is one which Moore sometimes expresses, in the terms belonging to his 'method of isolation' to which I shall return in section 2, by saying that it would be better that a thing of such and such a kind should exist than that nothing should exist at all. Thus, supposing that a certain characteristic C is positively value-implying, it does not follow that anything whatever *is* good, or that the world contains anything of positive value: that would only be the case if at least one existing thing possessed C. For example, if pleasure were good in itself, but no state of pleasure ever existed, there would not, in virtue of the goodness of pleasure, be anything at all of positive value.

The kind of universal judgements about intrinsic value with which Moore is concerned might therefore be formulated as follows: 'if anything of such and such a kind existed, then, by virtue of that thing's existence, something good in itself would exist'. Moore also holds that all such judgements, if true, are synthetic, self-evident, and necessarily true. That they are synthetic is said expressly, for example in *Principia* §§ 6, 35; and that they are synthetic and self-evident in § 86. I have already quoted, from § 18, the statement that these judgements, if 'true of one instance' of a thing, are 'necessarily true of all'. That by itself is ambiguous: for the sense might be either (1) that, those judgements being what they are, they must as such be universal; or

(2) that they are judgements whose content is a universal necessary truth, a universal proposition which is necessarily true. My contention that the latter is the right interpretation is supported by what Moore says in 'The Conception of Intrinsic Value'.

In that essay, Moore says that 'a kind of value is intrinsic if and only if, when anything possesses it, . . . anything exactly like [that thing] would *necessarily* . . . possess it in exactly the same degree'. In the course of explaining what is here meant by 'necessarily', Moore insists that, in order that the criterion should be fulfilled, neither empirical nor causal necessity would suffice. He adds that, if a certain 'predicate' were intrinsic, you could 'know *a priori*' that 'a thing *A* which did possess such a predicate, and a thing *B* which did not, could not be exactly alike'. He also speaks of an 'unconditional "must" ', which would occur in such a statement as 'if *A* possesses such and such a predicate, and if *B* is exactly like *A*, then *B* must possess it' (my illustration). Of this 'must' he says that 'the obvious thing to suggest is that it is the logical "must" ': but he gives reasons for being dissatisfied with that suggestion.

I think my summary of Moore's discussion in the essay in question shows that, in his view, a certain kind of truth concerning intrinsic value would be a necessary truth, in a sense of 'necessary' which Moore does not claim to analyse. The kind of truth to which Moore is here referring would not itself be a value generalization. Moore contrasted the theory that there are intrinsic values in the sense explained with some alternative theories. For example, according to an evolutionist theory, the statement that a certain type of human being, *A*, is better than another type, *B*, would mean merely that *A* is 'more favoured in the struggle for existence' than *B*. But that difference between *A* and *B* might not hold in other circumstances or under other natural laws than those which are assumed to exist. It cannot, therefore, be maintained that an instance of *A* would, unconditionally and in all circumstances, be better than an instance of *B*, and it follows that, according to the evolutionist theory, the difference in value between *A* and *B* would not be a difference in intrinsic value. In the argument which I have paraphrased, Moore implies that, if a kind of value is intrinsic, it belongs necessarily to a certain *type* of thing; that, if type *A* excels type *B* in intrinsic value, that relation of value must hold between instances of *A* and *B* always and everywhere: that is to say, he implies that a value generalization would be a necessary truth. I think it may be concluded that, in Moore's unanalysed sense of 'necessary', he holds it a necessary truth, not only that if something has a certain intrinsic value anything exactly like it has the same value, but also that if something is of a certain *kind* it has a certain intrinsic value.

Yet there is some vacillation in Moore's way of expressing himself. Given that, if anything has a certain quality it has a certain value, it follows that, if X has that quality, and Y is exactly like X, Y has that value: but given that if X has a certain value anything just like X has it, it does not follow that X has some one value-implying quality. The way of speaking in which value generalizations are framed in terms of a common quality is therefore not interchangeable with that in which they are framed in terms of exact likeness. I do not know whether Moore ever came down in favour of one way of speaking in preference to the other. I shall say more about the relation between them in my fourth section.

2. *Organic Unities and the Method of Isolation*

Moore expounds the principle of 'organic unities' at considerable length in *Principia* (§§ 18, 55, and ch. 6), and restates it in *Ethics* (pp. 240–7). I shall do my best to summarize the principle in my own words.

(*a*) Positive and negative intrinsic value may belong to wholes of various degrees of complexity, and also to parts of those wholes.

(*b*) The value which belongs to a whole is logically independent of the value which belong to its parts. For example, a whole, W, composed of parts X and Y, might have a certain positive value, even though neither X nor Y had any value, or even though X, or Y, or both had a negative value. If X, or Y, or both, had a positive value, the value of W might be different from the sum of the values of X and Y. Again, if X had a positive and Y a negative value, the value of W might not be the same as the difference between the values of X and Y. X or Y might itself be a whole composed of parts: and if so, the relation between its value and the values of its parts would be analogous to the relation just described between the value of W and the values of X and Y.

(*c*) The value of W, standing to the values of X and Y in the inconstant relation which I have described, is called by Moore (*Principia* § 129) the value of W 'as a whole'. But the value of W *as* a whole may not be identical with the entire value of the state of affairs consituted by the existence of W. For that entire value, which Moore calls the value of the state of affairs '*on* the whole', embraces all those values involved in W which are logically independent of one another. Thus, if W has a positive value *as* a whole, and one or more of its parts has a positive value, and none has a negative value, then the value *on* the whole of the state of affairs constituted by the existence of W is greater than that of W *as* a whole: if, on the other hand, one or more of the parts has a negative and none a positive value, then the value *on* the whole is less than the value of W *as* a whole. It is easy to see how quasi-computations on these lines may be extended.

It will be seen that Moore, like Bentham, seems to imply that comparisons of value might be expressed in simple arithmetic, analogous to the arithmetic of money accountancy. Moore is even further than Bentham from giving any specific examples of quantitative comparison. But it is hard to see what other construction can be put upon the passages in *Principia* (e.g. §§ 17–19) in which Moore refers to a 'sum of intrinsic value', or speaks of the 'proportion' which the value of a whole bears to 'the sum of the values of its parts'. In *Ethics*, pp. 240–4, Moore uses algebraic equations to illustrate the effects of compounding the positive and negative values belonging to a whole and its parts: and on p. 247 he says that 'whatever single kind of thing [pleasure, knowledge, virtue, wisdom, love] may be proposed as a measure of intrinsic value . . . it is . . . quite plain that it is not such a measure; . . . however valuable any one of these things may be, we may always add to the value of a whole which contains any one of them, not only by adding more of that one, but also *by adding something else instead*' (Moore's italics). In his denial that any single matter of fact is a measure of intrinsic value, Moore seems to presuppose that it is in its own nature quantitative. It is true that Moore speaks not only of amounts or sums, but of 'degrees' of intrinsic value: that the values of things should differ in degree does not, however, preclude them from differing in amount, any more than variation in degree of heat precludes variation in amount of heat. And it is true that such words as 'sum' are often used metaphorically, as in the poetic *cliché* 'the sum of things'. But Moore's use of a quantitative idiom with reference to intrinsic value is repeated and consistent: I cannot think of any place in which he offers any alternative mode of expressing comparisons of value; and, supposing Moore's usage here to be metaphorical, I can see no way of conveying his meaning in non-metaphorical terms, or in any alternative metaphor. I conclude that Moore literally means what he seems to say or imply, that amounts of intrinsic value are in principle arithmetically computable.

I have summarized the principle of organic unities in abstract terms. It will perhaps be more easily grasped if I attempt a concrete illustration of the kind of computation which Moore's use of quantitative expressions suggests to me.

Suppose a factory were conducted on a system of rewards and fines. There would be, I shall suppose, certain basic rewardable acts, such as the production of manufactured goods, paid for at piece rates; and there would be certain basic finable acts, such as the spoiling of some amount of raw material. There would be other rewardable and finable acts, wholes of the first order, which would include basic acts as logically necessary components: for example, there would be a reward for production accomplished with infectious gaiety, or for spoilt material successfully salvaged; a fine for production attended by infectious gloom. There might be second-order wholes, again rewardable or finable, which would contain as necessary ingredients first-order wholes: for example, there might be a fine for exciting envy by one's response to a first-order reward. The reader will readily continue the sequence. In this severe utopia, the wage-packet, positive or negative, would be calculated by adding together the rewards and fines for the basic acts; those for the first-order wholes; those for the second-order wholes; and so on. The most comprehensive whole would have its value, its reward or fine, *as* a whole: but the value *on* the whole resulting from its existence, the value embodied in the wage-packet, would be the sum of its value *as* a whole, of the values of each of its parts, of parts of those parts, and so on. The computation of the wage-packet is analogous to the computation of the value of a certain state of affairs *on* the whole which Moore's terminology seems to imply.

The doctrine of organic unities is closely connected with Moore's chief method of ascertaining the intrinsic value of anything, the 'method of isolation'. Moore describes this method in various places; for example, in *Principia* §§ 52–7, 112–13, and in *Ethics* pp. 57–8, 65–6. The method is first expressly recommended in Moore's discussion of hedonism: but the juxtaposition is inessential. 'The method which I employed in order to show that pleasure itself was not the sole good was that of considering what value we should attach to it if it existed in absolute isolation . . .' (*Principia* § 53). Here are some other formulations of the method. 'Could we accept, as a very good thing, that mere consciousness of pleasure and absolutely nothing else should exist, even in the greatest quantities?' (*Principia* § 55). To answer the question 'what things have intrinsic value, and in what degrees?', we must consider (1) 'what things are such that if they existed *by themselves* in absolute isolation we should yet judge their existence to be good', and (2) 'what comparative value seems to attach to the isolated existence of each' (*Principia* § 112). 'By saying that a thing is intrinsically good the theory means that it would be a good thing that the thing in question should exist even if it existed *quite alone* without any further accompaniments or effects whatever' (*Ethics* p. 65): of the intrinsically bad and the intrinsically indifferent a corresponding account is given. Again, 'to assert of . . . *A* that it is intrinsically better than . . . *B* is to assert that if *A* existed *quite alone* . . . if in short *A* constituted the whole universe, it would be better that such a universe should exist than that a universe which consisted solely of *B* should exist instead' (*Ethics* pp. 57–8). In the *Reply* (p. 557) Moore wrote, by way of recapitulation of what he has said in *Ethics* 'to say of a possible world that it would be a "good" world . . . is logically equivalent to saying that it would be *better* that the world in question should exist than that *there should be no world at all*': though he was not prepared to say that the two logically equivalent statements meant the same, or that 'the sense of "good" in question' was 'definable in terms of the sense of "better" in question'.

The method, then, consists in setting before one's mind something which might or might not exist, or several such things; comparing the existence of that thing with its non-existence, or the existence of one with that of another; and performing an act of 'intuition' (*Principia* § 86) or 'reflective judgement' (*Principia* § 122). And the possible state of affairs which is in question must be contemplated as though it existed 'alone, with no accompaniments or effects', or as though it constituted the whole universe. The effort of abstraction which Moore demands may seem difficult or bewildering; but I do not feel sure that the demand is absurd. Moore considers that those who apply his method will in the main reach the right conclusions—and therefore the same conclusions—as to the intrinsic values of things, and the relative values of different things. They may not always reach exactly the right conclusions because of the complexity of the subject, the variety and heterogeneousness of the kinds of valuable thing, and because of the difficulty of applying the method with sufficient rigour.

The principle of organic unities is itself established by the help of the method of isolation. In his discussion of hedonism (*Principia* ch. 3) Moore argues that (1) pleasure is not the sole good, because its positive value can be increased by the addition of consciousness; (2) consciousness of pleasure is not the sole good, because enjoyment of beauty has a much higher positive value than consciousness of pleasure as such; (3) the positive value of pleasure in isolation, of consciousness in isolation, and of beauty in isolation, is slight, but that of the enjoyment of beauty very great; (4) therefore the positive value of the enjoyment of beauty is not reducible to the sum of the values of its parts. This is the first of a number of discussions of the value of kinds of thing, each of which has as its outcome the conclusion that a certain kind of whole has a certain value, that the presence of certain parts is logically necessary to its being that kind of whole, and that the value of the whole is not reducible to the sum of the values, if any, of the parts. After the completion of one or more such arguments we might say, though Moore does not put the matter so, that there is inductive support for a policy of seeking organic unities. There may, it seems, be indefinite complexity in the relations of value between one whole and another, and between a whole and its elements. Every combination of elements which has not already been assayed, and every element of a whole which has not hitherto been isolated, requires an independent valuation.

Moore often speaks of the intrinsic value of a 'thing'. But if I have argued rightly in my first section, expressions of that kind must always be a short way of referring to the amount of good or evil which would exist *if* a state of affairs of a particular *kind* existed: the outcome of the method of isolation must be a value generalization. And Moore's language often bears out my conclusion, as when he says (*Principia* § 55) that it is 'essential to consider each distinguishable *quality* in isolation, in order to decide what value it possesses' (my italics): or again, at § 112, where he speaks of considering a 'property' in isolation.

The method of isolation is meant to be a safeguard against two kinds of confusion: (1) between the value which a kind of thing possesses in itself and the value which would belong to the effects it is assumed to produce; and (2) between the value which belongs to a kind of thing solely as being of that kind, and the value which arises from its having a part of a certain kind, or its being part of a whole of a certain kind. It might be thought that a less heroic form of abstraction would have served: might we not achieve the same result by asking, not 'what would be the value of X if it existed in absolute isolation?', but 'what difference would be made to the value of the world if X were brought into existence, or withdrawn from existence, on the assumption that the creation or annihilation of X would have no further effects?'. Moore occasionally uses language which suggests this alternative method of 'isolated addition'; for example, in *Ethics* p. 66 he interprets the phrase 'intrinsically good' by reference to the choice between 'an action of which A would be the sole or total effect and an action which would have absolutely no effects at all'. But that method would be open to objection, and I believe Moore only suggested it inadvertently. The method of isolated addition might be a sufficient safeguard against confusion between intrinsic and instrumental value: but it would not be a sufficient safeguard against confusions about organic unities. For if I were to judge that the world as it actually is, and a possible state of things differing from the world as it is only be the presence or absence of X, would differ in value by a certain determinate amount, I should not be entitled to conclude that the difference of value was identical with the value of X: the difference of value might result from the value of some whole formed by other things in conjunction with X.

Some problems about the method of isolation may be introduced by asking whether we can set any limit upon the kind of content to which the method is applicable. An obvious suggestion would be that it cannot be applicable to things whose isolated existence, or whose existence in abstraction from something else, is logically impossible. For otherwise I should have to ask myself a question of the form 'if X and X alone existed, would that state of affairs be good?', where the protasis stands for the existence of something logically impossible. And such a question is unanswerable whatever the apodosis may be. I cannot, for example, make anything of a question as to how things would be if there existed just one class of objects, a two-member class, and no unit classes.

Yet it is not clear that Moore would accept such a restriction, nor that he can afford to accept it if he is to make, by the help of his method, the distinctions he wishes to make. In *Principia* § 48 he considers, by way of illustration, the hypothesis that the only intrinsically good thing might be colour. He grants that colour could not exist unless some determinate hue existed. But he does not treat the possibility that colour, in abstraction from all hues, might be the sole good, as a hypothesis whose truth or falsity is unascertainable. Yet the supposition that colour might exist without hue seems to be impossible. And the attempt to apply the method of isolation to the hypothesis that colour, independently of hue, is intrinsically good, breaks down in the manner I have indicated.

The proposition that a thing is coloured, but of no determinate colour, is sometimes, with good reason, described as logically impossible. The reason is that the proposition that a thing is coloured entails the proposition that it has some determinate colour; the conjunctive proposition is therefore of the form '*P* and not-*Q*', where *P* entails *Q*, and the conjunctive entails a conclusion of the form '*Q* and not-*Q*'. The impossibility of that last conclusion is perspicuous as a matter of formal logic: it is therefore called, of right and not by courtesy, a logical impossibility. But the relation between '*X* is coloured' and '*X* has some determinate colour', by virtue of which the former proposition entails the latter, may well seem opaque: if so, the reasoning by which the logically impossible conclusion '*Q* and not-*Q*' was deduced contains an opaque element. It may therefore be held that the impossibility of '*X* is coloured but of no determinate colour' is logical only by courtesy. To avoid controversy on this point, I shall speak in such cases of 'conceptual' impossibility. I shall assume without argument that conceptual impossibility, and logical impossibility in the narrow sense, are distinct from the impossibility which arises from the breach of any empirically confirmable law of nature: and I shall call this last 'natural' impossibility. And I believe that my reasons for holding that the method of isolation cannot be applied to a logically impossible state of things would have equal force with reference to a conceptually impossible state of things.

Although the example of colour and hue illustrates the logic

of the matter as well as any other, a less factitious example may
be more easily grasped: and I shall therefore refer again to
Moore's discussion of pleasure and consciousness. In *Principia*
§ 17 Moore speaks of the intrinsic value, if any, of consciousness;
and in § 112 of 'the value of a certain amount of pleasure, *existing
absolutely by itself*'. In § 52 he says that pleasure is 'something . . .
which . . . may be distinguished from our consciousness of it',
and implies that it is uncertain whether consciousness is 'an
inseparable accompaniment of pleasure'. Yet even if it were, that,
he thinks, would not debar us from asking the question 'Is it the
pleasure, as distinct from the consciousness of it, that we set
value on? Do we think the pleasure valuable in itself, or must we
insist that, if we are to think the pleasure good, we must have
consciousness of it too?'. 'To maintain that pleasure is good as
an end', Moore says 'we must maintain that it is good whether
we are conscious of it or not.' There is one passage (§ 122) in
which Moore betrays some doubt about the isolability of something. He says there that 'it . . . is very difficult to imagine what
the cognition of mental qualities *alone*, unaccompanied by *any*
corporeal expression, would be like'. But since he goes on to
speak of the result which is obtained 'in so far as we succeed in
making this abstraction', he seems not to have thought the
difficulty insuperable.

It is hard to resist the impression that the passages about
pleasure contain some refractory implications. It seems to be
implied, in the first place, that Moore wishes to find out what
value, if any, belongs to pleasure, as such, to consciousness as
such, and to the complex, consciousness of pleasure, as such; and
that hedonistic doctrines cannot be assessed until each of those
questions has been settled. Secondly, as he expressly says in § 53,
Moore thinks that those questions may be tackled by the method
of isolation. And thirdly, he seems to imply that, even if the
existence of pleasure without consciousness were impossible, we
should still be able to answer those three questions.

Now if the second and third implications were accepted it
would follow that we can apply the method of isolation to the
question what value X would have, if it existed without Y, even
when it is impossible that X should exist without Y. On the other
hand, if either the second or the third implication were abandoned,
it would follow that the method of isolation was applicable only
to some, not all, questions about the intrinsic value of things.

Supposing the existence of pleasure without consciousness were impossible, as Moore allows that it may be, of what kind would the impossibility be? Perhaps, in Moore's view, it would have been only a natural impossibility, like the impossibility of consciousness existing without a supply of blood to the brain. Unless there is some general objection to the method of isolation, there is no difficulty about applying it to natural impossibilities.

It may well be thought, however, that the impossibility of pleasure without consciousness is conceptual: that to feel pleasure is to be conscious in a particular way, and that to try to contemplate pleasure as existing without consciousness is therefore as absurd as trying to contemplate colour as existing without hue. And it may well be thought that to apply the method of isolation even to consciousness of pleasure, as Moore must if he is to use his method in distinguishing between the value of enjoyment of beauty and that of consciousness of pleasure in general, is conceptually absurd: for the notion of enjoyment, it may be said, is related to that of particular modes of enjoyment in a way analogous to that in which the notion of colour is related to that of particular hues. It may be that Moore was misled by an ambiguity of the phrase 'consciousness of pleasure'. That phrase might stand for the state of being pleasurably conscious, or for the state of being conscious of being pleasurably conscious. There is probably no conceptual absurdity in isolating the former state, to the exclusion of the latter, even though there would be an absurdity in isolating pleasure to the exclusion of consciousness.

But even if the impossibility of pleasure without consciousness were merely natural, the method of isolation would not be vindicated. For there is no assurance that there may not be other things, besides pleasure and consciousness, whose values need to be independently established, even though it is logically or conceptually impossible that one of them should exist without another. Unless, in advance of particular valuations, some theoretical reason can be given for thinking that certain kinds of thing can never be bearers of intrinsic value, we must regard any characteristic whatever as a possible subject term of a value generalization. Moore gives no such theoretical reason, and I do not see how he could.

We can, of course, think about pleasure in abstraction from consciousness, or colour in abstraction from determinate colours; and the act of doing so is often spoken of as 'isolating' something in thought, or thinking of it in 'isolation'. But that sort of thinking, the drawing of 'distinctions of reason', does not ordinarily involve the hypothesis that such and such a kind of thing might constitute the whole universe.

In the *Reply* (pp. 581-2), in the course of disavowing part of what he had said in *Principia* on the question what is meant by calling a property 'natural', Moore rejects the view that natural properties, such as a penny's 'property of being brown or that of being round . . . could exist in time all by themselves, i.e. without being, at any time at which they did exist, properties of some natural object which also existed at that time': that suggestion, he says, was 'silly and preposterous'. Although Moore does not connect this statement with the method of isolation, it might be construed as implying disavowal of the method. But that construction is not certain. For he might mean to maintain, not that brownness, say, could not exist in isolation from all other natural properties: but that, if brownness so existed, it would follow that some natural object, namely a brown object, existed. The latter interpretation would be consistent with the method of isolation. Another passage in the *Reply* (p. 588) suggests that at the time of writing Moore was still prepared for a bold policy of isolation. He there says that 'an experience of mine, which was a tasting of caviare, might . . . be exactly like an experience of another person, which was a tasting of caviare, and that yet my experience might be pleasant to me, whilst his exactly similar experience was not pleasant to him'.

The assumption that there are true value generalizations, which may be discovered by reflective judgement, does not logically require that the method of isolation shall be used in discovering them. The reason for the method is prudential: that without it we may be in danger of contaminating our intuitions by not distinguishing sharply enough between the kind of thing whose value is in question and its effects and accompaniments. Perhaps that is carrying prudence to excess: or perhaps the method of isolation may be regarded as a fanciful way of dramatizing our power of making distinctions of reason. In *Principia* § 134 Moore says 'our only means of deciding upon . . . intrinsic value . . . is by carefully distinguishing exactly what the thing is about which we ask the question, and then looking to see whether it has or has not the unique predicate "good" in any of its various degrees'. A method so formulated would escape my criticisms.

My objections to the method of isolation leave the principle of organic unities undisturbed. If it is possible, by intuition or reflective judgement, to discover the intrinsic value which belongs to this or that distinct kind of thing, as being of this or that kind, independently of the accompaniments and effects from which we distinguish it, the values of different kinds of thing may prove to be interrelated in the ways which that principle foreshadows.

3. *Moore's Account of the kinds of thing which have Intrinsic Value*
Moore holds that it is possible to ascertain that certain general kinds of thing are intrinsically good in a high degree, and certain others intrinsically bad. The method he adopts in *Principia* and in *Ethics* is the method of isolation: but if I am right in the conclusions I have drawn in my second section, he might have reached equivalent results by some method of abstraction which would not be exposed to the objections I have raised. As to the kinds of thing which possess intrinsic value, there was a change in Moore's views after he had written *Principia*. When he wrote *Principia*, he held that 'personal affections and aesthetic enjoyments include by far the greatest goods with which we are acquainted' (§ 113, synopsis); and that 'great evils . . . consist . . . in the love of what is evil or ugly, or in the hatred of what is good or beautiful, or in the consciousness of pain' (§ 135). All these great goods and evils involve consciousness as an element. He held, however, that the existence of beautiful things was in some degree intrinsically good, and the existence of ugly things intrinsically bad, even if they were unperceived, but that their degree of value was very low in comparison with that of the wholes consisting in various kinds of consciousness of such things (§§ 18, 50, 113). When he wrote *Ethics* he seems no longer to have held that intrinsic value could belong to unperceived objects: for there (pp. 249–50) he says that 'nothing can be an intrinsic good unless it contains both some feeling and also some other form of consciousness', and that 'nothing can be intrinsically bad unless it contains some feeling'. In the *Reply* he states his change of view more explicitly, saying on p. 618 'I think now, as I did not when I wrote *Principia*, that the existence of some *experience* . . . does follow from the hypothesis that there exists a state of affairs which is good'.

I shall not examine Moore's lists of types of good and bad thing in detail, but I shall make some general comments on them.

In the first place, it is perhaps more accurate to say, not that Moore *applies* the method of isolation, but rather that he advocates it, explains how to practise it, and summarizes some results which he holds that he has reached by its aid. For most of Moore's statements about kinds of good and bad thing, even in *Principia* ch. 6 which is his fullest treatment of the subject, seem not to be themselves value generalizations, but rather statements to the effect that there are a number of true value generalizations of a certain type. Moore's account of aesthetic enjoyment is the clearest example. Those instances of it 'which we think most valuable' include 'not merely a bare cognition of what is beautiful in the object, but also some kind of feeling or emotion' (*Principia* § 114): 'different emotions', he continues, 'are appropriate to different kinds of beauty'. These appropriate emotions may be felt (*a*) towards beautiful qualities which a thing really has and is seen to have, (*b*) towards beautiful qualities which a thing is falsely supposed to have, (*c*) towards beautiful qualities which are merely imagined, without any belief that a thing possesses them, and (*d*) inappropriately, towards qualities which are falsely believed to be beautiful—I here paraphrase and simplify Moore's divisions in *Principia* §§ 115–16. Moore holds that the organic unities constituted by relationships (*a–c*) are intrinsically good in a high degree; whereas that constituted by relationship (*d*) is not good, and may well be intrinsically evil. It is clear that, in Moore's view there is a boundless range of 'beautiful qualities'—qualities by virtue of whose presence a thing is beautiful. In § 121 he expressly disclaims the attempt to classify 'all the different forms of beauty'. The proposition that the enjoyment, in the various forms I have listed, of beautiful qualities is intrinsically good, is not itself a value generalization. It is a generalization of higher order, to the effect that there are many qualities, and many emotions, standing in such a relation that, the emotion being appropriate to the quality and being combined with a certain kind of cognition, the whole constituted by that relationship is intrinsically good. A value generalization would be concerned with particular modes of the concepts which are involved, and would be to the effect that such and such an emotional and cognitive relationship to such and such a quality is intrinsically good, or possesses such and such a degree or amount of goodness.

In § 121 Moore says it is 'probable' that 'the beautiful should be *defined* as that of which the admiring contemplation is good in itself'. Given that definition, Moore's higher order generalization about the goodness of aesthetic enjoyments appears tautologous: for it resolves itself into the statement that all qualities the admiring contemplation of which is good *are* qualities the admiring contemplation of which is good. I do not think there is really a vicious circle. I take Moore's thesis to be that there *are* a great number of, let us say, 'pulchrific' qualities, each of which is such that the appropriate kind of admiring contemplation of it would be intrinsically good; not merely the tautology that if there were such qualities the admiring contemplation of them would be good. The distinction between pulchrific qualities, and other qualities which are involved in the subject terms of value generalizations, lies in their being ingredients of certain wholes of which another element is admiring contemplation. In the last paragraph of § 121, where Moore discusses the possibility of a 'criterion of beauty', he says some things which may possibly tell against my account of pulchrific qualities: but I find what he says there either obscure or confused, and since I am not concerned with the concept of beauty on its own account I shall not examine that paragraph.

By similar reasoning to the foregoing, it may be shown that Moore's statements about the intrinsic goodness of personal affection, and about the intrinsic badness of hatred of the good or beautiful, and of love of the evil or ugly, are not themselves value generalizations but statements of a higher order, about kinds of value generalization. There remains the intrinsic badness of the consciousness of pain; and in asserting that, Moore is perhaps stating a determinate value generalization. If so, that seems to be the only exception to my conclusion that, for the most part, he is merely describing general types of value generalization. Moore himself holds that pain is 'an exception from the rule [that] *other* great evils and *all* great goods . . . are . . . organic unities to which *both* a cognition of an object *and* an emotion directed towards that object are essential' (§ 127). That statement is not a direct corroboration of my conclusion, for the distinction I am drawing does not seem to have been noticed by Moore when he was writing *Principia:* but it helps to give colour to my contention that Moore's statements about the valuation of pain and those about the valuation of other things stand on different levels.

In order to put a defensible construction upon Moore's state-

L

ments about the things other than pain which have intrinsic value, I think, then, we must take him to be claiming (1) that he has himself applied the method of isolation, or at least some equivalent method, to a number of specific kinds of whole, and to all their distinguishable elements, and that by so doing he has established a number of value generalizations about the values of the wholes as wholes, and about the values belonging severally to the elements: (2) that he has surveyed the results of those specified valuations, and has found that whatever he has judged to have a high degree of value has been, to adopt his later terminology, a kind of experience: (3) that the specific kinds of intrinsically good experience which he has discovered fall into two or three generic kinds, and so do the specific kinds of intrinsically bad experience. The specific kinds of experience are, with one exception, not listed, but only summarized in the manner of the third of the foregoing clauses. But Moore seems to make a further claim, which he fails to distinguish from those which I have paraphrased in my second and third clauses; that 'by far the most valuable things which we can know or imagine are certain states of consciousness' (*Principia* § 113). Although, in the sentence from which I quote, the word 'valuable' is used in its positive sense, I think it is clear from the rest of chapter 6, and particularly its closing section, that Moore would be prepared to adhere to his statement if 'valuable' were given its comprehensive sense. And this statement goes beyond the three claims I have paraphrased. For in them Moore is only claiming that all the highly valuable things *he has* discovered fall under a certain classification. But here he is maintaining that the same classification embraces all the highly valuable things 'we'—that is, I think, human beings—*can* discover. And this last thesis cannot be supported by the method of isolation, or a counterpart of it, but only by some kind of induction from Moore's specific results.

If I am right, Moore has given few instances, perhaps only one, of the positive results of the method of isolation. And since his view of the great goods and the great evils is what it is it would have been difficult for him to do more: for the value of his organic unities depends on many fine gradations of feeling and perception, and an adequate vocabulary in which to express them might be hard to find. I shall say more on that point in my fourth section. But there is not the same difficulty about stating negative results of the method. In his discussion of hedonism, Moore has shown clearly enough how he would set about the disproof of such propositions as 'pleasure is intrinsically good in a high degree'.

4. Moore's Later Characterization of Intrinsic Goodness

It is well known that in *Principia* Moore maintains that goodness, or as he usually says good, is indefinable. 'That quality which we assert to belong to a thing when we say that a thing is good is incapable of definition' in the sense 'in which a definition states what are the parts which invariably compose a certain whole' (§ 10). I do not think that Moore has ever retracted the contention that, provided the word 'good' stands for any concept at all, it stands for a concept which is not definable in an analytical manner. In 'Is Goodness a Quality?' (p. 127) he says something which implies that he thinks goodness *might* be definable. But he does not avow that, as I shall argue below, he is in that essay giving a definition of it. He expresses another kind of doubt in the *Reply*, where he concedes that Mr. C. L. Stevenson may be right in holding that the word 'good' has only 'emotive meaning' and no 'cognitive meaning' (p. 554). I take it that if the word had no cognitive meaning it would not, as one would naturally say, stand for a concept at all; and the question of its being in any conventional sense definable would not arise.

In the essay 'Is Goodness a Quality?' Moore advances a thesis which has attracted less attention than it deserves. In *The Philosophy of G. E. Moore*, the thesis I am about to discuss is mentioned briefly by Mr. H. J. Paton: but the want of any sustained examination of it is one of several regrettable lacunae in that collection. On p. 122 of the essay mentioned above, Moore suggests that there is 'another way'—different, that is, from those adopted in his previous writings—'of explaining how the phrase "intrinsically good" is used'. The suggestion is that 'I use the phrase "intrinsically good" to mean precisely the same as "worth having for its own sake" ' (p. 123): the context shows that Moore intends the phrase 'worth having' to be applied only to experiences, and that it is not to be taken in the sense in which, for example, a piece of property might be said to be 'worth having'. He adds, referring to earlier discussions in *Ethics* and in 'The Conception of Intrinsic Value', that he is 'inclined to hold' that 'that experience was worth having for its own sake' means the same as 'that experience would have been worth having if it had existed quite alone'; and that the 'character' expressed by the phrase 'worth having for its own sake' is one whose possession by any experience, in a particular degree, 'depends solely on the intrinsic nature of that experience' (pp. 123–4). But he grants that on those two points he may be wrong, and he thinks that without committing himself to the opinions I have quoted he can still, by means of his new suggestion, 'explain fairly clearly' how he uses the term 'intrinsic goodness'.

The suggestion is not wholly new. In *Principia* § 113 he had said that 'if we consider strictly what things are worth having *purely for their own sakes*' (Moore's italics) we shall judge that nothing else has nearly so great a positive value as certain states of consciousness. But in *Principia* the phrase is merely one of a number of expressions which are meant to convey informally and discursively the notion of goodness which Moore there held to be indefinable. What is new in the later essay is the use of the phrase as a self-sufficient vehicle for expounding what is meant by the phrase 'intrinsically good'.

Surely Paton is right in thinking that here 'we have something complex substituted as an equivalent for something simple' (*Philosophy of G. E. M.* p. 116). If so, can it still be held that goodness is, as it is called in *Principia*, chapter 1, 'simple', 'indefinable', and 'unanalysable' (the last term is borrowed from Sidgwick, seemingly with approval)? And if not, can it be shown that Moore here gave what he ought on his own principles to acknowledge as an analysis of goodness?

Moore has often practised and advocated analytic procedures in philosophy, but less often undertaken a general account of philosophical analysis. The fullest discussion I known is in the *Reply* pp. 660–7. Among a number of penetrating things which Moore says there, I cannot find any statement of the sufficient conditions of something being an analysis of something else. He states certain necessary conditions, and the most I can hope to do is to argue that the fulfilment of some necessary conditions does at least give colour to the hypothesis that a given formula is in Moore's sense an analysis. Moore maintains there that his kind of analysis has always been concerned with 'an idea, a concept, or a proposition', never with a 'verbal expression'. He admits, however, that the giving of his kind of analysis requires that the verbal expressions in which it is given shall have certain characteristics: namely '(*b*) that the *expression* used for the *analysandum* must be a different *expression* from that used for the *analysans*'; and '(*c*) that the *expression* used for the *analysandum* . . . and that used for the *analysans* . . . must differ in this way, namely, that the expression used for the *analysans* must *explicitly mention* concepts which are not explicitly mentioned by the expression used for the *analysandum*' (*Reply* p. 666: Moore's italics). Condition (*a*) was 'that both *analysandum* and *analysans* must be concepts'. Moore also lays down on p. 664 a maxim which may be paraphrased as follows. If X and Y are two verbal formulae, and we wish to use Y in expressing the analysis of the concept or proposition for which X stands, it is advisable to avoid statements of the form 'X means Y': for they may give the false impression that the object of analysis is a verbal formula. In their place, Moore advocates expressions of the form 'the concept —— is identical with the concept ——', or 'to say that —— is the same thing as to say that ——'; where the expressions X and Y, with suitable grammatical adjustments, would be inserted in the blanks. In order that a statement shall give an analysis, the expressions X and Y must at least fulfil the conditions (*b*) and (*c*) which have been quoted. Moore admitted that in the past he had often used the word 'means' in what he had now come to regard as a misleading way, and his use of it in 'Is Goodness a Quality?' would no doubt have been an example of his doing so.

We may therefore reconstruct his thesis so that it will read as follows: 'the concept of a thing's being intrinsically good is identical with the concept of its being worth having for its own sake', or 'to say that something is intrinsically good is the same as to say that it is worth having for its own sake'. I shall refer to this reconstructed version as 'the worth-havingness thesis'.

Unfortunately this reconstruction, like the original thesis, is exposed to the following objection which Moore makes on p. 555 of the *Reply*: 'the sense of "good" with which I was principally concerned was such that to say of a state of things in which two or more people were all having experiences worth having for their own sake that it was "good" . . . would not be self-contradictory, whereas to say of such a state of things that it was *itself* an experience worth having for its own sake would be self-contradictory'. He therefore thinks that, although any experience worth having for its own sake must be good, to imply the converse was a 'sheer error'. Moore's objection is formally conclusive: yet it would not be difficult to preserve the substance of the thesis by a further reconstruction. Why should we not say that the concept of a thing's being intrinsically good is identical with the concept of its having a certain disjunctive characteristic: namely, that of being either an experience worth having for its own sake, or a state of things in which two or more people are having such experiences? This line of thought might be elaborated, but it is needless to do so, for the objection Moore has raised, though formally unanswerable, is shallow. For the sake of simplicity of discussion, I shall continue to consider Moore's thesis in its condemned form, as rephrased in the light of Moore's later remarks on analysis.

The question, then, is whether the worth-havingness thesis fulfils at least the necessary conditions for the giving of an analysis which Moore lays down on p. 666 of the *Reply*, namely (*a*), (*b*) and (*c*) which have already been quoted. The thesis fulfils condition (*a*) unless it is held, as some modern subjectivists might hold, that the word 'good' does not stand for a concept at all. It certainly fulfils condition (*b*), for its left and right hand parts are different expressions. The crucial question is whether the thesis fulfils condition (*c*): and it will be convenient to consider that condition together with another related but different criterion. Moore used sometimes in discussion to offer as a necessary condition of analysis that the expression standing for the analysans shall contain 'more words which have separate meanings' than the expression standing for the analysandum (I quote from memory). I shall call this last requirement (*c'*). (*c'*) seems less exacting than (*c*). For if the analysans expression 'explicitly mentions' concepts not explicitly mentioned in the analysandum expression, it must, I suppose, contain a word or phrase 'with a separate meaning' for each concept explicitly mentioned: but the converse principle, that every word or phrase 'with a separate meaning' has the function of 'explicitly mentioning' a concept, may not hold.

There is room for much doubt or disagreement as to what constitutes 'having a separate meaning' or 'explicitly mentioning' a concept. But I shall suggest two tests which may go a little way towards determining whether these requirements are fulfilled. When an expression consists of several parts (that is, words or phrases) there are two questions we may ask: in formulating them I shall speak of the parts as P_1 and P_2. In the first place, we may ask whether P_1 might be combined with some other expression, grammatically similar to P_2, in such a way that the sense of P_1 would be unchanged. Secondly, we may ask whether, if P_2 were omitted from a sentence in which P_1 and P_2 were juxtaposed, and nothing put in its place, the sentence would still make sense and the sense of P_1 be unchanged. If the answer to either question were Yes, that, I suggest, would tend to support both the conclusion (1) that P_1 and P_2 had separate meanings, and (2) that P_1 had the function of explicitly mentioning a concept. The support would be stronger for conclusion (1) than for conclusion (2), and would be given more strongly by an affirmative answer to the second question than by an affirmative answer to the first.

Here is an elementary illustration. Consider the phrase 'red book'. If we ask my questions about the first and second words of that phrase, we shall get the answers that in, say, the phrase 'green book' the sense of the word 'book' is unchanged; and that if the word 'red' were omitted from a sentence containing the phrase 'red book', and nothing put in its place, the sentence would still make sense and the sense of the word 'book' would be unchanged. It is possible to construct trick sentences which might make those answers seem doubtful, but I think the same ingenuity which allows us to devise the tricks would enable us to circumvent them. Given those answers, it would seem plausible to say, both that the word 'book' has a separate meaning and that it has the function of explicitly mentioning a concept. There is still room for uncertainty as to the grounds for saying that a word or phrase has the same sense in different contexts. But I shall now try to apply my tests for what they are worth.

The following sentences are adapted from Moore's examples in 'Is Goodness a Quality?'.

S_1. 'That experience was worth having.'

S_2. 'That experience was worth having for its own sake.'

S_3. 'That experience was worth having for the sake of the lesson it taught me.'

My suggestion is that, if we replace S_2 by S_3, or conversely, and if we replace either S_2 or S_3 by S_1, the sense of the phrase 'worth having' is unchanged. If so, by my tests, that phrase has a separate meaning, and has the function of explicitly mentioning a concept. Consider next two further sentences.

S_4. 'That action [*sc.* which I did] was worth doing for its own sake.'

S_5. 'That action was done for its own sake.'

I suggest that, if we compare $S2$ with $S4$, we find that the phrase 'for its own sake' has the same sense in either sentence. If so, by my first test, that phrase has a separate meaning and has the function of explicitly mentioning a concept. Next, if we compare $S4$ with $S5$, and if we may ignore the grammatical adjustment which requires the presence of the word 'done' in $S5$, then, by my second test, the same conclusion follows.

It might even be possible, by a further application of my tests, to argue for a corresponding relationship between the functioning of the word 'worth' and that of the word 'having'. But there is no need to go further. For if my tests have the force I have ascribed to them, and if they have been applied correctly, reason has already been given for thinking that the worth-havingness thesis fulfils Moore's condition (c), as well as the less exacting condition (c'). Then, if it also fulfils condition (a), and since it certainly fulfils condition (b), the thesis fulfils the conditions which in the *Reply* Moore laid down as necessary to an analysis, and there is at least some presumption that, according to Moore's own views, it is an analysis.

I must now mention two grounds for misgiving about the result I have reached. In the first place, might not a similar argument be constructed, which would support the conclusion that in the phrase 'intrinsically good' the two words which compose it have separate meanings and serve to mention distinct concepts? If so, a further conclusion would suggest itself, namely that Moore was mistaken all along in maintaining that the concept with which he was concerned was unanalysable, since he was himself giving an analysis of it in his own habitual designations of it. In that case, it would be a mistake to argue that he first gave an analysis in his later writings.

This difficulty may be met by distinguishing between two functions of adverbs and adverbial phrases. Their best known function is, as grammarians say, to 'modify' some other word. That function is illustrated by such phrases as 'slightly angry' and 'intensely angry', in which the adjective unquestionably stands for the same general characteristic in both of its occurrences, and the force of the adverb is to narrow its sense to a determinate degree of that characteristic. But another function is illustrated by such adverbs as 'literally', 'metaphorically', 'figuratively'. In such sentences as 'he literally exploded', and 'he exploded—metaphorically, that is', the force of the adverb is not to express some determination of the concept of explosion, but to discriminate between two senses of the word 'explode': a longer way round would have been to say 'he exploded—I am using the word "explode" literally/metaphorically'. In this latter kind of case, I shall say that the adverb has a 'sense-discriminating', as opposed to a 'concept-modifying' function. A sense-discriminating adverb is often superfluous, since the context, or the mutual understanding of speaker and hearer, makes misconception improbable. But a concept-modifying adverb can only be omitted—unless some other device takes its place—at the price of impoverishing the sense of what is said. The distinction may usefully be put in another form. If an adverb is sense-discriminating, it is not one of the words which carry the sense of the sentence, for it is a kind of gloss on the functioning of some other word. An alternative expedient, in my example, would be to write words used literally in black ink and those used metaphorically in red ink. Given that an adverb is sense-discriminating, it is not a part of the sentence which has a separate meaning, or serves to mention a concept. But if it is concept-modifying it is one of the words which carry the sense of the sentence, and is therefore not precluded from having a separate meaning or serving to mention a concept, thought it may still lack those characteristics.

The adverb in the phrase 'intrinsically good' seems, with little doubt, to be sense-discriminating. That Moore took it in that way, and that it is natural for a reader to take it in that way, is indicated by the ease and frequency with which Moore uses the word 'good' without prefix or suffix when he is concerned with intrinsic goodness. The same will be true of the adverbial phrases 'in itself', 'as an end', and so on. The same will be true also of the antithetical adverbial expressions, 'as a means', 'instrumentally', and so on. For the definiens of 'X is good as a means' will be to the effect that the existence of X tends to bring about the existence of other things, which are good in themselves. And the force of the phrase 'as a means' is, not to modify a generic concept expressed by the word 'good', but to direct attention to one of the senses of that word which, unlike the sense in which goodness is intrinsic, has a definition. My question in this section now becomes the question whether, in the worth-havingness thesis, Moore was offering an analysis of goodness, in that sense of the word 'good' which he discriminated by means of the adverb 'intrinsically'.

L*

My second ground for misgiving about my own answer to the question arises from the piece of semantic machinery which I have just used. Might not the same treatment be applied to the right-hand part of the worth-havingness thesis? May not the phrase 'for its own sake', attached to the phrase 'worth having', possess the force of a sense-discriminating adverb? If it has, my diagnosis of Moore's thesis is subverted.

I am inclined to reject this suggestion, but I cannot give conclusive reasons for doing so. It seems to me that prolonged discourse might be carried on in which the phrase 'worth having' was used without qualification, as in my sentence $S1$. If thereafter qualifications were added, as in my sentences $S2$ and $S3$ or in other ways, the effect would be to introduce one or more new elements of discourse, by expressing modifications of a concept which had until then only occurred generically. If I am right about that, and I see no way of proving that I am, the qualifications attached to the phrase 'worth having' are akin to concept-modifying rather than to sense-discriminating adverbs. I am therefore still inclined to argue that, in the worth-havingness thesis, Moore did offer what by his own standards may well be an analysis of intrinsic goodness.

I argued in my third section that for the most part Moore gives only general descriptions of the value generalizations he holds to be true, not determinate instances. In the light of the worth-havingness thesis, and the restriction which it places upon the subject terms of value generalizations, it appears difficult, if not impossible, to give determinate instances. The statement 'that experience was worth having' is capable of amplification in at least three ways. It might be taken as referring (1) only to the individual event; (2) to any event of a certain character; (3) to any event resembling the individual event, wholly or more or less. It is clear that (1) would not serve Moore's purpose, which requires that judgements of worth-havingness shall be generalizations. To decide between (2) and (3) is not easy, in view of the vacillation in Moore's way of speaking which I mentioned at the end of my first section. I have already argued that Moore's general position requires that what is value-implying shall be a quality or sort, rather than that which is common to two things which are alike. But the worth-havingness thesis puts the alternatives in a new light.

If a generalization is concerned with anything which has a

certain character, I shall call it 'Descriptive', and if with anything which resembles a certain standard object I shall call it 'Prototypic': so in cases (2) and (3) statements of worth-havingness will be Descriptive and Prototypic generalizations about experiences, and therefore about events of a certain kind. Value generalizations also might be either Descriptive or Prototypic. According to Moore's early views, they need not be concerned only with events. The argument of my first section would lead us to say that, in Moore's view, they were Descriptive.

Let us suppose that, according to the worth-havingness thesis, value generalizations are Descriptive: and to make as plain sailing as we can let us think of examples in which an experience consists of perceiving and responding to the same unchanged object, or indistinguishable objects: for instance, seeing the same picture or the same film, reading the same edition of a book, hearing the same recording of a piece of music, and so on. It is clear that Moore does not mean to commit himself to any such generalization as 'the experience of reading the *Inferno* is always intrinsically good'. For—to borrow the terminology of *Principia*— even if the *Inferno* possesses qualities the admiring contemplation of which is good, a particular experience of reading the *Inferno* may involve failure to discern those qualities, failure to admire them, admiration of qualities in the *Inferno* which are not ad-mirable, or mistaken perception and admiration of unadmirable qualities which the *Inferno* lacks. Not only is Moore precluded, by his own line of thought, from adopting value generalizations in which the subject term involves only sameness of the perceived object: but such generalizations have only to be framed clearly in order to seem unplausible to anyone.

On the other hand, if we try to construct a more adequate subject term, by specifying the admirable qualities of the perceived object and the feelings which are appropriate to them, we shall be hindered by the poverty and indefiniteness of the available vocabulary of criticism and appreciation. While that hindrance may be practical rather than theoretical, it is arguable that there is also a theoretical obstacle: there may perhaps be a frontier, beyond which the idiosyncrasies of experience are, if not in principle incommunicable, at least only roughly and imperfectly communicable. Yet anyone who attaches importance to what are called aesthetic experiences will probably think that whatever in them may be incommunicable, or imperfectly communicable, often contributes to their value. Although the notion of the incommunicable is out of fashion, I do not feel sure that the idea can be dismissed. In any case, whether theoretically removable or not, the obstacle is there, and it leaves us little hope of constructing Descriptive judgements of worth-havingness, with determinate subject terms, which will be anything more than dummies.

Would Prototypic judgements be more promising? Whatever difficulties there may be about communication will be just as great as they are in the framing of Descriptive judgements. The difficulties are greater if value is ascribed to fugitive events, such as experiences, than they would be if it were ascribed to enduring objects, such as pictures or musical compositions. If we are to make any use of a generalization which ascribes value to all events resembling a Prototypic event, there are three alternatives: the claim may be concerned (1) with any event exactly like the prototype, or (2) with any event resembling the prototype in some respect or other, or (3) with any event resembling the prototype in specified respects. I have given reasons in my first section for thinking that alternatives (1) and (2) cannot be taken seriously. But alternative (3) makes the reference to a prototype superfluous, for this alternative resolves itself into the combination of a Descriptive judgement and the assertion that some proto-typical experience falls under it.

My conclusion is that if, as Moore held in his later work, things are good only in virtue of being, or containing, kinds of experience, there is an inherent difficulty in framing determinate positive value generalizations. There would be a corresponding difficulty about negative value generalizations, except that which concerns the badness of pain, if we assumed that things are bad only in virtue of being, or containing, kinds of experience.

5. *A Reinterpretation of Moore's Later View*

So far I have followed Moore in taking as the object of discussion the statement or judgement that something has a certain value or is worth having. This practice suggests, if it does not necessitate, a cognitivist treatment of judgements of value. It will now be more convenient to consider second-order statements, to the effect that someone thinks or says that something has a certain value or is worth having. A statement of the form 'X thinks that S has P' might be analysed in two ways: as equivalent (1) to 'X thinks that S has such and such a complex character', or (2) to 'X adopts towards S attitude A'. The first type of analysis would be cognitivist the second non-cognitivist. The practice I am now adopting is therefore neutral between those two types of analysis.

When someone thinks an experience worth having, how far can we properly suppose that he may be mistaken? In the first place, it seems possible that someone should think a given experience of kind E worth having, and yet, on having a further experience of kind E, not think it so. Then the following suppositions are possible: (1) the two experiences, $E1$ and $E2$, are exactly alike in every way except being, or being thought, worth having; (2) there is no known or supposed difference between $E1$ and $E2$, apart from being, or being thought, worth having; (3) $E1$ and $E2$ are alike in being of kind E, but are in some other way known or believed to be unlike one another. Now in case (1), if $E1$ were intrinsically good, then, on Moore's principles, $E2$ also would necessarily be intrinsically good, and conversely; and if either were not, the other would not be. The only escape from this conclusion would be to suppose that worth-havingness, or the property of being thought worth having, might itself be value-implying. But if that were so worth-havingness could not itself be, or enter into, the definiens of goodness. So it may be concluded that in case (1), according to the worth-havingness thesis, the subject would be mistaken in at least one of his judgements of worth-havingness. We might argue similarly about case (2), but for one loophole: $E1$ or $E2$ might have some value-implying quality of which the subject was unaware, which made them different in value. But then he would still be mistaken so far as he was making contrary judgements about the qualities of which he was aware. In case (3), Moore's doctrine would not give us any ground for saying that he was mistaken.

Secondly, the worth-havingness thesis would require us to say, in any single case of a person judging an experience worth having, that he might be mistaken. For he always might make a contrary judgement about some other experience of the same kind: he could not be right on both occasions, and there is no reason to assume that the given occasion is superior in status to the other.

Thirdly, the worth-havingness thesis would imply that if different people had similar experiences, and made contrary judgements about their worth-havingness, one at least must be mistaken.

The question is, then, whether we can regard as intelligible the statement that someone might be mistaken in thinking an experience worth having, if we are taking the phrase 'worth having' in some natural undefined sense. There would be no great difficulty in supposing that he might be mistaken in thinking that, for some extrinsic reason, an experience was worth having: but I am of course still taking the qualification 'for its own sake' as understood.

We might be tempted to think that to be worth having is more or less the same as to be pleasant or enjoyable. If it were, then in a familiar way a person could not be mistaken in thinking an experience worth having: he might misdescribe it or misremember it, but if he did neither of those things, and if his mind were not confused in some similar way, the possibility of a mistake would not arise. It is not easy to give a clear account of this inerrancy which seems to belong to people's apprehension of their own feelings, but I am going to take the fact of such inerrancy as acknowledged.

But I do not think that worth-havingness is more or less the same as pleasantness or enjoyableness. For when a person thinks an experience worth having, there is a sense in which he is not merely taking note of his own feelings, but performing some kind of deliberation. Another thing which we might say of an experience is that it was of a kind which he would choose to have again: we might also say that he would choose that other people should have it. What is expressed by saying that 'he would choose' is the outcome of deliberation, and it seems to me that we might convey the same sort of sense by saying that he thinks the experience worth having. But there would be no absurdity in saying of someone that, although experience E was enjoyable, it was not of a kind he would choose to have; nor in saying that, although E was not enjoyable, it was such an experience as he would choose to have. So if the statement that he thinks E worth having were more or less the same as the statement that E is the sort of experience he would choose to have, worth-havingness could not be identified with enjoyableness.

What is meant by the statement that a person 'would choose' some state of affairs? A protasis seems to be understood, and I think it can be supplied. Part of it will be what is often expressed in the phrase 'other things being equal'. Another part will be the condition that the subject could bring about the state of affairs.

Nothing is implied about the degree of exertion which the subject would be prepared to make, beyond what is implicit in the 'other things being equal' clause; namely that there are a number of objects of choice, each of which he 'would choose', given that he could do so without sacrificing any of the others. Let us imagine that there are just two states of affairs, O_1 and O_2, to each of which, and to no others, a person, P, stands in the relation of deliberate election which is being described. If P thought he could effect O_1 without lessening the likelihood of effecting O_2, he would choose to effect O_1; and under the corresponding condition he would choose to effect O_2. The force of the phrase 'other things being equal' is to take account, without naming a number, of the possibility of constructing statements of the foregoing type in which any number of objects might be referred to. A more exact general formulation would be as follows. There is some class of possible states of affairs to each of whose members P stands in a certain relation: namely that, if O is the member in question, and if P thought he could effect O without prejudice to the other members, he would choose to do so. Of anything which is a member of the class in question we may say that it is an 'objective' of P's choice. My formula is not logically impeccable, but I hope the sense is clear enough for my present purpose.

The conditional statements about what someone would choose which I have framed possess a type of ambiguity which is widespread. I shall first use a different sort of example to illustrate it. Consider the statement (A) 'if I saw a flash of lightening, I should think there would shortly be thunder'. A may be taken as a compound of two propositions, of which if we were prepared to assert either one we should usually be prepared to assert the other; but we can distinguish them if we wish. They are (A_1) 'my opinion is that, if at any time I saw a flash of lightning, there would shortly thereafter be thunder'; and (A_2) 'if at any time I saw a flash of lightning, I should at that time expect thunder shortly'. A_1 states my present adherence to a generalization about a relation between lightning and thunder holding at all times: A_1 states a generalization about myself, that is to say about a relation at all times between my perception of lightning and my expectation of thunder. As soon as they are distinguished, it is obvious that A_1 and A_2 are logically independent of one another, and that, for either, grounds might be given which would not be grounds for the other. The grammatical form of A suggests interpretation $A2$ rather than $A1$. Although we may have just as great a need to make statements akin to $A1$ as to make those which are akin to $A2$, there seems to be a persistent tendency in English to give them a grammatical dress which disguises their logical form. In A and $A2$ a verb of intentionality stands in an apodosis which is subject to a condition stated in the protasis. But in $A1$ a verb of intentionality governs a conditional statement in *oratio obliqua*, in which both protasis and apodosis are subject to it. Verbs of intentionality, like expressions of modality, are of a nomadic habit. When such a sentence as A is used to convey a sense which might also be conveyed by such a sentence as $A1$, the sense of A may be called 'counter-grammatical'.

Although my conditionals about choices are, I think, idiomatically apt for my purpose, the sense I wish them to bear is counter-grammatical. Suppose a person were to make a statement of the form 'if I thought I could effect O, other things being equal I should choose to do so'. Someone else might try to rebut that statement by giving evidence that, under the relevant conditions, the first speaker did not in fact tend to choose in the way described. If the first speaker were convinced by the evidence, he might either retract his statement or stick to it. If he retracted his statement, it would follow that he was giving it the straightforward grammatical sense, and was using it to convey a generalization about the choices he would make at any time, under a given condition. But if he stuck to his statement, notwithstanding the evidence about his own character, he would be saying in effect 'I may be wrong in my forecast of my own conduct under conditions not now fulfilled, but that does not alter the fact that the choice I now adhere to is what I say it is'. He would then be giving his statement a counter-grammatical sense. A grammatically, though not idiomatically, apt expression would have been of the form 'I now choose that, if I thought I could effect O . . . I should do so'. In the former case we may say that the expression 'should choose' or 'would choose' bears a 'predictive' sense; in the latter case that it bears an 'elective' sense. A person who uses the verb electively is not expressing an actual choice, but, as it were, a mental act of voting. I shall describe such an act as a 'notional election'. A person who uses the verb predictively may be said to assert a 'choice-tendency'. The degree of coincidence between a person's notional elections and his choice-tendencies would constitute a variable trait of character for which I do not know the best name. The expression 'P chooses that', followed by a conditional in *oratio obliqua*, does not easily lend itself to the sense I wish to convey, and it will be better to use the less familiar expression 'P elects': and I shall use the formula 'P elects objective O' as short for the longer kind of sentence containing the conditional in *oratio obliqua*.

My present task is rather the construction of a concept than the analysis of a concept lying ready to hand. In what I have said, and shall say below, the construction will remain provisional and vague. It will be successful in proportion as it results in a counterpart of judgements of intrinsic value as conceived by Moore, retaining as much as possible of Moore's general description of them, while foregoing the doctrine against which so many have rebelled, that in such judgements we are adopting true or false opinions as to the kinds of thing which possess a certain 'non-natural quality'. It would be as though one were to shore up a mechanism balanced on a single fulcrum, change the fulcrum, and restore the original balance. If it is to do what is required, the concept of a notional election still has to be circumscribed and supplemented in various respects, some of which concern the objective and some the mental act.

In the first place, I have introduced my concept as a possible interpretation of the definiens in Moore's worth-havingness thesis. The statement that P thinks experience E worth having may be capable of bearing some quite different sense. The most I am claiming is that to assimilate it to the statement that P elects E is allowable, and that my interpretation is of some interest on its own account. The objective of a notional election need not be an experience: it may be any imaginable state of affairs. On the other hand, as Moore implied, only an experience can be worth having, for nothing but an experience can be 'had' in the sense in which an experience can be had. I might, therefore, circumscribe my concept by limiting the objectives of election to experiences. But it seems better to leave the point in suspense, in order to keep open a possible comparison with Moore's earlier, less restricted, conception of the objects to which intrinsic value may belong.

Secondly, a judgement of intrinsic value is held by Moore to be universal in the sense discussed in my first section. I have given no reason for thinking that a notional election might not have as its objective something which would happen at a particular place and time. But for my present purpose our attention is confined to the electing of universal objectives, those which consist in the coming about of some *kind* of thing or event.

Thirdly, in Moore's view there are negative as well as positive intrinsic values. The analogue is easily found, for what is elected may be that something of a certain kind shall *not* come about.

In the three foregoing respects, there seems to be no difficulty in bringing the objectives of election as near as we choose to the objects to which Moore ascribes intrinsic value. I come now to the further determination of the act of electing.

First, the distinction between thinking an experience worth having for its own sake and for some extrinsic reason must have as its counterpart a distinction between two forms of the act of election. So far as my discussion up to this point has given a clear idea of electing, what it has presented has been the idea of electing an objective for its own sake. For theoretical completeness we should have to add a counterpart of ascribing non-intrinsic value to something, though that counterpart will not be needed in the rest of my discussion. If we take electing an objective for its own sake as understood, other forms of election may easily be defined in terms of a combination of electing O_1 for its own sake and believing that O_2 stands in a specific relation to O_1, so that O_2 becomes an objective of election in the newly defined sense.

Secondly, a counterpart of comparisons between the values of several things has to be found. The first step is not difficult. Suppose that O_1 and O_2 are objectives elected by P. In addition to electing either of them other things being equal, P might make a further act of election, whose import would be that, if he thought he could effect only one of O_1 and O_2, he should effect O_1. In that case we might say that he 'notionally prefers' O_1 to O_2. The idea of notional preference might be extended over any number of objectives, so as to arrange elections in rank. The next step, the quantification of elections, seems to be demanded if we are to take seriously the metrical character which Moore ascribes to intrinsic value. Perhaps what Moore says on this point should not be understood over strictly. For the present I am content to leave the metricization of preferences in the obscurity in which, as I argued in my second section, Moore left the metricality of value. I hope to return to the subject in another article.

One other point of analogy has to be considered, which does not entail further determination of the concept of election, but only description of the possible outcome of someone's elections. In the deliberative process which leads to an election, any distinguishable characteristic of things might be picked out as a possible objective. The process of picking out would resemble Moore's method of isolation, in whatever toned down version we regard as intelligible. When a given characteristic had been isolated, further distinctions of reason might be made inwards or outwards: we might select for attention either some ingredient of that characteristic, or some compound characteristic of which it was an ingredient. Such discriminations might result in a network of notional preferences whose relationships would resemble the relationships of Moore's judgements about organic unities and their elements. Notional elections need not fall into any such pattern: and similarly the interrelations of the values of things which were ascertained by Moore's method might turn out not to fall into such a pattern. But if we have any foreboding that the values of things may be interrelated in accordance with Moore's description, we remain free to be guided by it in substituting the concept of election for Moore's concept of valuation.

I now return to the question in what sense, if any, a person might be wrong in a judgement of worth-havingness, which we may interpret as the question in what sense he might be wrong in making a particular notional election.

In the first place, given that P elected O, I might say he was wrong on no other ground than that my election was contrary to his. The possibility of calling someone wrong in that sense is trivial and uninteresting, and I mention it only to dismiss it from further consideration.

But secondly, there may be an analogy not hitherto mentioned between the objectives of notional elections and the subject terms of Moore's value generalizations. I argued in section 3 that Moore seldom specifies the subject terms of the generalizations he holds to be discoverable, but only refers to them generically; and in section 4 I argued that it would have been difficult for him to do otherwise. There may be a more radical difficulty than that which I mentioned there. When people discuss the value of a supposedly beautiful object, or a human mode of living, they may not really be discussing the same thing. One may be better qualified than another, by direct acquaintance or imaginative grasp, to apprehend the nature of the kind of thing whose value is in question. If there is such a difference, we may say that one person's valuation, or election, is more 'instructed' than that of another. It would then be natural to describe the less instructed valuation as less correct.

Yet even if two people's notions of a certain objective were equally instructed, and as highly instructed as we choose to imagine, might they not still elect differently? It is tempting to form the hypothesis that, in proportion as people's thoughts of their objectives were instructed, their elections would tend to agree. Cognitivist theories imply a corresponding hypothesis, that people must agree in proportion as their moral insight becomes greater. If some anthropologists and psychologists are right about the extreme diversity of 'patterns of culture', the hypothesis of ultimate elective agreement may seem far-fetched.

But that is not quite the end of the matter. If we failed to find any like-mindedness at all between ourselves and the people of a certain culture, and if that difference appeared unalterable, we should be tempted to say that they were scarcely human beings. And as soon as we began to think of them as almost another species, whether our theory of valuation was cognitivist or non-cognitivist, the ultimate diversity of their valuations would trouble us less. Yet it might still trouble us: for it is hard to forego the hope of ultimate agreement between rational beings, human or not. I do not know what grounds can be given in support of that hope.

6. *Conclusion*

I shall mention summarily some further questions which would take too long to examine.

In adopting the worth-havingness thesis, how far was Moore modifying the general account given in *Principia* of the kinds of thing which are intrinsically good? We have seen that the ascription of goodness to objects not involving consciousness had already been abandoned in *Ethics*. In *Principia* the greatest goods are described as being 'aesthetic enjoyments' and 'personal affections'. It seems to be implied (§ 119) that 'reciprocal affection' is good in a higher degree than unrequited affection. In discussing 'mixed goods'—those 'which, though positively good *as wholes* . . . contain, as essential elements, something intrinsically evil or ugly'— Moore implies that certain virtues, or 'virtuous dispositions', such as courage and compassion, may be intrinsically good in a high degree (§§ 129–32). The class of good things is impoverished if it is limited to experiences. It is hard to regard relations between human beings, and almost impossible to regard the existence of types of human character, as resoluble merely into experiences.

Perhaps even in *Principia* there was something undecided about Moore's position: for one name which he applies to his second class of goods is 'the pleasures of human intercourse' (§ 122). There seem to be two strands in Moore's thought about the great goods. Much of what he wrote in *Principia* gives the impression that there is a great variety of goods, and that among those compassable by human beings there are some at least which are not reducible to any kind of satisfaction: those goods, Moore sometimes seems to allow, may include the kinds of affection or nobility of character which consist in self-giving. But another strand, and that which expressed itself in the worth-havingness thesis, was a subtler form of the hedonism of Mill.

Secondly, if we think of judgements of value as relevant to conduct—not, in Moore's view, the only way of regarding them—is there not something romantic and *exalté* in the prominence which Moore gives to his great unmixed goods? To anyone acquainted, either with real ill fortune, or with the mere vexatiousness and humdrumness of human affairs, it may seem that only mitigations of evil, or mixed and mediocre goods, deserve much attention as goals of action.

Thirdly, is it not thinkable that a theory of value should depart even further than Moore conceived from a theory of ends and means? At this point the elective conception of valuation is an unsure guide. It is allowed by Moore, and by all utopian thinkers, and by all day-dreamers, that many things which are, so far as we can tell, impracticable, may none the less be the ultimate objects of our valuation. But usually, in such thinking, it is supposed that to aim at the ideal would be logically possible, even though practically fruitless. Yet there may be goods, and they may be the greatest goods, which, if they exist at all, can exist only as an unsought and unseekable blessing, and to regard them as the objects which in a happier world we might aspire to multiply may be to misconceive them wholly.

From the foregoing remarks I should like to distil one more. Philosophic debate in Moore's lifetime has often turned on what may be called the metaphysical nature of ethical concepts. Questions about the interconnections of ethical concepts, and their reducibility or irreducibility to those of other kinds, have been thought fundamental. Attention has been diverted from the question what things are of value in themselves, to which Moore himself devoted a large part of his discussion, to the superordinate questions, what constitutes being of value, or what constitutes thinking of something of value. Yet it seems possible, whether paradoxically or not, to carry on discussion of primary questions, about the values of things, while holding in suspense the supposedly fundamental questions about the nature of value or of valuation. I have found fault with Moore's discussions: but has any other philosopher given a better model? When I reopen his writings, from the earliest to the latest, all that I have said here seems slipshod in comparison. To praise what Moore has written would be superfluous and presumptuous: but by a fortunate custom tenacious criticism of a philosopher's work is deemed to be in proportion to the critic's high opinion of it.

MOORE'S UTILITARIANISM

by J. O. URMSON

Moore is frequently cited as a very clear and unambiguous exponent of what is called, in the jargon of recent philosophy, act
utilitarianism. If, indeed, we define an act utilitarian as one who
holds that the rightness of an individual action depends immediately and solely on the value of its consequences, then Moore is an
act utilitarian; for he maintained this thesis without any wavering
throughout his philosophical career. But Russell, in his *Portraits
from Memory*, says of Moore: 'I have never but once succeeded in
making him tell a lie, and that was by a subterfuge. "Moore," I
said, "do you *always* speak the truth?" "No", he replied. I believe
this to be the only lie he has ever told.' It would be strange that
such a story should ring so characteristically true of the man if his
relevant moral views could be adequately summarized in the thesis
that 'It is wrong to lie' is but an empirical generalization, admitting of exceptions, to the effect that the consequences of lying are
usually worse than the consequences of truth-telling. The purpose
of this short paper is to point out that Moore's views are much
more complicated than this and contain a remarkable combination
of act and rule utilitarianism. He was an act utilitarian in the sense
defined above, but Russell's story rings true because Moore held
that one could never be justified in telling a lie, not because he was
is an habitual rut of truth-telling.

In Chapter V of *Principia Ethica* Moore tells us that a third great
step in the argument is to be taken. So far the question of the
meaning of 'good' and the question about what things are good
have been discussed; now we turn to the third question: What
ought we to do? At first the argument moves along the well-known
lines of act utilitarianism, and so needs but a brief paraphrase here.
Truths about what things are intrinsically good are self-evident
and strictly universal; but if we ask what conduct is right we are
asking about the effects of certain types of conduct, and to such a
question the answer can be only a causal generalization (*P.E.*,
section 88). Moral laws are merely statements that certain kinds of
action will have good effects. For 'right' does and can mean nothing

but 'cause of a good result' and the assertion 'I am morally bound to perform this action' is identical with the assertion 'This action will produce the greatest amount of good in the universe'. To say that an action is a duty is to say that it will cause more good than any alternative, and to say that an action is right is to say that it will not cause less good than any alternative (89). Moore now acknowledges that, on this view, we can never know that an action is a duty or right (90). We can raise the question which among the alternatives likely to occur to anyone will produce the greatest sum of good (91); but an alternative that does not even occur to anyone may in fact be our duty (92). The most that practical ethics can hope to show is that one among a few alternatives will be generally productive of more good in the immediate future (93). But the generalizations so produced will be scientific predictions rather than moral laws.

I have summarized the argument so far very briefly. But it is clearly an exposition of classical act utilitarianism. The rightness of actions depends on their consequences, but the practical difficulty of determining consequences makes it advisable for us to have at our disposal certain rules of thumb of the kind 'Action X will generally produce the best results in situation Y'. It would be tedious to dwell on this familiar view at length. But now the arguments begins to take a rather different turn. First Moore acknowledges that certain basic rules recognized by universal common sense and generally observed at all times and all places (such as those forbidding murder and enjoining the keeping of promises) are necessary to the preservation of civilized society and that 'it seems certain that the preservation of civilized society, which these rules are necessary to effect, is necessary for the existence, in any great degree, of anything which may be held to be good in itself' (95). It is remarkable, however, that this important contention is not developed any further.

Having distinguished these basic and indispensable rules from the ideals of isolated cultural groups which have not been generally recognized nor generally practised even by those who recognized them (such as a rule of chastity), Moore asks, in section 99, what should be the attitude of the individual to these established basic rules, given their necessity for civilized society and the individual's own complete inability to determine what action is right on any occasion from first principles. His answer to this question needs to be given in full:

'It seems, then, that with regard to any rule which is *generally* useful, we may assert that it ought *always* to be observed, not on the ground that in *every* particular case it will be useful, but on the ground that in *any* particular case the probability of its being so is greater than that of our being likely to decide rightly that we have before us an instance of its disutility. In short, though we may be sure that there are cases where the rule should be broken, we can never know which those cases are, and ought, therefore, never to break it. It is this fact which seems to justify the stringency with which moral rules are usually enforced and sanctioned.'

This contention of Moore's that there are certain generally recognized moral rules which we ought never to break and are justifiably enforced and sanctioned with stringency has been accorded little or no attention. Yet it is not a casual observation but the culmination of what he calls the third great step of his argument. As other stages in his argument taken in isolation have seemed to display Moore as an extreme act utilitarian, this one taken in isolation displays him with equal clarity as a rule utilitarian. Moreover we have here an extreme form of rule utilitarianism, since most of those who have recognized the authority of secondary principles have been willing to admit that they were not utterly inviolable.

It is not impossible that some have ignored this aspect of Moore's position because they have failed to notice it. Perhaps others, more observant, have thought it so plainly incompatible with the general line of Moore's thought that they have charitably suppressed comment on the master's Homeric nod. It is not, it may be thought, open for one and the same philosopher to be an unambiguous exponent of both rule and act utilitarianism without inconsistency; if Moore is to be consistent one thesis must be withdrawn. But I believe in fact that Moore was not nodding, that his position, though perhaps false, is perfectly consistent, and that what is exposed is the ambiguity of our current notions of act and rule utilitarianism.

It is to be noted that Moore's act utilitarian thesis is primarily concerned with the rightness of actions and the rule utilitarian thesis is primarily concerned with the justification of actions. The right action is the one which has the best results whereas the justifiable action is in accordance with a moral rule (when some moral rule of the basic kind already noted is relevant). Now questions about whether one was right, correct or successful in thinking, speaking or acting in a certain way and questions about whether one was justified in thinking, speaking or acting in that way are normally, in non-moral as well as in moral contexts, settled by reference to quite different considerations. If I were now to predict an earthquake in Oxford in 1970 the prediction might turn out to be correct, but it would certainly be unjustified; whether the prediction would be correct is to be settled by reference to what happens in Oxford in 1970, whether it would be justified depends on what evidence is available to me now. I may be justified in buying a stock which it turns out to have been a mistake to buy. Herodotus was probably justified in saying that the claim of certain explorers that on sailing down the coast of Africa they found the midday sun to be to the north was ridiculous, but we know that he was mistaken in rejecting it. Insurance companies make a profit because for most people the taking out of insurance against theft or fire or burglary turn out to have been unnecessary, but it was still prudent for them to take out the insurance. To claim that I should not do the action which seems to me on my evidence to be likely to have the best results but should follow an established rule, as Moore does, seems to me to be like saying that even if I have every reason to believe that my house will not be burnt down I still ought to take out an insurance against it.

Thus there seem to be two quite distinct questions for the utilitarian to answer. The first is what principles determine whether an act is right or wrong; the second is what determines whether a person was justified in acting in a certain way. It is clearly theoretically possible to give either an act or a rule utilitarian answer to either of these questions, and so, in so far as a utilitarian does not make clear which of the questions he is answering, there is some ambiguity in his position. It would be very surprising if exactly the same answer were to be given to both these questions by any utilitarian who was aware of their difference. The most extreme act utilitarian would presumably hold that the right act was the one with the best consequences and that the justified action was the one that the agent had reason to believe would have the best consequences; but to say that this latter is the right action leads to the absurd consequence that one cannot make justified errors in moral matters, though elsewhere this is manifestly possible. It is also possible to give a rule utilitarian answer to both questions.

In his shorter book entitled *Ethics* Moore opts for an act utilitarian answer to both questions. There he says that the right action, the one which one *absolutely* ought to do, is the one with the best results but that the agent is praiseworthy if he does the one which he believes will have the best results and blameworthy if he does not. He acknowledges that he is committed to the paradox 'that a man may really deserve the strongest moral condemnation for choosing an action, which *actually* is right', but is willing to accept it. But in *Principia Ethica*, where he has laid far more emphasis on the virtual impossibility of forming a rational opinion on the merits of the total consequences throughout all time of an action, his position is different. There he holds an act utilitarian position on the question of what act is objectively right or a duty. An act will be a duty if it has better total consequences than any conceivable alternative and right if there is no alternative with better consequences. But, holding that we can never know what act is right or a duty, Moore maintains that we can never be justified in believing that an action contrary to certain generally accepted rules is right or a duty; consequently we ought never to break such rules and actions contrary to them can never be justified. This is plainly a rule utilitarian answer to the second question.

We can perhaps construct an analogue in the empirical field to Moore's position in ethics which will not be too impossibly artificial. Let us suppose that in some area of inquiry it is impossible to make predictions on the direct basis of scientific law and the actual situation, because all the relevant laws are not known and the situation is so complicated that we cannot establish accurately even those facts that we believe to be relevant. Let us further suppose that none the less when situations have contained feature A the feature B has followed in a high percentage of cases. Then perhaps we could not be justified in predicting other than B when the feature A was present, though the prediction might well be mistaken and our general scientific knowledge would render the presence of A quite unacceptable as a scientific explanation of the occurrence of B. Perhaps we could represent the view of the ancient medical *empirici*, in contrast to the *theoretici* and *methodici*, as being that though the right medical treatment was no doubt the one that would cure the patient, medical ignorance was such that no doctor was justified in going against rules based on experience of what had done good in other cases in the past. So, for

Moore, conformity to the common-sense moral rules does not make an action right, but we should be unjustified in breaking these rules based on experience, since any independent determination of the right action is rendered impossible by the complexity of the factors involved.

There is certainly some artificiality in insisting on Moore's preferred terminology, whereby the question which act is objectively suitable to the situation is called the question of rightness or duty and the question of the justification of actions is called the question of what we ought to do. In fact our terminology seems less rigid and much has to be understood from the context. Clearly one may properly say, for example: 'Not knowing that he was feeling ill, you were quite right to tell him to get on with his work', though here to say he was quite right is very like saying he was entirely justified. Similarly one might say: 'Knowing what I now know I can see that I ought not to have done it', which would not naturally be construed as saying that one had acted unjustifiably but, rather, mistakenly; Moore's own vocabulary indeed wavers in this sort of way. But that there are two questions to be considered is not called into doubt by the fact that which question is being raised cannot, in common discourse, be determined merely from the presence or absence of some such terms as 'right' and 'ought'.

There are then two distinct questions. First, we may ask for the criterion of an action's being a right action; second, we may ask for the criteria for determining how an agent is justified in acting. It is also clear that Moore, in *Principia Ethica*, gave an act utilitarian answer to the first question and incorporated rule utilitarianism into his answer to the second.

If we are willing to set aside for the present doubts about the viability of any form of utilitarianism, Moore's idea of giving an act utilitarian answer to the first question and incorporating rule utilitarianism into his answer to the second seems to me to be sufficiently promising to be worth investigation. I should regard the details of his answers to both questions as objectionable. With regard to his answer to the first, it is not merely difficult to determine the value of the totality of the consequences of an action, as Moore recognized; the very concept of the total consequences of an action is full of obscurities which Moore did nothing to dispel. Moreover, a rule utilitarianism which claims that one can absolutely never be justified in breaking such rules as those of truth telling and promise keeping is faced with great practical difficulties, as well as with notorious theoretical difficulties, such as that of the possible conflict between two such rules. Again, Moore quite overlooks the special status of rules which determine practices, which simply cannot be treated as having their origin in generalizations about the results of action.

But if one considers the various arguments used within the utilitarian fold for and against the act and rule versions, Moore's idea of giving different answers to the two questions emerges quite favourably. The principal argument in favour of rule utilitarianism has always been that it is plain that in moral thinking we simply do not treat moral rules always as mere generalizations or heuristic rules of thumb; the principal argument in favour of act utilitarianism is that it is clearly contrary to the spirit of utilitarianism to allow that an action with worse consequences could ever be preferred to one with better consequences; but a rule utilitarianism which does not allow this quickly collapses into act utilitarianism. Since the version of utilitarianism to be found in *Principia Ethica* allows that moral rules must sometimes finally determine our decision on how to act, it meets the point raised by the rule utilitarian. But since it claims that production of any but the best possible consequences must always involve error, it also meets the point raised by the act utilitarian.

Perhaps there are insurmountable objections to any form of utilitarianism, ones in no way met by the version offered in *Principia Ethica*. But Moore was surely right to distinguish the question of the theoretical criteria for the rightness of an action from that about how we ought to decide practical problems of action. In most discussions his answer to the second question has simply been ignored, and philosophers have therefore too often failed to realize that Moore had distinguished these two questions. Since most of us have failed to make the distinction clear for ourselves by our own unaided efforts, it is perhaps not of merely historical interest to go back to consider Moore's treatment of it.

G. E. MOORE'S LATEST PUBLISHED
VIEWS ON ETHICS[1]

by C. D. BROAD

The first six essays in the book *The Philosophy of G. E. Moore*, published in 1942 as Vol. IV in *The Library of Living Philosophers*, are devoted to Moore's ethical theories; and Moore's comments upon them occupy the first ninety-three pages of his terminal essay. I suppose that this part of the terminal essay must contain Moore's latest published pronouncements on ethical problems. As such, it is of considerable interest and importance. Of the six ethical essays and Moore's comments on them I propose to select three for discussion here, *viz.* those of Frankena, Stevenson, and myself. Between them they cover the following four main topics, viz. (I) The distinction between 'natural' and 'non-natural' characteristics, (II) The 'autobiographical' analysis of moral indicatives, (III) The interconnections of value and obligation, and (IV) Ethical egoism and ethical neutralism. I propose to treat each of these topics in turn.

I. THE DISTINCTION BETWEEN 'NATURAL' AND 'NON-NATURAL' CHARACTERISTICS

It is a well-known doctrine of Moore's that the word 'good', in one important sense of it, stands for a characteristic of a peculiar kind which he terms 'non-natural'. In *Principia Ethica* he gave certain criteria for distinguishing 'natural' and 'non-natural' characteristics. The two marks of a *natural* characteristic were said to be (i) that it 'can exist in time all by itself', and (ii) that it is a 'part' of anything that it characterizes. I tried to show in my essay that these criteria are utterly unsatisfactory. Moore accepted that criticism; and so we may henceforth regard that part of his doctrine as withdrawn.

In my essay I suggested that Moore was almost certainly intending to deal with the same distinction (though he does not use the words 'natural' and 'non-natural') in the paper entitled 'The Conception of Intrinsic Value' in his *Philosophical Studies* (1922).

[1] Reprinted from *Mind*, n.s., Vol. LXX, no. 280, 1961.

I understood his doctrine there to be as follows. (1) The characteristics of a thing may be divided into (*a*) those that *do*, and (*b*) those that do *not*, 'depend solely on its intrinsic nature'. (2) Those characteristics which do depend solely on the intrinsic nature of that which they characterize may be subdivided into (α) those which *are*, and (β) those which are *not* 'intrinsic'. (3) The *non-natural* characteristics of a thing are the members of the sub-class (*a*, β), i.e. those which *are* dependent solely on its intrinsic nature but are *not* intrinsic. The *natural* characteristics of a thing are the members of class (*b*) and the members of sub-class (*a*, α), i.e. they are those characteristics of it which *either* do not depend solely on its intrinsic nature *or* which depend solely on its intrinsic nature and are also intrinsic.

In his terminal essay Moore points out where I was right and where I was wrong in my interpretation of his doctrine in 'The Conception of Intrinsic Value'. I was right in thinking that he was concerned there with the distinction which he described in *Principia Ethica* by the words 'natural' and 'non-natural'. But I was wrong in thinking that he would admit there to be such a class of characteristics as (*a*, β), i.e. ones which *do* depend solely on the intrinsic nature of that which they characterize and yet are *not* intrinsic. Moore says that he held that *all* characteristics which depend solely on the intrinsic nature of that which they characterize *are intrinsic*. And he held that goodness, in the fundamental sense in which he is here concerned with it, is intrinsic.

He thinks that my mistake may have arisen from the very unfortunate terminology which he used in 'The Conception of Intrinsic Value'. He admits that he there used the term 'intrinsic property' in such a way that there would be no inconsistency between the following three statements, (i) '*P* is intrinsic', (ii) '*P* is a property', and (iii) '*P* is not an intrinsic property'. For, he says, his doctrine was that goodness (in the sense in question) *is* intrinsic and *is* a property and yet *is not* an intrinsic property of a good thing.

In view of this, I think that my misunderstanding was not only excusable but also fortunate, for it gave Moore an opportunity to remove what must have been a constant source of confusion even to wary readers. Henceforth, he says in the terminal essay, he will drop this terminology. In future, if I understand him aright, he would call *all* those properties and *only* those properties of a thing, which depend solely on its intrinsic nature, 'intrinsic properties' of it. He would then subdivide the intrinsic properties of a thing into 'natural' and 'non-natural'. And he would hold that goodness (in the sense in question) is a non-natural intrinsic property of a good thing. It will be noted that 'being an intrinsic property of a thing' is defined in terms of the notion of 'depending solely on the intrinsic nature of a thing'. The latter notion is elaborately expounded in 'The Conception of Intrinsic Value'. I did not criticize it in my essay, and Moore takes it for granted in his terminal essay; so I shall not discuss it here.

The verbal confusion is now removed, but we are left with the substantial question: What is Moore's criterion for distinguishing between those intrinsic properties of a thing which are *natural* and those which are *non-natural*? In 'The Conception of Intrinsic Value' Moore gave two criteria, and the first of these may be subdivided into two complementary parts. In the amended terminology they may be stated as follows. (1.1) A complete enumeration of the *natural* intrinsic characteristics of a thing would be a *complete description* of that thing. (1.2) An enumeration which omitted any *natural* intrinsic characteristic of a thing would be an *incomplete description* of that thing. (2) The *natural* intrinsic characteristics of a thing seem to contribute towards describing its intrinsic nature in a way in which predicates of value do not.

In my essay I confined myself to (1.1), and said nothing about (1.2) or about (2). Moore admits in the terminal essay that (1.2) cannot be maintained as it stands. Suppose that P and π are two properties, e.g. being red and being coloured, such that anything that had P would, as a necessary consequence, have π. Then a description which included P would not be made incomplete merely by omitting π. And yet π might be a *natural* intrinsic characteristic. So (1.2) would have to be amended to run somewhat as follows: No description of a thing would be complete, if it omitted any *natural* intrinsic characteristic of it which is not conveyed by some one or some combination of its other natural characteristics. (I use the phrase 'P conveys Q' to mean the same as 'If anything had P, it would necessarily follow from that alone that it would have Q'.)

Moore admits in the terminal essay that he did not clearly distinguish criteria (1.1) and (1.2), on the one hand, from criterion (2), on the other. He says that he is now inclined to rely mainly on the following amended form of (2), viz. that, in one sense of 'describe', the mention of *any natural* characteristic of a thing contributes to some extent to describe that thing; whilst the mention of its *non-natural* intrinsic characteristics does not, in that sense, describe it at all. He admits that this is extremely vague, unless we can give some more definite information as to the particular sense of 'describe' which is here relevant.

I think it is fair to conclude that Moore, at the time when he wrote this terminal essay, was unable to give any satisfactory definition of, or criterion for, a 'non-natural characteristic'. But I think that we can go further. His suggested criterion, with its admitted vagueness, due to the uncertainty of the relevant sense of 'describe', is surely grist to the mill of supporters of what I will call 'non-predicative interpretations of moral sentences in the indicative'. If, as that theory holds, the word 'good' is not the name of a characteristic at all, but its use is, e.g. to express or to evoke certain emotions, then to call a thing 'good' would *not* contribute in any way to the description of it. And yet, owing to the likeness of grammatical form between such sentences as 'That is a pleasant emotion' and 'That is a morally good emotion', e.g. there might well seem to be something paradoxical in saying that the former did, and the latter did not, contribute towards describing the emotion. So one could understand why those who never questioned that moral sentences in the indicative assign a predicate to a subject, should sum up the situation by alleging that the word 'good' stands for a property of a peculiar kind, which does not contribute to describe its subject in the familiar way in which, e.g. the property denoted by 'pleasant' does.

There remain two small points which are worth mentioning before leaving this part of the subject. (1) Moore says that, in his opinion, there are at least two kinds of intrinsic value, viz. goodness (in the sense in question) and beauty. But he does not hold, and never has held, that goodness, in that sense, is a determinable in W. E. Johnson's usage of that word. I must say, for my own part, that I should need a great deal of persuasion before I would admit that there is even a *prima facie* case for regarding beauty, in any sense of that word, as a form of *intrinsic* value.

(2) The other point is this. In the course of my essay I used an argument which presupposes that the pleasantness of a pleasant experience is dependent solely on its intrinsic nature. I assumed, e.g. that, in the case of a pleasant sensation, its pleasantness is always conveyed by some intrinsic pleasant-making sensible quality of it, such as its sweetness. Now Moore points out that the

M

relation between the pleasant-making characteristics of an experience and its pleasantness is almost certainly *not* that of conveyance, but is that of *causal determination*. I fully agree with that contention, and I will proceed to develop it in my own way, in which Moore might not have been willing to follow.

The essential point is that it is perfectly conceivable that two persons, or the same person on different occasions, should have sensations which were exactly alike in all their sensible qualities, and yet that one of them should be a pleasant experience and the other an unpleasant one. It is a very well-founded empirical generalization, e.g. that the vast majority of human beings, whenever they have a sensation of the 'toothachy' kind, dislike that sensation for its characteristic sensible qualities. That is why we call toothachy sensations 'unpleasant'. But there is no kind of necessity about that generalization. It is perfectly conceivable that there might be persons who, when they had a sensation of precisely the same kind, always, or on certain special occasions, *liked* that sensation for those very same sensible qualities for which most persons at most times *dislike* such sensations. For any such person, on any such occasion, a toothache would be a *pleasant* experience. I would suggest, then, that the words 'pleasant' and 'unpleasant', as applied to experiences, often imply a well-founded empirical generalization, to the effect that the vast majority of people, on the vast majority of occasions when they have an experience of a certain kind, would like it (or dislike it, as the case may be) for its characteristic experiential qualities. But there is also, plainly, a non-statistical sense of the words 'pleasant' and 'unpleasant'. To call an experience 'pleasant' (or to call it 'unpleasant'), in this latter sense, means that the particular person, who has it on a particular occasion, then and there *likes* it (or *dislikes* it, as the case may be) for its characteristic experiential qualities. There is no kind of contradiction in saying that a particular experience, which would correctly be called 'pleasant' (or be called 'unpleasant') in the *statistical* sense, occurring on a particular occasion in a particular person, might be correctly called 'unpleasant' (or 'pleasant', as the case may be) in the *non-statistical* sense.

II THE 'AUTOBIOGRAPHICAL' ANALYSIS OF MORAL INDICATIVES

Consider the sentence: 'It was right for Brutus to stab Caesar', uttered at a certain moment by a person who is really considering what he is saying and is not merely talking like a parrot or giving an example in an essay. What I call the 'autobiographical' analysis of this sentence is, on its positive side, that the speaker is intending to state, beside the historical proposition that Brutus stabbed Caesar, the autobiographical proposition that he himself is feeling a certain kind of emotion (viz. one of moral approval) in contemplating that historical proposition. On the negative side the theory is that the speaker is not intending to state anything else beside that historical and that autobiographical proposition and anything that may be logically entailed by them.

This must be carefully distinguished from what I have called 'the non-predicative theory of moral indicatives'. That holds that the speaker is stating nothing but the historical proposition; but that he would not have used the moral-indicative form of expression unless he were feeling moral approval towards it himself or had wanted to induce that emotion in his hearers. (The theory can, of course, take other forms, with something else substituted for 'moral approval'.) None of the essayists explicitly defends the non-predicative theory. But Professor Stevenson defends the autobiographical analysis against certain arguments which Moore had used in his paper 'The Nature of Moral Philosophy' in *Philosophical Studies*. Moore, in his reply, says that he would be more inclined to accept the non-predicative theory than the autobiographical analysis, if he were to accept either.

Before going further it is worth while to note that the autobiographical analysis might take two different forms, which I will call 'occurrent' and 'dispositional'. On the occurrent form of it, a person who says at a certain moment that X is right is saying that he is at that moment feeling moral approval for X. On the dispositional form of the theory, he is saying that he is generally disposed to feel moral approval when he contemplates actions like X. Moore distinguished those two forms of the theory in his paper 'The Nature of Moral Philosophy'. But Stevenson considered only the occurrent form, and therefore Moore also confines himself to that in his reply. This seems to me unfortunate, because the dispositional form is much more plausible than the occurrent form.

There is a matter, which seems to me quite simple, about which both Stevenson and Moore make terribly heavy weather. The essential point at issue can be put as follows. Suppose that the occurrent form of the autobiographical analysis were correct. Then A's utterance at t of a token of the type-sentence 'X is right' would be equivalent in meaning to his uttering a token of the type-sentence 'I am now feeling moral approval of X'. Similar remarks apply, *mutatis mutandis*, to 'X is wrong'. Now that makes the predicates 'right' and 'wrong' to be doubly relational, for it makes them involve a relation to a speaker and to a time. It follows that 'right' would have a systematically different meaning on every different occasion on which it is predicated, even by the same person, beside having a systematically different meaning corresponding to each different person who predicates it on any occasion. Now the word 'right' seems *prima facie* not to answer to those conditions. It seems to be used as if it could stand for precisely the same characteristic when predicated by different persons or on different occasions by the same person. Moore's arguments against the occurrent autobiographical analysis in 'The Nature of Moral Philosophy' are simply various ways of trying to exhibit strikingly certain aspects of this *prima facie* conflict between the common usage of the word 'right' and the usage which would seem to be required if the occurrent autobiographical analysis were correct.

One of Moore's arguments was concerned with the possible alteration in a person's emotional attitude towards the same action, if he should contemplate it on successive occasions. Stevenson's criticism of this argument brings out an important point about the use of tenses in such sentences as 'X *is* right', 'X *was* right', and 'X *will be* right'. The point may be put as follows. Suppose that A says at t 'I now approve of X, but I formerly contemplated it with disapproval'. Obviously his statement may be true. Now Moore has argued that, if the occurrent autobiographical analysis be correct, A's statement would be equivalent to 'X is now right, but was formerly wrong'. And he had pointed out that it is non-sensical to say, of *one and the same* action, that it was right at one time and became wrong later.

Now Stevenson quite justifiably challenges Moore's right to assert that the theory entails the equivalence mentioned above. Stevenson insists that the correct interpretation of the theory is as follows. If a person says 'X *is* right', he means that he is *now* feeling approval towards X, which is *now* being performed. If he says 'X *was* right', he means that he is *now* feeling approval towards X, which *has been* performed. The tense in the moral indicative refers only to the date of the action which is said to be right or to be wrong; and the principal tense in the autobiographical equivalent of that indicative is *always the present*.

If we accept this contention of Stevenson's, what really does follow from the autobiographical analysis, together with the fact of the change in A's attitude, is this. A can now correctly and truly say 'X was right'; and he could, at some former time, have said with equal correctness and equal truth 'X is (or was) wrong'. But at no time could he correctly and truly say 'X was right at one time and is now wrong'. For that would be equivalent to uttering the sentence 'I now approve of X, which happened in the past, and disapprove of X, which is happening now'. This is doubly nonsensical, since it asserts that the speaker had, at the same time, incompatible emotional attitudes towards one and the same particular action, and it implies that one and the same action was done at two different times.

Another argument in Moore's paper on 'The Nature of Moral Philosophy' may be put as follows. Suppose that A and B contemplate the same act X at the same time t. A may say 'I approve of X', and B may say 'I disapprove of X', and both may be telling the truth. Now, if the analysis under discussion be correct, A's statement is equivalent to his saying, 'X is right', and B's statement is equivalent to his saying 'X is wrong'. Now the two latter statements conflict logically, whilst the two former are logically compatible. Therefore they cannot be equivalent each to each.

The true account of this situation is admirably brought out by Moore in his terminal essay. It is this. If the analysis under discussion be admissible, A can correctly and truly say 'X is right', and B can at the same time correctly and truly say 'X is wrong'. But no one at any time can correctly and truly say 'X is both right and wrong'. For anyone who did so would, according to the proposed analysis, be saying 'I now approve and disapprove of X'. Now that could not be truly said by A, who approves and does not disapprove of X; not by B, who disapproves and does not approve of X; nor by any third person, since no one can entertain simultaneously incompatible emotional attitudes towards the same object.

This amendment, however, does nothing to diminish the force of Moore's original argument against the occurrent autobiographical analysis, viz. that, according to it, A and B do not differ in opinion when one of them pronounces an action to be right and the other pronounces the very same action to be wrong. This is recognized by Stevenson, who proceeds to meet it by making two additions to the proposed analysis.

The first is to point out that, although A and B would not differ in opinion, in the sense of holding incompatible beliefs, they would do so in the wider sense of having opposed emotional attitudes toward the same object. The second is to remind us that in such situations each person would generally seek to alter the emotional attitude of the other and make it resemble his own.

Stevenson admits that, even when due weight has been given to these two considerations, the occurrent autobiographical analysis is not wholly satisfactory. Suppose that A asks B 'Is X right?' A is not as a rule wanting to find out whether *he himself* now approves of X, but whether B or most other people would do so. Or, again, A may disapprove of X and may know that B approves of it, and the motive of his question may be to induce B to change his attitude. Lastly, if A asks *himself* 'Is X right?', he is certainly not trying to find out whether he now approves of X. The situation probably is that he has conflicting attitudes towards X, in respect of various aspects of it, and that he is seeking to straighten them out.

Moore does not seriously dispute anything that Stevenson here says. He tells us that he has always recognized that difference of 'opinion' covers opposition of emotional attitude, but that he used not to think it possible that moral conflicts could be merely of that kind. He is now inclined to think that moral disagreement *may* be nothing but opposition of emotional attitude; but he is also inclined about equally strongly to think that it involves a logical conflict between incompatible beliefs. Stevenson, he says, has given no reasons for his own alternative; he has merely shown that certain arguments against it are inconclusive. If Moore felt obliged to abandon his own theory, he would not be inclined to stop at the stage of the occurrent autobiographical analysis, but would prefer to accept some form of *non-predicative* theory. Moore says that he is, in fact, now quite strongly disposed to think that, when a person utters the sentence 'X is right', he is not asserting *anything* that could be true or false, not even the autobiographical proposition that he now approves of X. But Moore says that he also continues to have some inclination to hold his old view. And he cannot say which of these inclinations is the stronger.

III. THE INTERCONNECTIONS OF VALUE AND OBLIGATION

The longest and most complex essay in the ethical part of the book is that of Professor Frankena, and the part of Moore's reply which deals with it is also highly involved. The question at issue is the connection between the fact that a state of affairs would be *intrinsically good* and a person's being under an *obligation* to seek to *bring it into existence*. Moore had made certain statements on this topic in his various ethical writings, and Frankena discusses their truth and their compatibility with Moore's characteristic doctrines that good is a simple, indefinable, intrinsic, and non-natural characteristic.

The best way to convey an idea of the discussion is to take in turn the points which Frankena enumerates in the summary at the end of his essay, and to consider, in each case, Moore's treatment of them.

Point 1. This divides into two propositions, which I will call (1, *a*) and (1, *b*). The former is the contention that, if good (in Moore's sense) be *simple*, then the statement 'I am morally bound to do *Y*' cannot *mean* the same as the statement '*Y* will produce more good or less evil than any other act open to me'. The latter is the contention that the same negative consequence follows from the supposition that good (in Moore's sense) is *intrinsic*, in the sense explained by him.

(1, *a*) After a good deal of discussion on alleged obscurities and ambiguities in Frankena's reasoning, Moore proceeds to state formally what he takes to be Frankena's argument on this point. I have very little doubt that this is a correct account of what was present, in a less precise form, in Frankena's mind, and so I shall adopt it. The argument may be stated as follows. The proposition that good is *simple* entails that statements of the form '*X* is good' neither include nor are identical with statements of obligation. That entails that statements of the form '*X* is good' are *not normative*. That in turn entails that statements of the form '*Y* will produce the most good or the least evil of all the acts open to me' are *not normative*. And that entails that statements of the latter form are not identical in meaning with statements of the form 'I ought to do *Y*'.

Now Moore holds that the fundamental step in this argument is the second, viz. that if statements of the form '*X* is good' neither include nor are identical in meaning with statements of obligation it follows that such statements are not normative. The validity or invalidity of this step depends on what Frankena means by 'normative', and that (Moore alleges) is not made perfectly clear in his essay. But, setting aside minor verbal inconsistencies, it seems fairly plain that what he intends is the following. *S* is a normative statement about an action, if and only if it follows from the very nature of that statement that that action ought to be done. If we accept this account of 'normative', we see that the transition in step 2 depends on the tacit assumption that nothing can follow from the very nature of a statement except what is identical with or is a part of what is meant by the latter. There is in fact no doubt that Frankena does assume this premiss, for elsewhere in his essay he makes it quite explicit that he thinks that the two propositions 'Q *follows from the very nature of P*' and 'Q is *synthetically, though necessarily,* connected with *P*' are mutually exclusive. Now Moore rejects this premiss, and therefore sees no reason to accept step 2 of Frankena's argument.

As this is an important point, I will state all that is to be found in Moore's terminal essay on this topic. In the first place, he gives an example taken from Professor Langford's essay in the same volume. He says that, in his opinion, it *does* follow, from the very nature of the statement 'This is a cube', that this has twelve edges; whilst the latter is *not* identical with nor a part of the meaning of the former. Secondly, in another part of his essay, Moore makes the following general assertions. He says that he uses the phrase 'Q *follows from P*' to mean that the conjunction 'P & not-Q' is *self-contradictory*. But he holds that such a conjunction may be self-contradictory *without* 'Q follows from *P*' being *analytic*.

If we put all this together, we see that what Moore is maintaining is the following. Even though good be *simple*, the conjunction 'I ought to do Y, and Y will *not* produce as good consequences as some other action open to me' may be *self-contradictory*, in that sense (whatever it may be) in which the conjunction 'This is a cube, and this has *not* twelve edges' is self-contradictory. I should agree that this is quite possible, provided that *ought* itself is not simple, but contains *good* in its analysis. But, if *good* and *ought* were both simple, I cannot for the life of me see how the conjunction in question could be *self-contradictory*, in any generally accepted sense of that phrase. It might, however, be *self-evidently impossible*, without being self-contradictory in the formal sense, if we admit the possibility of necessary connections and disconnections which are synthetic, but obvious on inspection. I should add, perhaps, that I am extremely doubtful whether the conjunction 'This is a cube, and this has not twelve edges' *is* self-contradictory. I should suspect that what is so is the conjunction of this conjunction with certain of the axioms of three-dimensional Euclidean geometry. If so, it is not very helpful as an analogy to the ethical propositions under consideration.

Moore remarks that Frankena might reply to his criticisms on step 2 of the argument by saying that he uses the word 'include' in such a way that 'Q is included in P' covers *inter alia* 'Q follows necessarily but synthetically from P'. But that would not help Frankena's argument, since it would save step 2 only at the expense of step 1. For, if 'include' be used in this extended sense, there is no reason why the simplicity of *good* should prevent statements of the form 'X is good' from 'including' statements of obligation.

(1, *b*) This is the contention that, if good be *intrinsic* in Moore's sense of that word, then the statement 'I am morally bound to do Y' cannot mean what is meant by 'Y will produce more good or less evil than any other act open to me'.

Moore says that the argument is precisely the same as that in (1, *a*), with 'intrinsic' substituted for 'simple'. It therefore suffers from the same defect, viz. that the second step is unjustified, for the reasons given above. But it suffers from a further defect. For the first step, which was quite legitimate in (1, *a*), ceases to be so when 'intrinsic' is substituted for 'simple'. From the hypothesis that good is *intrinsic*, in Moore's sense, it would *not* follow that statements of the form 'X is good' neither include nor are identical with statements of obligation.

In order to discuss this, we must remember what Moore does and what he does not mean by calling a characteristic 'intrinsic'. To say that P is an intrinsic characteristic of X means that the possession of P by X depends solely on X's intrinsic nature. Now, in the first place, it does *not* follow from this definition that every intrinsic characteristic of X must be a *pure quality*. No doubt, if goodness were a pure quality, whether intrinsic or not, it would follow at once that 'X is good' could not be identical with or include any statement of obligation. For the latter would involve *relations* to an actual or possible agent. But Moore has distinguished between the 'external' and the 'internal' relational properties of a thing; and, whilst no *external* relational property of a thing could be intrinsic, there is nothing to prevent its *internal* relational properties from being so.

We may put the matter as follows. We must distinguish between what we might call 'categorical' and 'conditional' relational properties, though Moore does not use those terms. It would be a *categorical* relational property of a certain bit of arsenic to be poisoning Mr Jones at a certain moment. That property would be external and non-intrinsic; for that bit of arsenic would not be having it unless Mr Jones had existed and had swallowed it. It is a *conditional* relational property of any bit of arsenic to be poisonous, i.e. to be such that it *would* poison a man, *if* there were one and *if* he were to swallow it. This property, though relational, may be internal and intrinsic; for a bit of arsenic would have it even though there had never been any men or though no man had ever swallowed it. Similarly, if goodness be an *intrinsic* property of X, the statement 'X is good' cannot include or be identical in meaning with any such *categorical* statement as 'Z ought to desire X' or 'Z ought to try to produce X'. But there is nothing to prevent its including or being identical with some *conditional* proposition of the form 'If there were a person who fulfilled such and such conditions, he would be under an obligation to desire X or to try to produce X'. For X could have that property, even if there had never been any persons, or if no person had ever fulfilled the required conditions.

Whilst I admit the validity and the importance of the distinction which Moore draws here, I do think that it is rather misleading to say of even a *conditional* relational property that it 'depends solely on the intrinsic nature of its possessor'. Surely there is an important sense in which the poisonousness of arsenic depends just as much on the intrinsic nature of *a living organism* as on the intrinsic nature of arsenic. In the same sense and to the same degree the property of being such that, if there were a person and he were to fulfil certain conditions, he would be under an obligation to try to produce X, depends just as much on the intrinsic nature of *moral persons* as on that of X. No doubt arsenic would have been poisonous, even if there never had been and never will be any living organisms; but at least we can say that the very notion of poisonousness involves the notion of organisms and vital processes, and that no amount of reflection on arsenic in isolation could have supplied the latter notions.

Point 2. Frankena's second point really divides into seven interconnected propositions. It may be stated as follows. If value be either (*a*) *simple*, or (*b*) *intrinsic*, then it cannot be either (α) *normative*, or (β) *non-natural*, or (γ) *definable in terms of obligation*. And, that being so, (*c*) there is no reason to think that it is *incapable of being defined in non-ethical terms*.

It is evident that we thus have six hypothetical propositions, which arise by combining in turn each of the two antecedents (*a*) and (*b*) with each of the three consequents (*a*), (*β*), and (*γ*). In addition to these six hypotheticals there is the seventh proposition (*c*), which Frankena states in the form 'In that case there is no reason to regard value as being incapable of definition in non-ethical terms'. We may label the six hypotheticals as (2*a*, *a*), (2*a*, *β*), (2*a*, *γ*), and (2*b*, *a*), (2*b*, *β*), (2*b*, *γ*). The seventh proposition may be labelled (2*c*).

Moore claims to have dealt with (2*a*, *a*), (2*a*, *γ*), (2*b*, *a*), and (2*b*, *γ*) in his discussion of (1, *a*) and (1, *b*). He has admitted (2*a*, *γ*), i.e. that, if good be simple, it cannot be defined in terms of obligation, since it would be indefinable. He has rejected (2*a*, *a*), (2*b*, *a*), and (2*b*, *γ*). It remains, therefore, to deal with (2*a*, *β*), (2*b*, *β*), and (2*c*). That we will now proceed to do.

(2*a*, *β*). This is the proposition that, if good be *simple*, it cannot be *non-natural*. The essence of Frankena's argument is as follows. If good were simple, it would not be normative. If it were not normative, there would be no reason to think it non-natural. Therefore, if it were simple, it would be non-natural.

Now the first step has already been discussed and rejected. And, even if both it and the second step were accepted, the correct conclusion would be only that, if good were simple, there would be *no reason to think* that it is non-natural. There would be no justification for the stronger conclusion that it *would not be* non-natural.

(2*b*, *β*). This is the proposition that, if good be *intrinsic*, it cannot be *non-natural*. The argument is the same as before, with 'intrinsic' substituted throughout for 'simple'. The first step of this argument has already been discussed and rejected. And the argument has the same defect as (2*a*, *β*), viz. that of drawing a stronger conclusion than would be justified by its premisses, even if these were acceptable.

Before passing to (2*c*), it will be worth while to consider for a moment the second premiss, which is common to both the above arguments of Frankena's. This is the proposition that, unless good were *normative*, there would be no reason to think it *non-natural*. The essence of Frankena's contention on this topic is as follows. In his opinion, the main point of the doctrine that intrinsic value is non-natural is that it cannot be reduced to purely psychological, sociological, biological, or metaphysical terms. Now it seems to him that the only feature in moral judgements which can plausibly be held not to be so reducible is their ostensibly *normative* character, i.e. 'the fact that they seem to be saying of some agent that he *ought* to do something'. He concludes that, unless intrinsic value 'in itself possesses a normative character or obligatoriness', there is no reason to think that it is not essentially reducible to the terms enumerated above.

(2c). This proposition, which comes immediately after the six hypotheticals which we have now discussed, is stated in the very obscure sentence: 'In that case there is no reason to think that good is not definable in non-ethical terms.' We naturally ask: 'In *what* case?' In the context Frankena might mean *either* that if his six hypotheticals were true there would be no reason to think that good is not definable in non-ethical terms, *or* that if their three consequents were true there would be no reason to think this. Moore does not consider the first of these alternatives, but confines his attention to the second. This is the proposition that, if good be neither normative nor non-natural nor definable in terms of obligation, then there is no reason to think it is not definable in non-ethical terms.

The phrase 'not definable in non-ethical terms' needs a certain amount of unpacking. It will be best to start from the beginning. Good might be either (1) indefinable, or (2) definable. If indefinable, it might be either (1.1) identical with some admittedly non-ethical simple notion, e.g. pleasant, or (1.2) not identical with any admittedly non-ethical notion. If definable, it might be either (2.1) definable in wholly non-ethical terms, or (2.2) definable only in terms which are wholly or partly ethical. We could lump together the two alternatives (1.1) and (2.1) under the heading 'wholly *expressible* in non-ethical terms'; and the two alternatives (1.2) and (2.2) under the heading 'not wholly *expressible* in non-ethical terms'.

Now Frankena has argued that, if good were *simple*, it would be neither normative nor non-natural nor definable in terms of obligation. And we have interpreted (2c) to mean that, if good were neither normative nor non-natural nor definable in terms of obligation, there would be no reason to think that it is not definable in non-ethical terms. Putting the two together, we see that Frankena is committed to the proposition that, if good be *simple*, there is no reason to think that it is *not definable in non-ethical terms*. But, obviously, if it be simple, it cannot be *definable* in any terms whatever. So, in order to make sense of the above proposition, we must assume that Frankena is using the phrase 'not definable in non-ethical terms' in a loose sense which is equivalent to my phrase 'not wholly expressible in non-ethical terms'. What he is asserting is, in fact, the following proposition. If good be neither normative nor non-natural nor definable in.terms of obligation, there is no reason to think that it is not *either* (i) definable in wholly non-ethical terms, *or* (ii) identical with some simple admittedly non-ethical notion. If that is what Frankena means, it may be doubted whether (2c) is more than a tautology; for the only attempt which he makes to define 'non-natural' seems to identify it with 'not wholly expressible in certain enumerated non-ethical terms'.

Point 3. Frankena's third point may be put as follows. If good were either (*a*) *normative* or (*b*) *non-natural* or (*c*) *not wholly expressible in ethical terms*, then (α) it would be *definable in terms of obligation*, (β) it would *not be simple*, and (γ) it would *not be intrinsic*. The third point is therefore the conjunction of the nine hypothetical propositions which arise by uniting (*a*), (*b*), and (*c*) in turn as antecedents with (α), (β), and (γ) as consequents.

Now of these nine hypotheticals the following have already been dealt with. (3*a*, α) is the contrapositive of a step in the argument for point (1, *a*), which Moore has discussed and dismissed. (3*a*, β), (3*a*, γ), (3*b*, β), and (3*b*, γ) are the contrapositives of (2*a*, α), (2*b*, α), (2*a*, β), and (2*b*, β) respectively. And these have been discussed and rejected by Moore. Again, if (3*b*, α) be granted, then (3*c*, α) becomes superfluous. For it is admitted that, if good be not wholly expressible in non-ethical terms, it is non-natural. And, if this be combined with (3*b*, α), we can infer (3*c*, α). (3*b*, α) embodies Frankena's conviction, already discussed, that the only fundamentally ethical notion is that of obligation. We are thus left with only (3*c*, β) and (3*c*, γ). These are more simply expressed in the equivalent form of their contrapositives. If we do this, and combine them, they amount to the proposition that, if good were either *simple* or *intrinsic*, it would be *wholly expressible in non-ethical terms*, i.e. it would be *natural*. This will best be treated incidentally in connexion with the remaining points in Frankena's summary.

Point 4. Frankena's fourth point is that Moore has given no adequate reason for rejecting the view that 'good' is *definable in terms of obligation*.

Moore begins by admitting that he has given no *conclusive* reason. But he thinks that he can give *good* reasons. The gist of his argument is as follows. He considers three alleged definitions of 'good' in terms of obligation, which Frankena proposes. He rejects one of them on the ground that the two propositions suggested as definiens and definiendum do not even mutually entail each other. As regards the other two, he admits that there is mutual entailment between the definiendum and the suggested definiens. But he holds that that kind of logical relation can hold between two propositions without it being a case of two sentences with one and the same meaning. The test for the latter is to ask oneself the question 'Can I think of the one without *ipso facto* thinking of the other ?' In each of these two cases he holds that that is possible, and therefore that there is not identity of meaning. Now, Moore says, he cannot think of any *other* plausible instances of mutual entailment between a value-proposition and an obligation-proposition. Therefore he holds that he has given sound, though not conclusive, reasons for thinking that goodness cannot be defined in terms of obligation.

I will now say something about the three proposed definitions. (1) '*X* is intrinsically good' means what is meant by 'If one is capable of producing *X*, one has a *prima facie* duty (in Ross's sense) to do so'. This is rejected by Moore (rightly, I think), on the ground that the former proposition might easily be true when the latter was false.

(2) I am going to formulate the second in a slightly modified form of Moore's interpretation of Frankena's rather vague statement. It will run as follows. '*X* is intrinsically good' means what is meant by 'The mere fact (if it were a fact) that *A* could do *Y* and that *Y* would produce *X* would suffice to supply *some* reason for thinking that *A ought* to do *Y*'. Moore holds that these two propositions do entail each other. But he considers it obvious that a person could think of *X* as being intrinsically good, without *ipso facto* thinking of it as having this other complicated property, which is conveyed by and conveys its intrinsic goodness.

(3) Frankena quotes a certain alleged mutual entailment, which Moore gave in his *Ethics*, and asks why this should not be regarded as a definition. We need not trouble ourselves here about *this* particular alleged mutual entailment, because Moore says that he does not now think that it holds, or that the sentence quoted correctly expressed what he had in mind when he wrote his *Ethics*. Instead, we may confine our attention to the amended formula which he now proposes in its place. It runs as follows: '*X* is intrinsically good' entails and is entailed by 'If an agent were a

Creator, before the existence of any world; and if the only two alternatives open to him were (i) to create a world which consisted only of X, or (ii) to bring it about that there should never be a world at all; then it would be his duty to choose alternative (i), provided (*a*) that he knew for certain that these were the only two alternatives open to him, and (*b*) that he did not think it wrong to choose alternative (i)'. Moore says that it seems obvious to him (and who shall deny it?) that a person could think of the former proposition without *ipso facto* thinking of the latter.

Point 5. The main assertion in Frankena's fifth point, and the only one which Moore discusses, is the following. Frankena alleges that, even though it be *intrinsic value* which makes a thing such that it *ought* to be pursued or brought into being by a competent agent, still Moore has given no good reason why 'intrinsic value' might not be *definable in wholly non-ethical terms*.

What Frankena has in mind is no doubt this. He is alleging that there is no obvious reason why a *purely natural* characteristic, e.g. pleasantness, should not be such that the mere fact that a thing would have it would provide some ground for thinking that any agent, who could produce that thing, *ought* to do so.

In order to discuss this, let us begin by defining what Moore calls an 'ought-*implying* property', and what I prefer to call an 'ought-*inclining*' property. The sentence 'P is an ought-inclining property' is to mean what is meant by 'The mere fact that a thing would have P would suffice to provide *some* ground for thinking that any agent, who could bring such a thing into being, *ought* to do so'. Now Moore admits that *intrinsic goodness* is an ought-inclining property. He holds, moreover, that the intrinsic goodness of a thing always depends on the presence in it of some *natural* characteristic or other which is what I will call 'good-making'. Let Q be any *good-making* natural characteristic. Then anything that had Q would, of necessity, have intrinsic goodness. And the mere fact that anything had intrinsic goodness would suffice to provide some ground for thinking that any agent, who could bring such a thing into being, ought to do so. It follows at once that Q, though a *natural* characteristic, will also answer to the definition of an 'ought-inclining property'. And this can be generalized at once for every natural characteristic which is good-making.

There is no doubt, then, that Frankena is right in holding that there can be, and in fact are, *natural* characteristics which are ought-inclining. It is plain that he thinks that this fact entails that intrinsic goodness *either* (i) is *definable in terms of ought, or* (ii) is a *natural* characteristic. He thinks that, if the former alternative were fulfilled, there would be some reason to think that intrinsic goodness is *non-natural*. For, as we have seen, he regards 'ought' as *the* ethical notion *par excellence*, and as such the most plausible instance of a non-natural notion. On the other hand, he thinks that, if intrinsic goodness be *not* definable in terms of ought, then (in view of the fact that an ought-inclining property *can be natural*) there will be no valid reason for thinking that intrinsic goodness is non-natural.

Now Moore gives an argument which, he thinks, tends to show that intrinsic goodness cannot be identical with any natural property, even if it be not definable in terms of ought. The argument runs as follows.

Admittedly some *natural* characteristics are ought-inclining. But only *intrinsic* natural characteristics can be such. For a natural characteristic is ought-inclining only through being good-making. And only intrinsic natural characteristics convey intrinsic goodness. So the question reduces to whether intrinsic goodness could be identified with any *intrinsic* natural characteristic. After these preliminaries the argument continues as follows.

The number of ought-inclining intrinsic natural characteristics is, Moore asserts, certainly very great and possibly infinite. Plainly, we cannot identify intrinsic goodness with any particular one of them or with the aggregate of all of them. Moore thinks it obvious, moreover, that intrinsic goodness could not be identified with the *disjunction* of all these natural characteristics. Suppose that there were *one single* non-disjunctive intrinsic natural characteristic, which was (*a*) ought-inclining, and (*b*) was conveyed by each of the other ought-inclining natural characteristics. Then it might be plausible to identify intrinsic goodness with *it*. But there seems to be no one natural characteristic answering to these conditions. Therefore there does not appear to be any ought-inclining natural characteristic with which intrinsic goodness can be identified. And it certainly cannot be identified with any intrinsic natural characteristic which is *not* ought-inclining. Therefore it cannot be identified with any natural characteristic whatever.

I think that this argument is valid, so far as it goes. But it would not satisfy a person who might suggest that '*X* has intrinsic goodness' means what is meant by '*X* has *some* intrinsic natural characteristic or other which is ought-inclining'. I do not know whether Moore would count this as identifying intrinsic goodness with the *disjunction* of all ought-inclining intrinsic natural characteristics. I do not think that he would. But, if he did, I should be inclined to ask: What precisely is the objection to such an 'identification'? The advantages of the suggestion are that it avoids postulating *two* indefinable non-natural characteristics, and defines the less specifically ethical one ('intrinsically good') in terms of the more specifically ethical one ('ought'). The final objection would have to be that one can think of intrinsic goodness without *ipso facto* thinking of even so indeterminate a notion as that expressed by the phrase 'some intrinsic natural ought-inclining characteristic or other'. But is that really at all certain?

Moore's latest published Views on the Connection of Good, Better, and Ought. On pp. 606 to 611 of his terminal essay Moore formulates four very complicated pairs of mutually entailing propositions, which express the views, which he held at the date of writing, about the interconnections of 'good' and 'ought' and of 'better' and 'ought'. I am going to state them in my own way; but what I shall say is, I think, equivalent to what Moore had in mind and is perhaps somewhat easier to grasp.

I shall begin by defining certain statements. (1.1) '*P* is a *good-making* characteristic' means what is meant by 'If X did have or now has or will have P, it follows that X then was or now is or will then be intrinsically good; and if X should have had or should now have or should be going to have P, it would follow that X would have been or would now be or would be going to be intrinsically good'. (1.2) '*P* is a *bad-making* characteristic' is defined in a precisely similar way, with 'intrinsically *bad*' substituted throughout for 'intrinsically *good*'. (1.3) '*P* is a *valifying* characteristic' means what is meant by '*P* is either a good-making or a bad-making characteristic'. (2) '*P* is *more strongly good-making or less strongly bad-making* than *Q*' means what is meant by 'If X did have or now has or will have P (and *no other* valifying characteristic), and if Y did have or now has or will have Q (and *no other* valifying characteristic), it follows that X then was or now is or will then be better than Y; and if X should have had or should now have or should be going to have P (and *no other* valifying characteristic), and if Y should have had or should now have or should be going to have Q (and *no other* valifying characteristic), it would follow that X would have been or would now be or would be going to be intrinsically better than Y'.

N

We can now formulate the four pairs of mutually entailing propositions.

First Pair. (i) *P* is a *good-making* characteristic. (ii) If there had been, or in fact was, an agent who, before any world existed, (*a*) *knew* (*α*) that if he chose he could create a world characterized by *P*, (*β*) that he could so choose, and (*γ*) that if he did not so choose no world at all would ever exist; and who (*b*) *did not believe* that this choice would be wrong; then it would have been, or in fact was, the *duty* of that agent to make that choice.

Second Pair. (i) *P* is a *good-making* characteristic. (ii) *P* is an *ought-inclining* natural characteristic.

Third Pair. (i) *P* is a *more strongly good-making or a less strongly bad-making* characteristic than *Q*. (ii) If there had been or in fact was, an agent who, before any world existed, (*a*) *knew* (*α*) that if he chose he could create a world characterized by *P*, (*β*) that he could so choose, and (*γ*) that, unless he were so to choose, a world characterized by *Q* and not by *P* would inevitably come into existence; and who (*b*) *did not believe* that this choice would be wrong; then it would have been, or in fact was, his *duty* to make that choice.

Fourth Pair. (i) The world is *intrinsically better* because *A* chose to do *Y*, when he could have chosen to do something else instead, than it would have been if he had made any other choice open to him. (ii) *A did his duty* in choosing *Y*.

Moore holds that in each of these four pairs the two members are interconnected by *synthetic* mutual entailment, but are not identical in meaning. If either the first or the second or the third were *analytic*, it would provide a *definition* of intrinsic value in terms of obligation. If the fourth were *analytic*, it would provide a definition of obligation in terms of intrinsic value. For the reasons given, Moore does not regard any of them as analytic, and he therefore sees no reason to think that either notion can be defined in terms of the other.

(IV) ETHICAL EGOISM AND ETHICAL NEUTRALISM

In my essay in the *G. E. Moore* volume I defined what I call 'Ethical Neutralism' and what I call 'Ethical Egoism'. I pointed out that the latter might take milder or more extreme forms, but that it is in all its forms incompatible with Ethical Neutralism. I thought that Moore had claimed in *Principia Ethica* (pp. 96 to 105) to show that Ethical Egoism (at any rate in its extreme form) is *self-contradictory*. I argued that his attempt was a failure, and that all that could be proved was the tame proposition that Ethical Egoism is inconsistent with Ethical Neutralism.

Moore says, in his terminal essay, that what he was really trying to prove was not that Ethical Egoism *is self-contradictory*; but that Ethical Neutralism *would entail* that Ethical Egoism is self-contradictory, and not merely that it is false. Now Ethical Neutralism is at any rate highly plausible, and to some eminent moralists it has seemed self-evident on inspection. Therefore, if this argument of Moore's were acceptable, it would be at least highly plausible to hold that Ethical Egoism *is* self-contradictory, and not merely false.

Moore admits that his argument in *Principia Ethica* is extremely obscure and confused. He now produces a new argument and it is with this that we shall be concerned. It is extremely complex and hard to follow, and I am inclined to suspect that it contains a logical fallacy. In order to try to show this as clearly as possible, I shall exhibit formally what I take to be Moore's new argument.

In what follows I shall write '*p ent q*' for '*p* entails *q*', and I shall understand by this a kind of logical relation which holds, e.g. between the conjunction of the premisses of a valid syllogism and its conclusion. One way of describing it would be to say that the *conjunction* of *p* with not-*q* would be *impossible*, and that this impossibility does not depend on *p* being itself impossible or on *q* being itself necessary. I shall write '*p imp q*' for '*p* implies *q*', and I shall understand by this that the conjunction of *p* with not-*q* is *in fact false*. With these notational preliminaries, the argument may be stated as follows.

Let '*p*' stand for the sentence 'It would *not be wrong* for *X* to choose *Y*'.

Let '*q*' stand for the sentence '*X* does *not know* that the world would be *intrinsically worse* if he were to choose *Y* than if he were to choose some other alternative open to him at the time'.

Let '*r*' stand for the sentence '*X* knows that the choice of *Y* by him would procure *for himself* a more favourable balance of intrinsically good over intrinsically bad experiences than any other choice that he could make, and knows also that this choice would be at least as favourable to the development of *his own* nature and dispositions as any other that he could make'.

Then what Moore calls 'Proposition *A*' is that *p* would follow from *r alone*, even though *q* should be false. So we may write '*A*' for '*r ent p*, even though not-*q*'. Moore asserts, and I agree, that *A* is entailed by Ethical Egoism.

What Moore calls 'Proposition *B*' is that the falsity of *q* would entail the falsity of *p*. So we may write '*B*' for 'not-*q ent* not-*p*'. Moore asserts, and I agree, that *B* is entailed by Ethical Neutralism.

Now Moore asserts that *A* entails that *r* does *not* entail *q*. For, he argues, to say that *r* would entail *p*, *even though q were false*, entails that it is *logically possible* for *q* to be *false*, even though *r* were *true*. This contention of Moore's may be written

$$A \; ent \; \text{not-}(r \; ent \; q)$$

Moore's argument may now be stated formally as follows:

$B \; ent \; (\text{not-}q \; ent \; \text{not-}p)$ (by definition)	
Hence $B \; ent \; (p \; ent \; q)$ (by contraposition)	(I)
Again, $A \; ent \; (r \; ent \; p)$ (by definition)	

Therefore $(A \; \& \; B) \; ent \; ((r \; ent \; p) \; \& \; (p \; ent \; q))$

Whence $(A \; \& \; B) \; ent \; (r \; ent \; q)$ (II)

But, as we have seen, according to Moore

$$A \; ent \; \text{not-}(r \; ent \; q)$$

Therefore $(r \; ent \; q) \; ent \; \text{not-}A$ (by contraposition)   (III)

Therefore $((\text{II}) \; \& \; (\text{III})) \; ent \; ((A \; \& \; B) \; ent \; \text{not-}A)$

Since (II) and (III) can be asserted, we can drop them and assert what they together entail, *i.e.*

$$(A \; \& \; B) \; ent \; \text{not-}A \tag{IV}$$

Now up to this point the argument is valid, if we grant Moore's contention (which I shall not here question) that *A ent* not-(*r ent q*). But what he claims to have proved is that *B* entails that *A* is *self-contradictory*. Now this must be the proposition

$$B \; ent \; (A \; ent \; \text{not-}A) \tag{V}$$

(It must be clearly understood that it is *not* enough for Moore to show that

$$B \; ent \; (A \; imp \; \text{not-}A)$$

For *A imp* not-*A* is simply equivalent to (not-*A* or not-*A*), which is in turn simply equivalent to not-*A*. So the latter proposition would merely amount to the tame conclusion that *B ent* not-*A*, i.e. in effect, that Ethical Neutralism is incompatible with Ethical Egoism.)

The question is, therefore, whether it is justifiable to infer from (IV), i.e. from (*A* & *B*) *ent* not-*A*, to (V), i.e. to *B ent* (*A ent* not-*A*). The answer is that this is *not* justifiable. Consider, e.g. a valid syllogism (P & Q) *ent* R. Suppose that you could legitimately derive from this the proposition P *ent* (Q *ent* R). Then, if the premiss P were known to be true, you could drop it and assert the proposition Q *ent* R. That this is not justifiable can easily be seen by taking a concrete example of a valid syllogism with a premiss known to be true. Take, e.g., 'All men are mortal' for 'P', 'Socrates is a man' for 'Q', and 'Socrates is mortal' for 'R'. Then, if this kind of inference were valid, we could infer from the syllogism the proposition (All men are mortal) *ent* ((Socrates is a man) *ent* (Socrates is mortal)). Then dropping the true premiss that all men are mortal, we could assert that Socrates is a man *entails* that Socrates is mortal. Now that conclusion is certainly false. The mortality of Socrates is not a *necessary consequence* of his humanity *alone*.

So, unless I am much mistaken, Moore's new argument is fallacious, and he has failed to show that, if Ethical Neutralism were *true*, Ethical Egoism would be *self-contradictory*. It is a rash undertaking to accuse Moore of a logical fallacy, and it may well be that I have misunderstood his argument. On the other hand, it is very easy for the best of us to commit fallacies in *modal* logic, and so even Moore may have done so. But that consideration cuts both ways, and I myself may have committed some fallacy in modal logic in my criticism of his argument.

INDEX OF NAMES